The Binding of Proteus

The Binding of Proteus

Perspectives on Myth and the Literary Process

Collected Papers of the Bucknell University Program on
Myth and Literature
and the
Bucknell-Susquehanna Colloquium on Myth in
Literature
Held at Bucknell and Susquehanna Universities
21 and 22 March 1974

Edited by
Marjorie W. McCune
Tucker Orbison
Philip M. Withim

Lewisburg
Bucknell University Press
London: Associated University Presses

© 1980 by Associated University Presses, Inc.

Associated University Presses, Inc.
Cranbury, New Jersey 08512

Associated University Presses
Magdalen House
136-148 Tooley Street
London SE1 2TT, England

Library of Congress Cataloging in Publication Data
Main entry under title:

The Binding of Proteus.

   Bibliography: p.
   Includes index.
   1. Myth in literature—Congresses. I. McCune,
Marjorie W. II. Orbison, Tucker. III. Withim,
Philip M. IV. Bucknell-Susquehanna Colloquium on Myth
in Literature, 1974.
PN56.M94B5   809   76-49774
ISBN 0-8387-1708-X

Contents

174537

IV *Mythic Thought as Archetypal Patterns*

Preface

The papers in this volume are the result of two programs that were developed in the 1973-74 academic year: the one a year-long program on myth and literature, sponsored by the English Department of Bucknell University; the other a colloquium on myth-in-literature sponsored jointly by the Division of Language and Literature at Susquehanna University and the English Department of Bucknell. The purpose of the program on myth and literature was to bring to Bucknell a series of visiting professors who would discuss with faculty and students a literary problem of contemporary concern. Each visitor gave one or more lectures which form the substance of the papers presented here by the following: Professors Joseph Campbell, Deborah Austin, F. W. Bateson, Gene Bernstein, William Arrowsmith, and Eugène Vinaver. The paper by Tucker Orbison of Bucknell on Arrabal's *The Solemn Communion* describes and analyzes the production by a troupe of La Mama Experimental Theater Club, whose members took part in the myth and literature program by spending four days doing a workshop on the Bucknell campus.

The remaining papers, with one exception, were given as part of the second Bucknell-Susquehanna Colloquium, whose topic was more narrowly defined as myth-in-literature. The purpose of the two-day meeting on 20 and 21 March, 1974 was to encourage scholarly communication between the two universities by bringing faculty and students together with visiting scholars to discuss the problem of how myth works in the literary process. Three of the essays by our visitors—Professors John B. Vickery, Karl D. Uitti, and Charles Moorman—are given in this volume; the remainder are by members of the hosting universities: Lawrence Abler and Ron Dotterer of Susquehanna and Louis Casimir, Catherine Smith, and Philip Withim of Bucknell. To these is added the contribution of Professor René Galand, whose visit was sponsored by the French Department of Bucknell in the fall of 1973 and whose topic was coordinated with that of the myth and literature program.

As the reader will see, the topics of both programs provoked diverse reactions, an indication that consideration of the relation between myth and literature continues to command attention. The volume does not set out to establish any single point of view; rather, the editors' purpose is to suggest the kind of thinking now being done on a highly controversial topic: what directions it is taking and what limits some critics believe must be imposed on the myth-ritual approach to literature.

Neither program would have been possible without the cooperation of a number of people; nor would the publication of this volume. The editors wish to thank the Division of Language and Literature at Susquehanna and Dr. Wendell Smith, Provost of Bucknell, for providing financial support for the Colloquium. Dr. Smith's allocation of funds also made possible the myth and literature program. Our appreciation goes as well to President Gustave W. Weber of Susquehanna and to Dr. Smith for introducing the Colloquium sessions at their respective universities. To all those members of Bucknell's English Department who helped with organizing and running the myth and literature program and to those students who contributed their time and expertise, especially Laura Dabundo, Jane Curry, William Koehler, and Marc Powers, all of the Class of 1974, and Marjorie Cocke, Class of 1978, our gratitude. The Colloquium would have been the poorer without the moderating skills of Professors Charles A. Rahter and Dan A. Wheaton of Susquehanna and Professors Richard Smith and Michael Payne of Bucknell. For various kinds of editorial favors, we extend our thanks to Professors Rahter and Nancy L. Cairns of Susquehanna, Professor John B. Vickery of the University of California at Riverside, and Professors John Gale, Michael Payne, Joseph Fell, John Murphy, Karen L. Gould, and Catherine Smith of Bucknell. An especial debt is owed to Professor William G. Holzberger of Bucknell and to Professor Peter B. Waldeck of Susquehanna for aid in directing the Colloquium and for advising us on editorial problems. Naturally, the editors take full responsibility for whatever shortcomings the book may possess.

M. W. M.

T. O.

P. M. W.

Acknowledgments

The editors wish to thank the following publishers and individuals for permission to reprint copyrighted material or to publish translations of works already translated:

The American-Scandinavian Foundation for 14 lines from *The Poetic Edda* (1923).

Gioia B. Bernheim and Edmund R. Brill for an excerpt from Sigmund Freud, *The Basic Writings of Sigmund Freud* (1938). Copyright © renewed 1965 by Gioia Bernheim and Edmund Brill. Reprinted by permission.

Doubleday & Co., Inc. for various quotations from *The Poetry and Prose of William Blake*, edited by David Erdman (1970).

E. P. Dutton & Co., Inc. for reprinting of thirty-two lines and permitting the publishing of our translations of sixty-three lines from *The Romance of the Rose*, translated by Harry W. Robbins, edited by Charles W. Dunn. English translation copyright © 1962 by Florence L. Robbins. Reprinted by permission of the publishers, E. P. Dutton.

Editions Gallimard for fifty-two lines of "Le Cygne" and four lines from *Les Fleurs du Mal* in Pierre Charles Baudelaire, *Oeuvres complètes* (1961).

Harcourt Brace Jovanovich, Inc. for two excerpts from "The Archetypes of Literature" in Northrop Frye, *Fables of Identity* (1963).

Harcourt Brace Jovanovich, Inc. and Faber & Faber, Ltd. for three excerpts from T. S. Eliot, "Burnt Norton," *Collected Poems: 1909-1962* (1963).

Harvill Press Ltd. for permission to publish our own translation of material from Roy Campbell's *Poems of Baudelaire*, published by Pantheon Books (1952).

The Hogarth Press Ltd. for permitting the publishing of our translations from Rainer Marie Rilke, *Tagebücher aus der Frühzeit*, 1973.

Grateful acknowledgment is made to Alfred A. Knopf, Inc. for permission to quote from the copyrighted poems in *The Collected Poems of Wallace Stevens* (1954).

Libraire Honoré Champion for twelve lines from Chrétien de Troyes,

Cligés, edited by Alexandre Miche (1954); and for 395 words from Guillaume de Lorris and Jean de Meun, *Le Roman de la Rose*, edited by Lecoy (1966).

The Sterling Lord Agency, Inc. for seventy-five lines from *Dutchman* in *Dutchman & The Slave*. Copyright © 1964 by LeRoi Jones a/k/a Imamu Amiri Baraka. Used by permission of The Sterling Lord Agency, Inc.

Oxford University Press for four lines from *Prometheus Unbound* in *The Complete Poetical Works of Percy Bysshe Shelley*, edited by Thomas Hutchinson (1905, 1961).

Routledge & Kegan Paul Ltd. and Princeton University Press for an excerpt from *The Collected Works of C. G. Jung*, edited by Herbert Read, et al., translated by R. F. C. Hull. Vol. 10, *Civilization in Transition* (1964).

Vanguard Press, Inc. for permitting the publishing of our translation of twenty-two words from Charles Baudelaire, *My Heart Laid Bare and Other Writings*, edited by Peter Quennell and translated by Norman Cameron (1951).

William Carlos Williams, *Paterson*. Copyright 1946, 1948, 1949, 1951, 1958 by William Carlos Williams. Copyright © 1963 by Florence Williams. Reprinted by permission of New Directions Publishing Corporation.

William Carlos Williams, *Pictures From Brueghel and Other Poems*. Copyright 1954 by William Carlos Williams. Reprinted by permission of New Directions Publishing Corporation.

Introduction

1.

In Book Four of *The Odyssey*, Menelaus tells Telemachus how years earlier he had caught Proteus, the old man of the sea, and compelled the sea god to speak the truth and tell the future by holding him firmly through all his changes of shape. Myth and poetry also employ the agency of guise, yielding us their truth and telling our fortunes only if we grasp them firmly enough. Interpretation of their guises has never been merely a matter of using logic but of engaging all our powers of intuition and synthesis, of employing our whole mind until we break into truth. Any approach to myth and poetry that limits itself only to analysis, to what Ernst Cassirer has called "the discursive mind," is bound to fail simply by missing the central point.

Proteus ("first man") is the grandson of Sky and Earth, and this reminds us that our natures are a fusion of opposing characteristics such as spirit and matter, intellect and emotion, will and appetite. The parents of Proteus are Oceanus, god of the sea, and Tethys, a sea goddess, and when we remember that Homer calls Proteus the old man of the sea, it becomes clear that our natures reflect the characteristic of the ocean—its varying shapes and hues, its constant tides and currents. The sea does not easily surrender its secrets. Instead it lures the unwary into danger through its beauty, but the artist knows that changing shapes and hues make up a language revealing the secrets of the deep to those who can read, and he borrows those shapes and hues to project his own truth.

Because a myth is a mystery, it cannot be explained beyond a certain degree, for the point of a mystery is that it must be experienced. Art, though it is many other things as well, is the epiphany of a myth, as Joseph Campbell tells us; art is symbol and archetype manifested. Art, then, is its own mystery and beyond a degree may not be explained. It too must, like Proteus, be experienced, and only those who can grip very firmly are granted revelation.

The proper employment of myth by literary critics is not to explain, as so many have tried to do, the mystery of art by the mystery of myth. Rather,

11

it is to enable the reader to enter literature more fully, to see more clearly the ways in which mythic thought participates in the formative universe of art. Mythic awareness is weak and undeveloped in modern man; as a consequence we are in danger of losing its entire language. To the extent that art is involved with myth, we need a criticism that helps us enter its realms more easily and fully.

We bind Proteus to make him speak the truth; the essays in this volume explore ways of grappling with myth and art.

2.

The contributors to the colloquium and the myth program (described in the Preface) were given no direction other than the topic itself—the relationship of myth to literature—partly because the sponsors did not wish to tie the participants' hands and partly because they wished to see if myth criticism had progressed over the several years since Henry Murray's collection, *Myth and Mythmaking* (1960), and John Vickery's *Myth and Literature* (1966). As a result the papers move in a variety of directions, but after a bit it becomes clear that most of the essays share a common position—that myth and poetry are expressions of the same creative process, that creating and experiencing poetry always involve the mythic faculties. Though this idea is not novel, it here receives a variety of intriguing formulations and a number of applications to literary periods and genres. Several of our contributors, however, had strong reservations about the validity of myth criticism. Their essays have been placed at the beginning of the volume, where it is hoped that they will cause the reader to look searchingly at the remaining papers.

The essays are divided into four groups, moving from the most general to the most specific:

Section I (Mythic Thought as Levels of Symbolic Awareness) supplies a basis for myth criticism itself by demonstrating that the myths and symbols that pervade all of man's culture should be interpreted in the manner of poetry, and not as history or as primitive science; they then supply us with a universe of inexhaustible value and meaning.

Section II (Problems in Myth Criticism) deals with the kinds of difficulties that arise when myth is used to explicate literature, and also explores an approach in solving mythic awareness.

Section III (Mythic Thought as Process) extends the argument of the first section, showing how authors from a variety of periods believe that poetry involves mythic awareness on the part of both creator and audience. Several of the essays argue that poetry creates new reality, new myth.

Section IV (Mythic Thought as Archetypal Patterns) shows how a number of archetypes illuminate literature both in theme and in process.

Section I: Mythic Thought as Levels of Symbolic Awareness

A single essay constitutes the first section: Joseph Campbell's "The Interpretation of Symbolic Forms." It demonstrates how the symbolizing imagination enables man to lift himself by the bootstraps, so to speak, from level to level of awareness both in life and in literature. Campbell argues that the products of our creative imagination—symbols, legends, myths—must be interpreted poetically rather than as information or history. He provides us with forceful examples of myths and symbols that have meaning on varying levels of insight. He demonstrates how we can progress to higher levels of significance without losing the riches of those which are lower. The essay provides us with strong grounds for accepting the importance of mythic and symbolic images and processes in literature. We can now proceed to consider in Section II some of the problems that arise when we approach literature by way of ritual and myth.

Section II: Problems in Myth Criticism

There are four essays in this group. The first three point out ways in which a literary text can be wrenched to fit preconceived mythic readings; the fourth proposes a different kind of criticism, involving the arousal of our mythic awareness.

Charles Moorman's lively and rueful essay "Comparative Mythography: A Fungo to the Outfield" is a description of the author's movement away from the myth criticism he once employed. Moorman thinks that such criticism, as commonly practiced, gets too far from the literary text, that it abuses literature by using it primarily to support hypotheses about myth. He cannot quite believe that any single theory about myths can be made to fit the enormous diversity of literature, and he strongly doubts whether there is value in analyzing any text in terms of a body of information of which the author was unaware. After demonstrating the extra-literary nature of myth, he questions the usefulness of explaining the literary by the nonliterary. Lest myth criticism be completely abandoned, Moorman is willing to undertake his "fungo to the outfield," a fly ball on which we are to practice our critical fielding. He reminds us how much may be learned by comparing the uses that different texts make of "extended images," images around which has coalesced over a long period of time an enormous and significant range of responses. Through such comparisons, suggests Moorman, we may come to see more clearly, more precisely, what each work is in itself, without the semi-mysticism that frequently surrounds such concepts as rite of passage, archetype, and monomyth.

Deborah Austin in her essay "Threefold Blake's Divine Vision, Intention, and Myth" moves in a different direction. Where Moorman is chiefly worried about the potential vagueness in myth criticism, Austin deplores mainly its distracting power, which draws our attention away from the work conceived as a whole to its more intriguing, but also more localized aspects. Choosing Blake as an example, Austin shows how we are in danger of treating his great mythology as he treated those of Greece and Rome, as curiosities, as vestiges of dead religions that distract us from a steady vision of God and the eternal present. Through a series of sensitive readings informed by the perceptions of the poet that she is, Austin demonstrates that Blake must be considered not only as a creator of endlessly fascinating myths, but also as visionary, as prophet, and as artist. Blake, we are brought to see, is all these figures equally and simultaneously. He was under compulsion to see God and to exhort nations at the same time that he was also compelled to make a presentation of his vision, arousing his reader to something like the kind of comprehension that he had forged for himself. Austin sees modern scholarship as moving too easily into the swamps of Blakean mythology, locating and elucidating, with a loving but arid concern, all its seductive parts. Such a task must not be undertaken at the expense of equal attention to the threefold Blake, for whom vision was central and who regarded his myths and his art primarily as vehicles by which the windows of perception might be cleansed and understanding enlarged.

F. W. Bateson in his characteristic and vigorous essay "Myth—A Dispensable Term" connects his skepticism about myth criticism with the historical reluctance of the English language to adopt the term *myth* in the first place. For Bateson, myth criticism is unfortunately connected with that aspect of Romanticism which sees art as a substitute for failed religions, or which sees art as revelation. He suggests that myth critics feed on the "supernatural overtones" of art, and in this way evade the hard work of seeing, in his words, "the thing as in itself it really is," a task performed best by close reading, by the employment of historical knowledge, and by comparison of manuscript versions of the same work. Bateson cites Hazard Adams's commentary on Blake's "The Poison Tree" as an unfortunate example, arguing that Adams "escapes much too soon from the surface of the poem," with the result that his analysis constitutes a wrong reading. Bateson believes that great literature does not provide an easy escape route from duty; he thinks that the reader ought to expect hard work in his gradual understanding of the text, that he ought to earn it, "be worthy of it." Myth criticism, for Bateson, essentially attempts to find an easy road to understanding, a road that leads nowhere. In general, he agrees with Moorman and Austin that myth criticism distracts from the thematic and formal concerns of literature.

Amidst all his reservations about myth criticism, Moorman did propose the way of comparative mythography, in which he saw a chance for profitable analysis. The last paper in Section II points out another way of myth criticism. Philip Withim, in his essay "Mythic Awareness and Literary Form: Verbal Ritual in Whitman's 'Bivouac on a Mountain Side,' " argues that the way one looks at a literary work has a good deal to do with the kind of form or structure that can be perceived, and decides to study Whitman's poem through the lens of "mythic awareness." Drawing on a range of scholars from Cassirer and Freud to Eliade and Lévi-Strauss, Withim provides us with a descriptive definition of such awareness: it is kinesthetic, emotional, affective, imagistic, symbolic, and spatial; it obeys the laws of complementarity and association, reflecting the intrinsic patterns of the psyche. The kind of poetic structure perceived through mythic awareness mirrors its qualities and is therefore a structure primarily sensuous, emotive, symbolic, and open, as opposed to a form primarily abstract, aesthetic, symmetrical, and closed. The poetic structure is maintained and propelled through dialectical tensions of ideas, sounds, and images rather than through a linear logic. Although in analyzing the Whitman poem Withim begins with orthodox prosody, he demonstrates that formal approaches need to be supplemented by a criticism based on mythic awareness.

The essays in Section II are examples of a shifting in the focus of myth criticism. Moorman and Bateson both deplore the tiresome hunting for mythic parallels endemic in criticism for the last thirty years. They lament the tendency of some critics to leave the plain text in order to search for meanings at one and two removes in fields completely extra-literary. They desire a return to themes and images of the story or poem at hand, the interpretation of which is governed by the intrinsic structure of the work.

Austin joins Bateson and Moorman as she reminds us of the danger of losing Blake the poet and prophet in the seductive coils of his personal mythology. The shift in focus is signified in Withim's paper, which does not even mention mythic parallels but calls for a new emphasis on the texture, feel, and dynamics of the work itself. Withim argues that the faculties of the human mind and psyche that created the great myths are permanent capacities of mind and are drawn on by every poet in the act of creation and by every reader confronting literature. He asks that we read poetry in the spirit of mythic awareness, as he defines it. These considerations lead us into Section III.

Section III: Mythic Awareness as Process

These essays exemplify a renewed emphasis on the dynamics of literature and the literary process. Although each was originally written without prior reference to the other essays, all assume the same basic proposition, asserted by Campbell and underlying Withim's position, that the truth of poetry and the truth of myth are identical, and that the poets of the romance, the English lyric, and the nineteenth- and twentieth-century philosophical poem created their truth and poetry out of those qualities of mind and perception which scholars as diverse as Cassirer, Wheelwright, and Eliade call "mythic."

The first essay is Eugène Vinaver's "The Questing Knight," which demonstrates that to describe the courtly romance of the twelfth and thirteenth centuries is actually to describe a particular kind of imagination. This imagination cannot be characterized by the Aristotelean concepts of organic unity or of beginning, middle, and end. It is not concerned with a single center and a single purpose. On the contrary, the medieval imagination exhibited by the romances calls for many purposes, many centers, and for a cohesiveness derived from multiple relationships, all equally important, all mutually reinforcing: an imagination characterized by simultaneity in a psychological space rather than by hierarchy and sequence in time.

To understand these centuries we must move beyond the facts of economics and politics to the aesthetics of the medieval imagination. We must learn to see that different forms generate different meanings and that the image of the knight-errant plays a role in our own social thought. If we now include as part of our ideal selves such values as romantic love, generosity in a cause, willingness to reach beyond our grasp to the next adventure, it is at least partially because the literary imagination of the thirteenth century created these values in forms that still stimulate our imaginations.

It is profitable to look at Karl Uitti's essay "The Myth of Poetry in Twelfth- and Thirteenth-Century France" as exemplifying Vinaver's point that medieval form generates meanings different from those derived from Aristotelean form. Using the phrase *generic transformation*, Uitti argues that the literature of the twelfth and thirteenth centuries exhibits a development from the *chansons de geste* through the romances that concludes in their late fusion, so that the narrative, referential truth of the *chanson*, which concerned itself with the history of France, is merged with the lyric truth of the romance, which is created by the craft of the poet as he draws on the mythic materials of Troy and Britain. The truth of the romance is understood as existing only within the context of the poem itself, that is, within its form and fashioning. The result of such a distinction is to clarify the medieval "myth of poetry": poetry is seen as a way of discovering truth, a way by which mankind can participate with God in the very act of Creation, a way of transforming perishable truth into undying form, the final aim of *translatio studii*.

In support of his argument, Uitti takes us on a journey into literary history in which we examine such Old French texts as the *Cligés* by Chrétien de Troyes and *Song of the Saxons* by Jehan Bodel. Both poets distinguish between a truth of history and a truth of poetry created by the *bele conjointure* of literary craft. The *Cligés* actually celebrates the artificiality of poetry as the vehicle for remaking and preserving truth. The essay concludes with an examination of the *Romance of the Rose*, showing that its two authors see their poem as having three equally important elements: first, a poet-protagonist who acts as a centralizing ego, and second, an experience of life (such as love). This experience requires the poet to employ the third element—the craft of song, which narrates the experience, as in a *chanson*, and lyrically plumbs the experience so that its nature becomes clear, as in a romance. The result is a fusion of ego, craft, and life that together create a new reality, ready for experiencing by the willing reader.

The third essay of this section continues the concern with myth and process. Vinaver and Uitti have discussed how medieval forms worked mythically; Gene Bernstein, in his "The Mediated Vision: Eliade, Lévi-Strauss and Romantic Mythopoesis," deals with romantic conceptions of the mind. Bernstein argues that Wordsworth and Coleridge reject the

Augustan model of the mind as a passive recording mechanism, a Lockean *tabula rasa,* and turn to a conception of mind and poetry similar to that of the mind of primitive man uncovered by the studies of Cassirer, Eliade, and Lévi-Strauss—a mind vital, organic, sympathetic, and ordering. This portion of Bernstein's paper complements the description of mythic awareness given by Withim in Section II.

According to these views, man thinks in binary oppositions, using symbols for mediating between them. Primitive man employed the totem, based on metaphor and metonymy, as his chief symbolic mode for relating the natural, the cultural, and the spiritual worlds. Modern man has lost any sense of being at one with nature or with the divine; consequently, he cannot employ the totem, which is based on the natural world, as his symbolic resource. He is left with only language, with poetry. Fortunately, the roots of language and totemism are, according to Cassirer and Lévi-Strauss, the same; they are found in the infrastructures of the mind. Thus man still has a potentially mediating path. The English Romantics saw the Fall of Man as a fall into self-consciousness, which creates him as man but also isolates him from nature and God. Accordingly, his symbols drawn from nature shrivel, leaving man able to mediate only within his own cultural world.

At this point Bernstein offers an unorthodox interpretation of Coleridge's conception of the imagination. According to Bernstein, the primary imagination occasions man's isolating fall into self-consciousness and into linear history. Here we would be left to perish were it not for our secondary imagination, operating through metonymy and metaphor to dissolve the barriers between us and other orders of existence. In the absence of totems, we turn to language as our last symbolic resource. Poetry, then, is a function of the secondary imagination whose job is to arouse our faculties of sympathy and affection, and to stir in us the mythic powers of mind that enabled primitive man to relate to nature, God, and other men. The poet becomes a prophet exhorting us to salvation. However, says Bernstein, the burden the Romantics put on poetry was too great; they failed because poetry by itself cannot regenerate the world.

René Galand's study, "Baudelaire and Myth," stresses Baudelaire's agreement with Wagner that both myth and poetry are spontaneous products of the psyche and draw on the same roots, that myth arises from perceiving the supernatural in ordinary reality, and that art becomes great as it accomplishes that same task. Myth, says Baudelaire, is the anonymous poem of the people, manifesting those forces which are to be feared or adored, forces that escape the reason's capacity, while poetry derives from the deepest individuality of the artist's dreams and obsessions, revealing in everyday existence a spiritual and demonic nature. Galand points to the agreement of such positions with those of Freud and Jung forty years later. For Baudelaire, both myth and poetry strip away conventional appearances, which appeal only to the rational faculties, and present reality in concrete and specific forms that have the power to shock spectator and reader with the same emotional impact and to arouse the same perception of sacredness and essence as is experienced by the artist and the prophet.

Galand analyzes "The Swan" to illustrate Baudelaire's view that art manifests archetypal reality beneath ordinary appearance. In this poem, the archetype is the Fall. The bedraggled bird, lost in the city streets, dreaming of his former realms of water, symbolizes man's longing for his lost Paradise. Galand relates "The Swan" to several other poems to show that Baudelaire saw man as an innocent victim. It is God who falls from his original perfection when he creates an imperfect world filled with yearning, imperfect beings. The artist is both ridiculous and sublime in his vain efforts to reconcile that primal opposition through mythic and poetic faculties.

Lawrence Abler's essay "From Angel to Orpheus: Mythopoesis in the Late Rilke" shows how the poet created over a number of years a sequence of myths for himself in obedience to Nietzsche's insistence that the old god is dead and we must revert to the primitive within us to find new myths that will make possible new orderings. Rilke's work can be seen as a series of related myths growing out of each other: the myth of building God by our own effort to define and describe Him (the *Stundenbuch*, 1899); the myth of the God-wrestler, doomed to failure, as is the artist, in his attempts to transmute existence into Being by expelling all facile values and emotions until the emptiness of the abyss is reversed into the fullness of God's presence (*The Notebooks of Malte Laurids Brigge*, 1910); the myth of the invisible and remote Angel-artist, who has already moved the visible world out of time by internalizing it, a necessary model for man to aspire toward, but one that he can never reach (*The Duino Elegies*, 1922); the concluding myth of Orpheus, the artist as half man and half God (*Sonnets to Orpheus*, 1922).

Rilke says that "nowhere will the world come into being except inside us. Our life goes on in transformation." Man brings the world into human existence to the extent that he internalizes it and respects the actuality and specificity of every separate thing in it. Rilke's God or daimon is of the earth, which is the ground of all reality, but unless we transmute it through language, which alone grants significance, that reality remains in time. The Angel-artist could not remain the sole model for man, for he had never suffered or felt alone. Only Orpheus, who had experienced what Rilke calls "the great unity" of life and death, who like all of us has suffered, and who was man become divine, could complete Rilke's vision of the artist. Through the agency of song, Orpheus transforms reality from time into the "eternal present." Language is the creator of meaning and value, and song is the process of accomplishment. The poet sings reality into being.

Section III begins with medieval and concludes with twentieth-century poets, both agreeing that poetry is a vehicle for making and conveying truth through the agency of fiction and myth. Ron Dotterer in his essay "The Fictive and the Real: Myth and Form in the Poetry of Wallace Stevens and William Carlos Williams" carefully peruses their major poems, "Notes Toward a Supreme Fiction," and *Patterson,* to show that the common subject of these poems is the making of poetry. Stevens and Williams assert that only through art can man create his effective personal reality, but that its achievement distorts primal reality. To clear his vision, to see truly once again, man must revert to ignorance, symbolized for both poets by the sun. But ignorant reality blinds and overwhelms man. To bear it, man must cover it with a fiction, must transmute it through his art. In so doing, he once again distorts reality, a circular process from which man never escapes, but through which he grows, to become Stevens's "Major Man" and Williams's "Paterson." Poetry has a role as both artifact and process: artifact because a poem is a *made* thing that captures and freezes the flux of reality (the "made" quality of poetry is symbolized by tapestry in Williams and by crystal in Stevens); the poem is a process because the *making* of a poem both represents and is an instance of the creative process. Construction of the poem is a making of reality, symbolized in Williams by dance and in Stevens by song.

Each poet believes that reality and the mind must interact to make either a poem or a new reality. Williams says, "no ideas but in things," while Stevens speaks of "abstractions blooded." The opposing directions signified by these two statements are reflected in the form of the separate poems: *Paterson* is a tapestry in which many shapes, colors, ideas, facts, and fictions are so interwoven that one cannot be told apart from another; "Notes Toward a Supreme Fiction" is built on a process of thesis, antithesis, elaboration, and synthesis. Personal reality lies, on the one hand, in the tension of warp against woof and, on the other, in the tension of reconciled opposites.

For the editors the most important affirmation to emerge from the essays in Section III is that poetry is a truth-making process, working through mythic awareness. The poet grounds himself in daily reality, employing it with fidelity and affection, and passes it through the transforming lens of his imagination. The result is a reality neither merely objective nor loosely subjective: in short, a new truth. The poetic artifact is the consequence of a creative process, and it is the process that is the medium of truth-making. The poet has always undergone this process, which, as these essays make clear, he often makes the subject of his poetry. The reader in his turn participates in the process by submitting himself to the work; during this participation his sense of reality and his imagination are stimulated to create their version of the poet's world. To do this properly, the reader must lend himself to the occasion, exerting and employing precisely the same qualities of mythic awareness as the artist. Only then can art perform its creative function for the reader. Perhaps this is what Whitman meant when he asked for "athletic readers."

For all the impressive unanimity the poets share, however, these essays also make clear that their attitudes shift on a very important issue—the final efficacy of art. Uitti tells us that medieval poets believed that their craft participated in the work of Creation itself. They possessed a solid faith in the ability of the poetic process to create truths that would endure long after the death of poets. Vinaver asserts that new "forms generate new meanings"; he reminds us that values we hold today such as romantic love and self-sacrifice were partially determined for Western culture by the *chanson de geste* and the romance. He further says that imaginative literature is as important a determinant in human behavior as economics or politics.

But now we find a shift. Bernstein writes that the English Romantics found it necessary to restrict the role of literature in our lives. The Romantics diagnosed the malaise of modern man as a separation from cosmic rhythms, and they tried to use poetry to "mediate between the fact of the Fall and the hope of redemption." But their attempt failed because it was "too much to ask of poetry, whether mythic or otherwise," to "make a Heav'n of Hell." According to Galand, Baudelaire also saw the artist engaged in a necessary but vain pursuit, asserting that any gain art achieves over reality "remains illusory and transient." The artist is a buffoon—mad, ridiculous, sublime. Abler has something very similar to say of Rilke, whose only successful artist is the Angel of the Elegies, remote from humanity. The human artist of the *Malte* notebooks and the half-human-half-god-artist Orpheus are both doomed to vain or partial efforts, even though art is also our only victory. Dotterer concludes that while Stevens and Williams saw art as the only way man makes a personal reality, they also saw that art so distorts it that man must revert to naked and primal reality once again.

So it seems that while medieval poets were secure in their belief that art led to truth, we moderns, as in every other major concern, flounder in ambiguity; for us poetry and mythmaking are absolutely essential activities, but their validity remains uncertain.

Section IV: Mythic Thought as Archetypal Patterns

Each of the five essays that conclude the volume discusses a different archetype and uses it in a different way. The first two essays are overviews of culture and literature, moving through a wide sweep of reference, yet examining particular authors, such as Blake, and particular works, such as *The Bacchae*, with discrimination. The remaining essays focus on a single work—plays by Fernando Arrabal and LeRoi Jones and a film by Michelangelo Antonioni—showing how its meaning is deepened and its impact reenforced by the author's employment of archetype and ritual.

Artists employ archetypes because these repeated images connect one work with others. Since the archetype possesses an enormous range of cultural and literary meanings, it provides the author with a powerful instrument for augmenting the audience's receptivity to receding vistas of significance, to the stirring of primal sources of emotion, and to degrees of activated awareness. But beyond these sources of meaning lies another source, at least for those impressed by the studies of Freud, Jung, Cassirer, Eliade, and others. For these writers, the archetype is an imprint of reality upon the psyche; it is internalized as a symbol or as a network of symbols that becomes part of the enduring structure of that psyche. When an author uses an archetype, he triggers mental energies of great power. The employment of archetypes does not assure a resulting work of art—for there still remains the necessary transmission through the medium of language and formal structure—but it can provide necessary psychic force. Of course, an instrument of such potential does not always work simply toward the good, as the first essay shows.

Catherine Smith argues in her essay "The Invention of Sex in Myth and Literature" that the human imagination, "independent of observation, impels and preserves the notion of two sexes," and that we live in an "elaborate sexual cosmos" of which the principal inventors are "the poets and mythmakers." Smith takes us through four stages of existence—precreation, creation, experience, and apocalypse—showing how the characteristics of each are embodied in sexual images, usually to the derogation of women. She believes that the creator of the cosmos in the earliest myths was female and that the later myths displace her by a male figure—a mental revolution beside which those of Copernicus and Darwin are pale. As a result the functions formerly expressed by feminine imagery are now wrenched into masculine imagery—birth becomes male; the source of new life is now the brain or the mouth instead of the womb. Each phase of existence is similarly examined.

Smith then turns to the poetry of Blake, who, although dedicated to human equality, "limits his art by his use of sexual symbolism." Blake's artist is male; so is Albion, personification of the universe. Women are only emanations of male forces. Women, not men, are used to characterize materiality and fragmentation. Smith observes that there is a conservative time lag in metaphor, for just as the great chain of being has become an inadequate image for our universe, so have traditional images of sexuality. The enormous power of these archetypes still hobbles the mind and humiliates half the race.

In his essay "The Scapegoat: Some Kinds and Uses," John Vickery further examines an archetype that he studied with J. M. Sellery in *The Scapegoat: Ritual and Literature* (1972). Anthropologists have traced this ominous figure back to prehistory, and, of course, we still have many examples of it today, as Auschwitz, urban riots, and Moscow trials bear ample witness. Frazer calls such behavior the result of a mistaken association of ideas, while Freud cites it as an example of magical thinking. Why do we still act this way—why do we somehow still believe in the efficacy of self-purification through the suffering of others? Jung has explored the question more thoroughly than other psychoanalysts. The scapegoat, he suggests, represents the shadow, the image within our psyches of the alien other, that portion of our total personality which is suppressed for the sake of the ego-ideal. Such an explanation sheds some light on the reason why our literature today exhibits so many scapegoats that one critic claims almost all major characters as examples.

Vickery sees authors as employing two basic strategies for the scapegoat, a conscious or overt use and an unconscious or covert use. In either case there follow two possible consequences: society's self-degradation results in a waste of human life, or the victim can achieve heroism and transcendence by accepting his painful lot. In addition, Vickery, in his survey of Strindberg, Euripides, Hawthorne, Faulkner, Melville, Lawrence, Ibsen, and others, finds that there are three basic types: the king/hero, the criminal/knave, and the fool/clown. These figures can suffer an ironic reversal so that the king becomes a humble victim, the criminal a saint, and the fool a wiseman. In any case, Vickery sees literature as the only permissible area in our culture where the scapegoat may purify us through vicarious suffering.

Tucker Orbison's paper titled "Arrabal's *The Solemn Communion* as Ritual Drama" describes and analyzes a production directed by John Vaccaro and performed by the Playhouse of the Ridiculous, a member troupe of Ellen Stewart's La Mama Experimental Theater Club. The production was developed and presented at Bucknell University in May 1974 as part of the Myth and Literature program. Accepting Arrabal's word when he asserts that his plays are a form of ritual, Orbison undertakes to examine the structure of this play as presented both by the script and by the Vaccaro production. There is, of course, a wider implication in the undertaking—that much ritual is a form of drama, that much drama is a form of ritual. Eliade has asserted that in ritual the "novice emerges with a totally different being . . . he has become another." Ritual death prompts psychological and social rebirth; and art, as Norman Brown states, liberates us from our repressions by drawing them into our consciousness.

The analysis of Arrabal's play shows that it combines the ritual structures of holy communion and sexual initiation, motifs commonly associated in primitive ceremonies. But because the society depicted in *The Solemn Communion* is perverted, so are its rituals. Their effect on the protagonist, a young girl, would be to degrade and dehumanize her if, just at the end, she did not totally reject both the archetype of the Terrible Mother and the meanings of the ceremonies she is going through. Ironically, her rebirth comes about, not through the rituals as presented, but by her rejection of their perversion.

Having shown that the play embodies the structure of ritual, Orbison argues that it also *functions* as ritual in performance. The play publicly projects concerns that are the unconscious property of every member of the audience. John Vaccaro manipulates these concerns by means of image, word, and sound through a sequence of affects: arousal, shock, discontinuity, anxiety, and resolution—a sequence to which the audience is encouraged to surrender by the fictional frame and the communal setting. The audience lowers its defenses and introjects the performance, allowing its fears to rise into consciousness, where they can be dealt with. The participation of the audience in this process, sharing with others a common psychic response, leads Orbison to assert that this performance does function as a ritual to the extent that members of the audience have been able to open themselves sympathetically to the play. They emerge, if not new persons, at least changed—perhaps wiser and more perceptive. It becomes clear that both ritual and drama are manifestations of our mythic awareness.

Louis Casimir in his essay *"Dutchman:* The Price of Culture is a Lie" explores a paradox: the myths of an alien culture can infuse new life into a person whose passive acquiescence in that same culture results in living a lie that destroys true selfhood. This play by LeRoi Jones concerns a young Black named Clay who is accosted on the subway by a white woman named Lula. She tries to seduce him, outrages him, provokes him into an inspired outburst from which he relapses, and finally kills him. As automaton passengers carry off Clay's dead body, Lula sits down to await the next black victim, another in an unending series. Casimir argues that Jones deliberately constructed a ritual-drama to serve as manifestation and revelation of the paradox described above. The author draws on automatic and repetitive elements and on the resonances of a number of major Western myths, among which are Adam and Eve, Beauty and the Beast, the Flying Dutchman, and the myth of Hell. One way in which these myths are revitalized is the partial reversal in their story: Adam dies as a consequence of refusing to accept forbidden knowledge; the beast is blonde, the victim black; the Flying Dutchman is a woman trying to get herself killed. Finally, although Lula kills Clay when he fails to attack her, she also acts as his muse. She spurs him out of his acculturated passivity into an outburst of poetry and to the brink of an action that would have freed both the oppressed and the oppressor from an unending trap. In this play, murder becomes a saving act, execution "a simple act of sanity." When Clay refuses to take that action, he signifies his inability to rise out of his condition of death-in-life, his Hell. Thus he might as well be dead, as Lula's act of homicide makes clear. This play is a ritual action, for by using ancient myths translated into contemporary terms, it achieves for an audience of oppressed and oppressors a moment of revelation that might save both.

William Arrowsmith closes this volume on myth and literature with his paper "Antonioni's *Red Desert:* Myth and Fantasy," a penetrating analysis made precisely as if the film were a poem or novel. He shows how it manifests a process of psychological individuation painfully pursued by the protagonist, Giuliana. Through Arrowsmith's discussion, we come to see how the director constructed his film so that the audience, just as in the plays by Arrabal and LeRoi Jones, is led through a vicarious presentation of process. We are brought to see how the film is put together from techniques drawing on color, theme, image, sound, symbol, speech, echo and recall, parallels of characters, and spectrums of type and possibility. Antonioni uses all these elements of life and medium with precision and power. To receive the film's full effect, the audience needs to attend with sympathy and openness, as well as critical distance and awareness.

To this analysis, Arrowsmith brings Jungian insights, not in a reductive spirit but as provisional tools with which to present both the malaise of mankind and the processes of individual perceiving and willing that each person must go through. *Myth* and *Fantasy* in Arrowsmith's title refer to psychic resources, not to personal illnesses or delusions. Giuliana's fantasy of the Sardinian island is an archetype of Paradise, a projection of unchanging oceanic Being, of oneness with others and with nature; it represents a wholly subjective world. This vision is inadequate as a guide to life because it is cut off from the outside, changing world, but it contains, nevertheless, qualities and elements of life that may not healthfully be denied. The fantasy ambiguously prophesies the path that Giuliana must take. Her "myth" is the consequence of her deliberately willing to accept the intruding world of noise and change: a process in which subjectivity comes to terms with the objective, in which consciousness becomes aware of unconsciousness and comes to terms with that, and in which Being accepts Becoming. *Myth*, then, refers to a construct that a person makes in order to bring the phases of his personality into proper balance. The myth represents a victory always incomplete, always unstable, but a victory nonetheless, since, as Arrowsmith reminds us, while "the fantasy lives us," we live our authentic myth.

In this paper, awareness of mythic faculties is asked for in three ways: in Giuliana's necessary recognition of her unconscious self and its requirements; then, in the archetype of Paradise, which represents at once Giuliana's unconscious instincts and all mankind's need for a state of pure being; and, last, in the film as a process to which the audience submits with openness and critical distance simultaneously, the same process that brings Giuliana to face reality.

Although all five essays in Section IV have dealt with archetypes, those discussing plays and film have shown a more direct interest in literature as process. Orbison and Casimir point to their authors' own statements that they deliberately constructed their works as rituals designed to move the audience toward new stages of perception and awareness. Antonioni is not cited as making such a declaration, but Arrowsmith does assert that the point of *Red Desert* is to develop in the audience an increased self-awareness. Moreover, the awareness is not achieved through appeals to reason and logic, but through the manipulation of feeling and emotion by color, action, and symbol. Using the terms that Orbison applies to Arrabal's *The Solemn Communion*, we can say that *Red Desert* functions as a ritual as well as a film.

Interest in drama as ritual, myth, and archetype has been great in recent years and shows no sign of abating. Besides the examples offered in this volume, one has only to look to Grotowski's Polish Theater Laboratory, Julian and Malina Beck's Living Theater, Richard Schechner's Performance Group, André Serban's *Fragments of a Trilogy* for La Mama, and Peter

Brook, to say nothing of the scores of small groups in New York, San Francisco, Paris, London, and Berlin. The common effort in all these highly diverse enterprises is to revert, as we have heard Nietzsche, Wagner, Baudelaire, Rilke, Williams, Stevens, Arrabal, and LeRoi Jones say we must, to a direct and basic knowledge that allows us to regain contact with nature and with other human beings. Mythic theater is aimed at reawakening our essential selves.

3.

This survey of the essays tells us a number of things about the current state of myth criticism. First, it flourishes; next, it still has vigorous opponents; third, there has been no abatement of interest in the archetype as a governing literary structure. The papers by Smith and Vickery not only show how specific archetypes pervade our entire culture and shape works of literature, but they also provide us with occasion to consider how unfortunate the diffusion of such archetypes in history and literature can be, for those of sex and of the scapegoat have caused untold human misery; archetypes are powerful indeed, both for good and for evil. Then too, there has been a movement away from citing isolated parallels between the characters and landscapes of literature and those of myth. Only one paper in this volume examines such parallels. When Louis Casimir discusses the Adam and Eve myth, or the myth of the Flying Dutchman, he does so because the author made them part of his play. What primarily interests Casimir is the play as a ritual dramatizing its own myth. Finally, there is a movement in current myth criticism toward conceiving and exploring literature as a creative process rather than as a static artifact. Some further comments need to be made concerning the second and last of these points.

The papers by Moorman and Bateson make evident their distaste for the excesses of myth criticism. It is also clear that their charges are valid, since so much of myth criticism as practiced has turned reductive and abstract. At the same time, however, one should remember that each single critical approach suffers from similar problems. As a moment's consideration will show, all kinds of literary criticism tend toward reduction and abstraction. The literary work is richly various, sensuously concrete, evocative, suggestive, and many-layered; it works indirectly through metaphor and formal beauty; its concerns are precisely those which cannot be spoken of directly. Consequently, when we come to literature, trying to understand its structure, processes, and themes and trying to analyze our own reactions, we necessarily come with inadequate and reductive tools, tools that are useful to us, because, like a surgeon's knife, they do one job well. Each kind of criticism tends to reduce art in the direction of those principles and concerns forming the framework of the approach. Each critic moves from the individual work toward a particular kind of generality. Thus the historical critic, when he works at an extreme, tends to describe the work as a characteristic product of a certain time and place, or, more subtly, as a reaction against that time. The psychoanalyst, at his extreme, reduces the work to patterns of psychic determinism. The generic critic reduces the work to particular characteristics of specific literary forms, such as those differentiating the novel from the romance; or he sees the work largely as the product of technical devices, such as points of view rooted in specific genres. The formalist critic, at his extreme, reduces the poem or novel to a pattern composed of its parts. The ultimate patterns emerging from this approach can be very abstract indeed. Novels are described as hourglasses, X's, and spirals. *The Scarlet Letter,* an acknowledged triumph of form, is described in terms of three major scaffold scenes with two mediating scenes. Why that particular balance of scenes should contribute to the impact and success of that novel remains a mystery on which formalist critics shed little light. Although both the generic and formalist critics pride themselves on dealing with those aspects of the work which are peculiarly literary, they still cannot tell us, any more than can critics of other persuasions, why a particular assemblage of technical devices, or a specific harmony and balance of parts, should work. They are still perplexed by such questions as why Whitman, whose formal qualities evade adequate description, and Dreiser, whose style is lumpish and frequently sentimental, are major artists, while Housman's formal perfection does not raise him to greater heights.

The truth is that criticism tends to be a posteriori; that is, analysis by the mind follows evaluation by the heart, and is largely so governed. We know *independently* of formal or generic criticism that Blake's "The Tyger" is a very great poem. Consequently we might assert that the trochaic tetrameter, which opens the poem like the peals of a gigantic bell, is a stroke of genius. It may well be so, but we know so not from criticism but from our loins and heart. No single kind of literary criticism enables us to evaluate either fully or satisfactorily the success of a work of art. Such judgments can be made only by the whole person, calling on all the ranges of criticism available to him. The first judgment of a work, like the final one, is made by the aroused heart. The mind follows and supports; it influences, but it does not determine.

Myth criticism does not reduce, abstract, or fail to evaluate the success of a work more egregiously than other kinds of criticism. It remains true, of course, that myth criticism frequently offends, but that is the result of poor work, from which all critical approaches suffer. It is well to remember, when we find myth critics referring the work backward and downward toward archetype and to aspects of the monomyth, that such critics may well be right in specific cases. The question in the mind of the reader should concern not merely the act of calling on old legends, but also whether or not the literary work in question is thus illuminated. At the same time, myth critics ignore these criticisms at their peril. After all, the riches of literature should not be reduced to a pale archetype leaving no hint of the context and of the complex detail that give flavor and life. The myth critic has as much responsibility as any other literary critic to aid in the evaluation of the work, and, like him, he must do so as a whole person, not merely as advocate of a particular persuasion. As this volume exemplifies, skeptics like Moorman and Bateson have had their appropriate effect, since the tendency of myth criticism is to move away from myth-picking toward the exploration of literature as a process in which reader and audience mutually engage. Ten of the essays, those by Withim, Vinaver, Uitti, Bernstein, Galand, Abler, Dotterer, Orbison, Casimir, and Arrowsmith, either implicitly or explicitly, deal with literature as a way of making truth, and as a process for moving the reader or audience toward it by compelling participation in the continuing and universal need to organize one's personal reality.

The mythic faculties, whether those of the artist or the audience, are not concerned simply with strange stories or with justifying otherwise inexplicable rituals; rather, they are concerned with the experience of the oceanic feeling, with the mystery and otherness of the world, with awe and wonder. Nor is myth criticism concerned with explaining away these qualities when they are present in literature. On the contrary, it accepts that myth presents them through analogy and metaphor, leaving to science and logic explanations primarily causal and factual. The mythic faculties present and order the world precisely by including its mystery; consequently, the role of myth in literature is not to explain the world, but to order it through the dramatization of correspondences and oppositions. And just as the artist does not build by logic alone, so the reader must also call on mythic awareness. He too must apprehend by meditation and synthesis. The critic's job is to aid in that apprehension, not only by calling on all the traditional modes of literary criticism, but also by making clear the techniques, concerns, and structurings employed by mythic awareness. He must not use the myth to explain away the mystery—an effort destined to fail. Philip Rahv, in his notable essay "The Myth and the Powerhouse," argues that the mythic faculty belongs to an early stage in man's development that has been superseded by the superior forces of metaphysics and art. He says that the primitive mythic faculty is long past recall. But in the pages of the present volume alone, we see how the poets contradict him, how for a thousand years they have proclaimed the vitality and health of myth. Proteus still tells truths about all the imponderables concerning which science and logic are silent, and still helps to bring man through his necessary stages of growth and awareness. Myth criticism is trying now to reexamine that process, to reaffirm it, and to extend it.

The Binding of Proteus

Section I

Mythic Thought as Levels of Symbolic Awareness

Biographical Note on Joseph Campbell

A New Yorker by birth, Joseph Campbell was educated at Columbia University and at the Universities of Paris and Munich. From 1934 to 1973 he taught at Sarah Lawrence College and is now professor emeritus of literature. A renowned lecturer on James Joyce and on mythography, he gave a series of twenty-five talks at the Cooper Union in New York between 1958 and 1971, some of which were gathered together in *Myths to Live By* (New York: Viking, 1972).

Among his other publications are *The Hero with a Thousand Faces* (Princeton, N.J.: Princeton/University Press, Bollingen Series, 1949), the four volumes of *The Masks of God* (Viking, 1959-68), and with Henry Morton Robinson *A Skeleton Key to Finnegans Wake* (1944; reissued in 1961 by Viking). He has, in addition, edited *The Portable Jung* (Viking, 1971), six volumes of the *Eranos Yearbooks* for the Bollingen Foundation, and the posthumous works of the Indologist Heinrich Zimmer, notably *The King and the Corpse* (Bollingen, 1948). His latest book is *The Mythic Image* (Princeton/Bollingen, 1974).

"The Interpretation of Symbolic Forms" opens this volume because it supplies an explanation for being interested in myth criticism at all. Campbell, like Blake and Shelley, asserts an identity between the poet and prophet, between poetry and myth. He examines the multiple significance of the Cross, demonstrating why it cannot be attributed to history or science, but only to the organizing powers of the human imagination, our mythic faculties. The essay further makes clear that our understanding of myth exists along a continuum, a ladder of incremental meanings. In exemplification, Campbell explores a central symbol of Buddhism, the Chakra, explaining its continuum of meanings in terms borrowed from psychology. By demonstrating that the symbols and myths constituting our culture must be interpreted in the manner of poetry, Campbell has supplied a solid basis for the following essays, which seek to explore the symbols of literature.

The Interpretation of Symbolic Forms

JOSEPH CAMPBELL

1.

I was walking the other day in Washington Square, New York, and heard a little girl say to her father, "Daddy, why do all the churches have plus signs on top?" This I offer as an egregious misinterpretation of a symbolic form; but also as an occasion for asking how we would ourselves interpret the symbolic form of the Cross.

Actually, there are a couple of churches just to the south of Washington Square, one with a tall tower, the other not so tall, and each displays a cross. Interpreted in the simplest way in relation to that circumstance, the meaning of the cross would be: "This is a church." A postoffice, in that way of signaling, would have been flying an American flag; and in that sense the device is an emblem, sign, token, or signal, letting us know that this is a building of a certain kind. Or if one were driving along a highway and saw a yellow sign showing a black cross, one would know that there was a crossroad ahead. The signal is interpreted according to a context of conventional associations. The cross appears as a plus sign in mathematical equations, along highways as a warning, and over churches as an invitation to prayer.

But why, we now may ask, has this particular sign become the mark of a Christian church?. Let us ask somebody who knows: a member, say, of the congregation. His reply will very likely be that the sign is a reference to a historical event: the historical crucifixion of Jesus, who was the founder of the religion represented in the building that is here displaying a cross on its top. That is another way of reading symbolic forms, as references to significant historical events.

But why—or in what way—significant? What was it that was so significant about this particular historical event: the nailing to a cross of this historical personage, condemned to death by his community for the sin of blasphemy? Crucifixion was a common form of punishment in those days.

What was it about this particular case that transformed its sign from one betokening shame and disgrace to one befitting the designation of a church? As as knowledgeable informant would tell us, there is a great mythology associated with this particular crucifixion, namely, that of the redemption of mankind from the mortal effects of a calamitous event that occurred—according to report—long ago in a very distant period, when a serpent talked. The first man—the first example of the species *Homo sapiens*—had been forbidden by his creator to eat the fruit of a certain tree. Satan in the form of a snake tempted him (or rather his wife, who had been lately fashioned from one of his ribs) to eat of the forbidden tree. The couple ate, and thereupon both they and their progeny, the whole of the human race, were taken by the Devil in pawn. They could gain redemption only by the miracle of God himself in the person of his eternal son, Second Person of the Blessed Trinity, becoming incarnate in the person of that earthly Jesus who was crucified—not for blasphemy, finally then, but in order to redeem mankind from the Devil; or, according to another reading, to palliate the Creator's wrath by atoning through death for the heinous offense of that primal human act of disobedience.

Clearly, the historical reading of the emblem has here become anomalous, not to say even bizarre, what with a talking serpent, a devil, and an incarnate god entering into the action. Such are not the characters of a readily credible history. And the question becomes further complicated once we notice, and take into account, the fact that in the jungles of Guatemala there is a Mayan temple known as the "Temple of the Cross," at Palenque, where there is a shrine exhibiting for worship a cross that is mythologically associated with a savior figure, named by the Mayans Kukulcan, and by the Aztecs, Quetzalcoatl: a name that is translated "Feathered Serpent," and suggests the mystery of a personage uniting in himself the opposed principles represented in the earthbound serpent and the released free flight of a bird. Moreover, as the Scriptures related to this figure tell us, he was born of a virgin; died and was resurrected; and is revered as some sort of savior, who will return, as in a Second Coming. All this adds another, very troublesome, dimension to our problem of interpreting the symbolic form of the cross, since it must now be recognized, not simply or singly as a reference within one tradition to one historical event, but as a sign symbolically recognized in other traditions as well, and in significant association, moreover, with a number of related symbolic themes.

The figure of the Feathered Serpent linked with the Cross, for example, immediately suggests our own biblical Eden/Calvary continuity. Furthermore, on top of the Mayan cross there is a bird sitting, the quetzal bird, and at the base there is a curious mask, a kind of death mask. Now a number of paintings of the Crucifixion from late medieval times and the early Renaissance period show the Holy Ghost above, in the form of a dove, and beneath the foot of the cross, a skull. The name of the hill of the Crucifixion, as we all know, was in Aramaic, Golgotha, and in Latin, Calvary, both of which words mean "skull." We do not know what interpretation the Mayans gave to their death mask; but in medieval Christian legend, the skull out of which the cross appeared to have grown, as a tree from its seed, was said to be Adam's: so that when the blood of the crucified Savior fell upon it from his pierced hands and feet, the First Man was, so to say, retroactively baptized, and with him the whole human race. Had there been no Tree of the Fall, there would have been no Tree of Redemption—no Holy Rood, as the Cross was called in the Middle Ages. The answer, therefore, to our question as to why the crucifixion of Jesus holds for Christians such importance implies a complex of essential associations that are not historical at all, but mythological. For, in fact, there was never any garden of Eden or serpent who could talk, nor solitary pre-Pithecanthropoid "First Man" or dreamlike "Mother Eve" conjured from his rib. Mythology is not history, although myths like that of Eden have been frequently misread as such and although mythological interpretations have been joined to events that may well have been factual, like the crucifixion of Jesus.

Let us, therefore, examine further the mythological aspect of this symbolic form, which the little girl in Washington Square interpreted as a plus sign on top of churches.

Those familiar with Germanic myth and folklore will recall that in the Icelandic Eddas (specifically, in Hovamol, verses 139-140 and 142) it is told that All-Father Othin, to acquire the Wisdom of the Runes, hung himself for nine days on the world tree, Yggdrasil.

> I ween that I hung on the windy tree,
>   Hung there for nights full nine;
> With the spear I was wounded, and offered I was
>   To Othin, myself to myself,
> On the tree that none may ever know
>   What root beneath it runs.
>
> None made me happy with loaf or horn,
>   And there below I looked;
> I took up the runes, shrieking I took them,
>   And forthwith back I fell.
>
> Then began I to thrive, and wisdom to get,
>   I grew and well I was;

> Each word led me on to another word,
> Each deed to another deed.[1]

No one can miss the parallels here to the Gospel themes of Jesus' three hours on the Cross (3x3=9), the spear in his side, his death and resurrection, and the boon of redemption thereby obtained. The phrase, "and offered I was / To Othin, myself to myself," is interesting in the light of the Christian dogma of Christ and the Father as One.

Moreover, on top of Yggdrasil, this "Holy Rood" of Othin's suffering, an eagle is perched, like the quetzal bird on the top of the cross at Palenque; while at its roots a "worm" or dragon gnaws, Nithhogg by name, who corresponds there to the earth-bound serpent aspect of Quetzalcoatl, the Savior. And there is, further, a wonderful squirrel named Ratatosk ("Swift-Tusked"), who is continually running up and down the trunk, reporting to the eagle above the unpleasant things that the dragon is saying about him, and to the dragon below the abusive sayings of the eagle— which in a humorous way suggests to me a psychological process that C. G. Jung has termed "the circulation of the light," from below to above and above to below: the point of view of the unconscious conveyed to consciousness, and of consciousness to the unconscious. And there are, still further, four deer perpetually rotating around Yggdrasil, nibbling its leaves with necks bent back, like the four seasons of the year around the everliving Tree of Time, eating it away; and yet it continually grows. Yggdrasil, like that tree, is ever dying and simultaneously increasing. It is the pivotal tree of the universe, from which the four directions radiate, revolving as spokes of a wheel. And so, too, Christ's Cross has been represented symbolically as at the center of a mandala; just as in the old Testament image of Genesis 2:8-14, Eden is described as with "the tree of life in the midst of the garden, and the tree of the knowledge of good and evil," and with a river, moreover, that divides and becomes four rivers, flowing in the four directions.

2.

Mandala symbolism (with which, I take it, we are all, these days, fairly familiar) has been interpreted by Jung as grounded in what he identified as the four basic psychological functions by virtue of which we apprehend and evaluate all experience, namely, sensation and intuition, which are the apprehending functions, and thinking and feeling, which are those of judgment and evaluation. A life governed by prudent forethought may be undone by an upsurge of feeling, just as one swayed by feeling may, for a lack of prudent forethought, be carried, one day, to disaster. ("Never go out with strangers!") The cruciform diagram below makes it evident that in this view of Jung's "four functions" we are dealing with the claims and forces of two pairs of opposites; for as feeling and thinking are opposed, so too are sensation and intuition.

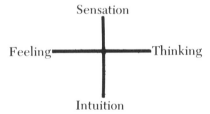

Sensation

Feeling —————|————— Thinking

Intuition

People aware only of the information of their senses, the most obvious actualities immediately present, may be disappointed or undone by unrecognized implications; whereas others, intuitive always of possibilities and implications, may be knocked down by a hard and present fact. In Jung's view, based on his work with patients, each of us tends to favor in the shaping of his life but one of the two functions of each pair—sensation and thinking, for example, which would leave intuition and feeling undeveloped; and any activation of the unattended functions tends to be experienced as threatening and is resisted. Moreover, since the resisted functions are undeveloped—"inferior," as Jung terms them—they are alien to the subject's understanding both of himself and of his world, and whenever they do break through, they overthrow controls and with compulsive force take over: the individual is "beside himself," out of control.

It is evident, then, that in our daily living we are but half men and that all societies actually favor and foster such a fractioning through their moral assignments of men's thoughts, words, and deeds either to the vice side or to the virtue side of their ledgers. Thus in the Christian system of symbolic forms, where the Cross is central, Heaven is above, to which the good go, and Hell below, to which the wicked are assigned; but on Calvary the cross of Jesus stood *between* those of the good thief and the bad, the first of whom would be taken up to Heaven, and the latter sent down to Hell. Jesus himself would descend into Hell before ascending to Heaven since, in his character as total man, eternal as well as historical, and transcendent thus of all pairs-of-opposites (male and female no less than good and evil, as was Adam before the Fall and before Eve had been taken from his rib), he transcends in his being all terms of conflict whatsoever, even that of God and Man. For, as Paul declared to the Philippians (Phil. 2:6-11): "though in the form of God, he did not count equality with God a thing to be grasped [or "held to"], but emptied himself, taking the form of a servant, being born in the likeness of men. And being found in human form he humbled himself and became obedient unto death, even death on a cross. Therefore God has highly exalted him and bestowed on him the name which is above every name, that at the name of Jesus every knee should bow, in heaven and on earth and under the earth, and every tongue confess that Jesus Christ is Lord, to the glory of God the Father."

In this beautiful passage an interpretation is given of the Savior as one uniting, as True God and True Man, eternal and temporal terms, transcending both (not "grasping"), yet to be known as both: as Christ, Second Person of the Trinity, and as Jesus, a once-living man, who was born and died in Palestine. Nailed to the cross, as a living historical man being put to death, he transcends death as he transcends life. The symbolism is obvious: to his left and right are the opposed thieves; himself, in the middle, will descend with one and with the other ascend to that height from which he has already come down. Thus Christ is bound to neither of the opposed terms, neither to the vertical nor to the horizontal beam of his cross, though historically he is indeed bound, even crucified— as we all are in our own lives. We, however, through faith in his image, are unbound and "saved."

If we read this metaphor of crucifixion in the psychological terms suggested by Jung's designation of sensation and intuition, feeling and thinking, then we recognize that in our living—in our temporal, historical living—we are bound either to one or to the other of the opposed terms of each pair, and hence to a knowledge or idea of good and evil that commits us to living as but part men. It follows that to be released from this limitation one must in some sense die to the laws of virtue and sin under which one lives in this world and judges, opening oneself to a circulation of energy and light through all four of the functions, while remaining centered in the middle, so to say, like the Tree of Life in the garden, where the rivers flow to the four directions; or like the point of crossing of the two beams of the cross, behind the head of the Savior, crowned with a crown of thorns. "Our old self," states Paul, "was crucified with him so that the sinful body might be destroyed. . . . For sin will have no dominion over you, since you are not under law but under grace" (Rom. 6:6 and 14).

The horizontal beam of the specifically Christian cross, by the way, is fixed, not at the middle of the vertical beam, but higher, at the level of the Savior's head. At the middle it would have crossed at the genitals and have thereby represented a phallic centering—like that of Yahweh's Old Testament law for those circumcised in the Covenant, where the religion is of race; whereas the Christian is of faith, belief, the mind and heart, to which members of any race whatsoever may be joined.

Hinduism, like Judaism, is an ancient religion of race, caste, or birth, and there, too, a phallic symbolism is recognized, the lingam and yoni (symbolized male and female organs) appearing in the central sanctuaries of temples; whereas in Buddhism, which, like Christianity, is a credal religion of belief and faith, not of birth and race, the central symbol is that of the Savior with the accent on his illuminated head.

3.

In mandala symbolism generally, the sign or figure at the center of the quadrated circle is crucial, in every sense of the word. Like the hub of a turning wheel, it is at the point where opposites come together: East and West, North and South, right and left, up and down; also, motion and rest, time and eternity; as in the words of T. S. Eliot in "Burnt Norton":

> At the still point of the turning world. Neither
>   flesh nor fleshless;
> Neither from nor towards; at the still point, there
>   the dance is,
> But neither arrest nor movement. And do not
>   call it fixity,
> Where past and future are gathered. Neither
>   movement from nor towards,
> Neither ascent nor decline. Except for the point,
>   the still point,
> There would be no dance, and there is only
>   the dance.
> I can only say, *there* we have been: but I
>   cannot say where.
> And I cannot say, how long, for that is to
>   place it in Time.[2]

The ancient cities of Sumer, Akkad, and Babylon, from whose mythological systems much biblical myth was derived, were organized roughly in quarters, with a towering temple of the presiding god at the center. This "height" or "ziggurat," as it was called, at the summit of which heaven and earth came together, was symbolic of the *axis mundi,* the world center, where the vitalizing energy of eternity entered the revolving sphere of space-time—as known from the revolving night-sky.

In Buddhist iconography, the Lord Buddha is represented as seated at the foot of a tree, that Bodhi-tree, or "Tree of Awakening," where he achieved illumination and thus release from the bondages of the senses, delusion, or, in Sanskrit, *Māyā,* which is a word referring to the way in which we generally experience life in the world. It is well defined as *a partial interpretation of a partial experience of the universe:* a misinterpretation of the totality of being, and the living of one's life. On the basis of that fractional glimpse, we are beset by fears and desires that are irrelevant to reality and only intensify the falsification. The Buddha's Tree of Awakening, known as the Immovable Point, is symbolic of that psychological state in which such desires and fears are quelled absolutely, and the mind, so cleared, comes to a knowledge of its own transcendence of all temporal terms and forms.

Plainly, we have a counterpart here to the Christian idea of salvation from sin, and the two historical saviors, Gautama the Buddha (563-483 B.C.) and Jesus the Christ (ca. 3 B.C.-A.D. 28?), are in similar roles. The Bodhi-tree of the Buddha and Holy Rood of the Christ are thus in some way homologous in their world-saving roles, even though the vocabularies of the two great religions differ significantly. The Christian is phrased in terms of sin and redemption, or atonement; the Buddhist, in terms of ignorance and enlightenment, or awakening. An essential question to be asked, therefore, in relation to the problem of interpreting these symbolic forms, is that of distinguishing the "vehicle" from the "tenor" of their arguments. We must ask if an essential identical message ("tenor") is not implicit in the two, one that underlies the differences in the vocabularies ("vehicles"). Are *ignorance* and *sin*, finally, two words for the same condition? Are *enlightenment* and *redemption* two ways of pointing to the same spiritual or psychological crisis? If so, then which vocabulary is the more explicit? If not, what are the essential differences in doctrine?

We are coming very close to some pretty serious questions of religious belief, touching the origins of mythological forms, as well as to a number of rather obscure historical and psychological problems.

What is sin? According to the "Catechism of Christian Doctrine" that I learned to quote by heart in primary school: "Sin is an offense against the law of God," and is of three kinds: venial, mortal, and original. "What," we were asked, "is venial sin?" "Venial sin is a slight offense against the law of God in matters of less importance; or in matters of great importance it is an offense committed without sufficient reflection or full consent of the will." "And what is mortal sin?" "Mortal sin is a grievous offense against the law of God." To make such an offense mortal, three things are necessary: "a grievous matter, sufficient reflection, and full consent of the will." "Why is this sin called mortal?" "This sin is called mortal because it deprives us of spiritual life, which is sanctifying grace, and brings everlasting death and damnation on the soul." "So what, then, is original sin?" "Original sin," runs the answer, "is the sin that comes down to us from our first parents; we are brought into the world with its guilt on our soul." "And what is the effect of this guilt?" "Our nature was corrupted by the sin of our first parents, which darkened our understanding, weakened our will, and left in us a strong inclination to evil."[3]

But are not this darkened understanding, weakened will, and inclination to evil exactly what the Buddhists mean by ignorance, fear, and desire; namely, maya? And is it really necessary, or even useful, to interpret these well-known effects of our normally deluded psychological condition as having been historically *caused* by the "sinful" act of an originally undeluded first parent of the human race? At what stage in the entire course of the evolution of our species are we to postulate the appearance of such a first parent? Indeed, is not the whole problem of our release from the "cloud of unknowing" in which we live only confounded and rendered the more dark by the literal acceptance of the imagery of such a symbolic tale as a chronicle of fact?

The crucial point of my argument is that the imagery of religions— whether of the high religions, or of the simpler nonliterate, primitive forms—is gravely misinterpreted, or rather, is interpreted misleadingly when it is understood to apply primarily to historical events. Such a mythologem, for example, as the Virgin Birth: Was that a historical event? If so, it presents a biological, medical problem, far indeed from anything that might properly be regarded as of spiritual interest. It cannot have referred originally to any specific historical event because we find it in mythologies throughout the world. It is a prominent motif in the mythologies of mankind, and many examples antedate by millenniums that of the Christian legend. The symbology of religion is, in many of its most essential elements, common to the whole of the human race; so that, no matter to what religion you may turn, you will—if you look long enough— find a precise and often illuminating counterpart to whatever motif of your own tradition you may wish to have explained. Consequently, the reference of these symbols must be to something that is antecedent to any historical events to which they may have become locally applied. Mythological symbols come from the psyche and speak to the psyche; they do not spring from or refer to historical events. They are not to be read as newspaper reports of things that, once upon a time, actually happened.

4.

So let us return to our consideration of the cross in relation to its mythological prelude, the fairy tale of the serpent who could talk, and the Fall of Man in the garden—which supplies the upbeat to the downbeat of our story of man's need for redemption. We all well know the amusing tale as recounted—without any sense, however, of its fun—in the second chapter of Genesis. It is based on a folktale-type known to folklorists as "the one forbidden thing"—of which "Bluebeard" is a good example ("You may open all the doors in my castle but one!") It commences with a scene of predawn peace, quiet, and wondrous solitude, as do many of the world's delightful early tales of the Earth-Shaper and his giving of life to creatures of his imagination.

In this version, God had a garden, and what he required for it was a gardener; and so he created a man of dust, breathed into his nostrils the breath of life, and there he was, alive, All-Father Adam, God's gardener. But, alone as he was, he was bored. God had formed out of the ground every beast of the field and every bird of the air, and now God brought them to Adam for his entertainment, but all he could think of to do with them was to name them—after which they went off to nibble grass or to eat each other somewhere else—as is the wont of beasts of the field. In any case, Adam still was bored. And so God—working this thing out as he went along—had a big idea. He put Adam to sleep, took out one of his ribs, and fashioned of it the first girl in the world, whom Joyce in *Finnegans Wake* calls "the cutletsized consort," All-Mother Eve. But now there *she* was with nothing to do, and now it was *she* who was bored. For there was Adam, after the first couple of hours of mutual surprise, back at his steady job of cutting the grass, watering trees, and taking care of the garden, while she simply stood around, watching for a while, possibly with some interest, but then, sitting, dreaming, eating candy perhaps. Then, as always occurs in such circumstances, along came this snake, the most subtle, we are told, of all God's wild creatures. The gardener having been warned by God not to eat the fruit of that one tree, of the knowledge of good and evil (this is the "one forbidden thing"), the serpent, seeing Eve idle, seduced her into doing just that. "God told my husband," she said to him, " 'You shall not eat of the fruit of that tree, neither shall you touch it, lest you die.' " But the serpent said to her, "You will not die. Rather, when you eat, your eyes will be opened and you will be like God." That was enough. Seeing that the tree was good for food and, moreover, a delight to the eyes, she plucked and ate and her eyes opened. Adam arrived when his work was done, and there she was, already wiser than he, and she gave him to bite, and he ate, and his eyes were opened too; and he realized what she must already have observed, namely, that both of them were naked. And so (for some reason that I can't figure out, but that must be known to the clergy), they sewed fig leaves together and made aprons for themselves. When God walked in the garden in the cool of day and saw them, he asked, "Who told you that you were naked? You have leaves on! Have you eaten of that tree?" Adam blamed Eve, Eve blamed the serpent, and the upshot of it all was that this god—who was, as he later explained, "a jealous god" (Exod. 20:5)—became fearful, because, as he told the angels, "the man has become like one of us, knowing good and evil; and now, lest he put forth his hand and take also of the tree of life, and eat, and live for ever; Therefore," as our Scripture says, "the Lord God sent him forth from the garden of Eden, to till the ground from which he was taken. He drove out the man; and at the east of the garden of Eden he placed the cherubim, and a flaming sword which turned every way, to guard the way to the tree of life" (Gen. 3:22-24).

A likely tale! Yet this is the famous story of the Fall, on which is founded the idea of our need for atonement with an offended God, and on this, then, the Christian religion. In fact, this is the authorized answer to the little girl's question in Washington Square, as to why all the churches have plus signs on top. Until only a few years ago, a person could be put to death for openly questioning the validity of this fairytale as *the* authorized, eyewitness account of an actual historical, or prehistorical, misadventure: the eyewitness, of course, being God himself, and this Word of God being revealed to the only people in the world who know what God is and how he should be worshiped. By this account, the gods of the Gentiles—of the Greeks and Romans, Germans, Hindus, and the rest—are, if not devils, then mere figments of man's misguided imagination, as Yahweh and the serpent in the garden are not.

What does this signify? Is the Christian religion founded on nothing more respectable than this museum piece of a misinterpreted folktale? If we accept such a position, do we have to jettison the whole shipload of symbols that have been the spiritual cargo of our passage in the Western World through the seas of two thousand years? Let us see if something can be made of this bit of nonsense by interpreting it, not as history, but as poetry, mythology: not by *de*mythologizing the Bible (as one school of theologians would have it, the book has already been demythologized enough through its interpretation as fact), but by *re*mythologizing it as symbolic of the spirit. The documents of religion—any religion, all religions—are to be read, not as early editions of the *New York Times*, but as poetry. Do we ask if the Ancient Mariner of Coleridge actually lived? or if there was a historical Huckleberry Finn? And if there was not, is the sense of the imagery lost? Popular religion, by and large, is a misinterpretation of great poetry, and the corollary of this statement is that the poet is the prophet and that the great poets of today are our prophets for today—not every little versifier, but those poets who in vision or experience have penetrated the mysteries of the veils of time to a knowledge transcending the foreground view of life that rules in the marketplace.

One of the most effective ways to rediscover in any myth or legend the spiritual "tenor" of its symbolic "vehicles" is to compare it, across the reaches of space, or of time, with homologous forms from other, even greatly differing traditions. The underlying core then is readily unshelled from its local, historically conditioned provincial inflections, applications, or tendentious secondary interpretations, and a shared psychological, or spiritual, ground is opened, transcending the conditions of space and time, and of history. For a tradition such as our own, where so much official emphasis has gone into insisting on the local historicity of the generally inherited symbols, such an opening of the eyes to wider horizons and other traditions may work as a marvelous restoration to life and sense of the apparently moribund forms.

Let us go to Nara, the holy city of Japan, where there is a prodigious image of the mythical Buddha known as Mahavairochana, "Great Sun Buddha" (in Japanese, Dainichi Nyorai). The statue is an image of bronze, fifty-three-and-a-half feet high, cast and installed in A.D. 749. What it represents is not the historical Buddha Gautama, who lived and taught in India and Nepal, 563-483 B.C., but a purely and frankly visionary figure, symbolic, in human form, of the light of unclouded consciousness. The counterpart in Christian thought is the Beatific Vision described by Dante at the end of *La Divina Commedia*. Gautama, the historical Buddha, is understood to be an incarnation of the consciousness here envisioned as transcendent; but so, according to Buddhist thought, are we all, only unawakened. The word *buddha* means "awakened." And Gautama's awakening to his Buddhahood at the foot of the "Tree of Awakening"—that "still point of the turning world"—Buddhists regard as a model for us all to follow, toward the realization of our own transcendence-in-truth of the nightmare of our lives in time. Wrote our own poet, Wordsworth: "Our birth is but a sleep and a forgetting"; and Shakespeare, in *The Tempest:*

> We are such stuff
> As dreams are made on, and our little life
> Is rounded with a sleep.

And then we have William Blake: "If the doors of perception were cleansed every thing would appear to man as it is, infinite." Thus we have the message in our own tradition, where it is known, however, as poetry, not religion, while our religion, actually, as I have already said, is being radically misinterpreted because it is read differently from a poem or enacted play.

So let us return for a moment to the poetry of that Japanese temple in Nara of the Buddha Mahavairochana. The approach from the south is guarded by an imposing gate, with a guardian standing at either side in the form of a large wooden statue, twenty-six-and-a-half feet high. The statues stand in threatening attitude, bearing weapons. The mouth of one is open, the mouth of the other is closed. Their look is frightening. They are known as "Thunderbolt Warriors"; in Sanskrit, *Vajrapani;* in Japanese, *Kongō-rikishi.* They are the counterparts, in the Buddhist mythic image, of the cherubim placed by Yahweh at the gate of Eden to guard "the way to the tree of life." I recall seeing in a New York newspaper, during the war with

Japan, a picture of one of these imposing images, with a caption that read: "The Japanese worship gods like this"—a piece of information, no doubt derived from what in journalese is known as a "reliable source," and published, of course, with high regard for the American public's "right to know." But I had a wicked, uncooperative thought. "No," I thought, "not they but we! It is we who worship a god like that." For in the Buddhist world the worshiper is instructed to walk right between those two gate guardians and approach the tree without fear; whereas, as told in the Book of Genesis, our own Lord God put his cherubim there to keep the whole human race *out*. The Buddha sits with his right hand raised in the "fear not" posture and his left in that of "boon bestowing." One is not to be intimidated by the death threat of those guardians, but to cast aside the fear of death and come through to the knowledge of one's own Buddhahood— or, as that thought would be rephrased, in biblical terms: one's own Godhood, as Yahweh himself recognized when, in Genesis 3:22, he expressed the fear to his angels that man might "become like one of us . . . take of the fruit, and eat, and live forever."

The tree, the gate, and the cherubim: it is a shared symbolic image that the two religions have inherited. But their interpretations differ. Let us ask, specifically, in what way. And let us begin by considering in Buddhist terms the force or meaning of the two cherubim, those "Thunderbolt Holders," at the gate.

5.

First, the mouth of one is closed, and of the other, open. They are thus a pair of opposites. Good and evil are a pair of opposites; so, also, male and female—as Adam and Eve realized when, having eaten of the fruit of the tree, they saw that they were naked. The exile followed this discovery of duality, opposition, separation: it was then that they became separated from God. Approaching the imposing gate of the Buddhist temple at Nara, we too are separated, being not yet within, but outside, the garden. Its two giant guardians are threatening; if they were not of wood, but alive, we should indeed be terrified on beholding them. We should become aware of another pair of opposites, our own fear of death and desire for life: fear and desire. But these, in the Buddhist legend of Gautama's achievement of enlightenment, were exactly the two chief temptations that he overcame while sitting on the "Immovable Spot" beneath the axial tree, at the "still point of the turning world." The god whose name is "Lust (Kama) and Death (Mara)" approached and, to unsettle him, displayed, in his character as the Lord of Lust, his three voluptuous daughters. Had Gautama, sitting there, had any thought of "I," he would have thought "They," and there would have been a response; but there was none; the temptation failed. Transforming himself, therefore, into his character as the Lord of Death, the Antagonist hurled an army of ogres against the one there sitting; but again there was no identification with ego; no sense of fear was evoked, and the temptation failed.

Likewise in ourselves, if our attachment to ego has not been conquered, so that the fear of death and a desire for continued life are still the governing principles of our experience and action, we are unfit psychologically to pass through the guarded gate to the Immovable Spot, where the Buddha sits. Physically we may go through the gate and walk along the broad path into the temple, there to stand taking pictures, or in prayer; but we shall not by that physical act have made the passage psychologically. Or we can even go to India, on pilgrimage to Bodh Gaya, where the tree still stands under which Gautama achieved illumination: we can view that tree, take pictures of it, worship it, and yet not be viewing the same tree at all under which the Buddha sat. For the Bodhi-tree is not geographically situated—as Eden was once thought to be—but is within us, and to be found there; and what is keeping us away from it is attachment to our separate lives as egos—to *ahamkara*, as the Indians say, "the making of the sound, *I*."

In other words: it is our own attachment to our temporal lives that is keeping us out of the garden. Could we get rid of this, we should walk in truth through what has been called, in a Japanese Zen Buddhist work, "The Gateless Gate," *Mu-mon*, since nothing is there, no cherub at either hand, only our own misidentification of ourselves with our mortal part.

In all mystical lore, a passage through the door of death leads to immortal life; not our merely physical, historical dying (that is the popular reading of the mystery), but a psychological dying to the fear of death. This means that one's center of self-identification has to be shifted from the temporal personality to that, within, which neither was born nor will die, but is eternal. And the whole sense of Buddhism, accordingly, asserts that only when our thirst for life and the life-chilling fear of death are quenched can we know that, within, which has always been there, antecendent to and transcendent of the limitations of the mortal personality. And in this knowledge, all categories, whether of experience, of thought, or of feeling, are transcended; all names and forms, all pairs of opposites, whether of I and Thou, good and evil, yes and no, life and death, or even being and nonbeing, God and the soul.

But returning from this Eastern, Buddhist sojourn for one more glance into our Western book of conundrums—not into its Old, however, but into its New Testament: is it not evident that Jesus, crucified on the Tree of Eternal Life, Holy Rood—that second tree of Eden, the way to which was guarded by Yahweh's cherubim and flaming sword—must have passed through the guarded gate to the Tree and thus opened the gate to ourselves? Indeed, is that not precisely the sense of the term *"New Testament"*? Fearless of death, and clinging neither to life nor (as we have read in Paul to the Philippians) to the form of God, he emptied himself altogether of both temporal and eternal categories, whether of experience, of thought, or of feeling.

"And at the ninth hour [Othin's ninth day!] Jesus cried with a loud voice, 'Éloi, Éloi, láma sabachtháni?' which means, 'My God, my God, why hast thou forsaken me?' " (Mark 15:34). For he had himself just broken past the bounds, the categories, within which gods and their laws, justices and mercies, operate; sprung like an arrow from its bow into the void, where Father and Son, all opposites, vanish. "And the curtain of the temple was torn in two, from top to bottom" (Mark 15:38).

"I am the door of the sheep," he is reported to have said, in the second-century "Gospel According to John." "I am the door; if any one enters by me, he will be saved, and will go in and out and find pasture. . . . I lay down my life, that I may take it again. No one takes it from me, but I lay it down of my own accord. I have power to lay it down, and I have power to take it again; this charge I have received from my Father" (John 10:7, 9:17-18).

But now, who was the Father so named? Yahweh? He who had blocked the road, and the veil of whose temple was rent? Throughout the early Christian centuries this question was in sharp dispute, and the answer that those called Gnostics gave was, to Yahweh, a definite "No!" The Father of the Savior was of another mythology entirely, of eternal light and grace, not of history and the law. "For Christ is the end of the law" (Rom. 10:4). The Greek word *gnosis*, "a knowing, knowledge," and especially "higher knowledge, deeper wisdom," is precisely a counterpart of the Sanskrit *bodhi*. Gnostics, or *gnostikos*, in their various sects, interpreted salvation as did the Buddhists, as the opening of an inward, intuitive eye, or door to illumination. In the second-century "Gospel According to Thomas," for example,[4] the following words are attributed to Jesus, when asked by his disciples, "When will the Kingdom come?" Jesus said, "It will not come by expectation; they will not say: 'See, here,' or: 'See, there.' But the Kingdom of the Father is spread upon the earth and men do not see it" (Saying 113). We are not, that is to say, locked out of the garden: it is here, over all the earth, and requires only a change in vision to be recognized. Moreover, this is the change of vision symbolized in the figure of Jesus on the cross: the crucifixion there of the temporal personality, but simultaneously also of the form of God, which was not held to, but was "humbled," becoming "obedient unto death." In other words, we have here, already in the Christian sphere, a spiritual, or psychological, nonhistorical interpretation of the mythic image, altogether in contrast to that which later gained supremacy with the victory in the fourth and fifth centuries of Byzantine orthodoxy. With that victory the opposition between the symbols of the Fall in Eden and redemption on Golgotha, of which Paul had made so much, was interpreted historically, first, as an original offense against God; second, as a subsequent act of atonement; and third, as an ultimate, general coming of the Kingdom at the end of time. The psychologically oriented Gnostic view, on the other hand, is in accord, not only with the Buddhist interpretation of symbolic forms, but also with the Greek, of the mystery cults—indeed, with the ways of all *poetic* approaches to life in its finally ineffable wonder. And since there are many grades, stages, or inflections, of insight recognized and recognizable in these nonhistorical, nondogmatic approaches to the mystery, let me now bring this discussion to a close by reviewing, in the briefest terms, one of the most illuminating systematizations of the graded orders of spiritual realization that has yet been given to the world. It will serve to show us that mythic images should be interpreted poetically, not literally or historically.

6.

I refer to the Indian system of Kundalini, or unfoldment of the so-called Serpent Power, which is an interpretation, in terms of seven steps, of the transformations of human insight by the vitalizing energies of the psyche rising from states conditioned by fear and desire to those of rapture and transcendent light. The Sanskrit noun itself, *Kundalini*, suggests a serpent coiled like a rope (*kundala*, the coil of a rope). It is a feminine noun and a feminine snake, since in India the moving energy of the psyche and body is symbolized as female. Pictured as coiled, asleep, within a "lotus" (*padma*) or "circle" (*chakra*) at the base or root of the body, situated between the anus and sex organs, this shining female serpent, fine as the fiber of a lotus stalk, is, through yoga, roused and caused to ascend, uncoiling, up the interior of the spine to the crown of the head, where it unites in ecstasy with the radiance of a thousand-petaled lotus known as Sahasrara, "Thousand Sectioned."

In this ancient system of symbology, which comes down apparently from Old Bronze Age times, 2000 B.C. or so, the human spine is represented as equivalent, in the individual body, or microcosm, to the axial tree or mountain of the universe, the macrocosm—the same mythical *axis mundi* symbolized both in the tree of Eden and in the towering ziggurats in the centers of ancient Mesopotamian cities. It may be recognized, also, in the Dantean Mount Purgatory, where the seven ascending stages represent steps in the purification of the soul on its way to the light of the Beatific

Vision. The stages of the ascending Kundalini also are seven, there being between the root base and crown five intermediate lotuses; and as each is touched and stirred by the rising serpent energy, the psychology of the yogi is transformed.

Now what I propose to do is to follow this ascent in its seven stages. My interest, particularly, will be to suggest something of the attendant transformations, not only in psychology, but also in the very ways of interpreting symbolic forms. The reader, if he likes, may try to identify the stations of his own manner of life—his own way of producing maya for himself—in the sequence of these archetypal steps in the amplification of human consciousness. However, the manner of my own discussion is to be neither hortatory nor moralistic, but—at least as far as I can make it so, enwrapped as I am in my own maya—objective, descriptive, and (to use the word rather loosely) scientific.

For this is an old, old, tried-and-true construction of insights that have been gained from centuries of inward, yogic explorations of a landscape that is interior to us all, and as real and actual to an inward view as are the landscapes of the external world to our outward-gazing eyes. Moreover, since each of us, from the point of view of others (and even of ourselves when we are looking into a mirror), is but a particle or feature of nature, so our inwardness in its transpersonal, archetypal, generically human charac-ter must be a portion of nature too. When we adventure into our own depths, we are adventuring into nature's depths, and the landscapes here disclosed are interior, not only to ourselves, but also to everything seen as outside. I have myself been interested for many years in the psychological formulations of this yoga, and am now completely convinced of its relevance to the interpretation of the symbolic forms, not only of all Oriental, but also of our own Occidental arts and religions.

To begin, then: the first station, circle, or lotus of the Kundalini, which, as already told, is at the root or base of the body, is called, appropriately, Muladhara, the "Root Base." One's spiritual energy on this level is without any impulse toward or zeal for life. One is simply gripping, hanging on. I think, when considering this chakra, of the character of dragons. We know a great deal about dragons. Their biology and sociology have been studied for thousands of years and described in legends from every part of the world. What dragons do is guard things. The typical situation is that each dragon has a cave, where it diligently guards captured things. These are, most usually, a beautiful virgin girl and a heap of gold (the symbolic values, namely, of the next two chakras up the line); but the dragon has no idea what to do with either. It simply hangs on, guarding. It experiences none of the joys of life generally associated with these two precious things. There are people like this; they just hang on; we call them "creeps." They have no impulse to adventure. They are not properly actors, but re-actors, responding unimaginatively to sheer stimuli. The system of psychology most appropriate to their state of consciousness is Behaviorism: the science of man as worm, and the art favored by such a person—if he has any taste for art at all—will be sentimental naturalism. His attitude toward living will be that which Nietzsche has called a groveling before "hard facts."

The first goal of any shining hero seeking to release the values of the spirit from the guardianship of such unimaginative worms must be to lance them, like a knight, and break the hold of their dragon grip. Accordingly the yogi, by deep and measured breathing, appropriate meditations, controlled body postures, hand postures, the recitation of stirring syllables, and so on, will strive to wake the torpid serpent of his spiritual life from its lethargy, its sleep, its unadventurous dream, to better things; lifting it, in its full, unfolding length, up the long spinal course to the crown, and rousing on its way all the other lotuses of our human potential to their flowering.

And so now, following him in this enterprise, we arrive with our own kundalinis at Lotus Two, the name of which, Svadhishthana, means approximately "Her Favorite Resort." It is the lotus of sexual zeal, desire, at the level of the genitals. At last we have a sense of excitement. We are no longer mere reactors, but originators of action; not grovelers before hard facts, for love, as they say, is blind. The facts, indeed, hardly matter; and when finally they do show through, we may find ourselves disillusioned. That is one of the standard crises of marriage. But in the meantime, this lout of a boy and goose of a girl shine for each other like gods. They are on Cloud Nine. They walk, a little on air. Or, described from another point of view, they may be said to have recognized, in their desire for each other, something of the godliness that is actually ingenerate in us all, but is normally encoiled in dragon brawn. One's psychology is, in any case, Freudian at this level. The whole view of life is sexually inspired: one's joys and frustrations are of sex; one's sublimations are of sexual zeal (Freud's libido); and though the frustrations are unremitting and the sublimations viable, a lot of distracting work gets done, and therein is the origin and meaning of civilization: one writes a Ph.D. dissertation, for example, say on Sexual Intercourse; and at the age of forty-five one gets the Ph.D., at the age of twenty having lost the girl.

Chakra Three is at the level of the navel and is known as Manipura, "The City of the Shining Jewel." The desire at this level is to consume things, to convert them into oneself or into one's own. The psychology is that of the conqueror, the winner, the master—or, if negatively aspected, the loser, the toady, or the seeker of revenge. In short, the psychology here is of Adler: the will to power.

We must recognize that mankind shares the modes of these three lower

Chakras with the animals, for they too hold on to life, no matter how dull it may be; they too have sexual zeal; and they too know the drive to conquer and to overcome. People living with these interests are fundamentally outward turned; their goals are outside, their happiness and fulfillments; and they have to be controlled by law and by inculcated ethical principles, lest they become wolves unto each other. In the main, therefore, it is to mankind on these three levels that the secular laws and institutions of a society are addressed.

But now we come to something else, something specifically human, at the Fourth Chakra, the lotus of the heart: an awakening of the spiritual life. For those aware only of the values of the first three levels of experience, the conditions of their own physical birth are what determine and govern their destinies. But when the rising Kundalini reaches the level of the heart, the spiritual birth occurs, a new inward life, specifically human; and this is symbolized in the mythological image of the Virgin Birth. The Savior so born—not in the natural way—is *symbolic* of the release of our own spirit from the bondages of unilluminated animality; and he is to be so born in each of us. For as the mystic, Meister Eckhart, phrased the argument in a beautiful sermon on this mystery: "It is more worth to God his being brought forth ghostly in the individual virgin or good soul than that he was born of Mary bodily."[5] The symbolical attribution of such a birth physically to an actual historical personage, accordingly, is not to be taken literally, but in its teaching sense, as representing the *meaning* of his life to us: the spirituality of his life, which is to become the inspiration and model of our own.

Reading such an upward-leading symbol downward, to the physical plane from which its imagery is meant to release us, only breaks the force of its effectuality—and this whether the physical misreading is of the Pope in Rome or of Dr. Freud. For the interpretation of mythic symbols is to be (using Eckhart's vocabulary) "ghostly," not "bodily"; their entire justification lies in their representation to our senses of an intuitable mystery-dimension that is meta-physical to physical things. However, the power or, rather, the willingness of the physically oriented intellect to waken to the ghostly metaphors and to follow them is a function of its own transformation—or in churchly terms, conversion—at the level of Chakra Four, prior to which crucial event the "Word behind words" cannot even be heard. Hence the oft-quoted saying of the ghostly born, historical Jesus; "Do not give dogs what is holy; and do not throw your pearls before swine, lest they trample them underfoot and turn to attack you" (Matt. 7:6).

In Sanskrit the name of the lotus-station of awakening, where (once again to use Eckhart's words) "God is born in the soul, and the soul reborn in God," is Anahata, a name that says, literally, "Not Hit," meaning specifically, "the sound that is not made by any two things striking together." Every sound that our physical ears can hear is made by two things striking together. The sound of my voice, for instance, is of the breath vibrating the vocal cords. The sound that is *not* made by any two things striking together is a sound of the energy of the universe, the interior of the atom, which is antecedent to things and of which all things are manifestations. And what this means is that beyond the range and ranges of all our scientific hypotheses of cause and effect and so on, there is an ultimate, irreducible mystery of being and becoming, which underlies the whole grandiose night-sky display of the galaxies and their suns. Moreover, the mystery of all-being is also the mystery of our own being. Becoming aware of the wonder of this mystery and of its fascination, like that of the sound of a seashell held to the ear, we are hearing, so to say, the sound Anahata, "Not Hit," which in the Indian tradition is described as OM. When pronounced, of course, the sound OM is made by two things striking together. However, its pronunciation supplies a directional clue for the inner ear, toward the sound to be secretly heard. And there is an allegorical extrapolation of the import of OM for the guidance of the mind, which has been provided in a brief but substantial piece of Scripture known as the *Mandukya Up-anishad.* It will be instructive, at this point, to review this explantation.

First, then, the sound OM may be written, alternatively, as AUM, since O is interpreted in Sanskrit as an amalgam of A and U. So pronounced, it is known as the four-element sound: A-U-M and a fourth, the fourth being the Silence out of which the sound emerges, back into which it will go, and which supports it throughout as a ground against which the A, U, and M are heard.

In the pronunciation of AUM, the beginning is with A, sounding at the back of an open mouth; U then fills the mouth cavity; and M closes at the lips. The whole mouth has thus been filled with the sound, so that all words are but particles of AUM, and their meanings but particles of its whole— much as we, in our limited temporal forms, are but particles or inflections of that Form of forms which is the Lord and our proper end.

Allegorically, as expounded in the Upanishad, A is associated with the world of Waking Consciousness, where things are seen as separate from each other; *a* is not *not-a;* an Aristotelian logic prevails: I see You, You see Me; Subject and Object are separate from each other. Further, the objects seen are of gross matter, weighty and not self-luminous, the only self-luminous objects here being fire, lightning, and the sun and stars, which are accordingly regarded as openings, gates, or doors to a higher, self-luminous sphere. And it is this higher sphere, represented in U, that is of Dream Consciousness. Here everything beheld is of a subtle self-luminous substance, wonderfully fluid and quick to change, weightless and fascinating. Furthermore, you the subject beholding them are at the same time they themselves; for dreams are of your own substance or energy, your own will. So that in this sphere, although Subject and Object appear to be different, they are the same.

Now comes the big point: the deities of vision are of this sphere and of the same luminous stuff as dream. Accordingly the vision and the visionary, though apparently separate, are one; and all the heavens, all the hells, all the gods and demons, all the figures of the mythic worlds, are within us as portions of ourselves—portions, that is to say, that are of our deepest, primary nature, and thus of our share in nature. They are out there as well as in here, yet, in this field of consciousness, without separation. Our personal dreams are our personal guides, therefore, to the ranges of myth and of the gods. Dreams are our personal myths; myths, the general dream. By heeding, interpreting, and following dreams we are led to the large, transpersonal fields of archetypal vision—provided, of course, that rational interpretations are not binding us back continually to our own Chakras One, Two, and Three. As the Hindus say, "To worship a god, one must become a god"; that is, one must find that part within that is the deity's equivalent. This is why (in mythological language) God the Son, Knower of the Father, has to become in each of us ghostly born before we can know, as He does, the Father, and say with Him, in knowledge and in truth, "I and my Father are One" (John 10:30); or with Paul, "It is no longer I who live, but Christ who lives in me" (Gal. 2:20).

Passing on to M: the reference here is to the condition of Deep Dreamless Sleep: no dreams, just darkness. There is consciousness, however, beneath the darkness, hidden, of no specific thing or things, whether of waking or of dream; undifferentiated; whole; sheer light. The ultimate goal of yoga is to enter that field awake; coming there to full union with that light. The experience is ineffable, beyond words, since words refer to objects and their relationships, whether of waking or of dream. Hence—Silence, the fourth part of the syllable AUM.

But now, just one more word about AUM and the states of consciousness to which its elements are referred. As the Upanishad points out: the objects known to Waking Consciousness are of the past; having already become, they are apprehended an instant later (or, if very far away, like stars, it will be light years before they are perceived). Consequently, our sciences and statistical analyses, dealing as they must with what is past, are telling us only of what has already occurred, projecting perhaps into the future, but on the basis only of a known past. No real novelty, no really new thing or event can be thus foreknown to science. But the forms beheld in Dream are of the present. Apprehended immediately in the moment of their life, our life, they are of our own becoming, right now, and of the powers that are moving us. Our effective myth, that is to say, is what is moving us as dream. However, this effective myth may not be the same as that which, in our waking state, we think we believe in, and to which we pay our worship on Sundays, in that building with the plus sign on top. A very important exercise should be that of getting our two mythologies— that professed and that actual—together in our present. And as for our future: that is what is hidden in the darkness of Deep Dreamless Sleep.

The hearing of the syllable OM occurs as the rising Kundalini reaches the level of the heart and wakens the lotus, Anahata, of Chakra Four, and it marks the beginning of our life as truly Man, aware of the mystery dimension of things. At this Moment our relationship to things changes. They are no longer simply objects of our lust or aggression, but vehicles of the syllable OM. We hear it everywhere, out there, in here. We are no longer desirous but in bliss, and the Indian Tantric saying, *iti iti*, "It is here! It is here!" is the Good News of our life. "The Kingdom of the Father is spread upon the earth."

However, a new zeal, a new yearning, may now arise in us, to know and to hear that sound directly, not through things, but unmediated—the zeal, that is to say, of the religious quest. And to this end one may abandon the world, as hermits do, and as Jesus did in his retreat to the desert, from which he returned only to teach. "Let the dead bury their dead" (Matt. 8:22). "Sell what you possess and give to the poor, and come, follow me" (Matt. 19:21).

I was reading some time ago (I forget just where) a list, published by the late Dr. Abraham Maslow, of the values for which men and women in our culture commonly live. They were: 1. survival, 2. security, 3. prestige, 4. personal relationships, and 5. personal development. And I thought, when I considered this list: "Well, those, precisely, are the values that are blown sky high when anyone becomes infected—not only with a religious zeal, but with any life-purpose at all." To which point we have another saying from the Gospels: "He who loses his life for my sake will find it" (Matt. 10:39). This, precisely, is the message of the next Chakra, number Five, the name of which, Vishuddha, means "Purification, Purgation": the cleansing and release of consciousness from its worldly infatuation in the passing features and forms of temporal experience. The seat of this center of transformation is at the level of the larynx, the organ of speech and the word. No animal, though it may bark or howl, can formulate by way of speech a concept, an idea representing the meaning of a universal term. We have entered the province of the human mind, the wonderful ornament of our species. The work to be achieved here is that of penetrating appearances to their source, their life, which is recognized with rapture as our own source and life, transcendent of our temporal birth and death. The function of art, according to this way of thinking, is to reveal through temporal forms the radiance of that unconditioned state: the supporting Silence of AUM. Or, to quote to the same point the words of the playwright Gerhart Hauptmann: "Poetizing consists in letting the Word be heard behind words." (*Dichten heisst, hinter Worten das Urwort erklingen lassen.*)

And so we pass from Chakra Five to Six, at that point just above and between the eyes which is represented in Indian images by a third eye, the inward eye, which opens to an inward view of the vision of God. Simultaneously the inward ear opens to the sound of AUM directly, in its full force; for the radiance of God is not only of light but of sound. And the name of this center is Ajna, meaning "Command," or "Authority in Knowledge." It is the counterpart, in our tradition, of the heavenly rose of Dante's empyrean, where the soul beholds in eternal rapture the Beatific Vision.

There was a great Indian saint of the last century, Ramakrishna (1836-86), a consummate master of yoga, who, when describing to his disciples the rapture of this sixth center of the Kundalini, declared that it was as though there were no more than a pane of glass there separating the visionary from his Beloved. Thus the experience is dualistic: that of a subject beholding an object; whereas the ultimate aim of the devotee is to be as one with the Beloved. The great Sufi mystic Hallaj (d. A.D. 922), compared the situation to that of a moth at night seeing a light shining in a lantern. Its zeal is to be one with the flame; but the glass, against which it batters its wings, prevents it from gaining that goal. And when morning comes it returns to its friends, to tell them of the wonderful thing it saw. "You don't look the better for it," they say on seeing its battered wings. (That is the condition and look of the ascetic.) But the next night, returning to its lamp, it manages to get into it and its passion is achieved, its love fulfilled. It becomes its beloved, and is itself, for one vivid instant, aflame.

Hallaj was executed in Baghdad for having confessed, Ana il-Haqq, "I am God," just as in Jerusalem Jesus had been for declaring, "I and the Father are one" (John 10:30). Such talk is heard as blasphemy wherever God and man are experienced as separate. And when Hallaj was brought to be crucified and beheld the cross and the nails, he uttered a prayer of thanks to God, and for mercy to those, who, to win God's favor, now were about to slay him: "For verily if Thou hadst revealed to them that which Thou hast revealed to me, they would not have done what they have done: and if Thou hadst hidden from me that which Thou hast hidden from them, I should not have suffered this tribulation. Glory unto Thee in whatsoever Thou doest, and glory unto Thee in whatsoever Thou willest!"[6] The orthodox community was giving him actually what he yearned for: union with his Beloved; so that it might perhaps be said that the highest religious function of an orthodox community is to give the mystic, in this cruel way, his ultimate release from that separation from God in which they have their pride.

In any case, we have now, in our own ascent of the lotus ladder, to mount beyond the level of Lotus Six to that at the crown of the head, Sahasrara, "Thousand Petaled," where dualism is transcended. The yogis speak of the experience of heaven as the last barrier to fulfillment: the rapture of the Beatific Vision of God—in whatever form He appears—so holds us to "the tasting of the juice of bliss" that we refuse to move on. In Meister Eckhart's words, "Man's last and highest leavetaking is leaving God for God."[7] Or we may think once again of those last words on the Cross: "My God, my God, why hast thou forsaken me?" The passage may be experienced either as the Self taking leave of God or as God taking leave of the Self; either way, duality is transcended and both the soul and its God—both Subject and Object—disappear.

That is the ultimate reading, I would say, of the plus sign on top of churches. Essential to the idea, however, is its realization by a willing victim, not in the fulfillment merely of some duty, but in love. For, once again to cite Meister Eckhart: "It is not the suffering that counts, it is the virtue. I say, to him who suffers not for love, to suffer is suffering and is hard to bear. But one who suffers for love suffers not and his suffering is fruitful in God's sight."[8] Moreover, the suffering of the cross of life is without end, as long as this beatifying crucifixion—which is our lifetime—lasts.

7.

And so, now, to summarize and conclude. What I have myself learned concerning the interpretation of symbolic forms from this Indian model of the lotus ladder of the Kundalini is chiefly this: that since one's way of experiencing—and so, of interpreting—phenomenality cannot but be a function of one's own level or state of consciousness, there can be no one true way of interpreting and evaluating life, symbolic forms, or anything else. The various psychological systems of our own competing Western schools are themselves committed—as I have tried to suggest—to one plane or another, and their interpretations, accordingly, commit all those who hold to them. Mythological symbols—when alive and working—are energy-evoking and directing signs, "affect symbols," like art; and where they grab you will depend on where you live. A symbol, for example, that in a person fixed at Chakra Two would evoke erotically toned fantasies, might for one moving toward Six lead to the opening of a mystical realization—as the sight of Beatrice did for Dante. For anyone of the first type to insist that *his* manner of experience is that from which the other must be interpreted is, from a larger view, unacceptable, as would be also that of any chap at Chakra Six who disparaged the dignity and values of a life lived at Chakra Two. There are values to be known at all levels, and the master of life is at home in all, responding appropriately to symbols in their context. Moreover, and here is another sobering thought: for the theologian at Chakra Six to anathematize, slay, or even cry down the mystic at Seven, is, from the larger view, intolerable. The Indian saint Ramakrishna used to ask those coming to talk with him: "How do you like to talk about God, with form or without?" Or perhaps you would like to think of God as one who will help you to pass an examination, or will give you the strength to fight and to win, and support you against your foes. "Arise, O Lord! Deliver me, O my God! For thou dost smite all my enemies on the cheek, thou dost break the teeth of the wicked" (Ps. 3:7). Well, you know where you are there; you are at Chakra Three.

And now, with that, just one more word. When all the symbols of religion are interpreted—as by Freud—as referring to Chakra Two, or—as by Adler—to Three, we are dissociated by such readings from the entire history of the human spirit; for the whole sense of specifically religious signs has always been to transport the mind *past* the ordinary One, Two, Three references of their images, onward to an experience of higher, more specifically human insights. And since all such imagery has to be drawn from the contents of normal experience, it is obvious that inferior readings should be possible, and, in fact, that neurotics fixed in one or another of the lower centers should inevitably read the signs to accord. But, as Jung has somewhere remarked—and with this remark I close: "The problem of the neurotic is that everything reminds him of sex. If it also reminds the physician only of sex. . . ."

Amen!

NOTES

1. Translation from Henry Adams Bellows, *The Poetic Edda* (New York: The American-Scandinavian Foundation, 1923), pp. 60-61.

2. T. S. Eliot, *Collected Poems, 1909-1962* (New York: Harcourt, Brace and World, Inc., 1930–63), p. 177.

3. Questions and answers from Lessons Fifth and Sixth of *A Catechism of Christian Doctrine*, published by Ecclesiastical Authority (Kinkead's Baltimore Series of Catechisms, no. 3; New York, Cincinnati, Chicago, San Francisco: Benzinger Brothers, 1885), pp. 54 and 57-60.

4. A. Guillaumont, H.-Ch. Puech, G. Quispel, W. Till, and Yassah 'abd al Masih, *The Gospel According to Thomas* (Leiden: E. J. Brill; New York: Harper and Brothers, 1959).

5. Franz Pfeiffer, *Meister Eckhart*, trans. C. de B. Evans, 2 vols. (London: John M. Watkins, 1947), 1:221.

6. Quoted by R. A. Nicholson in "Mysticism," in Sir Thos. Arnold and Alfred Guillaume, eds., *The Legacy of Islam* (Oxford: At the University Press, 1931), p. 217.

7. Pfeiffer, *Meister Eckhart*, 1:239.

8. Ibid., 1:422.

Section II

Problems in Myth Criticism

SECTION PREFACE

The above essay by Joseph Campbell argues that mythic symbols must be interpreted poetically. In Section II, Charles Moorman and F. W. Bateson attack myth criticism for deviating from the text, for confining the ranges of literature within the limits of a single critical hypothesis, and for employing literature as if it were a substitute for religion. Bateson concludes his paper by calling for a return to the morality of hard critical thinking based on looking at the thing as it is—a position that may remind some readers of Arnold's concepts of curiosity and disinterestedness. Moorman, though largely in agreement with Bateson, goes on to suggest that a comparative study of the ways different writers use the same myth constitutes a viable form of myth criticism.

Focusing on Blake, Deborah Austin's essay points out how the power of his mythology distracts his critics from his importance as a prophet and craftsman. In this manner, although she is not specifically attacking myth criticism as do Moorman and Bateson, Austin does reinforce their charge that myth criticism tends to lose the totality of the work in the particularity of the myth. Taken together, the three essays require that we ask whether or not Campbell's argument is invalidated, and whether or not the essays in Sections III and IV commit the critical errors against which they remonstrate.

The last essay of this Section proposes a road away from the kind of criticism objected to above. Philip Withim suggests that we view the work of literature through the lens of mythic awareness; that is, by seeking in literature what we find in the nature of the imagination. Drawing eclectically on a number of scholars, he summarizes what such a view might be. He analyzes a poem by Whitman to demonstrate how criticism based on a mythic awareness so described enables us to supplement the formal and thematic analysis with phenomenological and psychological responses, without reducing the work to a case history and without slighting traditional criticism.

60

Withim's paper closes this section because the essays of Sections III and IV complement and extend it by moving away from identifying characters and situations of literature with those of myth, and by tending to identify the power to create myths with the power to create poetry.

Biographical Note on Charles Moorman

Notably successful both as scholar and administrator, Charles Moorman is a specialist on medieval literature and myth criticism. A graduate of Kenyon College and Tulane University, he has been professor and chairman of the English department at the University of Southern Mississippi where he is now Dean of the graduate school. He has been a Guggenheim Fellow and a fellow of the American Council of Learned Societies.

He has published, among other works: *Arthurian Triptych* (Berkeley: University of California, 1960), *The Book of Kyng Arthur* (Lexington: University of Kentucky, 1965) and *A Knyght There Was* (Lexington: University of Kentucky, 1967), *The Precincts of Felicity* (Gainsville: University of Florida, 1966), and *The Pearl-Poet* (New York: Twayne, 1968).

Comparative Mythography: A Fungo to the Outfield

CHARLES MOORMAN

Toward the end of the *Purgatorio*, at the edge of a stream on the verge of the Earthly Paradise, Dante encounters:

> una donna soletta che si gia
> e cantando e scegliendo fior da fiore
> ond' era pinta tutta la sua via.[1]

This lovely handmaid to Beatrice, Matilda, who personifies the Active Christian Life, instructs Dante on the nature of the stream before him: "Da questa parte," she says, "On this side, it has the virtue of removing all memory of sin; on the other side, it restores the memory of every good deed."

This symposium allows me the rare opportunity, afforded, I think, only to Dante and Henry James while alive, of crossing both Lethe and Eunoe, of recalling past sin only, to quote Dorothy Sayers, "as an historical fact and as the occasion of grace and blessedness."[2] My past sin (*e pluribus unum*, I might add) is an essay entitled "Myth and Medieval Literature: *Sir Gawain and The Green Knight*," first published in *Medieval Studies* in 1956 and since anthologized a few times, most notably in John Vickery's collection.[3] I am not, you will understand, totally disenchanted with the ideas presented there, but I have come to agree with Dante that if I am ever to enter even the Earthly Paradise, I must join in the *Asperges me* and be immersed in the waters of scholarly contrition.

The fact is that I can no longer claim to be a myth critic or a mythographer or even a careful student of literature in the field. Not that I would not like to be, and I realize that I properly should be in order to take part in this symposium at all, but the field has become too vast for my garden-tractor mind, and even if I did have more time for study than I pretend not to have, I would still face the difficulties caused both by the enormous recent increase in the amount of myth criticism and also by its various, shifting, peripheral emphases.

The scholarly explosion of the last twenty years has resulted in an accumulation of critical commentary so vast that most of us do not have time to peruse even the highly selective anthologies of criticism in our areas that appear almost monthly, much less the total production. In preparing the piece on myth in *Sir Gawain and the Green Knight* to which I referred above, I read carefully all of the material that was in any way pertinent; now the mind boggles at even the prospect of such a task.

Along with this vast increase in the amount of scholarship devoted to myth has come what I referred to above in "an ill phrase, a vile phrase" as the "various, shifting, peripheral emphases" in myth criticism, by which I mean nothing more abstruse than the increasing tendency, noted in embryo by a number of people twenty years ago, of myth criticism to concentrate, like Marxist and Freudian criticism, on the fringes of literature, on theory rather than on practice. For example, in the introduction to his comprehensive anthology of myth criticism, John Vickery places as third among four "general principles" to which, he says, "most modern critics would subscribe," the idea that myth provides "concepts and patterns which the critic may use to interpret specific works of literature," the first two principles being that the "creating of myth . . . is inherent in the thinking process" and that "myth forms the matrix out of which literature emerges."[4] Vickery in fact ends the paragraph by stating that the "real function of literature [which term, as I take it, would necessarily include *The Miller's Tale* and *Emma* along with *The Bear* and *Moby Dick*] in human affairs is to continue myth's ancient and basic endeavor to create a meaningful place for man in a world oblivious to his presence," a concept rather far removed, one must admit, from the apparently naive "to delight and instruct" of Horace and the Renaissance. Now then, the New Criticism, whatever its faults (and they were mainly those of its second and third generations), at least insisted that one begin with the work; whatever theories one had concerning irony or organic unity had to follow *explication de texte*. But myth criticism, and indeed most contemporary literary criticism for that matter, has recently run pell-mell away from literature itself into a welter of generalized critical theory. Statistically, the number of theoretical courses in literature has increased enormously on my campus: freshman English is now universally as abstract a course as freshman philosophy; classes in Shakespeare, or in any other author, are taught generally as though the catalogue should read "Critical Theories on Shakespeare"; and my students are constantly flabbergasted when I ask them to open their Robinsons to page 40. They have not, it seems, brought their books to class, accustomed as they are to hearing prepared general lectures on the symbolic ambivalences in Shakespeare's bitter comedies rather than to examining at first hand and in detail the structure of the Knight's Tale.

The point is, I hope, self-evident, and I have labored it, I fear, much too long. But I am concerned at this retreat from the text, by the tendency among myth critics to argue over and over the same old general and peripheral anthropological, psychological, sociological, and essentially nonliterary questions of nature and origin, of transmittal and transference, of ritual and archetype. Even those pieces which claim to be close examinations of particular pieces of literature too often lay more emphasis on myth per se than on myth in literature and so end up not by demonstrating that the Jungian hypothesis casts light upon *Middlemarch*, which would be bad enough, but by pronouncing that *Middlemarch* supports the Jungian hypothesis.

To be somewhat more specific, my current discontent with myth criticism, my own and others, seems to settle on four points of concern: (1) the universality of myth as a tool, that is, its applicability to any and to all works of literature; (2) the "real presence" (and the theological reference is intended) of myth in literature, that is, its relation to the intent of the writer and hence to the theme of the work; (3) the authenticity of those myths chosen for critical use; and (4) the use of myth as an evaluative tool.

The first of these, the universality of myth in literature, is deceptive. It is a tempting panacea, but if one holds to Vickery's seemingly all-comprehending notion that myth forms "the matrix out of which literature emerges," one is in trouble. If you will forgive a personal word, I read last year for the first time, in addition to more professional readings in Chaucer and textual criticism, Dorothy Wordsworth's *Journal*, Woodforde's *Diary of a Country Parson*, Sassoon's George Sherston trilogy, and pages 333-766 of the *Complete Sherlock Holmes;* the year before, Kilvert's *Diary*, Loren Eiseley's *The Night Country*, a couple of Mary Webb's novels, *The Diary of a Nobody*, Isherwood's Berlin novels, the Wodehouse *Mulliner* stories, *White Fang*, some of the early Georgian poets, notably Andrew Young, some George Barker, and pages 1-332 of the *Complete Sherlock Holmes*. I am not, as you can see, pursuing any sort of self-improvement program, much less testing any theory of literature, but I should have a difficult time trying to apply any known theory of the function of myth across the board. Of the lot I could make a case perhaps for a thematic use of folklore and superstition as symbols of brutality and ignorance in Mary Webb and for the presence of a sort of "myth of the North" syndrome in *White Fang*, though I shall return to this kind of thinking in a moment. But patently myth criticism is, I am afraid, of limited use; one must pick his set texts too carefully. Like Freudianism and Marxism (each of which might also well claim to be "the matrix out of which literature emerges") it makes extravagant claims, but in the end myth is as useless in dealing with *McTeague* as is Marxism in coming to grips with *The Bear*, as is either in explicating Wodehouse.

Indulge me on this point a moment longer. One of the most perceptive, and most theoretical, pieces on myth I know is Northrop Frye's "The Archetypes of Literature," which first appeared in *The Kenyon Review* in the early fifties and is conveniently reprinted in the Vickery anthology. Having justified his concentration on peripheral materials by allying the myth critic, what he calls the "literary anthropologists," with his fellow "scientists," such as the rhetorician, the philologist, the literary psychologist, the literary social historian, etcetera, Frye proceeds to zero in on the archetype from which "all literary genres" are derived, the quest myth:

> The quest of the hero also tends to assimilate the oracular and random verbal structures, as we can see when we watch the chaos of local legends that results from prophetic epiphanies consolidating into a narrative mythology of departmental gods. In most of the higher religions this in turn has become the same central quest-myth that emerges from ritual, as the Messiah myth became the narrative structure of the oracles of Judaism. A local flood may beget a folktale by accident, but a comparison of flood stories will show how quickly such tales become examples of the myth of dissolution. Finally, the tendency of both ritual and epiphany to become encyclopedic is realized in the definitive body of myth which constitutes the sacred scriptures of religions. These sacred scriptures are consequently the first documents that the literary critic has to study to gain a comprehensive view of his subject. After he has understood their structure, then he can descend from archetypes to genres, and see how the drama emerges from the ritual side of myth and lyric from the epiphanic or fragmented side, while the epic carries on the central encyclopedic structure.
>
> Some words of caution and encouragement are necessary before literary criticism has clearly staked out its boundaries in these fields. It is part of the critic's business to show how all literary genres are derived from the quest-myth, but the derivation is a logical one within the science of criticism: the quest-myth will constitute the first chapter of whatever future handbooks of criticism may be written that will be based on enough organized critical knowledge to call themselves "introductions" or "outlines" and still be able to live up to their titles.[5]

That is fine for myth, we say, this movement out of "prophetic epiphanies" and local legends and rituals to quests and archetypes and genres, but what about particular works of literature? The answer comes two pages later:

> The importance of the god or hero in the myth lies in the fact that such characters, who are conceived in human likeness and yet have more power over nature, gradually build up the vision of an omnipotent personal community beyond an indifferent nature. It is this community which the hero regularly enters in his apotheosis. The world of this apotheosis thus begins to pull away from the rotary cycle of the quest in which all triumph is temporary. Hence if we look at the quest-myth as a pattern of imagery, we see the hero's quest first of all in terms of its fulfillment. This gives us our central pattern of archetypal images, the vision of innocence which sees the world in terms of total human intelligibility. It corresponds to, and is usually found in the form of, the vision of the unfallen world or heaven in religion. We may call it the comic vision of life, in contrast to the tragic vision, which sees the quest only in the form of its ordained cycle.[8]

Frye then introduces a table of images that sets forth what he calls the "central pattern of the comic and tragic visions." For instance, in the comic vision, we have images of community, gentle animals, gardens, and man-made structures; in the tragic vision, the opposed images of anarchy, beasts of prey, wildernesses, and deserts.

This table, which I am grossly oversimplifying, is itself a masterpiece of condensation, and I might add, without irony, a remarkably stimulating theory, particularly since it concentrates on specific patterns of imagery. One can check off *Lear* at every point of the tragic-vision scale rather as one does Arthur or Siegfried on the Lord Raglan-hero scale. But the categories do not fit the Miller's Tale or *The Glass Menagerie* or even one of the books I have been reading. And where one can, by stretching the seams, make them fit, they do not always yield the right results. The Holmes stories take place in a city, for example, rather than among "deserts, rocks, and ruins," yet surely they reflect a deeply pessimistic vision of man in society. Mary Webb's nature is more garden, more pastoral in the sense that it is allied with man, than it is wilderness, yet her vision of life is certainly more tragic than comic. And surely poor mad Dorothy Wordsworth is an extremely tragic creature whose images indicate a comic vision of the animal and vegetable worlds.

It will be clear, I hope, that I am not attacking Frye's theory: I hold nothing against it; I wish I had conceived it. But I simply cannot make it work universally, nor can I make any theory of myth work for all literature.

Point Two: the "real presence" of myth in literature, which is, of course, intimately related to Point One. We can set aside immediately, I think, those works which we might, borrowing a common literary distinction, call "primary" mythic works—those which are consciously and in their entirety based on a myth, Eliot's *Family Reunion* or John Updike's *The Centaur*, for example; those which are retellings of myths, with or without contemporary implications, *Prometheus Unbound* or the novels of Mary Renault or C. S. Lewis's *Till We Have Faces;* and those which contain conscious passing allusions to myths—*The Waste Land*, for example, or *Finnegans Wake*.

What I am concerned about is the application in "secondary" mythic works—works where references to myth never overtly appear, to *Huck Finn* or *Nostromo* or *To the Lighthouse*, to name only three from the ever-increasing number of works so examined. I have become more and more suspicious not only of the accuracy, but also of the real value, of statements such as "*Great Expectations* is [Dickens's] . . . most ironic (and sophisticated) use of the conventions of the fairy tale"[7] and "The journey of Gawain to the domain of the Green Knight amounts, in mythical terms, to a rite de passage. . . ."[8]

And on this last statement, if nowhere else, I have a right to comment. Just as I had spent much of the piece here quoted condemning Speirs and Zimmer *et al.* for identifying myth and poem, so in time I received my own comeuppance, principally from a distinguished medievalist, Morton Bloomfield:

> Of Moorman's attempt to save both the poem and the myth we may say that, however satisfactory his theory may be, it is hard to find in practice any specific evidences of a "rite de passage" ritual in *Sir Gawain* unless all testing is to be regarded as a type of *rite de passage.* Gawain is perhaps humbler at the end of his adventure than at the beginning, but just what has he been initiated into? He has perhaps learned that all human beings including the best are weak, but this lesson is not the purpose of the usual *rite de passage*, even a Christianized one. If he had been a good Christian, he should have realized this from the beginning; it is not secret knowledge. Then too the Court, as Moorman himself indicated, for which the whole affair was managed, is no better or wiser; and besides *rites de passage* are for individuals not institutions. To me at least Moorman has fallen into the trap he has so carefully delineated and whose dangers he has so vividly portrayed. Without being specific as to what a *rite de passage* means, without, in other words, establishing his *genus*, he makes the *differentia* he discusses lose the characteristics of *differentia*. Not only this; he has to force the plain meaning of the text to fit into his theory. The shade of the golden bough obscures the poem for one reader at least.[9]

The awful truth is that Bloomfield is right. I still think that the poem is about testing and about a journey from innocence to experience, but I also think that one does not need to make use of initiatory rites and of Campbell's monomyth in order to perceive these themes. And it may well be, though I cannot now be sure, that I used myth simply as a tool of explication rather than as a means of investigation. I did not, I am now afraid, really find a myth in the poem; I brought it there.

I adhere to the doctrine that "thought is free," but I wonder whether it is useful or valuable to bring to bear upon any work any body of outside information of which the author was not consciously aware or to which he at least made no reference. I cannot really believe, despite the visual evidence of the Olivier film, that Ernest Jones's application of Freudian doctrine to *Hamlet* really netted us any new insight into the play or that Christopher Caudwell has really contributed to our understanding of the *Agamemnon*.

I have, I suppose, read most of the classical literature on the writer's subconscious, or at least that beginning with Coleridge. I realize that matters subconscious may well creep unawares into a writer's work, willy-nilly; that Shakespeare was at times preoccupied with toothaches and building contracts and that these concerns reveal themselves in imagery; that, as J. L. Lowes demonstrated, Coleridge regurgitates a couple of years' reading in "Kubla Khan." But literary form and theme are still largely matters of conscious intent, and the literary iceberg is, unlike its natural counterpart, largely on top of the water. Thus, directly applying Freudian and Jungian *doctrine* to determine the themes of Shakespeare or Coleridge or to discuss the motivation of their characters is not the same as simply noting psychological undertones or patterns of image if for no other reason than that these authors did not themselves think or conceive in these patterns. Dorothy Sayers notes that she greatly resented the efforts of readers who sought to identify her with her characters, to offer her brandy because Lord Peter drank brandy or to assume that Lord Peter would end his days as a convinced Christian.[10]

Point Three is a corollary of Point Two: just as myths are often falsely applied to works that do not reflect them, so pseudo-myths are sometimes created by authors and critics in order to provide mythic depth to an otherwise shallow work. A pseudo-myth is thus a manufactured myth: not one inherited from a *bona fide* folk tradition, but one consciously manufactured in order to provide a clustering point, a convenient index symbol for a set of social phenomena or attitudes. One recalls the "Marilyn myth" and the "JFK myth" as attempts to create symbols, or rather to distill into symbolic personages (rather as Dante did, come to think of it) the essence of an era or a way of life, and then to use them as the bases of explication. How true, I have heard it seriously asked, is Norman Mailer to the truth of the Marilyn myth?

The use of such falsely conceived and even more nebulous "myths" in literary criticism has become, alas, increasingly legitimate. One hears of such mysteries as the "myth" of the river in Mark Twain or the "myth" of the small town in *Winesburg, Ohio*. I happen to come from a section of the country (Mississippi) where such myths abound, though the natives seem happily ignorant of them. The University of Southern Mississippi Center for Writers, like all creative writing programs, is positively inundated with the "myths" of rural Mississippi, the innocence, the simplicity, the folksy humor, the irony, the nobility, and particularly the much-touted, though as far as I am concerned really mythical, guilt thereof. I am sick to death of blood on the grits; of conjure women in smelly cabins; of moon pies, R-o-C Colas, crackers, and sardines at the country store; of decayed old gentlewomen in decayed old houses; of all the deflowered progeny of Temple Drake; and of blacks who have Brer Rabbit accents and Adlai Stevenson vocabularies. The only fresh thing I have seen in Southern literature in the last thirty years is Willie Morris's baseball-playing dog, and Willie played him for two pages more than he was worth.

Such pseudo-myth making, or at least its application to literary criticism, derives eventually, I suppose, from Maud Bodkin and the Jungians, but despite the occasional usefulness of legitimate archetypal patterns in elucidating works where they were seemingly intended to underlie structure and/or plot—*The Bear*, for example, or in another genre "High Noon"—the definition and application of such pseudo-mythic patterns is at best a circular and hence question-begging strategy, rather like the historians' use of *Piers Plowman* to construct a picture of fourteenth-century life with which to praise the realism of *Piers Plowman*. By such reasoning *Main Street* becomes a great novel because it so beautifully reflects the "myth" of small-town America, for which it is the chief source.

It will be seen that with the adjective *great* I have drifted into the realm of value judgments and hence of evaluative criticism, the last of my questionable areas. And it is precisely here that myth criticism has floundered, it seems to me, most disastrously. For one can forgive the zealous myth critic for seeing a myth lurking behind every title page or for digging up myths where their authors never buried them or even for constructing myths to fill abhorred vacuums, but not for making the use of myth an evaluative touchstone, a criterion for elevating an otherwise inferior work or denigrating a superior one.

On this point, I am again perhaps a model. I once wrote two articles on the fall of man in Melville's *Pierre*. Whatever you may think of the merits of my argument as to the mythic qualities of *Pierre*, I would hope that you would at least acknowledge my good sense and taste in not suggesting that the presence of a myth pattern in any way improves the wretched plotting and rhetoric that renders *Pierre* almost unfit for human consumption.

Pierre is an interesting book, a valuable book, I think. But it is not therefore a good book, and no amount of myth imagery can make it so. Ms. Grob's discovery of fairy-tale patterns in *Our Mutual Friend* fails to redeem that novel for me, and a number of hopeful rereadings have not convinced me that Tennyson's "insight into the nature of myth" makes *Demeter and Persephone* a "poetic triumph."[11]

Now then, as the Friar said, this is a long preamble of a tale, and I should like in conclusion to scrub for the moment my disillusionment with the theories and the applications, the controversies and the solutions, and to get down to actual myths and actual works of literature, to Heracles and *Hamlet*, to the voyage of the Argonauts and *The Hound of the Baskervilles*. What is their lowest common denominator, if one exists, and how do they impinge on each other, if indeed they do?

Their l.c.d. is, of course, narrative, for even the purest lyric poem, as the Chicago Aristotelians used to love to demonstrate, can be placed in a narrative context. But the narrative of the myth and that of the work of fiction essentially differ. Compare, for example, the following narratives:

As part of her dowry a beautiful young girl, the first of her sex, brought to her fiancé a jewelled box given her by a god who had commanded her not to open it. Eventually, however, curiosity overcame her, and she opened the box[,] thereby freeing a host of insects, all the diseases and plagues and terrors of man, in fact. Too late she closed the box. One creature, however, she did manage to capture—Hope, man's only solace in the world of grief Pandora had created.

A young hero, angered by his commander's dictatorial conduct, withdraws from battle and allows his comrades to suffer a series of humiliating defeats. Eventually, enraged by the death of a close friend, the hero returns to the field, kills the slayer of his friend, and is finally calmed only by the supplications of his enemy's father.[12]

I have tried to use the same technique in framing both, listing only the major events and motives. The first summary is moderately satisfactory; it at least conveys the central point, that man's best, indeed his only, hope is hope itself. That point is, moreover, completely contained within the narrative and is inseparable from it; one cannot tell the story of Pandora, perhaps because it is, like most myth, allegorical to begin with, without somehow saying that man will at least endure and may even, as another Mississippian has said, somehow prevail. Equally important perhaps is the fact that one could stretch out the narrative almost *ad infinitum* without saying much more than that.

The summary of the *Iliad* is, of course, totally unsatisfactory. One could not guess from it the subtleties of motive that underlie these simple actions or the complexities of theme (or even the theme itself) that derive from them. John Crowe Ransom used to say in class that the only way to explicate fully a work of literature in whatever genre was to read it aloud in its entirety. *No* summary of the *Iliad* will do in the way that *any* summary of the Pandora story will. The essence of myth is in the story, however well or badly, however briefly or lengthily, it is told. Delete one word of a Yeats poem or one paragraph of a James novel, however, and you have well-nigh created a new work.

The mythical narrative thus seems to me to be of itself nonliterary, or more accurately, extraliterary, and perhaps herein lies at least part of the secret of the ubiquity and the immediate appeal of the great myths. No real literary purpose is served in the search for myth origins; ritual, euhemerism, Jungian psychology—none of these theories affects or really explains, in my opinion, the impact of myth on even the most unlettered consciousness. A child understands Pandora perfectly; hence the popularity of children's collections of myth. The great myths sustain themselves; they do not need the embellishments of literature in the way that stories that are basically history, say the *Iliad,* do.

And not only do myths not need a literary setting, but they positively resist it. The Joseph narrative in Exodus is more powerful than Mann's novel, the simplest telling of the Cupid-Psyche story more appealing than C. S. Lewis's *Till We Have Faces.* Characterization, for example, interferes with the simplicity of myth narration; detailed settings are an intrusion on its universality.

The great myths thus best stand alone. They are immediately convincing, perhaps because they reflect universal experience; and they are immediately comforting, perhaps because they reflect the eventual triumph of man, the certainty that though the individual may suffer defeat, the race will somehow prevail. Eventually, somehow, somewhere, Prometheus will break his chains and Hercules finish his labors and the Comforter come. The hero will return to his native land bearing the elixir of life and "all shall be well/And all manner of thing shall be well."

Now then, if a piece of formal literature exhibits a "secondary" mythic structure and so can be shown to reflect, however unconsciously and in whatever form, no matter how ephemeral, the narrative pattern of one of these universally accepted, self-sustaining myths, cannot the work be said to partake of the myth's own enduring strength and appeal? The answer is, I hope, an unqualified "No"! For such broadly defined patterns are by their nature so universal as to apply indiscriminately at times to George Eliot and Dick Tracy, to Shakespeare and, as has been demonstrated, Mickey Spillane.

But, on the other hand, it seems to me that if a writer by allusion or by narrative pattern or by any other conscious evocation brings to his own work the already-known, already-understood and prejudged narratives of myth, he may well touch a chord of response in the reader deeper than he might ordinarily reach. I quote the conclusion of *Sweeney Among the Nightingales*:

> The nightingales are singing near
> The Convent of the Sacred Heart,
>
>
> And sang within the bloody wood
> When Agamemnon cried aloud,
> And let their liquid siftings fall
> To stain the stiff dishonoured shroud.[13]

Here the allusions, certainly consciously employed, to the rape of Philomela, to the Crucifixion, to the assassination of the priest of Diana in the sacred wood at Nemi, and to the murder of Agamemnon all serve to enforce a contrast between the passionate violence of myth and the purposeless, meaningless plot against Sweeney. The poet is certainly not concerned with the origins or the nature or even the importance of myth; he *uses* it as a literary device in the same way that Shakespeare consciously *uses* animal imagery in *Lear* or Hardy the heath in *The Return of the Native* or Chaucer the Song of Solomon in the Merchant's Tale as a means of enforcing meaning by allusion to a known and essentially prejudged body of information.

This "primary," conscious—and I find that I must keep insisting on this point—this *conscious* reference to myth in literature provides, I think, a very useful handle by which to pick up, and hence examine, a literary work, providing that one claims for it no special metaphysical powers or importance. And one of the most useful techniques of handling myth in literature is by a kind of comparative mythography.

One of the most provocative passages of literary criticism that I know comes from Charles Williams's book on Dante, *The Figure of Beatrice*, where he describes how the image of a wood appears so often in English verse that it is transformed into a great forest in whose green spaces the high episodes of English literature take place.

> Thus in one part there are the lovers of a midsummer night, or by day a duke and his followers, and in another men behind branches so that the wood seems moving . . . and in another a poet listening to a nightingale

but rather dreaming richly of a grand art than there exploring it. . . .
The forest itself has different names in different tongues—Westermain,
Arden, Birnam, Broceliande; and in places there are separate trees
named, such as that on the outskirts against which a young Northern poet
saw a spectral wanderer leaning, or, in the unexplored centre of which
only rumours reach even poetry, Igdrasil of one myth, or the Trees of
Knowledge and Life of another. . . .

The use of such an extended image is to allow the verse of those various
"parts of the wood" to point distantly towards each other, without the
danger of too hasty comparisons.[14]

Williams is, of course, discussing an image, the forest, not drawn from
myth, but I have had some luck in applying the same technique to myths as
they appear in literary works. For example, to paraphrase Williams:

The image of the Christ figure has appeared often enough among the
characters of Western literature. Our Lord has appeared under guises as
diverse as an American sailor who strikes down his accusing superior, the
son of Lancelot who alone among all the Round Table is worthy to
achieve the Holy Grail, a mystical Russian bourgeois, a Mississippi
sawmill worker, an Anglo-Saxon dragon-slayer, an Icelandic farmer, and
even a magnificent lion in the far off land of Narnia.

The usefulness of this kind of comparative technique does not of course
lie in this kind of simple listing, but in allowing the myths, *all consciously
employed*, as they appear in the various works to "point distantly towards
each other," as Williams says, to elucidate, literally to throw light on, one
another. A second paragraph might thus run:

But not all literary Christ figures are alike in that they reflect different
aspects of the Christ myth in order to fulfill the particular purposes of
their authors. For example, the sacrifice of Christ in behalf of an
essentially unworthy people is emphasized in *Beowulf* and in *The Lion,
the Witch, and the Wardrobe*; His unearthly holiness in contrast to the
worldly values of ordinary men in *Billy Budd*, *The Brothers Karamazov*,
and Malory's account of the Grail quest; His humility in contrast to the
pride and arrogance of the feuding families in *Njalssaga*.

Even in such a simple listing as this (and I have made no attempt to be
either systematic or definitive), it will be seen that one work serves to
define another. The austere, Christ-like Galahad—stern, icily pure,
untouched by human consideration—would seem to be far different from
the simple, Christ-like Billy Budd, whose dying words bless the judge who
condemned him, nor would Malory, a nostalgic, fifteenth-century, Tory

agrarian, seem to have much in common with Melville. But by placing the two figures together, one becomes conscious not only of the particular place of each within its own context, but also of certain similarities in the thematic uses to which they are put. Malory's Galahad, by comparison, becomes even more clearly a symbolic representative of a set of values to which worldly chivalry, even at its best, should not have aspired and which eventually contributes to its destruction, and Billy Budd, by comparison, even more clearly the symbol of what Melville elsewhere calls "chronometrical morality," a purity of absolute moral judgment that worldly justice cannot permit to exist. Both thus stand in opposition to worldly society, the Round Table and the *Indomitable*, and both threaten the expediency that is the basis of its existence. In *Le Morte d'Arthur* (and in *The Idylls of the King*, by the way) the Grail quest destroys the Round Table; in *Billy Budd*, the angel must hang. In both books, the Christ myth helps define the central theme and so serves as a convenient handle by which to grasp the Protean bag.

Again, by comparing Aslan, the Christ-lion in *The Lion, the Witch, and the Wardrobe*, with Beowulf, one first sees certain sharp differences in their treatment, each becoming more clearly defined in the light of the other. Aslan is a frankly allegorical figure, a way of presenting the essentials of the Christian faith by means of a set of terms borrowed from the fairy tale. *Beowulf*, on the other hand, is not in the least polemical; the sacrifical aspect of Beowulf's death is only vaguely alluded to, a means of adding a faint Christian coloration to what was in its original state a frankly pagan tale. Yet despite their obvious differences in tone and emphasis, both works use the Christ-figure as a means of defining the nobility of sacrifice; both Aslan and Beowulf die in order to save an essentially unworthy people.

What I am saying is actually quite simple, a rather poor paraphrase of what Eliot meant by saying that "the whole of the literature of Europe from Homer . . . has a simultaneous existence."[15] One can best understand and define an author's thematic use of a particular myth, it seems to me, if he places it within a tradition, if he sees Billy Budd not as a single Christ-figure, but as one of many Christ-figures. How does Billy Budd relate to Alyosha? To Hoskuld? How is he similar? How does he differ? And eventually through such questions one may arrive at the uniqueness of Billy Budd and hence at the meaning of the story. How does one define the taste of Coca Cola? By comparing it with Royal Crown and Pepsi. But in each case, note, there is nothing mechanically sure-fire in the operation; both coke-tasting and comparative mythography require a sensitive palate and considerable powers of description.

I am afraid that I have given a very skimpy demonstration. Comparative mythography is, according to my subtitle, a fungo to the outfield, a trial practice swing producing not even a hit, much less a run. This simple, impressionistic, nonscientific comparison of images drawn from myth is at best only a means of allowing the myth images themselves to be seen in relation both to their archetypes and to each other, both in and out of their contexts and their traditions, a means of allowing them to "point distantly towards each other."

It may be objected, of course, that I have not really treated myth in literature in any special way at all, that all of this is pedestrian and old hat, that the same technique could be applied to any nonmythical image, to forests, as in Williams, or to clothing or to colors, or to general statements of theme. But that is exactly my point, that there is nothing magical or metaphysical in the myth image per se: like any other image it brings to the work an already-formed body of knowledge and applies it to a fictional situation and so is best approached like any other image. To quote Shakespeare, it "gives to airy nothingness, / A local habitation and a name," and it does so very effectively.

NOTES

1. *Purgatorio,* 28: 40-42:

> a lady all alone, who wandered there
> singing and plucking flower on floweret gay,
> with which her path was painted everywhere.

2. *The Divine Comedy,* trans. Dorothy L. Sayers (Harmondsworth: Penguin Books, 1955), p. 68.

3. *Myth and Literature: Contemporary Theory and Practice* (Lincoln: University of Nebraska Press, 1966).

4. Ibid. p. ix.

5. Northrop Frye, "The Archetypes of Literature," in Vickery, *Myth and Literature,* p. 94. I am aware that Frye has written more recently and more fully on these matters, particularly in *The Anatomy of Criticism* (Princeton, N.J.: Princeton University Press, 1967). But he has nowhere revoked the view of the earlier piece, the conciseness and convenience of which make it a useful text.

6. Ibid. p. 96.

7. Shirley Grob, "Dickens and Some Motifs of the Fairy Tale," in Vickery, *Myth and Literature,* p. 269.

8. Charles Moorman, "Myth and Medieval Literature: Sir Gawain and the Green Knight," in Vickery, *Myth and Literature,* p. 179.

9. "*Sir Gawain and the Green Knight:* An Appraisal," *PMLA* 75, no. 1 (March 1961): 14,

10. Dorothy L. Sayers, *The Mind of the Maker* (New York: Harcourt, Brace and Co., 1941), p. 105.

11. G. Robert Stange, "Tennyson's Mythology: A Study of Demeter and Persephone," in Vickery, *Myth and Literature*, p. 367.

12. I am indebted to C. S. Lewis, *An Experiment in Criticism* (Cambridge: Cambridge University Press, 1961).

13. T. S. Eliot, *Collected Poems, 1909-1962* (New York: Harcourt, Brace and World, 1930-63), p. 50.

14. (London: Faber and Faber, 1943), p. 107.

15. "Tradition and the Individual Talent," *Collected Essays: 1917-1932* (New York: Harcourt, Brace and Co., 1932), p. 4.

SUGGESTED READINGS

Bidney, David. "Myth, Symbolism, and Truth." In *Myth and Literature: Contemporary Theory and Practice,* edited by John B. Vickery. Lincoln: University of Nebraska Press, 1966.

Brown, Daniel Russell. "A Look at Archetypal Criticism." *Journal of Aesthetics and Arts Criticism* 28 (1970): 465-72.

Eisenstein, Samuel. "Literature and Myth." *College English* 29 (1967-68): 369-73.

Hardison, O. B. *Christian Rite and Christian Drama in the Middle Ages.* Baltimore, Md.: Johns Hopkins University Press, 1965.

Herd, Eric V. "Myth Criticism: Limitations and Possibilities." *Mosaic* 2 (1969): 69-77.

Montgomery, Marion. "Shadows in the New Cave: The Poet and the Reduction of Myth." *Southwest Review* 55 (1970): 217-23.

Moorman, Charles. "Myth and Medieval Literature: *Sir Gawain and the Green Knight.*" In *Myth and Literature: Contemporary Theory and Practice,* edited by John B. Vickery. Lincoln: University of Nebraska Press, 1966.

Peck, Russell A. "Public Dreams and Private Myths: Perspectives in Middle English Literature." *PMLA* 90 (1975): 461-67.

Rahv, Philip. "Myth and the Powerhouse." In *Myth and Literature: Contemporary Theory and Practice,* edited by John B. Vickery. Lincoln: University of Nebraska Press, 1966.

Righter, William. *Myth and Literature.* London: Routledge and Kegan Paul, 1975.

Ryan, J. S. "Myth Criticism as Discipline." *Westerly* 2 (1973): 49-58.

Biographical Note on Deborah Austin

Deborah Austin graduated from Smith College with a B.A. degree and received her M.A. degree from Radcliffe and her Ph.D. from Bryn Mawr. She is a professor of English at the Pennsylvania State University, where she teaches Romantic and Victorian literature. Her articles on Meredith and James have appeared in *University of Toronto Quarterly* and *Journal of General Education*. She has published a volume of her poetry, *The Paradise of the World* (University Park: The Pennsylvania State University Press, 1964) and other poems have appeared in *Partisan Review, Yale Review, Atlantic, Massachusetts Review,* and elsewhere.

Threefold Blake's
Divine Vision, Intention, and Myth

DEBORAH AUSTIN

The world of Romantic scholarship contains an ever-growing band of hardy souls who, linked together like alpinists by the rope of scholarly discoveries stretching from S. Foster Damon through early Northrop Frye to the present, move fearfully forward into the vast universe of Blake's major poems, *The Four Zoas, Milton,* and *Jerusalem.* Tourists only, or determined scholarly cartographers, each one

> eagerly . . .
> O'er bog or steep, through strait, rough, dense or rare,
> With head, hands, wings, or feet pursues his way,
> And swims or sinks, or wades, or creeps, or flies . . .
> (Milton, *Paradise Lost* 2.947-50)

borne up or down as the commentaries of those who have gone before either illuminate their labors or add to their burden of uncertainty. The explorers are right to feel trepidation, and right also not to allow what Blake would call "nervous fear" to keep them from the journey. It will take help from as many as possible if they are to make all there is to be made of these extraordinary poems.

Yet the delights of spelunking in the depth of Blake's mythic meanings can become so enticing that certain other responsibilities devolving on the serious reader of Blake's prophetic books may be ignored or drastically curtailed. We shout to each other about the relationship between Zoa and emanation, about the difference between the fallen and the unfallen Tharmas, about why Reuben rather than another of the Twelve Tribes, about the sixfoldness of Ololon, about Los in *The Book of Urizen* and Los in *Jerusalem.* We search the sacred pages of Frye and Bloom for The Word on a particular passage, only to find that often it is just this particular passage about which neither Frye nor Bloom has any thing to say. More pleased about this than not, sometimes, we start an expedition of our own, and are last seen disappearing intrepidly into the interior.

There is nothing wrong with this, unless, as I hinted in the first sentence of the last paragraph, it is done at the expense of something else that Blake's readers should also be doing, which is to work as sensitively toward an awareness of the wholeness of these great poems, and of Blake's intention in composing them, as we do in apprehending the total resonances given off by parts of them. Obviously, the two ways of "seeing" the poems are interconnected. Yet it is possible to minimize our awareness of wholeness and intention in our eager concentration on some aspect of the whole. The reason I wish to speak of wholeness and intention at this time is quite simply that recent Blake scholarship has been fruitfully preoccupied with isolated aspects of the poems, and what this paper hopes to do is to correct an imbalance, rather than ask for a complete change.

Because *The Four Zoas, Milton,* and *Jerusalem* are so extraordinarily complex, of course, we must have concentration on the parts if we are to advance to an informed sense of the whole. Yet when we consider these poems, our sense of the whole must not be conditioned solely by internal evidence, or by internal evidence amplified by knowledge of Blake's sources, for Blake's sense of himself and his relationship to his work are both complex and highly original; to ignore them would be to cut ourselves off from a fuller understanding of some of the ambivalences of the poems that otherwise remain resistant to critical investigation.

Visionary, prophet, artist: Blake seems to have been born the first; to have considered his mission in writing *The Four Zoas, Milton,* and *Jerusalem* to have been that of the second; and to have used the tools and sensibility of the third to accomplish, or try to accomplish, what he seems to have believed were divinely imposed tasks. It would, of course, be ludicrous to try to disentangle the three roles to the point of attributing everything Blake says to one or the other. Yet criticism that ignores one or two of them does so at its peril, for there are aspects of each work, and of others of Blake's works, that will remain inexplicable in terms of only one. The critic aware of only one will find the work inadequate from his inadequate point of view, and such findings have led to, for instance, the sort of searching for the "key" to Blake's "system" that kept Ellis and Yeats from making a lasting contribution to Blake scholarship.

Theoretically, a visionary might be described as a man whose imaginative (Blake would have said his *real*) life is so extraordinarily rich that it seems to be more real than his nonimaginative life, even while seeming to explicate the nonimaginative life in various highly symbolic ways. Communication, however, is not an inevitable corollary of vision; the visionary may simply sit smiling in a state of solipsistic bliss; he may hint at what he sees; even if he does so hint, his visions may, after all, be a series of vivid but disconnected fragments, incapable of making sense when strung together, and so on. Blake's own confidence in his visionary capacity seems to have been lifelong and can be documented in various ways. Some of the most interesting evidence comes from the letters written by Blake to his patron, Thomas Butts, at the time Blake was living in Felpham working for his "corporeal friend and spiritual enemy," Hayley. Blake's move to the country and the promise of steady work had been approved, apparently, by all who felt concern for his worldly well-being. Yet once the move had been made, Blake found it harder and harder to combine (as he had been able to somehow in London) his professional work with his own original productions. Letters to the sympathetic Butts in January and November of 1802, and April and August of 1803, indicate that Blake's state of mind fluctuated between desperation at not being able to get on with his own compositions ("I find on all hands great objections to my doing anything but the meer drudgery of business & intimations that if I do not confine myself to this I shall not live. . . . I am not ashamed, afraid or averse to tell You what Ought to be Told. That I am under the direction of Messengers from Heaven Daily & Nightly . . . if we fear to do the dictates of our Angels & tremble at the Tasks set before us, if we refuse to do Spiritual Acts . . . Who can describe the dismal torments of such a state!" *Letter to Butts*, Jan. 10, 1802)[1] and growing confidence that he belonged back in London, where "I can alone carry on my visionary studies in London unannoyd & . . . converse with my friends in Eternity. See Visions, Dream Dreams, & prophecy & speak Parables unobserv'd & at liberty from the Doubts of other Mortals. . . . if a Man is the Enemy of my Spiritual Life while he pretends to be the Friend of my Corporeal. he is a Real Enemy . . ." (*Letter to Butts*, April 25, 1803). However, in spite of his turmoil there, it was in Felpham that he arrived at certain insights that strengthened him immeasurably in his determination to continue with his own work, whatever the cost.

Among his copious annotations to the *Discourses* of Sir Joshua Reynolds, Blake wrote on the back of the title page of Discourse VIII, "Burke's Treatise on the Sublime and Beautiful is founded on the Opinions of Newton & Locke On this Treatise Reynolds has grounded many of his assertions in all his Discourses. I read Burke's Treatise when very Young At the same time I read Locke on Human Understanding & Bacon's Advancement of Learning on every one of these Books I wrote my Opinion & on looking them over find that my Notes on Reynolds in this Book are exactly Similar. I felt the same Contempt & Abhorrance then that I do now. They mock Inspiration & Vision Inspiration & Vision was then & now is & I Hope will always Remain My Element, my Eternal Dwellingplace. how than can I hear it Contemnd without returning Scorn for Scorn?"

Bentley and Nurmi believe that Blake read Reynolds's *Discourses* in

1808, at which time he was forty-one. Two years later, in his prose piece describing one of his conceptions of The Last Judgment, he says, "The Last Judgment is not Fable or Allegory they are a totally distinct and Inferior kind of Poetry. Vision or Imagination is a Representation of what Eternally Exists, Really and Unchangeably. Fable or Allegory is formed by the daughters of Memory. Imagination is surrounded by the daughters of Inspiration . . . The Hebrew Bible & the Gospel of Jesus are not Allegory but Eternal Vision of Imagination of All that Exists. . . . The Nature of Visionary Fancy or Imagination is very little Known & the Eternal nature and permanance of its ever-existent Images is considered as less permanent than the things of Vegetative and Generative Nature yet the Oak dies as well as the Lettuce but its Eternal Image & Individuality never dies, but renews by its seed. Just so the Imaginative Image returns by the seed of Contemplative thought The writings of the Prophets illustrate these conceptions of the Visionary Fancy by their various sublime & Divine Images as seen in the Worlds of Vision. . . . The Nature of my Work is Visionary or Imaginative."

Later in the same piece, Blake indicates the state of mind in which the viewer should look at his picture:

> If the Spectator could Enter into these Images in his Imagination approaching them on the Fiery Chariot of his Contemplative Thought if he could . . . make a Friend & Companion of one of these Images of wonder which always intreats him to leave mortal things as he must know then would he arise from his Grave then would he meet the Lord in the Air & then would he be happy.

A situation conducive to vision, then, was not only essential to Blake if he was to get his own work done, but also was necessary for the reader or spectator if they were to comprehend it. Indeed, one of his aims in writing or employing any other creative medium is to arouse his audience to the same kind of visionary comprehension that he had himself. Regardless of our modern tendency to explicate his thinking in psychological terms, Blake believed absolutely in his own visionary capacities, and was willing to make any adjustments to his life that seemed necessary in order to preserve them unimpaired. The capacities themselves were not contingent upon his being an artist, but his art, of whatever kind, was contingent upon his preservation of the ability to function as a visionary.

There are two Hebrew words in use for the word *Prophet*, *nabi*, from a word meaning "to boil forth, as a fountain, hence one who speaks out freely from a full heart, impelled by God," and *ro'eh*, "from a verb meaning to see—hence a seer, one who saw Divine Visions, Divine Truths, and spoke what he had seen from God."[2] Both these definitions, I think, Blake would have found applicable to himself. Nevertheless, when it came to actually referring to himself as a prophet, and to his long poems as prophecies, the magnificent—or exasperating—assurance with which he speaks of his visionary or imaginative life is not found in his references to the prophetic role, nor does he speak of the three longer poems as prophecies. It was left to his readers to give them the familiar title of "prophetic books."[3] The best explanation for Blake's attitude here seems to lie in the fact that he deeply revered the Hebrew prophets for their vision, their discernment, and above all for their courage in speaking the truth as they saw it to a hostile and uncaring world. If anything brought out humility in Blake, it seems to have been the wish that his work might be lasting and effective in the same way as that of Jeremiah, Isaiah, and Ezekiel.

Blake's use of the words *prophet* and *prophecy* in his writing shows us that he believed the spirit of prophecy to be eternal, that he felt that the "ever-apparent Elias" manifested itself in every age, and that he intended the figure of the creator-blacksmith, Los-Urthona, to be his icon for it in the longer poems. The fact that he indicates (especially in *Milton*) a merging of the identity and power of Los-Milton-Blake is further evidence of his belief in the eternality of the spirit of prophecy, and of his conviction that in writing at least the last two of the long poems, he himself was assuming the mantle of prophecy.

Yet this conviction seems to have been one that he felt could best be conveyed through the medium of symbolic and indirect reference in poetry, rather than in direct prose statement. The only way for a prophet to proclaim himself a prophet was to get his prophecy into some form in which it could be absorbed by others. Simply to assert that one was a prophet would, if anything, tend to make the audience concentrate on the man rather than the message, and probably on the man as a harmless lunatic. Of the fifty-four references to *prophet, Prophecy*, and related words in Blake's poetry, almost none of them refer directly to himself, and of the thirty-five references found in the prose, again, except for the moments in the letters when he uses the word in the simple or colloquial sense, he seems to bring up the idea of himself as prophet only in the letter to Butts quoted earlier, when he says he needs to be in London to "prophecy."

The prophetic mode has always been unpopular, involving as it does the stern condemnation of current ways of life, and, particularly since the end of the Victorian period, the prophetic tone has seemed, in an uncertain world, unduly authoritarian; its original power remains inexplicable to many. The prophet's compulsion to exhort and to warn isolates him from most men, who prefer to be cheered up and told they are doing at least as well as can be expected. Moses (see *Num.* 11) once asked the Lord to create other prophets to help him (and to share the burden of opprobrium) when he was leading six hundred thousand Israelites in the desert. When the Lord did so, some astonished Israelites ran off to tell Moses that they thought interlopers were poaching on his exclusive prophetical preserve. "Enviest thou for my sake?" asked Moses, "would God that all the Lord's people were prophets, and that the Lord would put his Spirit upon them." Moses' wishes to the contrary, the number of prophets in the course of human history has remained small, and the prophetic insight, at once liberating and isolating, has continued to make the prophet himself feel burdened and misunderstood.

When Blake, in 1804, presented *Milton* to that invisible and indeed nonexistent audience which neither knew nor cared that it was being addressed, he clearly defined his own loneliness, his sense of prophetic responsibility, and his need for understanding by closing the prefatory material with his own version of Moses' words: "Would to God that all the Lords people were Prophets."

Unlike the visionary, the prophet has a compulsion to assess the life of his time, and whether he is a visionary as well as a prophet, or simply extrapolates with inspired common sense from what his time, his religion, and the past history of the human race have taught him, he must communicate with his fellow men because he cares what happens to them, to his country, and to the generations that will come after him. Though in the course of writing three long prophetic books Blake comes to identify himself more and more openly with Los, and, as he does so, to make Los more specifically an artist, a creator-figure, Los performs a prophet's task for a prophet's reasons when he searches Albion's "minute particulars" to find out why Albion has become alienated from the Divine Vision. What Los finds prompts him to fight his own feelings of fear and inadequacy until he subdues them enough to allow himself to start forging a better world from the ruins of the old. In a sense we could say that Los-the-Visionary gives Los-the-Prophet evidence enough to convince Los-the-Creator that he should act, redemptively, creatively.

The fact that Blake requires not only perception from his hero, and a change of heart, but also a method of action that is an act of the creative imagination, brings us to consider Blake's concept of the artist. For Los (and for the Milton of Blake's poem *Milton*, and for Blake himself), action is creative, is an imaginative and generative spending of self. It is not enough for Blake's hero, as it was for many older and more famous ones, to slay the dragon or dethrone a wicked king. He must indeed bring evil into a recognizable form and dispose of it, but he must also make anew the souls of men. The point to remember here is that this procedure is happening both within and without the poem: inside it, Los labors to make men worthy of the joyful intellectual tensions of conversing in eternity "according to the Wonders Divine/ Of Human Imagination" (*Jerusalem*, Plate 98), but Blake himself, by writing *Jerusalem* and *Milton*, is attempting to do the same thing.

Now, the artist differs from both visionary and prophet by his delight in making tough, beautiful structures having a value in and for themselves, whose wholeness, greater than the sum of its parts, has both multiplicity and resonance. These two characteristics interact with the beholder or reader of the work in such ways as to make him aware in varying degrees of the work's wholeness. That no two readers or beholders see precisely the same *Hamlet* or *Guernica* results from the fact that no two readers or beholders are endowed with identical powers of intellect and imagination. Moreover, what the artist makes may seem to the artist himself to be true, but will not necessarily be part of a coherent vision of life. He may profess one thing at one time and another at another, not, as Croce has pointed out, because he is a turncoat, but because it is endlessly interesting to him to make a structure that shows accurately what it is *like* to believe or feel in a certain way. In other words, while the prophet is a committed man, he is committed to warn and to exhort; style is to him what it is to the rhetorician—a skill, pure and simple. The visionary is committed to his role of Man Seeing; that is, man rightly seeing, unimpeded by the need to conform by seeing the same things his neighbors and contemporaries see. The visionary may or may not communicate, but if he does, style is secondary; vision is primary. The artist is also committed, but to Making— to causing to come into being a separate entity in which matter and method are so perfectly suited that one without the other is unthinkable. An inevitable corollary to this is that the artist is very much occupied with style.

Readers of Blake's prose annotations to the work of other men will find in them a large number of vigorous pronouncements on the value of suiting style to subject in painting, engraving, and writing, but probably the most important of these, and certainly one of the most frequently quoted, comes from the prefatory material to *Jerusalem*, chapter 1, where Blake says that in the poem to follow,

> Every word and every letter is studied and put into its fit place: the terrific numbers are reserved for the terrific parts—the mild & gentle for the mild & gentle parts, and the prosaic, for the inferior parts: Poetry fetter'd fetters the Human Race! Nations are Destroy'd or Flourish in proportion as Their Poetry Painting and Music are Destroy'd or Flourish!

Whether or not we are inclined to feel that Blake followed his own dicta with absolute consistency in *Jerusalem*, we know that to the prophet's compulsion to exhort and warn, and to the visionary's conviction of the truth of his vision, Blake adds the artist's scorn for craftsmen whose technique is inadequate to the demands they make upon it. Uncertainty and stylistic clumsiness in the professional artist were anathema to him, and his rejection of the possibility for himself is the source of some of his most unattractively arrogant statements. It is also the source of some of his most abusive remarks about the way in which people he considered bad artists ignore or fudge what he called the Minute Particulars, or the careful details of a picture, a poem, or an idea. Generalities infuriated him because they seemed to indicate a muddled mind, and, above all, a muddied eye, incapable of discerning the true nature of things. "Minute Discrimination is not Accidental," he says; "All Sublimity is founded on Minute Discrimination." Again, "Without minute Neatness of Execution, The. Sublime. cannot Exist! Grandeur of Ideas is founded on Precision of Ideas." And again, "Obscurity is neither the source of the Sublime nor of anything Else" (*Annotations to Reynolds*).

Northrop Frye, writing in 1966, says, "Blake soon led me, in my search for poetic analogues, to Dante and Milton, and it was clear that the schematic cosmologies of Dante and Milton, however they got into Dante and Milton, were, once they got there, poetic constructs, examples of the way poets think, and not foreign bodies of knowledge. If the prophecies are normal poems, or at least a normal expression of poetic genius, and if Blake nevertheless meant to teach some system by them, that system could only be something connected with the principles of poetic thought. Blake's message, then, is not simply *his* message, nor is it an extra-literary message. What he is trying to say is what he thinks poetry is trying to say: the imaginative content implied by the existence of an imaginative form of language."[4]

I am not entirely sure what a "normal" poem is, or what a "normal" expression of poetic genius" is, either. Both phrases seem to raise more questions than they answer. Yet it seems to me that the prophetic books are *not* "normal" poems in their intention or in their effect, and that they are simultaneously literary and nonliterary, because Blake was simultaneously a prophet, a visionary, and a poet. In other words, Blake's "myths" are specifically intended to enlarge the imaginative understanding and change the lives of those who read them. The poems were not composed to afford a viable container for resonant myths, so that we could enjoy them. Rather, the myths are the container for Blake's tough and demanding ideas of man's proper (i.e., fruitful and creative, rather than orthodoxly acceptable) relationship to God and to society. It is these ideas that are primarily important to Blake—and not only these ideas, but certain mores of feeling and imaginative empathy, which should accompany and provide a climate for the ideas.

Thinking that one is a prophet is a very different thing from being a literary man who assumes the prophetic stance for the purpose of all or part of a particular poem. And knowing that one is a visionary is a very different thing from couching one's poem in terms of, say, a dream-vision, as Shelley did in "The Triumph of Life," and Keats in "The Fall of Hyperion." In one sense, the urgency of one's conviction might shunt one away from the pleasures of "made" myth and into the experiential reality of actual religious experience. Keats, in the early poem "I Stood Tiptoe," closes his poem in praise of poetry-inducing landscape with a series of scenes in which he is concerned to show that myth-stories were engendered by the action of nature on poetic sensibilities. It is, as Wordsworth said of the "Hymn to Pan" in *Endymion*, "A very pretty piece of paganism." It is an experiment, a "What if—?" Though Keats and we who read the poem recognize it for the imaginative speculation that it is, we think no worse of the poet for having so speculated.

Blake himself was ambivalent about classical mythology. As poet, he was led by the strongly developed, symbol-perceiving aspect of his intelligence to share Keats's deep sense of the evocative power of ancient myth for the modern poet. Yet at the same time his conviction that Christianity, the "seventh eye of God," had rendered all other "eyes" obsolete appears to have led him to regard the presence of a body of myths as a sure sign of the deadness of the beliefs that generated them. Unlike Keats, who was relatively untroubled with religious musings, Blake saw such myths from the perspective of his own highly idiosyncratic Christianity, which depended on man's having a sense of himself as not only close to, but containing, God. On the first page of *Jerusalem*, the Savior says to Albion,

> I am not a God afar off, I am a brother and friend;
> Within your bosom I reside, and you reside in me:
> Lo! We are One . . .

and in *Milton*, Blake stands in the bosom of the fallen Satan, who has completely alienated himself from the Divine Vision, and says with terrible compassion,

> I also stood in Satan's bosom & beheld its desolations!
> A ruind man: a ruind building of God not made with hands;
> Its plains of burning sand, its mountains of marble terrible:
> Its pits and declivities flowing with molten ore & fountains
> Of pitch & nitre: its ruind palaces & cities & mighty works;

> Its furnaces of affliction in which his Angels & Emanations
> Labour with blackened visages among its stupendous ruins
> Arches & pyramids & porches colonades & domes:
> In which dwells Mystery, Babylon, here is her secret place. . . .
>   (*Milton*, Plate 38)

It was Blake's sense of the shared identity between men and deity that led to his hatred of what he called "Mystery"—the sense of a God so far off that he had to be interpreted to the believer by a priestly caste whose power came to depend on their preservation of the mystery of holy things and their own function as interpreters to laymen of things holy. Fallen Satan's desertlike interior has become a shrine for this type of mystery because Satan has lost the sense of himself as a "building of God," and has allowed the temple of himself to be perverted to other uses. Blake saw the Greek and Roman myths as examples of religion in another historical period when such "mystery" was rife. Not only that, but he saw the myths themselves as a way of perpetuating the mystery, and in *The Marriage of Heaven and Hell* he says (speaking of ancient religions), ". . . a system was form'd, which . . . enslav'd the vulgar by attempting to realize or abstract the mental deities from their objects; thus began Priesthood. Choosing forms of worship from poetic tales. And at length they pronounced that the Gods had orderd such things. Thus man forgot that All deities reside in the human breast" (*The Marriage of Heaven and Hell*, Plate 11). This firm stand was consistent in Blake's work when he was thinking of ancient religions, and leads to various slighting references such as that to "Bloated Gods Mercury Juno Venus & the rattletraps of Mythology . . ." in the description of a painting by Rubens in Blake's "Public Address." (In part, of course, this was a commentary on Rubens's style, but it was also characteristic of Blake's contempt for the general wrongheadedness of the religious system from which the mythology came.)

The Blake *Concordance* contains two references to *mythological* and five to *mythology*, all found in the prose. They are in general further evidence that Blake considered classical mythology a perpetuation of an untenable religious belief. Three of these references come from his "Descriptive Catalogue," where, in his notes to the pictures of Pitt and Nelson, he is concerned to show his contempt for Greek mythology because the "Greek Muses are daughters of Mnemosyne or Memory, & not of Inspiration or Imagination, & therefore not authors of such sublime conceptions." The "Descriptive Catalogue" is dated 1809. In 1826, the year before his death, he copied out the last paragraph of Wordsworth's Preface to *"The Excursion," being a portion of "The Recluse."* At this time, he was concerned not with the inadequacies of Greek mythology alone, but with all points in human history in which he saw an individual turning away from the Divine Vision. The strong convictions of his later life concerning God's mercy and man's capacity for alienating himself from God make the following annotation characteristic. First he copied Wordsworth:

> All strength, all terror, single or in bands
> That ever was put forth in personal Form
> Jehovah—with his thunder and the choir
> Of shouting Angels & the empyreal thrones—
> I pass them unalarmed . . .
>
> ("The Recluse," 5:31-35)

Then he added a comment in which Wordsworth's behavior is drawn together with that of Solomon:

> Solomon when he married Pharaoh's daughter & became a convert to the Heathen Mythology Talked exactly in this way of Jehovah as a very inferior object of Man's Contemplation he also pass'd him unalarmed & was permitted. Jehovah dropped a tear & followed him by his Spirit into the Abstract Void it is called the Divine Mercy Satan dwells in it but Mercy does not dwell in him he knows not how to forgive.

Blake's frequent use of the Old Testament Jehovah to represent a false, Urizenic god of power and destructive caprice rather than of loving concern does not seem to obtain here; rather, he shows Jehovah behaving to the apostate Solomon with the mercy and loving-kindness of Blake's "own" concept of deity. Blake's note indicates his own disapproval of what obviously seemed to him a clear case of "turning away from the Divine Vision" on the part of Wordsworth. It may seem a strangely inflexible censure from one who had been far from respectful to the "received" opinion of Jehovah in his own time, but what is important to us is Blake's implication (by comparing Wordsworth to Solomon) that it was "heathen" religions that had a mythology, not his own religion, and that "mythologies" are a collection of false beliefs.

Knowing how Blake felt here does not give us license to ignore or minimize the truth that the whole fabric of Blake's poetry is shot through with mythic overtones, or that the experience of the reader of these poems is contingent on his reacting to Blake's uses of myth as fully and as sensitively as he can. It is also incumbent on such a reader, however, to realize that Blake's reaction to the word *mythology* is not just a whim or an oversensitivity, but springs freshly and strongly from Blake's conviction that the religion he was writing about was alive and that others were, to all intents and purposes, dead.

Blake "uses" myth as the civilized poet must use it, working always at the growing-edge of creativity, where myth and metaphor meet and add their powers to each other. When this happens perfectly, more can be meant than needs saying, and no poet has ever been more aware of this than Blake. When he fails, he fails most often because he makes demands on us that we have not imagination enough to fill.

No one will ever, probably, arrive at a total and definitive reading of Blake's major myth of the fall and reintegration of Albion the Ancient Man. In part the reason is that Blake had not finished working out some of the details of it himself. Still, we have done better than Swinburne thought anybody could, and the work still goes on, with immense vitality. Blake taught the first great generation of his scholars, and they have shared their wisdom generously. A part of that wisdom, as Northrop Frye has repeatedly said, has been an increased knowledge of how poetry works, and this comes directly out of the struggle with Blake's enormous achievement.

It is the meeting of myth with metaphor that educates us, and it is this aspect of Blake's use of myth that remains endlessly generative, given, as it is, the emblematic pictorial quality that is part of the equipment of Blake the artist and engraver. One of these moments may be seen in a number of places in Blake's work, from the tiny "For the Children" (later, "For the Sexes") to much larger illustrations, and more indirectly in the written work. It shows a monumentally strong stone doorway, with an aged figure, supporting himself with a stick and slowly pulling himself toward its threshold. The entrance is Death's Door, the Gate of the Grave, and, like an emblem, the picture epitomizes the inexorability of man's end. However, familiarity with Blake's thought instructs us that the Gate of the Grave also means the door to (or from) what Blake calls "Eternal Death," or life (and death) upon earth. In Blakean terms "Eternal Death" is a "State." States themselves endure, but human beings may pass through them and emerge from them as their wisdom and self-knowledge permit them to do. Both the Gate of the Grave and the universal human pathos generated by the sight of the figure approaching it are, to Blake, the inevitable result of the conventional, unimaginative vision of most of us, which, when we regard death, becomes even more occluded than usual by our deep fear of the end of life. To Blake himself, the picture could, and probably did, have a double significance, which was the fruit of his own "cleansed" perception. He could see "through" the picture to a casting-off of imaginative inadequacy and to a continuance of intellectual energy more true and more certain than most men dare to postulate. He has recorded this vision in the endings of *The Four Zoas* and of *Jerusalem*. (It might be possible to say that Blake would probably regard the conventional interpretation of the Gate of the Grave picture as a "mythology" or defective vision engendered by an inadequate belief.)

In Night IX of *The Four Zoas*, when Albion begins to reintegrate, he calls on the fallen Urizen,

> Come forth from slumbers of thy cold abstraction come forth
> Arise to eternal births shake off thy cold repose.

Urizen, during the whole period of this fall, had assumed the figure of a bowed, ancient man, his long white hair stirred by the snowy winds and bitter cold that accompanied him. Now, at the sound of Albion's voice, this pitiful and erring figure

> Wept in the dark deep anxious his Scaly form
> To reassume the Human . . .

and eventually his cleansed vision allows him to repent and to change into his original glorious and "risen" self. He

> . . . shook his aged mantles off
> Into the fires Then glorious bright Exulting in his joy
> He sounding rose into the heavens in naked majesty
> In radiant youth.

Urizen is not a man, he is a Zoa, but he has passed out of a "state" and resumed his eternal self just as the man who reluctantly pulls himself toward Death's Door might do if his faith and imagination bore him up.

A variation of the Gate of the Grave appears in more complex form at the end of *The Book of Thel*, when the Matron Clay says to Thel,

> O Queen, enter my house, tis given thee to enter,
> And to return . . ."

What Thel sees in "the land unknown" is the necessary and terrifying interconnection between birth and death, between life on earth and the death of being separated from eternal life. Thel's tragedy is that she has not the vision to realize that if she enters into human life, with its inevitable concomitant of human death, she will enter into a "state" that can be passed through and transcended. Thel herself appears in the poem as a restless and seeking ego who wishes to take, but has ltttle idea of giving. The ministrations of the Cloud and the Clod remain unintelligible to her, and even though she sees the worm as a helpless babe, it does not occur to her to mother it herself. The vision that in *Jerusalem* prompts Albion to throw himself into the fire to save Los does not belong to Thel, and because it is lacking she turns away from human life forever and remains in a state of stunted visionary infancy, of which the conceivable outcome might be an endless future as a companion to Har and Heva of *Tiriel* in the "great cage" of senile innocence.

The counterimage, or myth-metaphor, to those involving the Gate of the Grave is that of a vital figure striding purposefully along through a dark landscape, or entering into a great door, with a lanternlike globe in his hand. We hear about such a figure in *The Four Zoas*; one performs the chief action in *Milton* and *Jerusalem*, and there are a number of illustrations, notably the Frontispiece and Plate 97 of *Jerusalem*, which show us what Blake has in mind. It is an image of combined energy and selflessness, and in each of the three long poems a character motivated by love and sacrifice goes down into the caves of Eternal Death to seek for and attempt to rescue someone who is lost there. There are, of course, many extant myths involving a similar search, of which the Orpheus myth comes most quickly to mind, but Blake's various versions, involving as they do *both* sacrifice and search, deal with the theme central to his major works—that of salvation of more than self, through a life of creative (i.e., imaginative) sacrifice and work.

In the Sixth Night of *The Four Zoas*, in a kind of earlier run-through of the story, Tharmas, the Zoa of Unity, searches the dens of Urthona for his lost emanation, Enion. Though he does not find her, and is, in fact, obliged to retreat in fear for his own life, the fact that he was impelled by love to search for her begins to move him, however slowly, toward wisdom and change from his fallen state, and to initiate the steps toward reintegration that culminate in Enion's eventual return in Night IX. The entire story of *Milton*, of course, shows Milton returning to Earth ("Eternal Death"), there to undo the misunderstanding caused by the faulty conception of the relationship between God and Man exhibited in his own writings.

In *Jerusalem*, chapter 2, Plate 45, Blake's great hero Los, blacksmith, artist-artisan, and fallen form of the Zoa of Creativity, Urthona,

> . . . took his globe of fire to search the interiors of Albions
> Bosom, in all the terrors of friendship, entering the caves
> Of despair and death, to search the tempters out, walking among
> Albion's rocks and precipices! caves of solitude & dark despair,
> And saw every Minute Particular of Albion degraded and murderd
> But saw not by whom; they were hidden within the minute particulars
> Of which they had possessed themselves; and there they take up
> The articulations of a man's soul, and laughing throw it down
> Into the frame, then knock it out upon the plank, & souls are baked
> In bricks to build the pyramids of Hever and Terah. But Los
> Searched in vain: closed from the minutia he walkd, difficult.
> Till he came to Old Stratford & thence to Stepney & the Isle
> Of Leutha's Dogs, thence thro the narrows of the Rivers side

And saw every minute particular, the jewels of Albion running down
The kennels of the streets & lanes as if they were abhorrd.
Every Universal Form was become mountains of moral
Virtue: and every Minute Particular hardend into grains of sand:
And all the tendernesses of the soul cast forth as filth and mire . . .

This mythic image of the friend who searches the depths of Albion's
personality in order to do what he can to bring him back to fully sentient
being seems to ramify endlessly if we consider it—outward to all people in
the largest sense, or singly and deeply inward, to the springs of action of
each individual. Blake's Albion is at once all Englishmen and all mankind,
and his Minute Particulars (in this case the individuals making up nation
and/or human race) suffer all the agonies of earthly life, including being
mutilated by that life until original potential is almost entirely lost.

In the course of evolving the prophetic books, Blake came to identify
himself more and more firmly with Los, who seeks to anatomize and
diagnose the ills of his "friend and brother" Albion. Blake's own mission to
England and humanity, he thought, was to perform, by making his poems,
the same task outside of them that Los was trying to perform inside
them—not only for *all* human beings, but for *each* human being; not only in
Blake's own time but for all future human history.

> All Life [he says] consists of these Two Throwing off Error . . . continually
> & receiving Truth . . . continually. . . . What are all the Gifts of the
> Spirit but Mental Gifts? Whenever any Individual Rejects Error &
> Embraces Truth a Last Judgment passes upon that individual.
> ("A Vision of the Last Judgment")

These lines bring us back once more to my initial concern with Blake's
intention and to our obligation to be aware that it was not solely literary.
The relationship between man and God, which forms the climax of
Jerusalem and which is adumbrated with varying success in *The Four Zoas*
and *Milton*, was something he strongly believed in himself, and thought of
as not only living, but as having invincible survival value. He was not
struggling to "save" a way of belief that he felt was dying. He was trying to
effect a cleansing of men's vision to that they might be able to perceive that
without such vision men themselves must continue to be less human.

Knowing the strength of his conviction and the incredibly inventive
energy with which he set about his task—and being aware also of the
inherent scorn in Blake's references to "mythologies":—we must, I think,
realize the irritation and bitterness with which Blake would probably react
if he found us regarding his major works as purely literary artifacts and

arguing with each other about his myth, rather than cleansing our perceptions and enlarging our capacities for creative interchange. That Blake *did* abandon *The Four Zoas* unfinished after many years of writing and rewriting it; did abandon his earlier plans for *Milton* and *The Book of Urizen;* did start, not anew, but differently, with *Jerusalem,* to cover a lot of the same ground he had been over before—all this indicates that the myth was less important to him than what he was trying to make the poems say.

Karl Kroeber, whose essay "Delivering Jerusalem" I read when this paper was nearly finished, had obviously been thinking along similar lines when he says that he would like to apply to Blake's work a passage from Frank Kermode's *The Sense of an Ending,* in which Kermode observed, "Myth operates within the diagrams of ritual, which presupposes total and adequate explanations of things as they are and were; it is a sequence of radically unchangeable gestures. Fictions are for finding things out, and they change as the needs of sense-making change."[5] Kroeber has indicated that he will write on this subject in the near future, and I have no wish to steal his thunder, but I think as he does that Kermode's word *fictions* is useful here. I think, for instance, that Blake's mythic situations are "for finding things out," and that he would rather have had his readers carry away from *Jerusalem* a full understanding of the *meaning* of Albion's throwing himself into the furnaces of affliction, than that they should tell the *story* of it over and over again. He did not mean his poems to be stories of the way things "used" to be between God and man, but of how they are. The drama of the fall and separation of the Zoas and emanations, and particularly of their reintegration and their achievement, through loving sacrifice, of the Divine Vision in fiery creative unity and freedom of the imagination is one that Blake wishes to show can occur at any time in human history.

His prophetic sense made him aware of the terrible distortions of human vision if it is not continually corrected by those whose imaginative sense is clear. Today the rash of current studies of human aggressiveness shows us that we have come to a moment in time in which Blake's prophetic sense of the dangers of our tendencies to exploit the weak, to make war on each other, and to extinguish the capacity for imaginative vision under a dead weight of scientific materialism speaks to us very clearly. Not Blake alone, but many hopeful and determined investigators are descending into Albion's depths to analyze his minute particulars, but none is so skillful and so perceptive as he.

When the reductive rationality of the fallen Urizen became complete in Night II of *The Four Zoas,* most of the people on earth were unaware of their own weakened capacities for vision. A very few, sickened by the grimness of life, "with trembling horror" cry,

What are we terrors to one another. Come O brethren wherefore
Was this wide Earth spread all abroad. not for wild beasts to roam
But many stood silent and busied with their families
And many said We see no Visions in the darksom air
Measure the course of that sulphur orb that lights the darksom day
Set stations on this breeding Earth & let us buy & sell
Others arose & schools Erected forming Instruments
To measure out the course of heaven.

(*The Four Zoas*, p. 28)

The man who heard the cry and recorded it had ended his own remarks on
the Last Judgment in 1810 with,

> I assert for My self that I do not behold the Outward Creation & that to
> me it is hindrance & not Action it is as the Dirt upon my feet No part of
> Me. What it will be Questioned When the Sun rises do you not see a
> round Disk of fire somewhat like a Guinea O no no I see an Innumerable
> company of the Heavenly host crying Holy Holy Holy is the Lord God
> Almighty I question not my Corporeal or Vegetative Eye any more than I
> would Question a Window concerning a Sight I look thro and not with it.
>
> ("A Vision of the Last Judgment," p. 555)

At some time in or about 1816, when he was illustrating Milton's
"L'Allegro," he seems to have painted a picture of this vision, and, calling it
"The Great Sun," used it to illustrate lines 60 ff. of Milton's poem.

But, however emancipated he knew his own vision to be, it was in just
such a painfully claustrophobic world of busy materialists as that described
in the quotation from *The Four Zoas, Night II*, that Blake knew himself to
be living. For these men and women, for these "Minute Particulars" of the
fallen Albion, the artist-prophet-visionary forged his prophetic books,
believing himself to be inspired by enabling love. "Do I sleep amidst
danger to Friends?" cries the revived Albion at the end of *Jerusalem*,

O my cities & Counties
Do you sleep! Rouze up. rouze up. Eternal Death is abroad. . . .

(*Jerusalem*, Plate 96)

Both the question and the warning might also have been spoken by Blake
himself, whose recognition of our plight was followed by his titanic struggle
for our enlightenment. Surely *The Four Zoas, Milton, and Jerusalem* are
meant to ride on the wave of time without being swamped by it, always
speaking directly to the condition of whatever historical present they find
themselves in. And regardless of our individual response to them, we
cannot approach them honestly without a full sense of that intention.

NOTES

1. All quotations from Blake in this essay are taken from *The Poetry and Prose of William Blake,* ed. David V. Erdman (Garden City, N.Y.: Doubleday, 1970).

2. *The Oxford Cyclopedic Concordance.* (London: Oxford University Press, 1947), p. 268.

3. The fact that "A Prophecy" appears on the title pages of "America" and "Europe" may be taken as the assuming of a literary stance in these two instances.

4. Northrop Frye, "The Keys to the Gates," from *Some British Romantics: A Collection of Essays,* ed. James V. Logan, John E. Jordan, and Northrop Frye (Columbus: Ohio State University Press, 1966; reprinted in *Romanticism and Consciousness,* ed. Harold Bloom, New York: W. W. Norton & Company, Inc., 1970), p. 234.

5. Frank Kermode, *The Sense of an Ending: Studies in the Theory of Fiction* (New York: Oxford University Press, 1967), p. 39. Quoted by Karl Kroeber in "Delivering Jerusalem," published in *Blake's Sublime Allegory,* ed. Stuart Curran and Joseph Anthony Wittreich, Jr. (Madison: The University of Wisconsin Press, 1973), p. 359 n. 12.

SUGGESTED READINGS

Abrams, M. H. *Natural Supernaturalism: Tradition and Revolution in Romantic Literature.* New York: W. W. Norton and Co., Inc., 1971.

Bloom, Harold. *Blake's Apocalypse: A Study in Poetic Argument.* Garden City, N.Y.: Doubleday, 1963.

Curran, Stuart, and Wittreich, Joseph Anthony, eds. *Blake's Sublime Allegory: Essays of the Four Zoas, Milton and Jerusalem.* Madison, Wis.: University of Wisconsin Press, 1975.

Erdman, David V. *Blake, Prophet Against Empire.* rev. ed. Princeton, N.J.: Princeton University Press, 1969.

Erdman, David V., and Grant, John E., eds. *Blake's Visionary Forms Dramatic.* Princeton, N.J.: Princeton University Press, 1970.

Frye, Northrop. *Fearful Symmetry: A Study of William Blake.* Princeton, N.J.: Princeton University Press, 1947.

Hagstrum, Jean H. *William Blake, Poet and Painter.* Chicago: University of Chicago Press, 1964.

Raine, Kathleen. *Blake and Tradition.* Bollingen Series 35:11. Princeton, N.J.: Princeton University Press, 1968.

Rosenfeld, Alvin H., ed. *William Blake: Essays for S. Foster Damon.* Providence, R.I.: Brown University Press, 1969.

Biographical Note on F. W. Bateson

F. W. Bateson went to Trinity College, Oxford, and to Harvard, where he was a Commonwealth Fellow. Until his retirement in 1969 he was a Special University Lecturer at Oxford and a Fellow and Tutor of Corpus Christi College, where he was Emeritus Fellow. During his long and distinguished career he had been a Visiting Professor at Minnesota, Cornell, Berkeley, and Pennsylvania State University.

For ten years Mr. Bateson edited and was the chief contributor to the *Cambridge Bibliography of English Literature*. In 1951 he founded and subsequently edited the influential quarterly *Essays in Criticism*. Among his works are *English Comic Drama* (1929), *English Poetry and the English Language* (1934), *English Poetry: A Critical Introduction* (1950), *A Guide to English Literature* (1965), *The Scholar-Critic* (1972), and *Essays in Critical Dissent* (1972), a collection of twenty-four skeptical and provocative polemic essays.

Mr. Bateson died 16 October 1978.

Myth—A Dispensable Critical Term

F. W. BATESON

That the term can be dispensed with in English literary criticism is at least suggested—the parallel can hardly be denied—by the curious reluctance of the English language to adopt the word *myth* at all. In the early fifteenth century Lydgate was already using *mythology* (in the plural spelling of "methologies"); and *mythic, mythical, mythographer, mythologer, mythologian, mythologic, mythological, mythologically, mythologist, mythologize, mythologizer* all make their appearance in the seventeenth century. The eighteenth century added *mythistory* and *mythologue*, but it is not until 1830, according to the *Oxford English Dictionary* (from which all this information is derived), that *myth* itself occurs. It is almost as if pre-Victorian England and early nineteenth-century America were skeptical of the whole mythic concept per se, though its compounds might be accepted as learned importations, loud in the mouth but meaning little or nothing. A couplet in Butler's *Hudibras* is openly contemptuous:

> Though Love be all the worlds pretence,
> Mony's the Mythologic fence.[1]

The use of *myth* or *myths* in a critical context is even more recent. This may seem odd since the Greek *muthos* is a key term in Aristotle's *Poetics*, the foundation stone of all later European literary criticism. But Aristotle's translators have not rendered his *muthos* by the word *myth*, though etymologically they were, of course, entitled to. Instead we find Butcher using *plots* (and once *themes* and *plots*); Bywater prefers *Fable* or *Plot* for the singular, *stories* for the plural; L. J. Potts uses *Fable* for both with creditable consistency, though at one point he too breaks down and uses *Plots* for the plural. It seems clear that Aristotle himself tended to confuse the concepts of (1) narrative (E. M. Forster's "The king died and then the queen died") and (2) plot (Forster's "The king died, and then the queen died of grief").[2] What is more surprising perhaps is that none of Aristotle's

98

translators thought of evading the latent confusion by using *myth* or *myths* wherever he used *muthos* or *muthōi*. It is possible, as we shall see, that they were anxious not to allow the ordinary connotations of *myth* (=popular fallacy) to intrude. Gilbert Murray, who added in 1920 a lucid and persuasive "Preface" to Bywater's translation, divorced from his Greek text and severely technical notes, got round the difficulty by proposing, simply as an experiment, "a ruthlessly literal translation," which would begin:

> MAKING: Kinds of making; function of each and how the myths ought to be put together if the Making is to go right.[3]

He was then able to abandon the "literal translation" and speak of the "heroic saga, the myths."[4] And so myth criticism was at last let loose on an unsuspecting world, though with Murray—with his emphasis on the ritual origins of Greek tragedy—we are still closer to anthropology than to literature.

But Murray was an Englishman, the Regius Professor of Greek at Oxford, and it was not until the 1940s that American myth criticism began to spread its wings in such minor masterpieces as Northrop Frye's *Fearful Symmetry* (1947) and Francis Fergusson's *Idea of a Theater* (1949), the latter specifically continuing and generalizing where Murray left off. The later history of American myth criticism has been judiciously, if unsympathetically, surveyed by René Wellek in a number of essays collected in *Concepts of Criticism* (1963) and *Discriminations* (1970). I find it difficult to resist his conclusion that the term "has today so wide a range of meanings that it has become difficult to argue about it with any clarity of reference."[5] It is even, apparently, already out of date. " 'Vision,' " Wellek tells us, "is momentarily the fashionable key-term, as 'myth' was a little while ago, and 'ambiguity' and 'irony' even earlier."[6] To a member of Wellek's own generation all this will irresistibly recall Arthur O. Lovejoy's 1927 trumpet call as President of the Modern Language Association. "The word 'romantic,' " Lovejoy told us then, "has come to mean so many things that, by itself, it means nothing,"[7] and should therefore be abandoned.

It is one of the ironies of literary history that it was Wellek who should have come to the rescue of *romantic* against the skepticism of Lovejoy by proposing three criteria that, as he applied them, would justify the use of the term *Romanticism* to describe a coherent literary movement. And one of the three was "symbol and myth" as a characteristic of Romantic "poetic style."[8]

The crucial essay, antedating Wellek's own attacks on myth-criticism by many years, is his "The Concept of Romanticism in Literary History." All the relevant facts are here assembled, many of them for the first time, and up to a point Wellek's defense of "The Unity of European Romanticism," as he puts it, must certainly be conceded. But it is only up to a point, and the point has become a very blunted one when *symbol* and *myth* have been conjoined for the *thirteenth* time in this one essay as apparently almost synonymous. (The conjunction is repeated six more times in Wellek's later "Romanticism Re-examined."[9]) And in any case to limit *myth* to an aspect of "poetic style" seems as eccentric as the uses the most irresponsible myth-critics put the term to. The plain man, male or female, expects a myth to be untrue, a fiction or delusion; his more sophisticated brother or sister may also think of a myth as the component part of a "mythology," a still conceivably usable fragment, that is, of the detritus of some extinct or discredited religion. The criterion in either case is not a stylistic one but one either of logical validity or of social value. Has the symbolic narrative still some justification as intellectual explanation or communal ideal? Or is it, as the context in which the word is used today generally implies, mere myth—one of civilization's discarded hypotheses?

I I

Wellek's limitation of *myth* to the primarily aesthetic area of "poetic style" clearly does the use of the term by modern myth-critics less than justice. The "myths of concern" in which Northrop Frye, as he recently has told us, is now principally interested are more a matter of social function than of stylistics. They are essential to "hold society together, so far as words can help to do this."[10]

The special attraction of myth today is, however, in its *subject matter*. No doubt subject matter wholly divorced from form or style is a preliterary or even subliterary area. Consider, for example, the "sources" of Shakespeare's plays. But the example of Shakespeare—almost unable to write without source material (the tediously schematized plot of *Love's Labour's Lost* shows what happens when he tried to)—sufficiently demonstrates the dependence of even the greatest literature on what I have called preliterary subject matter.

The case of William Blake, a poet particularly dear to modern myth-critics, demonstrates or at least suggests in his best work (which is not, as Frye seems to imagine, the long and stylistically pretentious later Prophetic Books) the relation between symbolic statement and traditional mythology. "A Poison Tree," one of the best of the *Songs of Experience*, may be used as a test case. Although written circa 1790, the poem was not engraved in Blake's special "Illuminated Printing" until circa 1793 and was not actually published until 1794. The title, to start with, raises a hitherto overlooked problem. The earliest extant version—that almost at the end of the so-called *Notebook*[11] that Blake had inherited from his favorite brother Robert—is in autograph and originally had no title, though "Christian Forbearance" (in Blake's hand) was squeezed in later in the narrow space that was all that was available to him at the beginning of the poem. This title was not used in the engraved text, however, which substitutes "A Poison Tree" for it, the reference being to the fabulous Upas (the Malayan word for poison) that Erasmus Darwin had just popularized in *The Loves of the Plants* (1789). (This "myth" was in fact the fabrication of an eccentric Englishman who wrote it up in the *London Magazine* of 1783.[12])

If "A Poison Tree" is a better title for Blake's poem than "Christian Forbearance," to what does it owe its superiority? (That it *is* a better title will hardly be disputed.) The superiority is surely because "Christian Forbearance" is a premature and over-explicit summary of the poem's theme. That a forgiveness unto seventy times seven may be malicious, like the hypocritical humility of Dickens's Uriah Heep, is no doubt the conclusion, or at any rate one of the conclusions, that a reader will ultimately draw from the poem; but it is a conclusion reached *after* the poem has been experienced as poetry. Christian "charity" is not *explicitly* under attack in it. A parallel may be relevant here to a traditional proverb—or indeed to Blake's own "Proverbs of Hell" (in *The Marriage of Heaven and Hell*), which were also composed circa 1790. A social or moral generalization is implicit in the image or miniature drama of a proverb, but the effectiveness and memorability of a proverb depend upon the generalization's remaining implicit, only to be worked out as it were by the alert auditor or reader. Blake was right therefore to prefer "A Poison Tree" as a title. It titillates the reader's curiosity—as the enormously long corpse, lying on its back apparently in a nightgown, titillates it in the illustration to the engraved text of 1794.

So far, however, *myth* (in the myth-critics' various senses) has not entered my discussion of the poem. It will be remembered that the first verse runs as follows in both the *Notebook* and the engraved text (except that the *Notebook* version has no punctuation):

> I was angry with my friend;
> I told my wrath, my wrath did end.
> I was angry with my foe;
> I told it not, my wrath did grow.

It will not be necessary to quote the whole poem. The unspoken anger with his enemy festers and is externalized as a carefully tended tree bearing a beautiful but deadly apple. The "foe" is fascinated by it, eats the apple one night and is poisoned by it:

> In the morning glad I see
> My foe outstretched beneath the tree.

The "I" of the poem—who is perhaps at a literal level Blake reflecting with shame upon his own irascibility—is gladdened by his success as a *murderer*. "A Poison Tree" is a better title, if only because it is less explicit, demanding more from the reader.

A revision within the poem confirms a general point I have been hinting at: that this may be a successful poem because—being only halfway to a conceptualization—it *resists* a satisfactory prose paraphrase. The sarcastic comment on Christian forgiveness remains implicit, to be read between the lines, not to be handed to the reader on a plate. And the deadliness of a hypocritical charity is nicely symbolized in this home-grown, beautiful, but immediately poisonous apple. So far then, paraphrase *is* possible. But by deleting in the manuscript the original line 11, which ran

> And I gave it to my foe[13]

and substituting for it, as in the engraved text,

> And my foe beheld it shine

the parable is given an extra twist. And, as the identical spacing between the new line 11 and line 12 proves, this change must have been made in the course of writing the poem, *currente calamo*.

What is the thematic effect of this revision? The change seems to me a crucial one. Instead of the melodrama of the speaker's offering his enemy the poisonous apple as a gift, the enemy *destroys himself by stealing it*. The theft now puts the enemy in the wrong morally—and so in a sense he deserves what he gets, even if death must seem an excessive punishment for stealing an apple, however superb. But Blake has made his point about the hypocritical Christianity that gets its own way by a pretended forgiveness of sin. I find it difficult, however, to translate the beautiful but both corrupting and destructive apple into the language of discursive prose except at intolerable length. Is the "I" of the poem to be equated in some way with the Jehovah of Genesis, or the God of *Paradise Lost* that Blake called "Nobodaddy," who deliberately planted the Fatal Tree in Adam and Eve's innocent sexual Garden of Eden? There are certainly defiant echoes of Genesis (as interpreted by Milton) throughout *Songs of Experience*, especially in the obscure "Introduction," which was apparently intended to summarize the dominant themes. At this point myth-criticism of a sort may seem to be entering my interpretation of the poem, but the reason why

Blake deleted "And I gave it to my foe" was primarily, it is clear, a technical one: the English language did not provide him with an appropriate rhyme here to *foe*. (He had already used *grow*.) The unconscious or subconscious mind—which Coleridge was about to call "the genius in the man of genius"—may then have come to his rescue. This poem, like almost all of Blake's poems, is all about "I," "me," "mine." (Blake uses the first-person singular more often than any other English poet.) And so via *mine* Blake may well have reached shine—and thus achieved the brilliant succulent fruit as it presented itself to the "foe." By what may have been subliminal thinking, his sympathy is transferred, however briefly, from the "I" to the "non-I," and an ethical statement of much greater subtlety emerges.

This tentative reconstruction of the new turn Blake's revision gave the poem proposes very tentatively an unconscious extension of the theme to one superior to and more intelligent than what the conscious mind had planned for the poem. The reconstruction cannot be proved; the revision *may* have been the work of the reasoning faculty. (There is nothing about it that the reason could object to.) But it is still a fact to which most poets can bear witness that the mind, in certain lucky moments, sometimes works with a special intensity and rapidity—works, indeed, so fast that the conscious mind cannot follow its operations. I am a very minor poet, but I can remember an occasion many years ago when the apparent miracle occurred with me. I was struggling with two lines in the middle of a lyric that just wouldn't "come." I was in Norway at the time and, as I opened a woodshed door (I can still smell the pinewood logs), the lines "came" in a sudden flash. They did not exist as my hand pressed the latch, and in the fraction of a second spent in stepping into the shed, they were fully formed in my mind. No doubt it was not great poetry, but the lines, which rhymed and had the "correct" number of syllables and stresses, were probably the best in the poem. But the difference—this is my real point—was one of degree and not of kind.[14]

Now, Blake's change of title and revision of the eleventh line in "A Poison Tree" were also changes of degree rather than of kind. A myth-critic, however, goes much further. Here is Hazard Adams's interpretation of the poem in his *William Blake: A Reading of the Shorter Poems* (1963):

By repressing the initial emotion the speaker has created a monstrous situation. For everyone but him, the usually bright and true image of morning becomes the blackest of nights. Without knowing it, he is playing the part of Satan in a perverse Eden of his own construction. Like Blake's Satan, he has no science of wrath. He is merely a negation, consumed by an "abstract" which preys upon other spiritual bodies as well as his own. Ironically his own gladness demonstrates that he too has fallen into the condition of his foe. His only joy is the joy of the primitive

god of materialism, who is apparently happy to see Albion stretched in a
dream beneath the tree of the knowledge of good and evil.[15]

Here we have a reading of "A Poison Tree" that escapes much too soon
from the surface meaning of Blake's poem. To say that "the usually bright
and true image of morning" has become "the blackest of nights" is to
impose a meaning on the words that they simply will not bear. The speaker
saw what had happened to his "foe" in the morning because the coming of
daylight is a necessary condition for the human eye to function. Again, to
describe the speaker as an "abstract" is to introduce a term from Blake's
later vocabulary that did not exist for him in 1790. (The poem engraved in
Songs of Experience as "The Human Abstract" was called "The Human
Image" in its original form in the *Notebook*.) And to introduce Albion, the
central figure in *Jerusalem*, is to force Blake's final mythology on a poem
essentially free from any explicit mythologizing at all. The difference
between Adams's interpretation and the natural meaning of "A Poison
Tree" *is* a difference of kind rather than degree. To interpret early Blake by
late Blake is to defy the processes of historical reality. Even Wordsworth
did not expect the Child to be *identical* with the Man.

III

The apparent emergence of great literature—or at the very least of some
of the constituent elements in literature agreed by common consent to be
great, such as Blake's *Songs of Experience*—from unconscious or subliminal parts of the mind was a discovery of the Romantic period. The one hint
of an awareness of any such faculty in Aristotle's *Poetics* is his comment on
metaphor, which Bywater translated:

> But the greatest thing by far is to be a master of metaphor. It is the one
> thing that cannot be learnt from others; and it is also a sign of genius,
> since a good metaphor implies an intuitive perception of the similarity in
> dissimilars.[16]

(Bywater's rendering is also an example of the way Romantic notions
then permeated even the severest scholarship; *genius* is a good deal more
than Aristotle meant and *intuitive* is entirely Bywater's gloss.) The
"myths," however, remained for Aristotle and his neoclassic successors a
matter of conscious choice or, on occasion, of conscious invention by the
dramatist, as to which a variety of recommendations could usefully be made
by a critic.
The Romantic exaltation of the unconscious mind led above all to a new

extension of the subject matter of literature. Much the most remarkable
material now made available to the poet was, of course, the dream and the
drug-induced "reverie." "Kubla Khan" combines both elements. I have
not been impressed by recent attempts to discredit the account of the
poem's composition that Coleridge prefixed to the first edition of 1816 and
that is substantially the same as that in the Crewe MS (which cannot be very
much later than the autumn of 1797 when the poem was "given" to
Coleridge, as he put it in 1816). To skeptics like Elisabeth Schneider,
whose *Coleridge, Opium and Kubla Khan* (1953) accuses Coleridge of
having fabricated the dream—and the account of its dramatic interruption
by the "person on business from Porlock"—it has always seemed sufficient
to me to give Wordsworth's comment (which Schneider ignored). It occurs
in the diary of Henry Alford, who was an undergraduate at Trinity College,
Cambridge, when Wordsworth paid a short visit in 1831 to his brother,
Christopher, who had by then become the Master. Alford and five other
undergraduates spent the evening of December 19 asking Wordsworth
questions:

> Then we spoke of the "Kubla Khan," as to whether it was actually
> composed in a dream; certainly Coleridge believes so. Wordsworth
> thinks it might very possibly have been composed between sleeping and
> waking, or, as he expressed it, in a morning sleep; he said some of his own
> best thoughts had come to him in that way.[17]

But most dreams are at the best preliterary. The most vivid dreams are those
recorded in treatises on morbid psychology such as Freud's *The Interpretation of Dreams*—a masterpiece in its own field that has proved a total
will-o'-the-wisp as an aid to literary criticism. The best poets are *not*
morbid, and, though no doubt they dream, they will often, like the rest of
us, have difficulty in recalling their dreams. One great poet who did so was
W. B. Yeats. As it happens, Yeats lived in Oxford when I was an
undergraduate there, and I came across him occasionally, wildly waving his
monocle on its black tape. An ingenious fellow student called William
Force Stead is said—on excellent authority (that of L. A. G. Strong)—to
have exploited Yeats's deficiency of dream material of his own by supplying
the poet with *his* dreams and sometimes even fabricating dreams that he
thought Yeats would like—peacocks, unicorns, princesses without clothes
on and the rest of the Pre-Raphaelite menagerie. Yeats swallowed the lot.
   From dreams to magic, astrology, spiritualism, table-turning and similar
pseudo-sciences, the transition has proved easy. Tom Gibbons has summarized it in *Rooms in the Darwin Hotel: Studies in English Literary
Criticism and Ideas 1880-1920* (1973), an important work of research into

the occultist reaction against Darwinian theories of evolution. Gibbons calls his last chapter "A Kind of Religion," by which he means, as he explains, the "ultra-Romantic quasi-religious view of the status of art,"[18] of which traces exist in Joyce, Pound, Eliot, and D. H. Lawrence, and more specifically in the substitution in prose fiction of "the fundamental archetype or myth which the novel or story allegedly embodies"[19] for the words on the page.

It is these supernatural overtones that perhaps present modern criticism with its greatest challenge to see the thing as in itself it *really* is. The mythicists tend to feed on them. As Gibbons demonstrates, *myth*, in the sense in which some literary critics use the word, is the product of Romanticism *plus* "a sort of religion"—in the failure, that is, of institutional religion to satisfy the imagination.

But were not, it may be asked, the supernatural overtones already present in Romanticism itself? In his *The Use of Poetry and the Use of Criticism* (1933) T. S. Eliot quotes with approval two sentences from Jacques Rivière's "La Crise du concept de la littérature" that he had already translated in *The Criterion:*

> If in the seventeenth century Molière or Racine had been asked why he wrote, no doubt, he would have been able to find but one answer; that he wrote "for the entertainment of decent people" (*pour distraire les honnêtes gens*). It is only with the advent of Romanticism that the literary act came to be conceived as a sort of raid on the absolute and its result as a revelation.[20]

But Rivière's crucial sentence, immediately following those quoted by Eliot is "literature at this time gathered to itself the religious heritage and organised itself on the model of what it was replacing," which may have come too near the bone of *The Waste Land* and *Ash-Wednesday* to be comfortable for him. The mythic odor has displaced that of sanctity, as Shelley had already attempted in *Prometheus Unbound*, by compromising with it. The difference from such cheerfully irreligious mythological poems as Marlowe's *Hero and Leander* and Shakespeare's *Venus and Adonis* is due more to a cultural gap than to a change of genre.

The connection between *myth*, as the word is used in a literary context, and religion in its traditional sense is stressed in such critical works of reference as M. H. Abrams's *Glossary of Literary Terms* ("a religion in which we no longer believe"), Karl Beckson and Arthur Ganz's *Reader's Guide to Literary Terms* ("established myth satisfied a metaphysical hunger"), Joseph Shipley's *Dictionary of World Literary Terms* (which begins "Myth is essentially a religious term"), and Roger Fowler's *Dictionary of Modern Critical Terms* ("an *absence* in literature"—lost gods or lost childhood). In the light of the evidence such textbooks provide, Wellek's limitation of the terms to a stylistic litmus paper for the detection of Romanticism would seem all the more perverse. On the contrary, as Claude Lévi-Strauss and both Freud and Jung have made abundantly clear, its usefulness is confined to the analogies it may call our attention to between the content of Romantic literature and the findings or speculations of anthropology and psychology.

Unfortunately—this is the final basis of my mythic scepticism—such reversions to primitive man and early childhood have no adult validity. They are either *lies,* more or less innocent deceptions ranging from Father Christmas to Hitler's Master Race, or they are escape routes from one's duties as a lover, a father, and a citizen to various more or less irresponsible Never-Never-Lands. Sir Philip Sidney's logical conjuring trick (the poet "nothing affirmeth, and therefore never lieth"[21]) demands a blunt answer; poetry that affirms nothing cannot be taken seriously. Great literature is essentially meaningful, significant, affirming all the time. And, though there is a proper place for such symbolic narratives as Blake's "A Poison Tree" or the parables of Jesus Christ, they must still not be used in defiance of intellectual honesty. To use myths as a Birnam Wood screening one's own attempts to escape from reality is not so much "a kind of religion" as a pseudo-religion.

The great Romantic poets were not, in a final analysis, escapists. They took their stand, as Wordsworth put it in an extract from *The Prelude* that he allowed Coleridge to use in *The Friend,*

> Not in Utopia, subterranean fields,
> Or some secreted island, Heaven knows where!
> But in the very world, which is the world
> Of all of us—the place where in the end
> We find our happiness, or not at all![22]

By giving the extract the title "French Revolution as it appeared to enthusiasts at its commencement," the middle-aged Wordsworth—if it was not a middle-aged Coleridge—may seem to be disparaging the lines, but it should be remembered that by October 1809, when *The Friend* first printed the extract, Wordsworth was no longer, except occasionally and erratically, a poet. He was now a noisy adherent of the Church of England. The conjunction may not be merely a coincidence.

No such reservations need affect our judgment of a younger Romantic poet writing exactly ten years later.

> Away! away! for I will fly to thee,
> Not charioted by Bacchus and his pards,
> But on the viewless wings of Poesy. . . .

In drawing his parallel between alcohol (in Coleridge's case it was opium) and poetry as methods of escape, Keats was being perfectly explicit. And the lines from the last stanza of his "Ode" are sufficiently skeptical:

> Adieu! the fancy cannot cheat so well
> As she is fam'd to do, deceiving elf.

We have only one life to live, one world to live in—and the literature most worth reading derives its value from our responsibility to ourselves and to our neighbors here and now. Blake's aphorism in *The Marriage of Heaven and Hell*[23]—"Thus men forget that All Deities reside in the Human Breast"—applies equally to literature. The masterpieces of literature acquire their greatness for us when we have earned them as human beings—*and not before*. Literature is not a patent medicine. You must work for it—and understand and criticize it and be worthy of it—to be entitled to enjoy it. The enticing shortcut by myth leads in the end only to the Slough of Despond.

I am thinking not only of poetry but of such a novel as *The Great Gatsby*, in which, especially in the final pages, some excellent social satire is invaded by the Great American Myth, a bootlegger being implausibly elevated to heroic proportions. At the risk of being hauled before the House's Un-American Activities Committee, if that disreputable body still functions, I may be forgiven for wondering if the Great American Myth (in some mythic-critics' sense of the word) is not itself a myth, a nonconcept that Henry Ford, a sort of Gatsby himself, might well have called *bunk*.

NOTES

1. Samuel Butler, *Hudibras* (Oxford: Clarendon Press, 1927), 2. i. 443-44.

2. E. M. Forster, *Aspects of the Novel*, (New York: Harcourt, Brace and Co., 1927), chap. 5.

3. Ibid., p. 6.

4. Ibid., p. 8.

5. René Wellek, *Concepts of Criticism* (New Haven, Conn.: Yale University Press, 1963), p. 335.

6. Ibid., p. 342.

7. Arthur O. Lovejoy, *Essays in the History of Ideas* (Baltimore, Md.: Johns Hopkins Press, 1948), p. 232.

8. Wellek, *Concepts of Criticism*, p. 161.

9. Ibid., pp. 199-221.

10. Northrop Frye, "The Critical Path," in *In Search of Literary Theory*, ed. Morton W. Bloomfield (Ithaca, N.Y.: Cornell University Press, 1972), p. 105.

11. Often called the Rossetti Manuscript because owned for some twenty years by D. G. Rossetti, who "improved" some of the poems in it.

12. The *OED* refers us for details to *Hobson-Jobson* by Henry Yule and A. C. Burrell (1886), *s.v.* Upas.

13. The variant is not recorded either in the excellent edition of Blake's *Poetry and Prose* by David V. Erdman (Garden City, N.Y.: Doubleday, 1965; rev. ed. 1970) or in W. H. Stevenson's edition of the *Poems* (Longmans Ltd., 1971). John Sampson has it in his Oxford edition (1914), and such facsimiles as that in Joseph H. Wicksteed's edition of *Songs of Innocence and Experience* (New York: Dutton, 1928) seem to confirm Sampson's reading of the deleted line. Complete certainty is now provided by the infra-red photographs Erdman has used in his edition of the *Notebook* (Oxford: Clarendon Press, 1973).

14. A. E. Housman has told us of a similar experience of his own (*The Name and Nature of Poetry* [London: Macmillan & Co., 1933], p. 50). Two verses of the four-verse poem that concludes *A Shropshire Lad* "came" as he crossed a road on Hampstead Heath, and a third "came with a little coaxing after tea." But a necessary fourth verse "did not come" and required thirteen drafts before he was satisfied with it. Housman did not specify which the reluctant verse was; to his modern readers they all seem much of a muchness, whether "given" subconsciously or sweated out by the conscious mind. My own guess is that it was the fourth verse that gave him so much difficulty.

15. Hazard Adams, *William Blake: A Reading of the Shorter Poems* (Seattle: University of Washington Press, 1963), p. 244.

16. Aristotle *Poetics* trans. Ingram Bywater (London, Oxford University Press, 1960), p. 78.

17. *Life, Journals and Letters of Henry Alford, D.D.* (London: 1873), p. 61 of 1874 edition.

18. Thomas Gibbons, *Rooms in the Darwin Hotel: Studies in English Literary Criticism and Ideas* (Nedlards, W.A.: University of Western Australia Press, 1973).

19. Ibid.

20. T. S. Eliot, *The Use of Poetry and the Use of Criticism* (Cambridge, Mass.: Harvard University Press, 1938), p. 128. Eliot does not provide a reference or even the title of Rivière's article. I am obliged to Roger Kojecky for both. The article will be found in *La nouvelle revue française*, 1 Feb. 1924. The sentences used by Eliot are on p. 161. For the sentence following those that Eliot quoted, I have used Kojecky's translation.

21. *The Defence of Poesy* (written ca. 1585), ed. Albert Feuillerat (London: Macmillan & Co., 1923), p. 29.

22. From the 1805–6 text of *Prelude*, 10, lines 724-29; 1850 text, 11, lines 140-44.

23. Erdman ed., *Blake's Poetry and Prose*, p. 37.

Biographical Note on Philip Withim

Philip M. Withim did his undergraduate work at Pomona College and Fordham University and his graduate work at New York University. His present position is associate professor of English at Bucknell University, where he teaches courses in American literature, critical theory, and the relation between literature and psychoanalysis. In addition to being an editor of the present volume, he has published articles on Melville, Milton, and the psychodynamics of literature in such journals as *Modern Language Quarterly, Psychoanalytic Review*, and *Journal of General Education*. His special interests are Whitman, theories of American literature, and Freudian theory.

Mythic Awareness and Literary Form: Verbal Ritual in Whitman's "Bivouac on a Mountain Side"

PHILIP WITHIM

Myth criticism, when employed in the exploration of specific works of literature, usually concerns itself with the application of the more pervasive ancient myths and rituals that deal with journeys, fertility figures, and rites of passage. In this essay I wish to outline the description and application of a somewhat different criticism: a criticism that draws on our faculty of mythic awareness, and that accounts both for features of the work and for the dynamics of the reader. Such criticism employs but is not limited to formalism, close reading, and the responsive self-consciousness of phenomenology. It will take into account the reader's prelogical awareness—his visual, aural, kinesthetic, affective, and metaphorical awareness right down into unconscious responses and defenses with which the phenomenologists do not deal.

I

No work of literature has a single structure; it has a variety of structures depending on the perspective from which it is viewed. Thus we can discuss the themes of a novel and come to speak of its thematic structure, that is, the ways in which the themes engage and combine in dialectical and cumulative relationships. We can also discuss a structure of images, as is frequently done with Shakespeare. Or we can discuss structures of characters in conflict like those provided by Laertes, Hamlet, and Fortinbras, or in a paired relationship like Lear and Gloucester.

We can see the literary work as a structure of plot, with a beginning, middle, and end, with rising action, climax, and resolution. We can see a given work as a sequence of structural units such as chapters or books

111

which, having a certain completeness in themselves, also create an edifice of relationships through comparison and contrast, through before and after. We can also speak of other kinds of structure, more formal, such as points of view or variations in the reliability of internal commentary. We can speak of a structure of paradoxes and ironies, of tone tensions and emotional sequences. The final structure of any work must surely be all these structures apprehended simultaneously. It is from such perspectives that we realize what is meant by the inexhaustibility of art.

This survey of literary approaches demonstrates that each form of criticism has, as Richard Blackmur says, its own "job of work"; that none can pose as the only or the best criticism. Accordingly, if we speak of mythic awareness and literary structure, we recognize that the structure we come to see through the lens of mythic awareness will be an appropriate one. Thus we must now go beyond myths and legends; we must go behind them to that faculty of the mind which engenders not only the myths, but dreams and art, and which is shared by both the creating author and the responding reader. The following description of mythic awareness is a recension drawn from many contributors to the theory of myth; it employs as its primary base the philosophy of Cassirer and, where appropriate, turns to the psychologies of Freud, Jung, and D. H. Lawrence and to the cultural anthropologies of Joseph Campbell, Mircea Eliade, Lévi-Strauss, and Philip Wheelwright. These men are not in full agreement with each other, approach their subject from different directions, and frequently work at cross purposes. Yet there are many constants, many unifying threads. The test of this approach, as with any theory of literature, will always be whether or not the text is illuminated.

Mythic awareness is a psychic activity differing significantly from that rational discursiveness which is founded upon causality and logic, and which works by abstraction and subordination.[1] Mythic awareness draws on the kinesthesia of the body, the movement of the organs, the tone of the muscles, the sheer sensuous organic life. It is experienced as an emotion or a feeling, as opposed to an idea.[2] It is inherently metaphorical, expressing ideas and feelings through images rather than words.[3] "No ideas but in things," says William Carlos Williams.

According to Ernst Cassirer, mythic awareness consists of the faculty of the human mind to *notice* something, whether externally or in the domain of internal reality. The mind notices with such sharpness of focus, such passion of intense observation, that an imprint of essences is etched upon it. Cassirer calls this imprint a symbol.[4]

He asserts that the noticing is experienced as either an influx of external power, which man calls divine, or as an upwelling of inward force, which he calls demonic. These divinities of inward and outward reality flood the psyche. Thus every place has its own specificity, its own god; the trees have their dryads, the springs their nymphs; the earth becomes our holy mother: all the world is experienced as sacred or demonic. As D. H. Lawrence puts it," . . . the spirit of place is a great reality. The Nile valley produced not only the corn, but the terrific religions of Egypt." This he calls the "polarity" of place.[5] The symbol constitutes then an intuition of reality, a recognition of sacredness, and the foundation of religion. Logically, the first noticings occurred in the dawn of man's history, but the capacity to notice and therefore to symbolize, according to such diverse authorities as Cassirer, Eliade, Lawrence, Freud, Jung, Wheelwright, and Campbell, is still alive within us today, however repressed by logical discursive thought.

Before man thinks rationally, he orders his reality in terms of the images and symbols created by the noticing process.[6] When these symbols become part of the mind, they must obey the dynamics of the mind. The symbol, as it were, takes on vitality and interacts dynamically with other symbols. The resulting network becomes our language of reality, our a priori way of knowing reality. We have internalized reality; we have condensed it into symbols that are ordered by the dynamics of our psyches into complicated relationships both with each other and with outside reality. Consequently we are limited in our knowledge of reality by the structure of our mind. To put is more affirmatively, we create, within very sharp limits, our own reality; we certainly metamorphose it.[7]

This symbolic language of reality has a number of characteristics very different from the language of logic. First, mythic reality does not subordinate; it coordinates. Its reality is of coequal essences and qualities. It knows no hierarchies.[8] Ideas and emotions exist in it simultaneously without regard to the laws of contradiction.[9] The noticing process operates by the principle of complementarity in which the act of noticing engenders its opposite. Thus darkness evokes brightness, as death evokes life; the valley calls forth the hill, and hate coexists with love.[10]

Second, the symbols of mythic awareness are ordered by the law of association, which says that any ideas, qualities, images, or things resembling each other in appearance or function can stand for each other. In a dream as in a poem the room symbolizes a tomb, the tower a phallus, and explosions the orgasm.[11] In the mythic world, the part stands for the whole. According to Cassirer, it does more than stand for: it is felt and experienced as identical to that which it symbolizes, possessed of all its indwelling power and force.[12] In Catholicism the Communion is not merely a symbol of God, but is actually His divine presence veiled by the appearance of bread and wine. In these great laws of complementarity and association lie the secret of metaphor, the currency of poetry, and the heart of the primary imagination.

Third, according to Jung, Erich Neumann, and the principles of analytical psychology, the symbols of archetypes operate as agencies of development, obeying intrinsic laws of transformation. As the human race moved in its art through images of the line, the circle, and the mandala, so also moves the psyche of the individual. The appearances and transformations of these symbols are both expression and vehicle of the growing psyche.[13] Northrop Frye's system of literary criticism is based on an analogous approach. The various modes of discourse are regarded by Frye as archetypal forms subject to laws of change governing all symbols. The various modes metamorphose through ascending and descending stages and finally engender their own opposite forms.[14]

Fourth, in psychoanalysis, those symbols by which our psyche binds and channels its energies are subjected to the principles displayed in the dreamwork—displacement, substitution, condensation—all resulting in the overdetermined (having more than one adequate cause) and plurisignificant symbol.[15] This position agrees with that of Lévi-Strauss on the structural analysis of myth, in which he has demonstrated that it is not merely the elements of a myth that transmit its meanings, but, as in art, the structure of those elements. Components, drawn from all the variants of myth, are arranged in a grid in which the horizontal lines represent the recounting of a variant, while the vertical lines represent the elements common to all or to several. In order to read the story of myths one reads across; but in order to understand the myth one reads vertically.[16] A major virtue of this approach is that it sees mythic symbols as having their meaning in layers of development in which no stage is ever fully abandoned any more than in the developing psyche. Thus, in Freudian terms, the myth is condensed and overdetermined.[17]

In addition to the dynamics of the dreamwork, the symbols of mythic awareness are subject to the dynamics of the ego's resources and defenses that the unconscious ego develops to manipulate the great flood of external and internal reality that forever collides with it, tending to overwhelm it. Some of the most important of these ego dynamics are introjection, in which outside images are internalized by the psyche and are identified with; repression, in which the ego pushes an undesired reality into the lower unconscious and holds it there at great cost by a constant expenditure of psychic energy; repetition compulsion, in which the ego masters a hateful or confusing reality by making rituals out of its material, repeating and repeating them until the psyche slowly gains control over anxieties that normally would have paralyzed it; reaction formation and reversal into the opposite, in which the ego disguises the unpleasant by intensifying its opposite.[18] Psychoanalysis and the structuralism of Lévi-Strauss put a common emphasis on substitution and reversal as standard metamorphoses of myth.

In summary, let me describe mythic awareness as being founded in the kinesthesia of the body, as emotional and affective, as imagistic and symbolic, obeying the laws of complementarity and association rather than the laws of contradiction and logic, as reflecting intrinsic patterns of progression evolving from those dynamics of the psyche characteristic of dreams and the resources of the ego.

Some implications of this description for literary criticism ought already to be clear. Certainly the structures that myth criticism will help us perceive will be primarily sensuous, emotional, and symbolic and will not be primarily formal or symmetrical; the structures will be more open than closed, more spatial than temporal, more layered in meaning than monosignificant. They will be better grasped through images and affective tensions than understood through linear logic. They will work through episodes and analogues rather than through a single plot with a beginning, middle, and end. They will be closer to medieval literature and romantic poetry than to the classic literature of Greece and the neoclassic literature of Pope, Dryden, and Swift. We can perhaps now see that greatness in art is the result of a fusion of mythic awareness and discursive thought. To the flooding images, the sensuous rhythms, and the chaotic emotions is added the controlling power of logic, harmony, and proportion: Nietzsche's fusion of Dionysus and Apollo. Such control is at once an additional mode of discourse through which the poet can further explore his concerns, and a powerful distancing factor defending the mind from the overwhelming impact of what Freud calls pure primary process.

I I

Criticism of Whitman's poetry is confined largely to thematic approaches. This may be occasioned by the failure of traditional formal criticism to explain the relation of his form to his undoubted power and impact. Let us analyze a poem drawn from *Drum Taps* (1865), to see whether a criticism based on the description given above can relate Whitman's form to his content and to the reader's response.

Bivouac on a Mountain Side

1. I see before me now a travelling army halting,
2. Below a fertile valley spread, with barns and the
   orchards of summer,
3. Behind, the terraced sides of a mountain, abrupt,
   in places rising high,
4. Broken, with rocks, with clinging cedars, with
   tall shapes dingily seen,
5. The numerous camp-fires scattered near and far,
   some away up on the mountain,

6. The shadowy forms of men and horses, looming,
            large-sized, flickering,
7. And over all the sky—the sky! far, far out of reach,
            studded, breaking out, the eternal stars.[19]

This lyric presents itself as a simple description of soldiers around their campfires at night. If, a priori, one feels, as I do, that these lines compose a highly effective poem, we must go beyond the usual formal and dramatic reasons in order to establish this position critically. I say this because Whitman draws only slightly on traditional modes of ordering. The poem has no story to speak of, no characters as such. It simply presents, in almost conversational tones, a rather static situation. The poet's technique as such seems to consist of little more than a series of factual statements. Whitman is not employing blank verse; the essentially iambic meter is very level, is, in fact, relaxed to the point of monotony. As a result the poem may strike many readers as barely a poem at all. Where, for example, is that felt intensity, so urged by T. S. Eliot, or artistic pressure fusing varied elements into the unity of a poem? Where, in Mark Schorer's terms, are the manipulations of craft and technique that alone afford exploration of subject matter and the engagement of the reader? Since Whitman has, one way or another, eschewed not only character and story, but also the security of a traditional stanza and the comforts of meter and rhyme, we must look for other kinds of order. To do this, I will first draw on traditional criticism of form to see what it can tell us, but I will then search for fuller guides to Whitman's form in a different kind of criticism.

Let me begin by employing formal prosody. I can see in this poem a movement from lesser to greater intensity partly caused by lines of increasing length, and by additional stresses and pauses in succeeding lines. The poem moves from a first line of fourteen syllables to a last line of twenty-three. It moves from a first line of six stresses to a last line of twelve. The number of caesurae increases from two (l. 3) to four (l. 7). Furthermore, the pauses get sharper and stronger as the poem gathers energy. But this increasing intensity of technical devices is not unqualified; though the drift is toward increased length of line, the actual movement is more like pulsing waves, alternately shorter and longer, each successive wave-unit on a larger scale than the preceding one, until the last is the largest wave, the longest line of all. With twenty-three syllables, twelve stresses, and four caesurae, it breaks the limits set up by the two earlier waves, moving out, as it were, into unexplored areas—a movement very appropriate to a poem asserting that beyond the camp fires burn the mysterious stars. This order is characterized not by the formalism of symmetry and balance, but by impulse and growth. Prosody has brought us to a point at which we should not be surprised to enter an area of poetic construction where criticism based on formal prosody is less useful. There is a strong kinesthetic basis in this poem that can be felt in key words pushing against each other; for example, the way *halting* works against the muscular push of *travelling;* the way *spread* works against *halting,* and *rising* against *spread.* Each of these movements, based on our sense of the body, creates tensions and relaxations. These contraries work in harmony with the law of complementarity innate to the psyche and, arousing its latent dialectic, create an effect of vitality and vividness.

The kinesthesia of the poem is further developed by the sequence contained in the words *before, behind, below,* and in the direction *above* indicated by the stars and sky. This movement is coupled with still another, uniting distance with sharpness, and nearness with vagueness. In the beginning of the poem the army is clearly visible in the middle distance. In the second line the speaker's vision takes in somewhat more closely the barns and *orchards of summer.* This last phrase is less precisely an image and more an evocation. The "orchards of summer" works on our imagination like Blake's "the forests of the night," giving us in an image of one orchard a generic orchard and a generic summer. The use of this phrase in the second line suddenly deepens the poem, making us aware of broader, less obvious concerns. In the third line we move neither nearer nor farther, but from the front of the speaker to behind him, while the degree of clarity remains about the same. In the next line we are close enough to make out "rocks" and "clinging cedars," yet they are mere shapes "dingily" seen. Realistically, of course, it is simply night falling, but the psychological effect is that the nearer we move toward objects, the less clear they become and the more indefinite is their reality. In line five the campfires are scattered about the mountain, some way up. The increase in distance is accompanied by a sense of increased visual sharpness caused by the points of firelight. In line six we move near the shadowy forms of men and horses, which loom and flicker—very close, shadowy, almost illusory. In the last line the sky suddenly wrenches our vision up to the infinitely remote, as the stars break out, studding the heavens with campfires—far and sharp.

This movement of the poem upward and out is enhanced by Whitman's choice of line endings. These words are in no sense rhymes or even half-rhymes, but they do reflect appropriate common qualities. "Halting" (1. 1) and "flickering" (1. 6) are participles signifying actions not yet finished, continuing actions; again, "halting" (1. 1) "summer" (1. 2), and "mountain" (1.5) are each feminine endings creating an effect of indefiniteness; "summer" (1. 2), "high" (1. 3), "seen" (1. 4), and "stars" (1. 7) are each an open-ended or resonant sound that continues to vibrate in the air after speech has ceased. Thus each of the words chosen to end the lines of the poem provokes visual and aural images of the vague and the unconcluded.

The poem's last line ends two movements, the linear outward one I have just described and another, a complementary one, involving an intricate placement of scattered images of barns, orchards, rocks, trees, men, horses, fires, all suddenly collected under the enveloping unity of the dark sky stretching over all. Another effect of the numerous pauses becomes clearer. They separate the images of the poem, creating of them a lonely list, all of which are then swept into a common unity by the vision of sky and stars. Each pause marks a syntactical unit, bearing its own image, making clear that the line movement of the poem is not based on a metrical beat but on the flow and catch of phrases and clauses, not on prosody but on syntax. The linear movement outward is countered by a circular movement toward unity. Every device in the poem is bent toward achieving a complementary tension of enormous vitality, a tension that is a major reason for the success of the poem.

The ease with which these devices have been located and explored demonstrates that the form of the poem is highly ordered, that it matches both Schorer's description of technique as "any selection, structure, or distortion, any form or rhythm imposed . . .,"[20] as well as Eliot's insistence on artistic pressure fusing the poem into unity. But a criticism based on mythic awareness encourages us to say more about the form of this poem. I shall leave the purely objective technical devices discussed so far, and turn to others more subjective. What kind of mental state does this poem release us into? What process does it put us through? It seems to me that Whitman's abandonment of tradition for a form more open, more kines-thetically organized, has created a kinetic tableau, itself a fusion of complementary opposites. We have both a progressing line of vision and a scene frozen eternally, forever caught from the flux of the world. Such a fusion of opposites provokes meditation. Let us examine this sequence of thought and emotion.

This poem rehearses a customary action we all love, that of gazing into darkness, the fire, the sky. We surrender to this poem so as to re-create in ourselves the sense of wonder and mystery such communions always arouse. But the meditation here is not so free and drifting as that arising from an actual gazing into the heart of things. On the contrary, it is highly organized, and we are guided by it. If we speak of dream-process: of displacement, condensation, and overdetermination, we can perhaps see that this poem moves us as a dream does. The images stand for themselves, surely, but they stand for, evoke more. The poem gives us images of an army resting above fertile fields and summer orchards: images of death looming over images of life—a conflict arousing uneasy emotions. The army fades into shadows and vague forms—further images of death, desirable in their restfulness but frightening in their strangeness. In this poem we find the familiar and cozy images of fire, men, horses, and trees, becoming the carriers of a mystery. They hint in their flickering at the insubstantiality of all reality. It is only the remote that is clear, sharp, and bright, but that is also frightening in its grandeur; and it is infinitely mysterious. Our world has metamorphosed before our eyes; we realize that this poem is about death as a relief from the uncertainties of life, but it is also about our fear of having to depart from all we know, of having to enter another world.

Ordinarily we have little desire to expose our psyches to such frightening concerns, but the poem invites us through its beauty and fictionality. So protected, we are encouraged to enter its oral and symbolic process, which allows us to explore our anxieties about life very much as does a repetition compulsion through which the psyche handles confusing and frightening situations, internalizing them by constantly repeating them in symbolic and ritualistic forms. I suggest that the poem is such a repetition— Whitman's rehearsal of life—and that through our responsive reading the poem becomes a ritualistic repetition of our own. Because it is disguised in the warm and cozy language of the familiar, we are finally brought to confront the alienage of the *other*. In the safety of a fiction, under the veil of beauty, manipulated by the devices of the author, we undertake a journey into mystery and return refreshed. If we are afraid in life to entertain conjecture of the frightening, we may yet in every achieved work of literature engage it vicariously. We may engage with a rehearsal of life through verbal ritual. Let me expand on this.

A ritual is a pattern of action having several functions: to celebrate life, to thank the benign gods, to placate hostile ones, to coerce indifferent ones, and to signal rebirth into such new conditions as puberty, marriage, and death: the so-called rites of passage.[21] It is important that a ritual be performed without error, that the charm be done right, because the coercive force lies in its net of symbolic actions, thus revealing ritual's source in the dynamics of the repetition compulsion.

Can a poem do all this? I would answer, yes, it can; but we must recognize that we may ask of the poem only that it does for the reader in its way what the rites of passage do for the acolyte in their way. In its way then, a poem is like a ritual; it must be exactly right in all its features or the magic is lost, that ability of words and verbal shapes to rouse and shape our affections, sensibilities, kinesthesia—and through this magic, this ordering, allow us to celebrate life or to be drawn on a journey testing its dark hostilities, to emerge, if not reborn, then moved from what we were. This is what I mean by poem as verbal ritual. The steps are always the same: first, as in this poem, we are alerted to a tension—the army, symbol of death, rests above the life-giving fields; second, we are brought to a sense of mystery—aroused by the lines dealing with the near-vague and the far-sharp, with the familiar becoming alien; and finally, we are brought to a moment of resolution and emergence by the image of overarching sky, deepened by our sense of the eternal order. We have come to perceive more; thus we can stand more; we are more than we were.

Joseph Campbell, drawing from Joyce, says that a work of art is the epiphany of an archetype, a manifesting of it.[22] This little poem, in its gentle way, is an ephiphany of its archetypal idea: transient man confronting eternal order.

We need to employ a criticism based on mythic awareness because it lies behind all myths, poems, and dreams; because it is still a living if dormant faculty in each of us. Art is a result of mythic awareness and it requires mythic awareness from its audience. Formalism and New Criticism can tell us about the work per se, but myth criticism explores the experiencing of the work from within; it explores the interaction of the work and the reader, both consciously and unconsciously. We need an attitude toward art that goes beyond those which are historical, intellectual, aesthetic, and moral. We need to explore that modification. The art work brings the reader to the point of noticing; we need a criticism able to discuss that process.

In conclusion, let me tell a fable. A mathematician once was asked by a friend the sequence in which these numbers were arranged: 8, 5, 4, 9, 1, 7, 6, 10, 3, and 2. He put in an hour on the task, then an evening; finally he spent an entire weekend. He still could not uncover the basis of the sequence. In exasperation he called his friend and was told that the numbers were arranged in alphabetical order. The mathematician had been blinded by his expectations of seeing a different kind of order.

A criticism drawing from mythic awareness will reveal its appropriate orders. Let us be free to see them.

NOTES

1. Ernst Cassirer, *Language and Myth*, trans. Susanne K. Langer (New York: Dover Publications, Inc., 1946), pp. 32-36; idem, *The Philosophy of Symbolic Forms*, vol. 2; *Mythical Thought*, trans. Ralph Manheim (New Haven, Conn: Yale University Press, 1955), pp. 33-45; Philip Wheelwright, *The Burning Fountain: A Study in the Language of Symbolism* (Bloomington: Indiana University Press, 1954), pp. 52-55.

2. Cassirer, *Language and Myth*, pp. 32-33; idem, *Mythical Thought*, pp. 29-34; Wheelwright, *The Burning Fountain*, pp. 45-50; Sigmund Freud, *General Psychological Theory*, ed. Philip Reiff (New York: Collier Books, 1963); "Repression," trans. Cecil M. Baines, pp. 110-11; Mircea Eliade, *Myths, Dreams and Mysteries*, trans. Philip Mairet (New York: Harper & Rowe, Harper Torchbook, 1967), p. 74.

3. Cassirer, *Language and Myth*, p. 88; idem, *Mythical Thought*, p. 40; Wheelwright, *The Burning Fountain*, p. 159; Wheelwright, *Metaphor and Reality* (Bloomington: Indiana University Press, 1962), p. 130.

4. Cassirer, *Language and Myth*, pp. 29-33; Wheelwright, *The Burning Fountain*, pp. 78-82.

5. Cassirer, *Language and Myth*, pp. 33-37; Wheelwright, *Metaphor*, p. 136; Eliade, *Myths*, chap. 7, "Mother Earth and the Cosmic Hierogamies," pp. 155-89; D. H. Lawrence, *Studies in Classic American Literature* (New York: Viking Press, 1964), p. 6.

6. Cassirer, *Language and Myth*, p. 37.

7. Ibid., p. 10; Joseph Campbell, *The Masks of God*, vol. 1, *Primitive Mythology* (New York: Viking Press, 1969), p. 33.

8. Cassirer, *Language and Myth*, pp. 32-33; idem, *Mythical Thought*, p. 65; Wheelwright, *The Burning Fountain*, p. 82.

9. Cassirer, *Mythical Thought*, p. 37; Wheelwright, *The Burning Fountain*, p. 96; Sigmund Freud, *An Outline of Psychoanalysis*, trans. James Strachey (New York: W. W. Norton & Company, 1963), p. 53.

10. Sigmund Freud, *Character and Culture*, ed. Philip Rieff (New York: Collier Books, 1963), "The Antithetical Sense of Primal Words," trans. M. N. Searl, pp. 45-46; C. G. Jung, *Two Essays on Analytical Psychology*, trans. R. F. C. Hull (New York: World Publishing Co., Meridian Books, 1956), pp. 63-71; Wheelwright, *The Burning Fountain*, pp. 70-73.

11. Cassirer, *Language and Myth*, p. 92; idem, *Mythical Thought*, pp. 50, 64; Wheelwright, *The Burning Fountain*, p. 181.

12. Cassirer, *Mythical Thought*, pp. 45, 67; Wheelwright, *The Burning Fountain*, p. 181.

13. C. G. Jung, *Two Essays*, "The Archetypes of the Collective Unconscious," pp. 100-123; Erich Neumann, *The Origins and History of Consciousness*, vol. 1; *The Psychological Stages and Evolution of Consciousness*, trans. R. F. C. Hull (New York: Harper Torchbooks, The Bollingen Library, 1962), pp. xvi-xxiv.

14. Northrop Frye, *An Anatomy of Criticism* (Princeton, N.J: Princeton University Press, 1957), p. 42.

15. Sigmund Freud, *Outline*, pp. 46-57; Wheelwright, *The Burning Fountain*, pp. 112-17.

16. Claude Lévi-Strauss, "The Structural Study of Myth," *Journal of American Folklore* 78, no. 270 (Oct.-Dec. 1955): 428-44, as reprinted in *The Structuralists from Marx to Lévi-Strauss*, ed. Richard DeGeorge and Fernande DeGeorge (Garden City, N. Y.: Doubleday and Co., Inc., Anchor Original), pp. 169-94.

17. Sigmund Freud, *The Basic Writings*, trans. and ed. A. A. Brill (New York: Random House, The Modern Library, 1938), "The Interpretation of Dreams," pp. 330, 338, 403n.

18. Otto Fenichel, *The Psychoanalytic Theory of Neurosis* (New York: W. W. Norton and Co., 1945), pp. 146-55.

19. Walt Whitman, *Leaves of Grass*, Comprehensive Reader's Edition, ed. Harold W. Blodgett and Scully Bradley (New York: New York University Press, 1965), p. 300.

20. Mark Schorer, "Technique as Discovery," in *The Modern Critical Spectrum*, ed. Gerald Jay Goldberg and Nancy Marmer Goldberg (Englewood Cliffs, N.J.: Prentice-Hall, Inc., 1962), p. 71.

21. Cassirer, *Mythical Thought*, p. 109; Wheelwright, *The Burning Fountain*, pp. 175-83; Joseph Campbell, *Myths to Live By* (New York: Viking Press, 1972), pp. 44-60; Mircea Eliade, *Birth and Ritual: Religious Meaning of Initiation in Human Culture*, trans. Willard Trask (New York: Harper, 1958), p. x.

22. Joseph Campbell, "Bios and Mythos: Prolegomena to a Science of Mythology," in *Myth and Literature: Contemporary Theory and Practice*, ed. John B. Vickery (Lincoln, Neb.: University of Nebraska Press, 1966), p. 17.

SUGGESTED READINGS

Lyons, Charles R. "The Movements of the Creative Process from Playwright to Actor in the Avant-garde Drama of the Sixties and Early Seventies," *Mosaic* 8 (1974): 139-50.

Munz, Peter. *When the Bough Breaks: Structuralism or Typology?* London: Routledge and Kegan Paul, 1973.

Murray, Henry A., ed. *Myth and Mythmaking*. Boston: Beacon Press, 1969.

Newman, Robert. "Myth and Creative Process," *Centennial Review* 9 (1965): 483-93.

Norris, Margot C. "The Function of Mythic Repetition in Finnegans Wake," *James Joyce Quarterly* 11 (1974): 343-54.

Payne, Michael. "Origins and Prospects of Myth Criticism," *Journal of General Education* 26 (1974-75): 37-44.

Piaget, Jean. *Structuralism*. New York: Basic Books, 1970.

Schechner, Richard, and Chwat, Jacques, eds. "An Interview with Grotowski," *TDR* 9, no. 1 (1968): 29-45.

Wheelwright, Philip. "The Archetypal Symbol." In *Perspectives in Literary Symbolism*, edited by Joseph Strelka, vol. 1. University Park, Pa.: The Pennsylvania State University Press, 1968.

Section III

Mythic Thought as Process

SECTION PREFACE

Section II closed with Philip Withim's paper arguing that criticizing poetry through the lens of mythic awareness is a necessary complement to traditional and formal analysis. His position is reinforced by the essays of Section III, which show that poets of various ages have viewed their work as creating, through the terms of their forms and within the context of the genre, new truths and new realities. The essays describe in detail the nondiscursive methods and devices employed by the poets. Eugène Vinaver points out that the medieval romance is organized on the principles of simultaneity and polycentrality. The result is the creation of a new value system of honor, love, and self-sacrifice, which forms part of our self-image today. Karl Uitti particularizes that point by showing how different kinds of medieval poetry embody their different truths in different ways: for example, the matter of France is true as history, the matter of Rome is true as clerkly wisdom, and the matter of Britain, first viewed as a diversion, becomes true as fiction is true, truth achieved through artifice.

Gene Bernstein describes how the English Romantic poet, employing ideas similar in certain respects to those adapted later by Eliade and Lévi-Strauss, sought to remake man through the power of the sympathetic and synthesizing imagination. René Galand shows how, in effect, Baudelaire retreats from the high-water position of Wordsworth and Coleridge by viewing the creative effort of the artist to heal the split between man and world as glorious and necessary, but also as doomed to failure. Art can not redeem the primal fault.

Lawrence Abler shows Rilke going a step beyond Baudelaire in creating for himself a sequence of myths embodying different concepts of reality and of the poet's role, but each myth is only a temporary stay against confusion. We come full circle when Ronald Dotterer makes clear the profound ambivalence at the heart of the poetry of William Carlos Williams and

123

Wallace Stevens. They, like Baudelaire and Rilke, see their poems as process, as spinning fictions, creating the only realities by which man can live. But they also perceive that such "supreme fictions" fundamentally distort the primal reality to which man must inevitably return.

Thus each of these essays makes two points about poetry: it produces truth, and it does so through a process, mythic in nature, that the poet employs and the reader joins.

Biographical Note on Eugène Vinaver:

Eugène Vinaver was born in St. Petersburg and was educated at the University of Paris and at Oxford. His distinguished career has included appointment as Reader in French Literature at Oxford and Professor of French Language and Literature at Manchester. In addition, he has held visiting professorships at Chicago, Stanford, Wisconsin, and Northwestern. His honors are many. In 1967-68 he was Visiting Scholar for Phi Beta Kappa, he was elected President of the Modern Language Association in 1961 and of the Modern Humanities Research Association in 1966, and he served as president of the International Arthurian Society from 1966 to 1969. Two Festschrifts have been presented to him in recognition of his work and influence in medieval literature (*Medieval Miscellany*) and in modern French literature (*Modern Miscellany*).

Professor Vinaver has authored more than fifty articles and reviews, as well as several books. His most important work is probably the publication in 1947 of the unique and long-lost manuscript of Malory's tales: *The Works of Sir Thomas Malory*, in three volumes (Clarendon Press); this work was revised in 1967. His most recent book is *The Rise of the Romance* (1971).

The Questing Knight

EUGÈNE VINAVER

In the context of this colloquium it seems appropriate to pay some attention to the appearance in the Middle Ages of a type of hero whose impact on European imagination was very great, but whose origins are not easy to determine: a knight who goes on a quest, and as soon as one quest is over undertakes another and again another. Some knights do even better than that: they undertake the second quest before the first one is finished, and the third before either the first or the second is finished, and they never forget what they have left behind: they always return to their unfinished tasks. All such characters, whether they belong to the first or the second category, are called *knights-errant*—a term borrowed from the French without much attempt at translating it or even altering the French word order. *Chevalier errant* means literally "wandering knight"—a man whose life is spent in adventurous wandering. Nor does he wander just anywhere: the place where he follows his unending path is usually a forest—that ancient symbol of man's uncertain fate.

Various questions come to mind when we read stories about these restless travelers. First of all, did they really exist? And second, whether they did or not, why did the people who wrote about them make them behave in such strange fashion? Why were they not allowed to settle down to a quieter life, especially in times of peace? What was the motive behind their constant search for adventures?

I shall try to answer these questions as best I can, but my answers will, I hasten to say—and this may be a disappointment to some—have nothing to do with the social, political, or military history of the Middle Ages for the simple reason that at the time when people began to write and talk about knight-errantry there was, so far as we know, nothing like it in real life. It

This paper is a sequel to my essay on *Form and Meaning in Medieval Romance* (Presidential Address of the Modern Humanities Research Association, 1966). For the sake of continuity I have found it necessary to reproduce some of the examples quoted there.

126

was neither an established profession nor even a type of social behavior, and to describe its origin and development means describing a particular kind of imagination, not a social phenomenon. What Oscar Wilde said about life and literature was less of a paradox than he thought. It is not, he said, literature that imitates life, but life that imitates literature. This is certainly true of the finest examples of imaginative prose and poetry in the Middle Ages. It is a fact that the romances of chivalry and some of the things they stood for had a profound effect on people's lives both during the later Middle Ages and after: they influenced life, but they were not a reflection of life, and to build up a picture of medieval society on the basis of the romances as some historians tend to do is to misunderstand the very nature of medieval poetic fancy, if not the nature of all great literature.

But, you may ask, granted that we *are* concerned with literature only, why is it that in the imaginative writings of the Middle Ages the heroic characters—the knights-errant—do not behave like normal human beings? The answer is that they certainly do, but is there any reason why they should not? Why indeed should a character in a story move rationally from step to step, with each step being determined by the one before? Why should he follow the rules of rational behavior? And who can say for certain that in the last analysis what we call reason is not the madness of many, and madness the dream of one?

We know the story of one such dream—the dream of Don Quixote, inspired by his reading of late medieval romances of chivalry. It was by that time "the dream of one"—the dream of a man who imagined himself to be a knight-errant in a world that seemed to have rejected the mode of feeling and thinking that has conditioned the very existence of knight-errantry. The inquisition held by the curate and the barber on the books of chivalry in Don Quixote's library was a means of putting an end to this "fabulous extravaganza," as Cervantes calls it in the Preface to his great novel. As soon as the housekeeper who accompanied the curate and the barber saw the books, she ran hastily out of the room and returned with a crock of holy water and a bunch of hyssop, saying: "Take this, your reverence, and sprinkle the room: we may then avoid being bewitched by one of the many enchanters from these books." What in her simplicity she did not and could not know was that it was not the enchanters from those books, but the books themselves that had fired Don Quixote's imagination and made him into an out-of-date knight-errant—and not so much the stories told in those books, but the way they were told, the way the characters were made to behave in order to enact the stories. The fire that the curate and the barber lit in the courtyard of Don Quixote's house was not meant to destroy the enchanters or even the enchantments; it was meant to destroy—at least symbolically—a particular brand of imagination that, they thought, was contrary to orderly human life. The books, they felt, were dangerous because they had no beginning, no middle, and no end, because they were a living negation of what by that time had become the "madness of many"—the belief in rational organization in any form of art.

That the fire lit in Don Quixote's courtyard did not in the end destroy anything but a few well-worn volumes from his library is an indication of the extraordinary vitality of the imaginative process to which it was intended to put an end. There were two important events in medieval literary history, both of which occurred in the twelfth century, and both of which had a profound effect on the modern age despite all the changes undergone since then by our civilization. One was the rise of a new doctrine of love, which has since become known as the "courtly doctrine," and the other was the rise of a new form of imaginative narrative known as "romance." The two were sometimes combined—the ideology of courtly love was sometimes brought into this new type of fiction—and the combination of the two produced what is known as "courtly romance"—the most original and the most influential literary genre in medieval Europe. Its founder and its chief exponent was a French twelfth-century poet, Chrétien de Troyes, the author of the very first romances dealing with the adventures of the knights of King Arthur. Here is how one of them—perhaps the most famous of all—begins:

An unknown knight appears at Arthur's court. "I have in my castle," he says to the king, "knights and ladies from this court whom I hold captive; but if you want them to be set free, do as I tell you. Let one of your knights lead the queen after me into the forest, and if that knight defeats me in single combat, not only the queen, but all the other captives will be set free." The challenge is answered by Kay—one of the least distinguished of Arthur's knights—who immediately departs with the queen. Gawain, one of Arthur's best knights, then tells the king he should not have entrusted the queen to so unreliable a champion, and the quest for the queen then begins. Gawain rides out into the forest, and the first thing he finds is Kay's horse without its rider. He then meets a knight whose name at first is not revealed to us, but who, as we discover much later, is Lancelot, the best knight in the world. Lancelot says that his horse is unable to go much farther and begs Gawain to lend him one. Gawain does as he is asked, but the next time we see Lancelot he seems to have lost his horse again, for he is walking in his heavy armor, with his shield hung round his neck. Suddenly a cart appears, driven by a dwarf, and Lancelot asks the dwarf if he has seen the queen. The dwarf replies: "Get into my cart and you will soon discover where she is." To understand the meaning of this offer and the dilemma to which it gives rise we must remember that the cart was considered in those days a degrading and humiliating vehicle normally used for taking criminals to the place of punishment. And so for a few seconds—for two steps, to be precise—Lancelot hesitates: Reason is telling him not to accept the dwarf's offer, but while Reason dwells only on his lips, not in his heart, Love, which rules his heart, is telling him to get into the cart and secure the rescue of his lady, Queen Guinevere. And so he accepts the humiliation. The rescue is, of course, successful, but many strange things happen before Lancelot gets to the place where Guinevere is held captive, and many dangerous adventures are undertaken by the faithful and fearless knight, including the most terrible of all, the crossing of a bridge known as the "sword bridge"—*pont de l'épée*—made of the blade of a sword lying across a deep stream. Lancelot's hands, knees, and feet are bleeding, but Love, which inspires his every step, comforts him so that he finds joy in his suffering. When at last, after a fierce battle with the queen's abductor, he rescues her, she refuses to speak to him and gives no reason for her displeasure. His distress nearly causes his death, and he bitterly regrets having allowed the dwarf to drive him in the ignominious cart which, he is convinced, is the cause of his disgrace. He soon discovers that he is mistaken and that the queen is angry with him simply because he hesitated to get into the cart: there should have been, she thinks, no question in his mind as to where his duty lay, and the thought of rescuing her a little sooner should have taken immediate precedence over everything else, including his honor and dignity as a knight.

All this, however, is only a small part of the story of Lancelot as told by Chrétien de Troyes. There is much more to it than the tale of Guinevere's rescue and the problem of honor versus love. There is an exciting series of adventures and exploits, some of which are related to the rescue, but some are not, because in the character of Lancelot as portrayed by Chrétien de Troyes there is a significant convergence of two distinct concepts: the concept of a courtly lover whose whole life is dedicated to the service of his lady, and the concept of a knight who undertakes whatever challenging adventure he may come across. Of course, these two concepts can ideally be merged into one if the author and the reader bear in mind that part of the courtly lover's task is to make himself worthy of his lady's love. Insofar as Lancelot's exploits add to his reputation, they can all, at least in theory, be said to be part of the courtly way of life. But one cannot help seeing that already in this romance, which was to become the fountainhead of all later Arthurian fiction, being a knight-lover and being a knight-adventurer could mean two different things, and that even when the author had some overall purpose in mind in relating the many and varied adventures upon which his indefatigable characters were engaged, these characters themselves were not necessarily aware of any such purpose; and to the extent to which they did *not* know where their adventures were leading them, where exactly they were going and what they were fighting their battles for, they could be said to inaugurate the great tradition of knight-errantry.

A lot of valuable time and energy has been spent by scholars on attempts to explain this phenomenon in terms of the social, political, and even economic conditions of the time. The predicament of such scholars is understandable. They cannot conceive of literature as being anything other than an expression of a particular state of society, and therefore, if the known historical facts provide no means of relating one to the other, they have to be supplemented from the historian's own imagination. One such historian, Erich Köhler, has recently put forward the view that because in the second half of the twelfth century, between the Second and the Third Crusade, there was not much general fighting going on in Europe, knights had to divert their energies from warfare to questing and tourneying. A tourney was, of course, a recognized form of chivalric exercise, and we know it existed, both in times of war and between wars, but there is not a shred of evidence to show that knight-erranty existed at the time when Chrétien de Troyes wrote his romances, and the only reason why some people assume that it did is their belief, nay, conviction, that otherwise there would have been no cause for poets and prose writers to write about such things.

I believe that the motive for the creation of knight-errantry is to be found *within* the works in which it appears and nowhere else. I have just said that although Lancelot is primarily concerned with the rescue of Guinevere from captivity, he does become involved in adventures that interrupt his quest, and that as long as he thinks of them in those terms, that is to say as long as they are additional to his main task, he is well on the way to becoming a knight-errant. But this is only a beginning. Chrétien wrote two romances after the *Lancelot*, and in both he placed more emphasis than he ever did before on the itinerant aspect of knighthood. The real flowering of knight-errantry, however, belongs to the first half of the next century, the thirteenth, which saw an impressive development of romantic fiction in the form of greatly enlarged adaptations and remodelings of Arthurian romances. These were mostly written in prose and copied in magnificent, beautifully illuminated manuscripts, widely read throughout the last three centuries of the Middle Ages. One of the most famous among them, and one of the longest, was the prose adaptation of the story of Lancelot. Here a very important change occurred. Lancelot, no longer the protagonist of a single adventure, is a figure in a complicated series of interlocked situations and actions, and the work itself is reminiscent of those vast frescoes in which the same figure appears from time to time in different postures. It is not the hero's concentration on a single purpose that counts but, on the contrary, his ability to spread himself over a vast range of enterprises, all happening more or less simultaneously and requiring therefore a very special technique of presentation. To be side-tracked from any given task ceases to be an unfortunate accident and becomes a necessity, and a desirable one, for otherwise how could so many simultaneous tasks be performed? The resulting form is not so much an *expression* of the new chivalric mode of behavior, as its *mainspring* and *origin*, for the substitution of the multiple for the single inevitably leads to the substitution of the knight-errant's philosophy of life for the earlier, less varied mode of thought; the structure of the work in which the knight now appears becomes the structure of his own existence: a structure consisting of a vast number of themes forming a multiple whole, but so conceived that no part of it can be removed without somehow affecting the whole.

You may wonder how this kind of structure can be fitted into what we normally regard as the right sort of pattern of dramatic or narrative composition. The answer is that it *cannot* be so fitted because it is different from anything that we are familiar with, unless we happen to have more than a superficial acquaintance with the literature and art of our own time. But if we think of narrative or dramatic organization in classical or Aristotelian terms, we shall have great difficulty in understanding the romances of chivalry; for they are a negation of everything that we have been brought up to regard as essential in any art, visual or literary. The classical doctrine assumes that there can be no proper cohesion, or integrity, in a work of art without singleness of purpose; that is what we call the doctrine of *unity*. In the great cycles of chivalric romances there is cohesion without unity. What is more, it is precisely this feature of medieval romance that seems to have assured its vitality and its prodigious growth. It fascinated the reader of the late Middle Ages—and particularly the enlightened reader—by the elaboration of a variety of themes succeeding and echoing one another, by the sense of their simultaneous presence. It was the joy of remembering, or half-remembering a number of unfinished stories, and waiting for their reappearance while following others. Each sequence of incidents seemed to call for an extension that would serve either as a preliminary or as a sequel to it.

It is precisely through the narrative medium, as a result of its acceptance, that Lancelot and all the other knights of King Arthur's court became knights-errant. The early chronicles speak of Arthur as a great king whose victorious campaigns had enabled him to extend his sway to the whole of the British Isles and beyond. Lancelot in the thirteenth-century romances is concerned neither with this political and military side of the Arthurian epic nor with the exclusive service of love. When he first arrives at Arthur's court he is immediately made part of the world of knight-errantry. A wounded knight is found lying in a room in Arthur's palace, with two lance-points buried in his body and a sword driven into his head. But he survives, and his survival is due not to any physician's skill or even to the powers of some magician; it is the result of a literary device that consists in using each adventure as a means of introducing several others in such a way that neither the characters nor the author ever forgets to return to the initial point of departure. Lancelot sees the wounded knight, pulls the deadly weapons from his wounds, and swears to avenge his plight. But before he can embark upon this task, an equally urgent adventure is announced, that of a lady whose castle is being besieged by the King of Northumberland. On the way to that castle other adventures occur. Lancelot conquers the Dolorous Gard, which will play an important part in his life, defeats a formidable opponent of the name of Brandus of the Isles, and, when this is done, a story completely unrelated to Lancelot's many tasks is introduced—that of Arthur's quarrel with the King of the Land Beyond the Marches—*le roi d'Outre-Marches*. At long last, after an interval which in any modern printed book would have filled at least one hundred pages, we hear of Lancelot's first battle on behalf of the wounded knight. The theme is then abandoned again, but it keeps recurring, while in the intervals other themes rise to the surface, each broken into comparatively short fragments and carefully interwoven with fragments of other themes.

There is a significant parallel to this type of composition in medieval ornamental painting and sculpture. Art historians have known for a long time that the Western ornament of the eleventh, twelfth, and thirteenth centuries had two characteristic features, a negative and a positive one. The negative feature was the absence of any single center around which in a classical ornament everything would normally organize itself. We call it a negative feature as long as we think of it from the standpoint of classical aesthetics; but once we realize that there are in fact *several* centers instead of one, we can just as easily call it a *positive* feature. Instead of seeing the absence of a center we would then see a *polycentric* design of correspondingly greater complexity. A clearly positive feature of Romanesque and Gothic ornament is something that could be described by the term *cohesion:* the fact that the various elements of the composition are somehow *related* to one another, not *subordinate* to a central point or theme, but brought into a close relationship with one another in such a way that none of them can be cut off from the rest without damaging the whole. This combination of *polycentricity* and *cohesion* is a remarkable aesthetic achievement, difficult to understand until we have actually seen it in operation.

In the initial *T* of the GRADUAL OF ALBI (Plate I), cohesion and polycentricity are amply illustrated, but what we also see is a very careful

PLATE I. The Gradual of Albi (eleventh century).

PLATE II. The Sacramentary of Figeac (eleventh century).

PLATE III. Detail of the West Portal of the church of St. Lazare in Avallon (twelfth century).

PLATE IV. Beatus Initial from the Gloucester Psalter (early thirteenth century).

working out of two basic *patterns* of ornamentation, *both* polycentric and *both* highly cohesive. One of these patterns is called the *interlace;* it is what we see inside the stem of the letter; the other is what is known as a *coiling spiral*, a pattern modeled originally on a floral design, usually on the acanthus leaf, which was found to be particularly suitable as a model. And we also see that the two patterns are here kept *strictly apart*, as they will be in manuscript painting throughout the eleventh and the greater part of the twelfth century.

Another example of the same two patterns and of the way they are being kept in separate compartments is the initial *A* from another liturgical manuscript, the words being *Ad te levavi animam meam* (Plate II); but what we are expected to do when we see it is not just to read the letter and the word to which is belongs, but also to grasp the extraordinary complexity of the linear ornament, to understand how the interlace works inside the letter, how the coiling spiral develops outside it, and thus to discover the subtleties of this amazing design.

Plate III shows a detail of the Western Portal of the church of St. Lazare in Avallon. It is an example of a development characteristic of the second half of the twelfth and of the whole of the thirteenth century: the merging of the two processes and the appearance of a design in which the acanthus leaves become coiling spirals intertwined in a pattern of interlace. Possibly the most striking illustrations of this phenomenon are found in the decorated initials of the thirteenth century, such as the famous Beatus Initial from the Gloucester Psalter (Plate IV). The precision, sobriety, and balance exhibited here is unequaled in medieval painting; knight-errantry is admirably represented in the carefully drawn curves with their endless offshoots, entwined, latticed, knotted or plaited: an indefinitely extensible, but strictly controlled itinerary through the forest of adventure.

This is one way of seeing infinity in a grain of sand; it is also a way of realizing two things that are essential for the understanding of our own civilization and its true values. The first is the simple fact that our conventional standards of aesthetic judgment, our ideas as to how literary form should function, are applicable only to the very restricted range of works from some of which these ideas were originally evolved. There are vast stretches of our creative imagination that have been consistently excluded from our aesthetic horizon, and to do real justice to our literary and artistic heritage we have to adjust our perception accordingly and so widen the range of our sensibility. It is not enough to study history to understand what history has bequeathed to us; what is important above all is to make room in our lives for aesthetic experiences of which we have too long been deprived, for sources of both understanding and enjoyment that our conventional aesthetics have caused us to ignore. We tend to regard complexity as a fault; medieval writers and artists regarded it as a virtue, as a means of conveying certain things that could not be conveyed to the onlooker or the reader in any other way. When Gawain lends Lancelot his sword so as to ensure his victory in a dangerous contest with three strong knights, and Lancelot exclaims: "Ah! good sword, he who bore you must have a noble heart," we must take notice of the event and of Lancelot's words because hundreds of pages later on they will acquire a deep ironical significance. When the harmony of the Round Table is broken and Lancelot has to meet Gawain in single combat, the sword that was once a symbol of their mutual devotion will become a reminder of the broken bond between them and the source and emblem of their own destruction. Simultaneously present in our minds, the two events will interact in such a way as to bring forth, as no other device could have done, the meaning of both: *form will generate a new meaning*, just as the form of the romance as a whole generates a new mode of feeling and a new way of life that otherwise would not have been.

Such is the first lesson to be drawn from this brief exploration of knight-errantry: respect for those forms of art which are not dreamt of in our traditional philosophy of art. But there is still another lesson to be learned from the same exploration. I began by saying that so far as the romances of chivalry were concerned, it was not a case of literature's imitating life, but of life's imitating literature. By this I did not mean, and if I remember rightly I did not in fact say, that from the thirteenth century onwards, knights-errant stepped out of the pages of the romances and began to wander through the forests of Western Europe in search of adventure. There *are* such cases on record, but they are extreme cases, and I was not referring to them when I said that life sometimes modeled itself on literature. But there was in the romances of chivalry, especially in those of the thirteenth century, an important *ideological* content, which was not the doctrine of courtly love in its original extreme form, but rather the doctrine of *perfect knighthood*, made perfect by a deepened sense of devotion, by the recognition of a freely chosen allegiance to what Malory was to call much later the High Order of Knighthood. This too was the effect of the change from the knight-lover with a single object of worship in mind to the knight-errant whose virtues must of necessity include qualities other than fidelity to his lady. Lancelot's confidence in his ability to accomplish *any* adventure he undertakes stems at this later stage of his development not simply from his faith in his love, which gives him joy and strength, but to an equal degree from the fact that he possesses all the other qualities required of a perfect knight: *loyalty, bravery, courage, goodness of heart, graciousness, generosity,* and the quality described by the almost untranslatable French word *fierté*, which connotes both contempt for the wicked and gentleness toward the good. It was through this enlarged image of perfect knighthood that the chivalric romances exerted the most profound influence on the living concept of chivalry. There is even documentary evidence to show this, for we know that one of the most important statements of medieval political philosophy, Beaumanoir's *Coutumes de Beauvaisis*, written about half a century after the Prose Romance of *Lancelot*, was largely inspired by that romance, especially in its definition of the nature and purpose of knighthood. And therefore something that began as part of a poetical ideal, unrelated to any real social phenomenon, something that developed toward its most sophisticated and complete form within the framework of imaginative literature finally became a powerful factor in the genesis of modern social thought. It may well have been at first simply an escape from reality; the fact is that this imaginary chivalric life has had the effect of transforming in the end reality itself. If it seems natural to us nowadays, as indeed it has seemed natural for some time to all civilized mankind, that love should be the dominant theme of serious imaginative literature, it is because certain medieval poets, more than eight hundred years ago, made it the dominant theme of *their* verse; if the notion that generosity, graciousness, and dedication to a cause regardless of sacrifices has become part of our moral culture, it is because these things were part of an important literary tradition that held the whole of civilized Europe spellbound for over three centuries. And finally, if a constant search for marvels, for unfamiliar experiences, for opportunities of measuring one's spiritual and physical powers against odds has become part of human reality, it is because while walking on the clouds we have discovered that there was firm ground beneath our feet, and we ourselves have created that reality by following in the footsteps of great poets.

We live at a time when it is only too fashionable and too easy to talk about the social, political, and economic "determinants" of human behavior. It is perhaps time that we reminded ourselves of some other equally important determinants operating less ostensibly, but quite as effectively, upon mankind. The greatest among them is human imagination—the capacity for creating something that starts as a dream and ends by fashioning human life. It takes time before it is ready to be translated into a reality. An escape, a protest, a refusal to accept things as they are—those are the most powerful manifestations of the mind, and their effect can be slow; but it is lasting. After all, the people who escaped from the social injustices of their time into Utopia did create our modern notion of liberty and human dignity, and it may well be that those who rebel against the world of today are at the same time creating a better one for us all. The example of the medieval man's endowing us with something alien to the reality of his own age is an encouraging reminder of the inexhaustible strength of human thought at its imaginative best. The fate of Don Quixote may suggest to some people the idea that knight-errantry was an absurd fancy of a deranged mind; in fact it means something totally different; it is an expression in a deliberately grotesque form of something very real, and true, and profound—of the idea that greatness lies in the urge to look for greatness, and the real butt of the satire is not Don Quixote, but the people around him who think that by burning his books they can destroy what these books had taught him—and us all.

SUGGESTED READINGS

Auerbach, Erich. *Mimesis.* Berne, Switzerland: A. Francke, 1946; Princeton, N.J.: Princeton University Press, 1953; New York: Anchor Books, 1957.

Bogdanov, Fanni. *The Romance of the Grail.* Manchester University Press; New York: Barnes and Noble, 1966.

Ker, W. P. *Epic and Romance: Essays on Medieval Literature.* London: Macmillan & Co., 2nd ed., 1897; Oxford Macmillan & Co., 1908; New York: Dover Publications, 1957.

Loomis, R. S. *Arthurian Literature in the Middle Ages.* Oxford: Oxford University Press, 1959.

Saintsbury, George. *The Flourishing of Romance and the Rise of Allegory.* New York: Scribners, 1897.

Tuve, Rosamond. *Allegorical Imagery: Some Medieval Books and Their Posterity.* Princeton, N.J.: Princeton University Press, 1966.

Vinaver, Eugène. *The Rise of Romance.* New York: Oxford University Press, 1971.

Biographical Note on Karl D. Uitti

Before receiving his doctorate from the University of California at Berkeley in 1959, Karl D. Uitti held a French Government Assistantship at the Universities of Nancy and Bordeaux. During his tenure in the Department of Romance Languages at Princeton, where he is now full professor and chairman of the department, he was awarded a Guggenheim Fellowship and several visiting professorships at other universities.

His many publications include *The Concept of Self in the Symbolist Novel* (Paris: Mouton, 1961), *La Passion littéraire de Remy de Gourmont* (Paris: Presses Universitaires, 1962), *Linguistics and Literary Theory* (Englewood Cliffs, N.J.: Prentice-Hall, 1969), and *Story, Myth, and Celebration in Old French Narrative* (Princeton, N.J.: Princeton University Press, 1973). His main fields of interest are poetic and linguistic theory, nineteenth-century French literature, and medieval poetics.

The Myth of Poetry in Twelfth- and Thirteenth-Century France

KARL D. UITTI

My subject, I am afraid, is evanescent; when one believes one has a purchase on it, it escapes, refusing to let itself be pinned down. Few categories of theory help out. Straight criticism, at this juncture, will be less useful to our purposes than a critically oriented literary history—a history, in turn, based on philological reading. For I shall deal with the possibility of poetry's being itself an indispensable ingredient of myth in literature, of its being itself and *as such* mythic. (I do not claim that poetry is *invariably* indispensable to myth; rather I believe that it can be, and indeed that at times in the past—as in twelfth- and thirteenth-century France—it has been.)

Of course, everything depends on what one means by *myth*. When Claude Lévi-Strauss speaks of myth, he means a type of study that translates structural components out of the play (e.g., *Oedipus*) or out of the folktale (verse or prose narrative) into a new kind of paradigmatic framework designed to establish correlations and graphs (analogies and sequential possibilities) which, in turn, are meant to further the science—the language—of ethnology and, one hopes, our understanding of humanity. Indeed, to an important extent, our underlying humanity—what all societies share—resides in the universality/particularity of Lévi-Strauss's constructs. These contain "our" mythic sentences, our utterances.

However, the fact that the Oedipus myth "occurs" in a play—and in a tragedy to boot—is irrelevant to Lévi-Strauss. Its peculiar poetic shape—its *parole*like "reality"—is peeled away. What is significant to Lévi-Strauss may be reduced essentially to the relationships obtaining between elements of plot and theme (or motif). Analogously, we recall, phonologists were wont to peel away whatever in language they deemed pertinent to utterance and impertinent to code, namely, all historicity. As the German philologist, Harald Weinrich, has put it: "La première démarche de la

142

méthode est toujours d'éparpiller le mythe en mythèmes et le texte littéraire en je ne sais quels -èmes, pour quitter le plus vite possible la séquence narrative."[1] He adds: "Le style narratif en tant que tel n'intéresse guère les auteurs [like Lévi-Strauss] auxquels seul l'ordre paradigmatique semble traduisible dans le langage argumentatif de la science." Weinrich goes on to remark—and I concur—that Lévi-Strauss's emphasis on paradigm has led to admirable findings, but that these good results have been obtained at the expense of what he calls equally important research into the syntagmatic orders of text. "Structural mythology," he avers, stands to benefit from the syntactic study of myth.

As Weinrich suggests, literature—especially narrative—is characterized by the importance it must accord to sequential linearity. I should add here that sequence is built into paradigmatic constructs too; the two are inseparably conjoined. This *reality* ought to be taken into account when that which is expressed by and in literature—for example, myth— ostensibly concerns us. Why are certain legends (like that of Charlemagne) within given cultural contexts (twelfth-century France) invariably couched in the same type of sequential verbal constructs (*chanson de geste*)? And what of the equally important play between these generic constructs or processes (e.g., Béroul's *Tristan*)? Literature—whether we mean literary process or poetic artifact—does not lend itself entirely to phonological or ethnological abstraction; neither, then, can the study of myth *in* literature so lend itself. Those of us who deal with literary theory often tend to forget that a text as fundamental to our critical concerns as Aristotle's *Poetics* is based largely on empirical observation of Greek practice: a kind of typologically oriented literary history. Much the same applies to Dante's *De vulgari Eloquentia*. In order to understand how poetic texts work, then, a proper first step might be to take a close look at some texts, not to elaborate beforehand a theory, say, of textuality or what have you. One's observations, when handled with care, might well lead to some interesting—albeit provisional—generalizations, even with respect to the specific concerns of our symposium.

It is in this context, then, that I propose to study poetry as myth; literary and poetic structuring (as discourse, tradition, and value) function—*can* function, *have* functioned—mythically, in their very nature, every bit as meaningfully as the paradigmatically structured relationships isolated and accounted for by contemporary ethnology. I shall concern myself with poetic processes as such, with respect both to texts and to literary traditions.

Old French literature, in the period starting around 1050 and ending, roughly, at 1300, provides a fascinating area of exploration. "Form" and "content," in the Aristotelian sense, were distinguishable but inseparable during this period. Moreover, the vernacular lyric, various kinds of narrative, a new theater, vernacular prose—all these genres were developed as significant expressive processes at this time in the Northern French *langue d'oïl*.

Around the year 1200, the late epic poet Jehan Bodel (who also wrote lyric verse and highly innovative drama) made some remarks usually interpreted by Romantic and Positivist critics as concerning Old French narrative subject matter. However, these remarks lend themselves with equal pertinence to treatment, as well, of manner and style—of poetic construction. The term he uses is *matere*. In the first stanza of his *Song of the Saxons* (ca. 1200)—a poem that nobly tells of Charlemagne's eventual victory over the rebellious Saxons, a victory gained despite Roland's death at Roncevaux—Jehan Bodel distinguishes between the "matter of France," the "matter of Rome," and the "matter of Britain." The *matere de France* is "true" *(voir)* because the crown of France enjoys primacy among kingdoms: God created through His command the first king of France. Meanwhile, the matter of Rome is "wise and clerkly" *(sage et de sens aprendant);* the tales of Britain, conversely, are "vain and pleasant" *(vain et plaisant)*—at best entertaining.

Though much should be said of this distinction, I shall try to be as concise as possible. The matter of France stands for the narrative material contained in (and expressed by) the *chansons de geste*, for example, the *Song of Roland* or poems of the *William* cycle. These poems, couched in *laisses* made up of decasyllabic verses, sing the "imperial" myth of the crown of France—heir to Roman universality and guardian of Christian unity; they recount the poetic history of Charlemagne and the twelve peers. The earliest surviving texts date from the close of the eleventh century; all are immediately recognizable in their form though considerable variation within the form is possible. Conversely, Bodel describes the matter of Britain—essentially the Arthurian stories, which became popular in the vernacular first among the Anglo-Norman and subsequently among the French aristocracy during the second half of the twelfth century—as a kind of amusing diversion; the octosyllable rhyming couplets were meant to be read, not sung, before refined, courtly audiences. This is the world we have all come to associate with romance, with knights and ladies, with Celtic fictions, and with the elaborate poetic techniques taught in the schools. Stories about Arthur, Guenevere, and the Round Table are not "true" in the sense that stories about Roland, Oliver, Turpin, and their companions are "true." For Jehan Bodel, then, two orders of "myth" are at issue; they are moreover indistinguishable from matters of literary— indeed of generic (i.e., generative)—form.

Of course, Jehan Bodel's continental French patriotism weighs heavily in his judgment. The "French" Charlemagne, not the Anglo-Norman kings of England, *really* vanquished the "pagan" Saxons and converted them to Christianity. (The Anglo-Norman kings considered Arthur, the last Celtic king to conquer the Saxons, as a kind of precursor; it suited their politics to do so.)

Yet it would not do to categorize and then dismiss Bodel's arguments merely on grounds of nationalist bias. Bodel has identified a crucial literary problem: How does one go about deciding what is "true" within a piece of discourse—a poem—that in turn depends entirely upon an organic relationship obtaining between a subject matter and a poetic form? Let us not forget that the intellectual and spiritual atmosphere around 1200 was not completely favorable to poetry. By the close of the twelfth century the literary curricula of the cathedral schools had given way—or were about to give way—to new university curricula based on logic and—to oversimplify somewhat—philosophical, not poetic, discourse. Furthermore, years of attack on the part of churchmen such as Bernard of Clairvaux had also taken their toll: poetry was on the defensive. Finally, some of the vernacular genres had apparently been worked out; Bodel himself hoped to create anew a *chanson de geste* form that, in the view of many, had seriously decayed. Villon's poignant query, "Où est le preux Charlemagne?," had become an appropriate question and a motif of regret already by the year 1200. (Bodel's renewals also extended themselves to hagiography: his *Jeu de St Nicolas* recreates the genre by translating it into theater.) Meanwhile, courtly romance itself had also become increasingly oriented toward sheer entertainment. One thinks of *Floire et Blanchefleur*, the poems of Jehan Renard, of *Aucassin et Nicolette*. The balanced and complex narratives of a Chrétien de Troyes were giving way to transitional forms. But then had not Chrétien himself, throughout his *Cligés* (ca. 1176), emphasized the artifice inherent in romance entertainment in order to expose the romancelike artificiality of the Tristan stories? In this fashion he wished to show that these stories—stories that many people had started to "take seriously" (as they took seriously the *matere de France*)—were "true" only within their purely romance context. The veracity of what a romance says derives from what Chrétien called its *bele conjointure*, a term meaning "putting together"—what Bernard of Chartres had described a generation or more earlier as *iuncturæ dictionum*, the "joining of words." In fact what a romance "says" *is* its "putting together."

My task would be easier (and far less interesting) if we could simply equate romance form and falsehood, *chanson de geste* and poetic truth. Thanks to its romance form, *Cligés* serves "truth"; it is true to itself and, in so being, it provides an understanding of a kind of reality, a literary reality, with important connotations for our comprehension of the real world. We recall as well that Bodel was much less severe in his appreciation of the "matter of Rome" than in his judgment of the Breton material. Retold in the vernacular according to the poetic arts of the time, these classical stories of Thebes and Troy, of Alexander the Great and Aeneas are "wise and clerkly." The issue of truth and falsehood as such is simply not raised. The *matter* (or subject) is specifically subordinated to what might be called a kind of *manner*, a manner that represents continuity in literature and devotion to poetic activity. Moreover, this activity—a creative process—was frequently viewed by twelfth-century thought (e.g., Bernard Silvester) as itself participating, so to speak by definition, in the work of the Creation.

Yet, on the surface at least, there is little to distinguish most Breton romances formally from texts belonging to the matter of Rome; one finds the same octosyllabic versification, identical technical developments (descriptions, monologues, figures). Texts pertaining to the matter of Rome as well as poems belonging to the matter of Britain display, at times quite ostentatiously, the same high degree of concern for questions of literary form, the same poetic self-consciousness that can be noted in Chrétien's notion of *conjointure*. Thus, the forematter to Chrétien's *Conte du graal* (*Perceval*) describes this romance as the "best narrative of all," as, in his own words, ". . . le meiller conte/ Qui soit contez a cort roial."[2] Analogously, Wace and Benoît de Sainte-Maure, who flourished a generation before Chrétien, also underscore the importance of clerkly activity. Without clerks—in other words without "wise and clerkly" narrative—who set down in writing what they know, we should all live like beasts, unaware of our ancestors' deeds, ignorant of the glories of Troy, of Rome, of Ninevah, deprived of our *memory*, of the book that is our past.

Interestingly, in *Cligés*, the romance that even in its plot conjoins "ancient" and Arthurian material— the Greek hero Alexander and, later, his son Cligés both remove to Britain in order to win knighthood at Arthur's court—Chrétien articulates a specific critical and historical justification for vernacular poetic activity in 12th-century France. Chivalry and clergy (knightliness and clerkliness) were born in Greece, transferred to Rome, and have now come to dwell in France, where as the narrator to *Cligés* explains, "may the honor of it all remain forever":

> . . . Grece ot de chevalerie
> Le premier los et de clergie.
> Puis vint chevalerie a Rome
> E de la clergie la some,
> Qui or est an France venue.
> Dex doint qu'ele i soit maintenue
> Et que li leus li abelisse
> Tant que ja mes de France n'isse
> L'enors qui s'i est arestee.[3]

Literary self-consciousness reaches one of its highest peaks in *Cligés*, a fiction based in its totality on the ramifications of its author's faith in the efficacy of poetic artifice. The text is *about* the celebration of poetry through poetic artifice: from Greece to Rome to France—Chrétien expresses here, and imparts new life to, the old topos of the *translatio studii*. The status of our discussion will therefore remain impossibly confused until we understand the nature of this topos. Memory, we recall, is also brought into Chrétien's articulation:

> Par les livres que nos avons
> Les fez des ancïens savons
> Et del siegle qui fu jadis.[4]

These lines introduce the *translatio* articulation. Let us not forget that Chrétien is himself "remembering" the opening lines to Wace's *Roman de Rou* in this adaptation, and that, still more important, "memory" was considered by ancient rhetorical theory as well as by 12th-century poetic theory as, precisely, part of the *art* of writing.

Had I time and space enough, I should look closely into the meaning of Bodel's favorable view of the *matere de Rome* (as opposed to his rejection of the Breton matter) in terms of what he himself had set out to do in the *Song of the Saxons*. Prologues in Old French works have a way of telling us what their texts are all about and how they should be read. Once again, however, *Cligés* might be pressed into service in order to help us better understand Bodel.

Too complex to admit of easy summary, the story of *Cligés* closely parallels the story of Tristan and Yseut. Cligés's parents die; meanwhile his uncle Alis has occupied the throne at Constantinople. Cligés is therefore Alis's nephew, a relationship duplicating that of Tristan and King Mark. Alis decides to marry, despite his previous promise to Cligés's father to make Cligés his heir. His betrothed, Fénice, is the daughter of the emperor of Germany. Of course she and Cligés fall in love. She is disconsolate. How can she marry a man she does not love? And yet *she will not be another Yseut*, she says; only he who has her hand in marriage will possess her body. All is not lost. Fénice's nurse, Thessala, will of course prepare a magic potion that will be served to Alis on their wedding day; this potion will cause Alis to dream that night that he has enjoyed his wife's favors whereas that will not have been the case. After many episodes Fénice and Cligés will finally get together and even marry.

The potion, as M. A. Freeman[5] has pointed out, is described at the midpoint of *Cligés*, that is, at the spot in which, frequently, Chrétien's protagonists earn (or reveal) their identity (e.g., Lancelot's name; Yvain's identification with the lion). Thessala's potion is a central element in *Cligés*:

its centrality is, so to speak, double. Without it, of course, the story would stop. It is a device, then, borrowed from the repertory of romance devices, that allows the romance to go on, *just as*, without *their* potion, the *story* of Tristan and Yseut would never have got off the ground. Thessala's potion is therefore a central element of plot. Just as importantly, however, the potion *in its description* both sheds light on and receives illumination from the prologue to the romance: the artifice-device of poetry is doubly related to the artifice-device of the potion; verbal illusion and magical illusion are identified with one another. The potion is described as "clear," but it is described at considerable length in terms of how it was concocted: *put together*. It stands in a metaphorical relationship to the book just as the book, in *its* formal identification with the story of Tristan and Yseut, constitutes a kind of metaphor of "life." (Later on in the romance, Cligés and his presumed-dead Fénice take refuge in a marvelously contrived tomb—lavishly described in traditional *descriptio* terms—built for them by their friend Jean, the artisan, and including running hot water! This isolation of the lovers in so artificial a *locus amoenus* perpetuates the motif of artifice and, of course, plays off on Tristan's stay with Yseut in the forest of Morois.) The artifice of poetry itself is celebrated as such by *Cligés*, internally within the romance and also with respect to poetic process; thus, *Cligés* tells us (and as I suggested above), the essence of the *Tristan* lies in *Tristan's* similar participation within an analogous poetic context. That is its identity: it is *poetry*. To return to Jehan Bodel, then, the service of truth, clearly, is inseparable from poetic intention; careful reading is indispensable because the poem is everything. Indeed, the reader's task is to collaborate in the *poetic* creation.

In what I have just briefly described (and which is fully examined in M. A. Freeman's dissertation) may be found a kind of authentication or authorization of Jehan Bodel's praise of the "wise and clerkly" *matere de Rome*. And here at last I reach the point of what I am trying to say: in poetry, without poetic craft, that is, without our having a sense of poetic craft, there is no truth. At least that is the lesson of the Old French romance of the second half of the twelfth century. Even the self-styled epic poet Jehan Bodel holds this view. It no longer suffices to sing—in, so to speak, a straight manner according to the old forms—the self-evident and "referentially" true myth of Charlemagne and his peers. His poetic enterprise must be explicitly identified with the clerkly craftsmanship he finds epitomized by the *matere* of Rome. (Bodel thus turns the Charlemagne story into a kind of novel.) What he knows how to do as a clerk, as a poet, constitutes then an indispensable ingredient of the myth he endeavors to serve and propagate. His mastery, that is to say, his "medium," is built into what he does. Let me add at this juncture that Bodel is not overly successful in this task. Yet what he set out to do in the *Song of the Saxons* foreshadows (and justifies) the most impressive poetic accomplishments of the thirteenth and fourteenth centuries, namely, the *Romance of the Rose* and Dante's *Divine Comedy*, two narratives of the romance type constructed on the basis of what may be called lyric intensity and the creative faith in the *translatio studii*. (Some might wish to add—but for different reasons—the *Prose Lancelot* and the *oeuvre* of Rutebeuf to this short list.)

The broad outlines of Dante's poetic career are too well known to bear detailed repetition here. The autobiographical prose of the *Vita Nuova*, studded with highly wrought songs derived from the twelfth and thirteenth-century lyric tradition, as well as the proclamation of faith in the poetic authenticity of the vernacular that his *De vulgari Eloquentia* propounds, lead to the text of the *Comedy*, the story of a journey in which the clerk-poet protagonist is led—up to a point—by Vergil, the matter of Rome incarnate. But Vergil can go only so far; Dante must continue with the Christian Statius, and then proceed alone. Truth is served—articulated by poets—but truth is dynamic in history: Greece to Rome to Christian Europe. And poetic craft, as well as language (i.e., the vernacular, opposed to Latin), must move apace. (Both Vergil and Statius, moreover, had been "translated" into twelfth-century Old French romance form.) Grammar, said Alain de Lille in the *Anticlaudianus*, provides the chassis for Prudence's trip to heaven; yet, to be sure, it is the trip itself that counts. Conversely, without what for lack of a better term I shall call poetic consciousness—the sense of self and of craft—no trip is possible, no truth discovered. Scholastic syllogisms *in Latin*—in a thoroughly revised "logical Latin" of speculative grammar—win the day.

We observed that in *Cligés* Chrétien de Troyes comments upon the Tristan myth through formal means. Quite literally he *transforms* that myth. In so doing he provides the model for Bodel's transformation of the Old French epic. The matter of France undergoes a generic sea-change that is designed at once to serve the myth and to renew the manner; Bodel's *Saxons* really develops what Chrétien had attempted in *Cligés* and, though certainly a partial failure, this work is a kind of stepping-stone in the history of generic transformations that lead to Dante's *Comedy* and beyond.

Let us recall at this point that genre in the Middle Ages is something quite different from our post-seventeenth-century Aristotelian classifications. Just as the clerk-poet saw himself as participating in a process—in a sense he is the Roman orator, the guardian of knowledge, the creator of beauty, the defender of values—so the "genre" or various "genres" within which he worked must be viewed as process. What *is* the *Song of Roland*? It is a manifestation—in several very distinct shapes imperfectly related by the several surviving manuscripts—of the matter of France. Nowadays most of us like best the Oxford text; but by no means may we be thereby authorized to consider this text, even when competently edited, as, say, a monument ontologically comparable in status to Flaubert's *Madame Bovary* or Joyce's *Ulysses*. I oversimplify certainly, but throughout the twelfth and thirteenth centuries given texts are in effect *versions*. It makes sense to see in *Cligés* a version of the Tristan corpus every bit as authentic as Béroul or Gottfried. It is not unreasonable to view the *Divine Comedy* as a version—albeit a masterpiece—of what the medieval romance could do. This generic process is moreover a conscious one; it is *poetically* relevant and as such it has much to do with what poems mean.

In the space remaining, let us consider the *Romance of the Rose* (1240, 1280), medieval France's greatest poem, a work without which Dante's *Comedy* would have been inconceivable. Here what Bodel tried to do, from a clerkly-poetic as well as from a generic point of view, results in a *chef-d'oeuvre*. Mythic constructs—for example, the Narcissus story, the personification of Nature, established poetic *récits*, etcetera—are used; but they are, as it were, ground up and refashioned in order to serve a new kind of organization.

The *Rose* is based on a dream; it proclaims that dreams are not necessarily lies. It makes the proclamation by putting *songs*, "dreams," in rhyme position with *mençonges*, "lies," in the very first couplet (Lecoy ed.), with (in ll. 3f.) an *annominatio* development stressing the same idea: *songier*, "to dream," rhymes with *mençongier*, "lying." Truth is very much at issue.

The structure of the *Rose* is lyric, its development is narrative. Thus, to be brief, informing the entire poem is the generic triangular construct composed of poetic ego (the poet-protagonist), love experience, and song (poetic craft). This "triangle"—I am tempted to say this equilateral triangle, since the angles are all equal—derives from the great courtly love lyric of the twelfth century in which the poet sings his love, affirms his noble identity in the experience, and, if I may say so, loves his song. The language, the experience, and the self are at once inextricably combined and mutually interchangeable.

It has often been remarked that the so-called first part of the *Rose*, some 4,000 lines composed by Guillaume de Lorris around 1240, celebrates something scholars since the 1880s (following Gaston Paris) have called the "myth of courtly love," but that in the second part—the continuation, dating from about forty years later—Jehan de Meung undermines this myth completely. From the point of view of "mythic content," it has been averred, the two parts are virtually opposed to one another. However, any interpretation of this sort presupposes—in my view, mistakenly—the a priori existence of a doctrinal myth of courtly love that, then, poets may

either celebrate or negate. The poetry is peeled away. This is dead wrong;
it is contradicted by the historical process of medieval vernacular literature, by what I have been trying to show. The *Rose* must be looked at as a
creative example of the poetic exploitation and transformation of generic
constructs—of what I call "generic transformation"—and, in particular, as
the transformation through narrative means of a type of lyric in which
protagonist, experience, and poetry are coequal. The true mythic purport
of the *Romance of the Rose* lies in the poem's relationship to poetic process.
Moreover, the text itself is explicit in this regard.

The first forty-four lines of Guillaume de Lorris's work constitute a
prologue; we must put it to good use. Here is the text:

Aucunes genz dient qu'en songes	[1 a]
n'a se fables non et mençonges;	
mes l'en puet tex songes songier	
qui ne sont mie mençongier,	4
ainz sont aprés bien aparant,	
si en puis bien traire a garant	
un auctor qui ot non Macrobes,	
qui ne tint pas songes a lobes,	8
ançois escrit l'avision	
qui avint au roi Scypion.	
Qui c'onques cuit ne qui que die	
qu'il est folor et musardie	12
de croire que songes aviegne,	
qui se voudra, por fol m'en tiegne,	
quar endroit moi ai ge fiance	
que songes est senefiance	16
des biens as genz et des anuiz,	
que li plusor songent de nuiz	
maintes choses covertement	
que l'en voit puis apertement.	20
El vintieme an de mon aage,	
el point qu'Amors prent le paage	
des jones genz, couchier m'aloie	
une nuit, si con je souloie,	24
et me dormoie mout forment,	
et vi un songe en mon dormant	
qui mout fu biaus et mout me plot;	
mes en ce songe onques riens n'ot	28
qui tretot avenu ne soit	
si con li songes recensoit.	
Or veil cel songe rimeer	
por vos cuers plus feire agueer,	32

qu'Amors le me prie et comande.
Et se nule ne nus demande
comant je veil que li romanz
soit apelez que je comanz,   36
ce est li *Romanz de la Rose,*
ou l'art d'Amors est tote enclose.
La matire est et bone et nueve,
or doint Dex qu'en gré le receve   40
cele por qui je l'ai empris:
c'est cele qui tant a de pris
et tant est digne d'estre amee
qu'el doit estre Rose clamee.[6]   44

This text is divided into two parts, of twenty and twenty-four lines respectively. The shape and sense of lines 1-20 correspond exactly to what theorists of the time prescribed for narrative, namely, to start off with a proverb or general *sententia* (dreams/lies), to cite authority in defense of the idea (Macrobius), to conclude by a general justification. Interestingly, the justification here is an antisyllogistic conclusion: "often people dream at night/of many things covertly/ that one sees later openly" (ll. 88ff.). This antirationalist stance—a defense of poetry in fact—constitutes a veritable theme of the poem.

The second section of the prologue introduces the lyric motif: "In my twentieth year, at that time when love takes its toll of young men . . . [twenty is the canonical age of falling in love] I went to bed one night as usual . . . and saw a dream as I slept, a most beautiful dream . . ." (ll. 21ff.). Protagonist and poet are one and the same; the experience is love—a personal experience, existentially authentic, but an experience nevertheless that can be shared by other noble hearts. "Now I wish to put this dream into poetry [*rimeer*] . . . for love begs it of me and commands me" (ll. 31ff.). Our triangle is complete. In my romance, that is, *in my poeticization*, the art of love is enclosed (l. 38): "the matter [*matire*] is good and new" (l. 39). What I have done—dare I say, "my kind of transformation"?—has never been done before. *Nueve* can and does mean "new" as well as "renewed."

The lyric construct underlies this *romanz*, then, imparting to it truth and authenticity: the hero is an eye-witness to love, so to speak. Moreover, it is thanks to poetry that the truth can be grasped by others, since—and this is astounding—it is through poetry that the poet-narrator seizes his *own* truth, a poetry at once lyric *and* narrative. For at the beginning of the narrative proper, at l. 45, we read: "Avis m'iere qu'il estoit mais, / il a ja bien .v. anz ou mais, / qu'en may estoie, ce sonjoie, / el tens en moreus . . ." ["It seemed to me that it was in May, / *at least five years ago,* / that I was in May, this I dreamt, / in the season of love . . ."]. The lyric Springtime, of course, when love holds sway, the birds sing, and when Nature renews herself. . . . But in and through the time reference—"at least five years ago"—our protagonist turns himself into a "romance type" of narrator. He is recording his own history in the same way that a Chrétien de Troyes had recorded, say, the history of a Lancelot or of a Perceval. The experience is given as experience and also as something filtered through the kind of poetic witness that the tradition of romance narrative, in the persona of the clerkly narrator, would allow: two kinds of witness, two kinds of truth, conjoined, indeed fused. The "I" of the *Rose* is at once "courtly lover" and "wise and clerkly." (Dante, of course, will later take up this same device in the *Comedy.*) A new kind of poet—a new myth of poetry—is born in the European vernacular. The transformation-*conjointure* of the two genres is incredibly creative and fertile.

All this, we see, is quite consciously brought off by Guillaume de Lorris in his prologue; and, we recall, the prologue is one of the two most strategic points in the continuum of a romance. Yet further and still more significant confirmation of Guillaume's enterprise is forthcoming from his successor, Jehan de Meung.

If we combine both parts of the *Rose*, it is at the midpoint—that is, starting at around l. 10463 and ending at l. 10650 (there are, all in all, 21750 lines in the Lecoy edition)—that Amors (Love) exhorts his troops to attack Jealousy's castle. In this speech Amors laments the loss of those poets who had served him and his mother Venus so well: Tibullus, Gallus, Catullus, and Ovid. They are dead and gone. But now Guillaume de Lorris stands before us, and he too, because of Jealousy, risks death. Let us all help him; then he will begin the romance in which all my commands will be incorporated *(mis)*. Jehan de Meung has taken over the poem as well as the clerk-narrator role played by Guillaume in Part I, but Jehan identifies *his* protagonist—the Lover—as Guillaume, the lyric hero. The process invented by Guillaume provides for—indeed, *invites* and *generates*—further development, in true medieval fashion. And let us not forget that the second most strategic point in Old French romances is precisely the midpoint.

What I have said does not tell the whole story. Love goes on to say that Guillaume will write only so much before he too will die; experience is subject to mortality, but poetry is not. The poem, as such, is never finished, at least not in one of its most important dimensions, that is, *as it participates in poetic process*. It is to be completed only *as a text*. Amors's discourse is extraordinary; let me provide a few extracts: "Puis vendra Johans Chopinel, / . . . qui nestra seur Laire a Meün / . . . [he] me servira toute sa vie, / sanz avarice et sanz envie, / et sera si tres sages hon / qu'il n'avra cure de Reson. . . . / Cist avra le romanz si chier / qu'il le voudra tout parfenir.

. . . / je l'afubleré de mes eles / et li chanteré notes teles / que, puis qu'il sera hors d'enfance, / endoctrinez de ma sciance, / si fleütera noz paroles / par carrefors et par escoles / selonc le langage de France, / partout le regne, en audiance, / que ja mes cil qui les orront / des douz mauz d'amer ne morront . . . / que tretuit cil qui ont a vivre / devroient apeler ce livre / le Miroër aus Amoreus" (ll. 10535–621). Here is a rough translation: "Then will come Jehan Chopinel . . . who will be born at Meung on the Loire. . . . He will serve me all his life, without avarice and envy, and will be so clerkly *(sages)* a man that he will pay no heed to Reason [the personification of a sirenlike dialectic in the poem]. . . . He will so love the romance that he will wish to finish it. . . . I [Amors] will give him my wings and will sing him much music that as soon as he is old enough and sufficiently indoctrinated in my science he will sing our words at the crossroads and in the schools, in the language of France, throughout the realm, in public hearing, so that nevermore will those who hear them have to die of the sweet pangs of love. . . . Everyone will call this book the *Encyclopedia* ["mirror," or *speculum*] *of Lovers.*"

Immortal poetry—the poetic process—endures, then, in defiance of death as well as of scholastic dialectic. Jehan, we see, has incorporated the myth of the *translatio studii*—the myth of poetry itself—into his story at the very center of the combined texts of Guillaume and himself. He was able to do so because of his faith in poetry—in this process—and because, both formally and structurally, the tradition to which Guillaume belonged had provided the framework for him to do so (and also because Guillaume provided the example). The myth of poetry in all its dynamism and self-consciousness is an inseparable part of the poem. I have tried to suggest how the Old French literary tradition gives us a purchase on the workings involved in this accomplishment. I believe firmly that students of literature and of myth today stand to profit from a still closer scrutiny of these old poetic texts.

NOTES

1. Harald Weinrich, "Structures Narratives du Mythe," *Poetique* 1 (1970): 34.

2. Chrétien de Troyes, *Le Roman de Perceval; ou, de Conte du Graal,* ed. Roach (Genève: E. Droz, 1956), ll. 64 f.)

3. Chrétien de Troyes, *Cligés,* ed. Alexandre Micha (Paris: Champion, 1954), C.F.M.A. 84, 11.29ff: Greece enjoyed the initial glory that was knightly heroism (chevalerie) and refined humanism (clergie). Next, chivalric honor removed to Rome, as well as the entirety of accumulated learning that has now arrived in France. May God grant that it (she) be cared for: may the surroundings delight her in hopes that the honor that has come to rest here never take its leave of France.

4. By means of books that we possess, we are apprised of the deeds of the ancients and of the world that once was.

5. M. A. Freeman, Ph.D. dissertation, Princeton University, 1975.

6. *Le Roman de la Rose*, ed. F. Lecoy (Paris: Champion: 1966), ll. 1-44.

> Many a man holds dreams to be but lies,
> All fabulous; but there have been some dreams
> No whit deceptive, as was later found.
> Well might one cite Macrobius, who wrote
> The story of the Dream of Scipio,
> And was assured that dreams are ofttimes true.
> But, if someone should wish to say or think
> 'Tis fond and foolish to believe that dreams
> Foretell the future, he may call me fool.
> Now, as for me, I have full confidence
> That visions are significant to man
> Of good and evil. Many dream at night
> Obscure forecasts of imminent events.
>   When I the age of twenty had attained—
> The age when love controls a young man's heart—
> As I was wont, one night I went to bed
> And soundly slept. But then there came a dream
> Which much delighted me, it was so sweet.
>
> No single thing which in that dream appeared
> Has failed to find fulfillment in my life,
> With which the vision well may be compared.
> Now I'll recount this dream in verse, to make
> Your hearts more gay, as Love commands and wills;
> And if a man or maid shall ever ask
> By what name I would christen the romance
> Which now I start, I will this answer make:
> "*The Romance of the Rose* it is, and it enfolds
> Within its compass all the Art of Love."
> The subject is both good and new. God grant
> That she for whom I write with favor look
> Upon my work, for she so worthy is
> Of love that well may she be called the Rose.

English translation by Harry W. Robbins (New York: E. P. Dutton & Co., 1962), vol. 1, ll. 1-33.

SUGGESTED READINGS

Frappier, Jean. *Chrétien de Troyes*. Paris: Hatier-Boivin, 1957; 1965.

Freeman, Michelle. "Problems in Romance Composition: Ovid, Chrétien de Troyes, and *The Romance of the Rose*." *Romance Philology* ("Jean Frappier Memorial Issue") 32 (August 1976): 158-68.

Lévi-Strauss, Claude. "The Structural Study of Myth," *Journal of American Folklore* 78, no. 270 (October-December, 1955): 428-44, as reprinted in *The Structuralists from Marx to Lévi-Strauss*, ed. Richard DeGeorge and Fernande DeGeorge (Garden City, N.Y.: Doubleday and Co., Anchor Original, 1972), pp. 169-94.

Uitti, Karl D. *Story, Myth, and Celebration in Old French Narrative Poetry, 1050-1200.* Princeton, N.J.: Princeton University Press, 1973.

Vinaver, Eugène. *The Rise of Romance.* Oxford: Clarendon Press, 1971.

Zumthor, Paul. *Essai de poétique médiévale.* Paris; editions du Seuil, 1972.

Biographical Note on Gene M. Bernstein

After completing his undergraduate work at Alfred and his M.A. at the University of Wisconsin, Gene M. Bernstein received his doctorate from the University of Massachusetts in 1974. He has taught at the University of Arizona, was a short-term guest professor at Bucknell, and is now assistant professor of English at Notre Dame. Professor Bernstein publishes regularly on Romantic poetry from such perspectives as Jungian psychology and the structuralism of Lévi-Strauss.

The Mediated Vision:
Eliade, Lévi-Strauss, and Romantic Mythopoesis

GENE M. BERNSTEIN

"We have barely started to attempt to understand literature as a distinctive mode of knowledge in which the processes, or, better, the desires of the human mind find their clearest expression," wrote Geoffrey Hartman in 1954,[1] and it remains a valid observation twenty years later. It is within the context of Hartman's statement that I wish to discuss myth and literature—in particular, mythic thinking and Romantic poetry. The relationship between the two can be mutually enlightening since Hartman's statement applies to myth as accurately as it does to literature. By examining several works of Mircea Eliade, I hope to show that myth is indeed "a distinctive mode of knowledge," or a way of organizing perceptions of the world into a meaningful pattern. And in turning to Claude Lévi-Strauss I intend to suggest how "the processes, or, better, the desires of the human mind find their clearest expression" in mythmaking poetry. Without attempting to define myth comprehensively, I will nevertheless suggest several ways in which Romantic poetry, at least a substantial portion of the most significant Romantic poetry, is mythic and therefore illustrative of the desires and processes of the human mind.

My title, as the readers may already have inferred, is based on Hartman's *The Unmediated Vision*, an illuminating study of Wordsworth, Hopkins, Rilke, and Valéry. Hartman's concept of the unmediated vision is in many ways analogous with the mythic state of mind, as we shall soon see. For Hartman, the unmediated vision represents a perception of reality in which "cognition and statement are not relational, but immediate and in relation"; thus, "neither effect nor value comes from each relation taken separately; they both exist as a function of an immediately perceived identity, and this identity reposes upon the mind's capacity for non-

158

relational and simultaneous apprehension" (pp. 44, 45). This is what we find in "Tintern Abbey," according to Hartman. The poets of unmediated vision also strive for "pure representation, which we have sometimes called the imageless vision" (p. 129), as in Shelley's "Mont Blanc" and "Hymn to Intellectual Beauty." They try to "conceive a pure representation distinguished from that of Jewish or medieval Christian thought in that its motive and terminal object is identified not with the God of the Testaments, but with Nature, the body, or human consciousness" (p. 154). These terminal objects—nature, the body, and human consciousness—are what Coleridge was referring to when he pronounced that "the poet, described in *ideal* perfection, brings the whole soul of man into activity."[2] It is in the Romantic age, after all, that nature becomes an object of study, and not a mere poetic ornament. And it is also in this period that human consciousness becomes a central focus in poetry and aesthetics.

Coleridge's all-encompassing definition invites mythicoreligious and sociopolitical as well as literary considerations, all of which should help us "understand literature as a distinctive mode of knowledge," in Hartman's words. Before proceeding, however, I think it necessary to make explicit what has been implicit in my remarks thus far, namely, that myth and poetry, at least certain types of poetry, are analogous if not one and the same. Ernst Cassirer notes, for example, that both language and myth

> stand in an original and indissoluble correlation with one another, from which they both emerge but gradually as independent elements. They are two diverse shoots from the same parent stem, the same impulse of symbolic formulation, springing from the same basic mental activity, *a concentration and heightening of simple sensory experience.*[3]

Thus we may infer that *language* that describes "a concentration and heightening of simple sensory experience" *is related to myth* in that they both descend "from the same parent stem, the same impulse to symbolic formulation." Such language is poetic, or in Milton's words, "simple, sensuous, and passionate." Its relation to Romantic poetry is clearly articulated in Wordsworth's "Preface" to the *Lyrical Ballads*—a volume dedicated not only to *simple, sensuous,* and *passionate language,* but to "a concentration and heightening of *simple sensory experience*" as well.

If it is hardly fair to classify all poetry seeking to celebrate "simple sensory experience" as mythic, this is a substantial beginning toward describing mythopoesis nevertheless. Though Wordsworth's "spots of time," Coleridge's "conversation poems," Shelley's encounters with Mont Blanc and the West wind, and Keats's great odes do concentrate upon and heighten sensory experience, they are mythic in other ways too, each of them fitting Cassirer's description of mythic thinking as a mode in which

> thought does not dispose freely over the data of intuition, in order to relate and compare them to each other, but is captivated and enthralled by the intuition which suddenly confronts it. It comes to rest in the immediate experience; the sensible present is so great that everything dwindles before it.[4]

In mythopoesis, then, not only does language magnify simple sensory experience. In addition, the thought is antithetical to strictly rational minds in that it does not seek cause-and-effect relationships. Wordsworth addresses the reader of "Simon Lee: The Old Huntsman" as follows, making explicit what has been implicit throughout the *Lyrical Ballads*:

> My gentle Reader, I perceive
> How patiently you've waited,
> And now I fear that you expect
> Some tale will be related.
>
>
> O Reader! had you in your mind
> Such stores as silent thought can bring,
> O gentle Reader! you would find
> A tale in every thing.[5]
>
> (ll. 61-68)

There is no effort in "Simon Lee" (nor in countless other Romantic poems) to relate and compare the data of intuition, but rather an attempt to present the immediate experience itself, confident that the latent "tale" will be grasped by the "gentle" reader. Moreover, the unmediated vision is "captivated and enthralled by the intuition which suddenly confronts it," entering into what Martin Buber calls an "I-Thou" relation with the world, not an "I-It" experience. Of the latter, Buber says:

> Those who experience do not participate in the world. For the experience is "in them" and not between them and the world. The world does not participate in experience. It allows itself to be experienced, but it is not concerned, or it contributes nothing, and nothing happens to it.[6]

The "I-It" experience is the relational view of Lockean epistemology, of Augustan poetry. The "I-Thou" relation is immediate and overwhelming; it is Hartman's unmediated vision. There are three spheres in which the world of relation arises: life with nature, with men, and with spiritual things,[7] or "the numinous," as Rudolf Otto refers to it in *The Idea of the Holy*.

In this intuitive, subjective "I-Thou" relation, the poet refuses "to employ the language of analysis either on himself or on external nature," for he recognizes that the outer world of sensory experience and the self are "both partners of the act of understanding" (Hartman, p. 5). This is central to the Wordsworthian imagination and the Coleridgean organic mind; it is the fluid give and take between mind and matter that distinguishes Romantic epistemology from the Augustan concept of mind as mechanism. It is, then, the intercourse between *language* seeking to heighten sensory experience and *thought* eschewing rational, cause-and-effect analysis that eventually bears that precocious child—mythopoesis. Needless to say, in the act of creation the two parents, language and thought, are so unified as to be nearly indistinguishable. Yet they provide a taking-off point for our study of Eliade.

According to Mircea Eliade, a myth is a story narrating the sacred history of an event that took place in primordial time. A myth therefore "is always an account of a 'creation'; it relates how something was produced, began to *be*." If it is a living myth "it supplies models for human behaviour and, by that very fact, *gives meaning and value to life*."[8] The importance of this aspect of myth can not be emphasized enough for, as modern, existential man has come to realize, "neither the objects of the external world nor human acts, properly speaking, have any autonomous intrinsic value. Objects or acts acquire value, and in so doing become real, because they participate, after one fashion or another, in a reality that transcends them."[9] For the archaic man, all life is sacred because his reality is composed of nature, man, and the numinous. For the modern man, on the other hand, life is primarily profane, because the only reality is man; nature and the numinous are of little or no consequence.

How and why archaic myth imparts value and meaning to objects, events, or persons is brilliantly explained by Eliade in *Cosmos and History*. He begins by focusing on "the image of himself formed by the man of the archaic societies and on the place that he assumes in the Cosmos," and proceeds to assert that

> the chief difference between the man of the archaic and traditional societies and the man of the modern societies with their strong imprint of Judaeo-Christianity lies in the fact that the former feels himself indissolubly connected with the Cosmos and the cosmic rhythms, whereas the latter insists that he is connected only with History. (p. vii)

In short, for the archaic man, myth was a comprehensive way of life because everything about him had a reality that was constantly being reaffirmed.

Conversely, modern man is out of touch with nature and the numinous, and thereby left to his own devices to ameliorate what Eliade calls "the terror of history." For history is linear, nonrepeatable, and thus unredeemable.

> Time present and time past
> Are both perhaps present in time future,
> And time future contained in time past.
> If all time is eternally present
> All time is unredeemable. . . .[10]

wrote T. S. Eliot, overlooking the fact that in mythic thinking there is no conception of time as Western man thinks of it—of past, present, and future. Because mythic thought is cyclical, an event or an act is redeemed through recurrence rather than explanation. Such a way of thinking has no place in the modern man's perception of the world and he must therefore search out bridges linking cause-and-effect so as to justify the reality of an historical act or event that is unique and unrepeatable. Or else he must accept existentialism, though as Eliade points out, "justification of a historical event by the simple fact that it is a historical event, in other words, by the simple fact that 'it happened that way,' will not go far toward freeing humanity from the terror that the event inspires" (p. 150).[11]

Nor will it suffice, in the case of suffering and evil, to transform them from a negative to a positive, even a redemptive experience, as Christianity tries to do. Where modern man has failed to justify pain and evil, the archaic man succeeded, as Eliade explains:

> The critical moment of the suffering lies in its appearance; suffering is perturbing only insofar as its cause remains undiscovered. As soon as the sorcerer or the priest discover [s] what is causing children or animals to die, drought to continue, rain to increase, game to disappear, the suffering begins to become tolerable; it has a meaning and a cause, hence it can be fitted into a system and explained. . . .
> The important thing for us is that nowhere—within the frame of the archaic civilizations—are suffering and pain regarded as "blind" and without meaning. (p. 98)

The source of suffering could always be identified among the exemplary models embodied in myth and subsequently exorcized by the priest or medicine man.

It is worth noting, in this connection, that modern man's efforts to justify evil and suffering often rely upon just this type of archaic, mythical thinking. The Nazi holocaust is seen as an archetypal repetition of Jahweh's retribution against his wayward "chosen people," the exemplary models to be found in the Old Testament. And the threat of nuclear destruction is seen as an archetypal repetition of the biblical Deluge.

How the archaic man "fell" out of the cyclical, mythic perception of the world and into the linear, historical one is a fascinating subject, albeit outside the range and scope of this paper, except for its relation to art. David Bidney offers the following explanation of man's evolution from a mythic to a historical being:

> Man's interpretation of the world is said to have evolved through three stages: a mythic stage, an epic stage, and a historical stage. The mythic stage changes into the epic stage when man bases his conduct on some notion of "the model man," or the cult hero. The historic stage emerges when man ceases to look to the exemplary past and sets up for himself rational objectives and means for their attainment.[12]

These three stages are easily correlated with the three stages of art as outlined by Otto Rank.

> And so we have *primitive art*, the expression of a collective ideology, perpetuated by abstraction which has found its *religious* expression in the idea of the soul; *classical art*, based on a *social* art-concept, perpetuated by idealization, which has found its purest expression in the conception of beauty; and lastly, *modern art*, based on the concept of individual genius and perpetuated by *concretization*, which has found its clearest expression in the personality-cult of the artistic individuality itself.[13]

These two explanations, especially the latter, accord with the concept that modern man has moved away from the sacred myth incorporating man, nature, and the numinous and accepted the profane or political myth of historical man instead.

Though these explanations of how man and his art evolved are helpful, they raise some serious questions too. If, for instance, primitive, mythic art represents "the expression of a *collective ideology*, perpetuated by *abstraction*," how can Romantic art "based on the concept of *individual genius* and perpetuated by *concretization*" be mythopoeic? Or, how do we account for Shelley's individual genius, a Romantic trait, expressing itself through abstraction, a primitive characteristic? To resolve these questions we must turn to Lévi-Strauss, whose anthropological studies, psychologically oriented as they are, provide some answers.

We should begin by noting that for Lévi-Strauss the idea of *History* is a delusion. Throughout *The Savage Mind*, and particularly in the last chapter, he rebuts Sartre's defense of history in *Critique of Dialectical Reasoning* by arguing that *history* is as much a part of one's present state of mind as it is of the irrecoverable past. If history is reduced to a unique event in the unrepeatable past, man is seemingly in control of it because he can label and define it. But if, on the other hand, as Lévi-Strauss maintains, the past is really a part of one's present mental equilibrium, then man is not yet, nor will he ever be, in a position to define his own life, and value must therefore lie outside man's control. This is the point at which modern man has erred, for he deludes himself into believing that he is enlightened and therefore in control of his destiny, and that the poor ignorant primitives are slaves to nature and superstition. Such is not the case, of course. Modern man's use of concrete taxonomies, seemingly superior to the archaic man's use of abstractions, is merely *a different* mode of classifying knowledge, *not a superior one*. "In fact," Lévi-Strauss writes,

> the delimitation of concepts is different in every language, and, as the author of the article "nom" in the *Encyclopedie* correctly observed in the eighteenth century, the use of more or less abstract terms is a function not of greater or lesser intellectual capacity, but of differences in the interests—in their intensity and attention to detail—of particular social groups within the national society.[14]

Thus we can understand why archaic, or magical thought is not to be seen as a nascent form of modern, or scientific thought. On the contrary, magical thought represents a well-articulated system that functions as a parallel, rather than a contrasting mode of acquiring and organizing knowledge. "Both science and magic . . . require the same sort of mental operations and they differ not so much in kind as in the different types of phenomena to which they are applied," observes Lévi-Strauss (p. 13). I would add that not only do these two parallel ways of thinking apply themselves to different phenomena, but they differ as well in the relation of the phenomena themselves to knowledge. By this I mean that for the archaic man knowledge acquired through sensory experience is an end in itself; for the modern man it is a means to an end, hard though that end may be to define. Knowledge is dealt with in relational, cause-and-effect terms rather than direct, unmediated ones. Recognizing, then, that the thought processes of archaic and modern man "differ not so much in kind as in the different types of phenomena to which they are applied," and in the relation of experiential phenomena to knowledge, is a first step in understanding why certain characteristics of primitive thought and art are found in modern thought and art.

Also helpful in resolving this apparent paradox is Lévi-Strauss's theory of infrastructures. In *Totemism* he argues that the foundations of human consciousness are the same for the archaic and the modern man. In so doing, he relies upon Rousseau, who "sees the apprehension by man of the 'specific' character of the animal and vegetable world as the source of the first logical operations and subsequently of a social differentiation which could be lived out only if it were conceptualized."[15] Archaic man conceptualized this logical operation through totems, which transfer "relations, posed ideologically, between two series, one *natural,* the other *cultural.* The natural series comprises on the one hand *categories,* on the other *particulars;* the cultural series comprises *groups* and *persons*" (p. 16). Lévi-Strauss is therefore the first to explore and expand upon Rousseau's observation that "the animal world and that of plant life are not utilized merely because they are there, but because they suggest a mode of thought" (p. 13).

It is this mode of thought that is of interest to our study of mythopoesis, which, as I have already suggested, represents both a way of thinking about sensory experience and a way of expressing said mode of thought. The mythic way of thought used by the archaic man relates to the total cosmos—man, nature, and the numinous—as we have already seen. Such thought, according to Lévi-Strauss, *originates in the unconscious arrangement of sensory experience into binary opposites and the subsequent mediation of these oppositions through symbols.* For the archaic man the totem is the mediator between the most basic of binary oppositions, nature and culture, for this is that first logical operation to which Rousseau alluded above. The modern man is unaware of such tensions because he is concerned solely with culture; unlike the archaic man, who "abandons himself solely to the consciousness of his present existence,"[16] the modern man is preoccupied with both past and future, cause and effect.

Unable to rely upon totems as mediating agents because nature and the numinous are too far removed from his daily life, the modern man must rely upon language for symbolic expression. Moreover, unable to perpetuate the unmediated vision as a way of perceiving reality because subject to a cultural mediation that imposes a mental equilibrium from without, the modern man is left with but one hope of establishing an unmediated, intuitive "I-Thou" relation with the cosmos. This hope is based, according to Rousseau, on "the only psychic state of which the content is indissociably both affective and intellectual, and which the act of consciousness suffices to transfer from one level to another, namely, *compassion,* or as Rousseau also writes, *identification with another*" (p. 101, my emphasis). This emphasis on sympathy is, of course, precisely what Wordsworth, Coleridge, and Shelley sought to arouse in their contemporaries through poetry and prose.

Their use of language as "a synthesizing operator between ideas and facts" (p. 131) is based on the same structures that give rise to totems, namely, metaphor and metonym.

> Metaphor is a means toward association, a means of connecting "things," whether objects-to-objects, relations-to-relations, levels-to-levels, domains-to-domains, objects-to-domains, people-to-birds, people-to-people, etc. The justification for the connection is the *similarity* that is sensed to exist between things. Metonymy is a means of connecting things by the notion of their juxtaposition, whether temporal or spatial. . . . The critical conclusion is that metonymy and metaphor are principles which underlie any lexical substitution set in language.[17]

In this connection it is worth recalling that "connecting things," whether through metaphor or metonym, is the very basis upon which Buber establishes the "I-Thou" primary word that is so quintessentially mythic. The emphasis therein is on affectivity, on feeling and sensing the immediate moment, rather than on intellectuality or reasoning and understanding in terms of past, present, and future. Metaphor and metonym are also, as we have already seen, the principles upon which totems are based, thus accounting for the similarity perceived between natural and human orders, which is in turn transformed into a cultural order. We have now returned full cycle to Cassirer's claim that language and myth are offshoots of the same stem, particularly in their mutual reliance on metaphor for symbolic formulation, that stem being the human mind with its infrastructures.

To turn now to Romanticism, we must pose the basic question inherent in all interdisciplinary studies: Are the relations between the various disciplines involved genuine or fortuitous? I hope, in response to this implicit question, to illustrate that the analogies I have suggested between the mythic state of mind as characterized by Eliade, and the structuralist theory of the mind's infrastructures as described by Lévi-Strauss, are genuinely related to Romantic aesthetics and epistemology. We have already established that the three primary spheres of the "I-Thou" unmediated, mythic relation are nature, man, and the numinous. In attempting to define Romantic mythopoesis we must consider Romantic attitudes toward these three spheres, albeit summarily. Toward this end it seems altogether appropriate to extend Cassirer's metaphor and think of the three spheres as offshoots of the same root, the organic theory of mind, to which I shall turn presently.

First, however, I would like to consider Romantic attitudes toward nature. Fortunately M. H. Abrams's recent book, *Natural Super-*

naturalism, offers what should be the definitive work on the subject for years to come.[18] Quite accurately, Abrams dismisses any sentimental notions surrounding the "back to nature" cliché and focuses instead on Wordsworth's call for a "spousal verse" celebrating the marriage of mind and nature. Abrams makes it abundantly clear that both Wordsworth and Coleridge sought "to redeem man by fostering a reconciliation with nature, which because man severed himself from his earlier unity with it, has become alien and inimical to him" (p. 145).

The return to nature is not merely a naive longing for simplicity in an increasingly complex society, nor is it an escape from the harsh realities of life. It represents a profound rejection of Lockean epistemology, in which the mind is like a passive machine recording sensory data received from without, or in Locke's own words, a "tabula rasa." Instead, relying upon nature and its inherent principles of process, the Romantics conceived of the mind as essentially vital and organic, shaping and coloring sense impressions, acting and reacting to both intuitions from within and inspirations from without. But above all else, the organic mind was the one hope upon which they sought to, as Wordsworth expressed it, "arouse the sensual from their sleep/ Of Death."[19]

Thus, the Romantics thought of the poet as a prophet seeking man's salvation. This was indeed a difficult as well as a heroic task, a task at which Milton had failed, they believed, because of misguided reliance upon Urania. Wordsworth sought a greater muse, "for," he writes,

> I must tread on shadowy ground, must sink
> Deep—and, aloft ascending, breathe in worlds
> To which the heaven of heavens is but a veil.
> All strength—all terror, single or in bands,
> That ever was put forth in personal form—
> Jehovah—with his thunder, and the choir
> Of shouting Angels, and the empyreal thrones—
> I pass them unalarmed. Not Chaos, not
> The darkest pit of lowest Erebus,
> Nor aught of blinder vacancy, scooped out
> By help of dreams—can breed such fear and awe
> As fall upon us often when we look
> Into our Minds, into the Mind of Man—
> My haunt, and the main region of my song.[20]

From this poetic posture there can be no doubt that the pun on "fall" is intentional, for to the Romantics the Fall of Man is coterminous with the birth of self-consciousness. Prior to the Fall, Adam "is in the fortunate condition of not knowing that he has a self, and therefore of not being worried about it, as is the archaic man," according to Peter Caws.[21] It is after the Fall, a fall into history that is unredeemable, that Adam becomes aware of himself as distinct not only from his natural surroundings, but also from his fellow human being, Eve. In this respect the Romantics, like both Eliade and Lévi-Strauss after them, realized that, as Caws explains, the archaic man was "nearer the truth than we are, and that a good deal of our trouble arises out of the invention of the self *as an object of study*, from the belief that man has a special kind of being,"[22] independent of both nature and the numinous.

But the Romantics were not content merely to diagnose the malaise of modern, historical man; they prescribed an antidote as well. Recognizing that man was cut off from the cosmic rhythms and thus alienated from the world about him, they called upon the most puissant power of the mind—imagination—to lead them to salvation. The most famous discussion on the subject, and the most cryptic, is, of course, Coleridge's distinction between the primary and secondary imagination in *Biographia Literaria*.[23]

The following explanation of Coleridge's definition is, to say the least, highly unorthodox. Yet I believe that Romantic self-consciousness and the concomitant faith in man's ultimate redemption through regenerated imagination can justify such a reading. This is particularly true when we bear in mind the preceding discussion of Eliade on myth and Lévi-Strauss on structural thought. The primary imagination is defined by Coleridge as "the living Power and prime Agent of all human Perception, and as a repetition in the finite mind of the eternal act of creation in the infinite I AM." Now, the power and agent of human perception is obviously the mind which, according to Lévi-Strauss, is composed of infrastructures. And "the eternal act of creation in the infinite I AM" is that moment in which self-consciousness is born within the individual; it is both eternal and infinite because it exists within each man's life and within the life of the species. It is also a "repetition in the finite mind," because once the individual becomes self-conscious he becomes historical and thus has a beginning and an end. To achieve the "infinite I AM" the individual must use the self as mediator between nature, which is infinite and eternal, and which man is a part of, and culture, which is historical and finite. This is to say that the mind constantly adjusts itself to new situations, as does the body to effects of geography and climate, so as to maintain a healthy equilibrium between fact and idea. As Shelley says, "There is a principle within the human being, and perhaps within all sentient beings, which acts otherwise than in the lyre and produces not melody alone, but harmony, by an internal adjustment of the sounds of motions thus excited to the impressions which excite them."[24] This process of mediation by the mind depends upon symbols that neutralize the disharmony between polar oppositions (i.e., finite-infinite; historical-eternal) by transforming them through metaphor and metonym. For to Lévi-Strauss "It is because man originally felt himself identical to all those like him (among which, as Rousseau explicitly says, we must include animals) that he came to acquire the capacity to distinguish *himself* as he distinguishes *them,* that is, to use the diversity of species as conceptual support for social differentiation";[25] accordingly "the eternal act of creation in the infinite I AM" originally took place. In other words, when Adam became conscious of himself as distinct from all about him, including Eve, he engaged in the eternal act of creation. In this sense the myth of the Fall is a true myth; that is, it is "an account of a 'creation'; it relates how something was produced, began to be" (see n. 8), and that something is man.

The secondary imagination is, according to Coleridge,

> an echo of the former, co-existing with the unconscious will, yet still as identical with the primary in the *kind* of its agency, and differing only in *degree,* and in the *mode* of its operation. It dissolves, diffuses, dissipates, in order to recreate; or where this process is rendered impossible, yet still at all events it struggles to idealize and to unify.

This is the very essence of secondary creation, or all creation other than that of the self. It is based on the same principles of metaphor and metonym, though it varies "in the *mode* of operation" because as a consequence of the primary act of creation man has become self-conscious, hence historical. And that in turn leads to an "I-It" experience with the world in which things are disconnected, in which a subject-object position is maintained. Thus it is necessary in secondary imagination to dissolve, diffuse, and dissipate our fallen way of perceiving the world, and re-create a new world by celebrating what Shelley calls "the before unapprehended relation be-tween things."[26] Those who are unable to do so are not true poets; they rely on fancy, which, as Coleridge says, "has no other counters to play with but fixities and definites." Because it represents the fallen world of "I-It" experience, fancy is unable to dissolve and dissipate in order to re-create and therefore must, according to Coleridge, "receive all its materials ready made from the law of association."

Romantic mythopoesis, then, represents a mode of thought which, based on the profound recognition that the mind can "make a Heav'n of Hell, a Hell of Heav'n," opted for the former. This was, and remains, too much to ask of poetry, whether mythic or otherwise, and so the Romantics failed. In so doing, however, they revealed through their literature "a distinctive mode of knowledge in which the processes . . . [and] desires of the human mind find their clearest expression" (n. 1). That mode of knowledge, as I have tried to illustrate, is the mythic mode long abandoned by modern, historical man. This in itself is a magnificent contribution to man's search for meaning and value in life.

The Romantics recognized that self-consciousness is the inevitable price we must pay to be human, an observation since corroborated by the work of mythologists like Eliade. But even more important than their diagnosis of this disease[27] was their belief that the very same mind that gave birth to self-consciousness was capable of producing an antidote. By using poetry to mediate between the fact of fall and the hope of redemption, just as the archaic man had once used totems to mediate the opposition between nature and culture, the Romantics sought to transform the profanity of self-consciousness into the sacrament of sympathetic love, a love not only of man, but also of the entire cosmos, including nature and the numinous. Imaginative sympathy, or love, is "the great secret of morals" ("Defence," p. 118), Shelley wrote, adding that

a man, to be greatly good, must imagine intensely and comprehensively; he must put himself in the place of another and of many others; the pains and pleasures of his species must become his own. The great instrument of moral good is the imagination; and poetry administers to the effect by acting upon the cause. (p. 118)

Imaginative sympathy was and is the only state of mind that is both affective and intellectual, and thus the only state of mind capable of maintaining an equilibrium between feeling and fact.

The mythopoeic mode of consciousness, as Philip Wheelwright puts it, is characterized by "a strong tendency of the different experiential elements to blend and fuse in a non-logical way. And not only that, but the self-hood of the worshiper tends to blend with them; that is to say, he becomes a full participant, not a mere observer."[28] Aware that "poetry is connate with the origin of man," the Romantic poets sought to escape selfhood by identifying with nature, man, and the cosmos, through worship of the imagination. Starting from the hell of self-consciousness, they sought to find the heaven of cosmic harmony; hoping to regenerate a fallen world, they regenerated hope instead, and fell.

NOTES

1. Geoffrey Hartman, *The Unmediated Vision* (New York: Harcourt, Brace and World, 1966), p. xi.

2. Samuel Taylor Coleridge, *Biographia Literaria*, ed. J. Shawcross, 2 vols. (London: Oxford University Press, 1969), 2:12.

3. Ernst Cassirer, *Language and Myth*, trans. Susanne K. Langer (New York: Dover Publications, 1954), p. 88; italics mine.

4. Ibid., p. 32.

5. William Wordsworth, *Poetical Works*, ed. Thomas Hutchinson and rev. Ernest de Selincourt (London: Oxford University Press, 1971), p. 379. All subsequent citations are from this edition.

6. Martin Buber, *I and Thou*, trans. Walter Kaufmann (New York: Charles Scribner's Sons, 1970), p. 56.

7. Ibid., pp. 56-57.

8. Mircea Eliade, *Myth and Reality*, trans. Willard Trask (New York: Harper and Row, 1963), pp. 5-6, 2.

9. Mircea Eliade, *Cosmos and History*, trans. Willard Trask (New York: Harper and Row, 1959), pp. 3-4.

10. T. S. Eliot, "Burnt Norton," *Collected Poems: 1909-1962* (New York: Harcourt, Brace and World, 1963), p. 175.

11. I have dealt with this subject in greater detail in chap. 2 of "Structuralism and Romantic Mythmaking," Ph.D. dissertation, University of Massachusetts, 1974.

12. David Bidney, "Myth, Symbolism, and Truth," in *Myth: A Symposium*, ed. Thomas Sebeok (Bloomington: Indiana University Press, 1971), p. 19.

13. Otto Rank, "Art and Artist," *The Myth of the Birth of the Hero and Other Writings*, ed. Philip Freund (New York: Vintage, 1964), p. 146.

14. Claude Lévi-Strauss, *The Savage Mind* (Chicago: The University of Chicago Press, 1970), p. 2.

15. Claude Lévi-Strauss, *Totemism*, trans. Rodney Needham (Boston: Beacon Press, 1963), p. 99.

16. Ibid., p. 100 n. 13.

17. James Boon, *From Symbolism to Structuralism* (New York: Harper and Row, 1972), p. 74.

18. M. H. Abrams, *Natural Supernaturalism* (New York: W. W. Norton and Co., 1971).

19. Wordsworth, Preface to the 1814 edition of "The Excursion," *Poetical Works*, p. 590.

20. Ibid.

21. Peter Caws, "What is Structuralism?" *Partisan Review* 35, no. 1 (1968):82.

22. Ibid.

23. *Biographia Literaria*, 1:202. All subsequent citations of Coleridge's definitions are from this page.

24. Percy Bysshe Shelley, "A Defence of Poetry," *The Complete Works of Percy Bysshe Shelley*, ed. Roger Ingpen and Walter Peck, 10 vols. (New York: Gordian Press, 1965), 7:109. All subsequent citations are from this edition.

25. *Totemism*, p. 101.

26. "A Defence of Poetry," 7:111. Cf. the entire passage with my analysis of the secondary imagination herein.

27. Geoffrey Hartman, "Romanticism and 'Anti-Self-Consciousness,'" reprinted in *Romanticism and Consciousness*, ed. Harold Bloom (New York: W. W. Norton, 1970), p. 47 n.

28. Philip Wheelright, "The Semantic Approach to Myth," in *Myth: A Symposium*, p. 159.

SUGGESTED READINGS

Burnham, Jack. *The Structure of Art*. New York: Braziller, 1971.

Chomsky, Noam. *Language and Mind*. New York: Harcourt Brace Jovanovich, 1972.

Gardner, Howard. *The Quest for Mind: Piaget, Lévi-Strauss, and the Structuralist Movement*. New York: Alfred Knopf, 1972.

Leach, Edmund. *Claude Lévi-Strauss*. New York: Viking. 1970.

Lévi-Strauss, Claude. *The Raw and the Cooked*. New York: Harper and Row, 1970.

Piaget, Jean. *Structuralism*. New York: Harper and Row, 1971.

Biographical Note on René Galand

René Galand did his undergraduate study in mathematics and philosophy at the Lycées of Brest and Rennes (1936-41); attended the University of Rennes (1941-1944); served in the French underground "maquis" during World War II; and was an officer in the French Forces of Occupation in Germany. He resumed his studies to complete his doctorate at Yale in 1952. He has taught at Yale and is now professor of French at Wellesley College, where he was chairman of the French department from 1968-1972.

He has published four books: *L'Ame celtique de Renan* (New Haven, Conn.: Yale University Press, 1959), *Baudelaire: poétique et poesie* (Paris: A. G. Nizet, 1969, *Saint-John Perse* (New York: Twayne, 1972), and *Baudelaire as a Love-Poet and Other Essays,* coauthor (University Park, Pa.: Pennsylvania State University Press, 1969); and has written nearly two dozen articles appearing in *Yale French Studies, PMLA, French Review,* and elsewhere. He is an assistant editor of *French Review* and is a Chevalier, Ordre des Palmes Académiques (1971).

A native of Brittany, he is keenly interested in the language and culture of the Breton people. The poet and author France Galand is his wife.

Baudelaire and Myth

RENÉ GALAND

Myth criticism rests on a fundamental assumption: the belief that literature owes much of its magic to its mythic dimension. In the *Iliad* and the *Odyssey*, in the ancient Sumerian poem of *Ishtar's Descent into Hell*, in *Jerusalem Delivered*, or in *The Charterhouse of Parma*, modern readers respond to the eternal archetypes that haunt the human imagination.[1] The enduring fascination that some poets exert over their readers may well be due to similar causes. Such is, I believe, the case of Baudelaire. Mythic motifs abound in *Les Fleurs du Mal*, awakening innumerable echoes within our unconscious: the struggle of light and darkness, the conflict of order and chaos, the war between God and Satan, the ecstasy of Eden and the horror of Hell, the duality of woman, who appears as heavenly Angel or infernal Siren. Although the mythic dimension of Baudelaire's poetry has been fully explored, less attention has been paid to his understanding of myth; it is apparent, however, that his views on myth are closely related to his theories of poetic creation and aesthetic value.[2]

Baudelaire's most detailed comments on myth are to be found in his celebrated article on Richard Wagner.[3] To be sure, this essay comes fairly late in Baudelaire's literary career. It was written in 1861, four years after the publication in book form of *Les Fleurs du Mal*, but the ideas expressed in this study reflect concerns that had been his since he first started to ponder the mystery of artistic creation. Baudelaire's initial encounter with Wagner occurred early in the year 1860, when he attended a concert given at the Théâtre-Italien. The experience came to Baudelaire as a revelation. He immediately wrote an enthusiastic letter to Wagner and became one of his first and fiercest supporters in France. Seizing every opportunity to listen to Wagner's music, Baudelaire also decided to investigate Wagner's theories. His efforts culminated in the publication, one year later, of the study that earned him Wagner's undying gratitude. In this undertaking, Baudelaire had at his disposal a number of articles and pamphlets occasioned by Wagner's concerts of 1860 and the *Tannhäuser* performance

174

of 1861 at the Paris Opera, an English translation of *Oper und Drama*, and the *Lettre sur la musique*, which served as a preface to Wagner's *Quatre poëmes d'opéras traduits en prose française*. In this text, Wagner recounted how he had come to write *Art and Revolution, The Art-work of the Future*, and *Opera and Drama*. The *Lettre sur la musique* is also an original presentation of his conception of a new art form in which music and drama would best accomplish their union. In addition, Baudelaire was acquainted with Wagner's letter to Berlioz and Liszt's study of *Lohengrin and Tannhäuser*. Although he made considerable use of the available sources, Baudelaire's study of Wagner bears the unmistakable mark of its author's originality.[4]

In his essay, Baudelaire takes as his point of departure the striking similarity between the program notes distributed for the concerts given at the Théâtre-Italien and written by Wagner himself, the comments made by Liszt in his study of Lohengrin and Tannhäuser, and his own experience in listening to the overture of Lohengrin. In each case, there is "la sensation de la *béatitude spirituelle et physique; de l'isolement;* de la contemplation de *quelque chose infiniment grand et infiniment beau;* d'une *lumière intense* qui réjouit *les yeux et l'âme jusqu'à la pâmoison;* et enfin la sensation de *l'espace étendu jusqu'aux dernières limites concevables*" ("the sensation of *spiritual and physical beatitude;* of *isolation;* of contemplating *something infinitely great and infinitely beautiful;* of *an intense light* that brings such felicity to *the eyes and heart that one would swoon;* and finally the sensation of *space extending to the last conceivable limits*") (*OC*, p. 1214). For Baudelaire, this empirical observation warrants some explanation. He offers two, between which he sees a necessary connection. One is based on plain common sense: if the music is eloquent enough, if the artist has succeeded in making its power of suggestion both quick and accurate, then chances are that sensitive listeners will conceive ideas related to the ones that inspired the composer (*OC*, p. 1211). Baudelaire's power of empathy is such that, listening to Wagner's music, he almost felt it to be his own.[5]

This readiness to identify with another artist is a characteristic feature of Baudelaire's sensibility. With Poe, he had the uncanny feeling that sentences that he had just thought up had actually been written by Poe twenty years earlier.[6] After reading *Madame Bovary* and *La Tentation de Saint Antoine*, he felt himself fully able to enter the "chambre secrète" of Flaubert's spirit (*OC*, pp. 656-57). The paintings of Delacroix recalled to his memory feelings and poetic thoughts that he already knew, but that he had believed doomed to remain forever buried in the night of the past (*OC*, p. 1117). Baudelaire concludes his letter to Wagner with these words: "Une fois encore, Monsieur, je vous remercie; vous m'avez rappelé à moi-même et au grand, dans de mauvaises heures" ("Once again, Sir, I thank you; you have recalled me to myself and to greatness, in wretched times") (*OC*, p. 1207). For Baudelaire, this is the hallmark of true art: it awakens within man an echo of the artist's greatness; it enables man to experience, if only for a fleeting moment, the noblest feelings and the most intense passions. Experiences of this nature constitute proof of the essential unity of mankind. If the paintings of Delacroix are seen by Baudelaire as a reminder of the greatness and native passion of universal man, Wagner's music has the same power (*OC*, pp. 1117, 1206). It stems from the universal heart of man, since true dramatic music is but "le cri ou le soupir de la passion noté et rhythmé" ("the cry or the sigh of passion written down in note and rhythm") (*OC*, p. 1217). It follows that different men, if they are endowed with a measure of sensitivity, will normally experience similar reactions when exposed to the same work of art.

These considerations lead Baudelaire to adopt Wagner's conclusion that a truly universal art must be free from any extraneous details, be they technical, political, or historical, which would be an obstacle to this similarity of reaction among the readers, the listeners, or the viewers. A truly universal art must be based on the purely human motives that govern the human heart. Wagner saw this truth and searched for the raw material of such art. He found it in the realm of legend. As examples, Baudelaire lists a number of operas: "*le Tannhäuser*, légende; le *Lohengrin*, légende; légende, le *Vaisseau fantôme*" ("*Tannhäuser*, legend; *Lohengrin*, legend; legend, *The Flying Dutchman*") (*OC*, p. 1220). No mention is made of *Tristan and Isolde* or the *Nibelungen* tetralogy, but Baudelaire was well aware of their existence and could have included them as additional illustrations.

According to Wagner, as Baudelaire quotes him, "la légende, à quelque époque et à quelque nation qu'elle appartienne, a l'avantage de comprendre exclusivement ce que cette époque et cette nation ont de purement humain . . ." ("legend, whatever the time or the nation to which it belongs, has the advantage of comprising exclusively what is purely human in this time and this nation . . .") (*OC*, p. 1221).[7] Following Wagner's example, Baudelaire makes no significant difference in his use of the words *legend* and *myth*, and he quotes Wagner's definition of myth with obvious approval:

Le mythe est le poëme primitif et anonyme du peuple, et nous le retrouvons à toutes les époques repris, remanié sans cesse à nouveau par les grands poëtes des périodes cultivées. Dans le mythe, en effet, les relations humaines dépouillent presque complètement leur forme conventionnelle et intelligible seulement à la raison abstraite; elles montrent ce que la vie a de vraiment humain, d'éternellement compréhensible, et le montrent sous cette forme concrète, exclusive de toute imitation, laquelle donne à tous les vrais mythes leur caractère individuel que vous reconnaissez au premier coup d'oeil. (OC, p. 1221)[8]

Myth is the primitive and anonymous poem of the people, and we find it taken over in every period and ceaselessly recreated by the great poets of civilized ages. In myth, human relationships almost completely lose their conventional forms, which are understandable only for abstract reason; they show what is truly human and eternally comprehensible in life, and they show it in this concrete form, exclusive of any imitation, which gives all true myths their individual character, which one recognizes at first glance.

No artist can therefore claim greatness unless his art can rival the power of the primitive and anonymous poem of the people. Great art must present the essential feature of myth: the concrete form, which does not speak to abstract reason, but which is apprehended at first glance. In ancient Greece, the deepest poems, those of Aeschylus and Sophocles, could be presented to the people with the certainty that they would be perfectly understood (OC, p. 1219). Myth has the power to throw the mind into a state akin to dream. It creates a kind of second sight, which enables the mind to discover a new concatenation of phenomena that it could not perceive in its normal state (OC, p. 1221). There is, moreover, a striking similarity between the myths of different races and nations.

Baudelaire cannot accept the simple-minded explanation according to which myths and legends born in different areas of the earth have been transmitted like seeds that a traveler brings from distant places for replanting in his own land (OC, p. 1229). The similarities that can be observed between myths of different periods or cultures lead him to a more satisfactory explanation. Baudelaire thus makes a comparison between the story of Psyche and the legend of Lohengrin. Under the evil influence of Ortrude, Elsa could not refrain from asking the fatal question: where does Lohengrin come from? what are his name and his nature? When she breaks her promise to respect his secret, he must reveal his identity and return to his miraculous homeland. Psyche also fell victim to a curiosity inspired by evil influences. When she unveiled the mystery of her divine lover, she lost her happiness forever. When Eve listened to the serpent, she fell from God's grace and was forever exiled from the Garden of Eden. Eternal Eve falls into the eternal trap. Thus a myth resembles another just as a man resembles another man. Differences are only superficial, just as the difference between a white man and a black man is only skin-deep (OC, pp. 1228-29). This holds true whether myths come from different places in space or in time.

Baudelaire is well aware that Venus, depicted by an artist who has been influenced by centuries of Christian tradition, no longer has the radiant innocence that was hers in ancient Greece. Although he does not fully account for this change, he gives the impression that he understands why it occurred and that he considers it relatively unimportant. Under the influence of a more ascetic tradition, the sexual fascination embodied by Venus came to be associated with sin (OC, p. 1219). For the austere Fathers of the Church, carnal delights were an object of horror. Ancient Greeks may have been awed by the power of Aphrodite, but her victims were to be pitied rather than blamed or castigated; nor was it expected that they should feel consumed by guilt. Such cultural differences must not overshadow a deeper similarity. Wagner's Tannhäuser is no ordinary libertine; he is universal man under the sway of the eternal and irresistible Venus (OC, p. 1225). For Baudelaire as well as for Wagner, the analogies to be found between myths originating from the four corners of the universe or from widely separated periods in history offer conclusive proof of the essential eternity and universality of man, of his permanent identity.

Baudelaire might be considered as a forerunner of the structuralist approach to the study of religion and myth exemplified by Mircea Eliade and Claude Lévi-Strauss were it not for one major difference. To put it as concisely as possible, Baudelaire is not entirely satisfied with the explanation that he himself offers. The analogies that he has observed cannot be explained solely by the identity of mental or psychological processes in men belonging to different races, different cultures, or different moments in history. To the psychological explanation derived from the comparative study of myths, Baudelaire adds a theological one: the absolute principle and the common origin of all beings, God, who created the world as a complex and indivisible totality (OC, pp. 1213, 1229). The opposing poles that Baudelaire discovers in Wagner, the nostalgia for order and the violence of passion, are linked to the deadly struggle of the flesh and the spirit, of Heaven and Hell, of God and Satan. In the overture to Tannhäuser, the conflicting orgiastic and mystic themes appear to the listener as the divided halves of his own soul (OC, p. 1224). This leap from the psychological to the theological level must be recognized, but it does not invalidate Baudelaire's essential conclusion, which can be summed up in the following terms: there is in all men a mythmaking faculty, and this faculty operates in identical fashion in all men, regardless of time and place.

This conclusion has a direct bearing on Baudelaire's theory of poetic creation, since he believes the creative process of the individual artist to be identical with the universal power through which a people creates its mythology. In every part of the world, primitive religions and poems prove that myth is indeed "un arbre qui croît partout, en tout climat, sous tout soleil, spontanément et sans boutures" ("a tree that grows everywhere, in any climate, under any sun, spontaneously and without cuttings") (*OC*, p. 1229). Like myth, authentic art is "un produit naturel, spontané" (*OC*, p. 1222). The development of the individual mind reflects on a smaller scale the history of the universal spirit. For Baudelaire, the ontogeny of the work of art reproduces the phylogeny of myth. The artist creates first; then, and only then, he reflects upon his creation in order to discover the obscure laws that govern the creative process. The same sequence obtains in the spiritual evolution of mankind: poetry came first, and its existence led to the study of its laws. In the history of civilization as in the psychological growth of the artist, art precedes criticism (*OC*, p. 1222). Baudelaire's use of the word *spontaneous*, within this context, leads one to suspect that he was influenced by the theories on the evolution of the human mind that prevailed in France during his formative years and that are most closely associated with Victor Cousin. Cousin's study of the mental process had brought him to the conclusion that the phenomenon of human consciousness is identical in all men. The unity and the identity of the human race need no other explanation. In its most primitive state, human consciousness is unable to distinguish between its constitutive elements, which are three in number. Primitive man cannot conceive his own identity, the *me*, without at the same time encountering the *not-me* which is the *me*'s boundary. Nor can he conceive the *me* and the *not-me*, which are both finite, without conceiving an infinite Being. For primitive man, the *me*, the *not-me*, and the infinite are perceived simultaneously, not separately. This perception is the result of a purely instinctive activity. It is so vivid and so rapid that it precludes any possibility of reflection or negation. It appears as pure affirmation, as the revelation of a truth, and it is accompanied by a feeling of enthusiasm. This is the phenomenon known as inspiration. The absolute affirmation of truth without reflection is experienced as having a divine origin. When man, hurried by this vivid and rapid perception of truth, attempts to express it by words, he is able to express it only by words as marvelous as the phenomenon that these words strive to render intelligible. This is why, according to Cousin, the natural language of inspiration is poetry, and sacred hymns its necessary form. Cousin uses the expression *spontaneity of reason* to designate the activity of reason anterior to reflection, the power that human reason has to seize upon truth without demanding or rendering to itself an account of it. Spontaneous and instinctive thought gives us a synthesis in which the clear and the obscure are mingled. Little by little, reflection and analysis are applied to this complex phenomenon: prose follows poetry, philosophy succeeds mythology.[9] Whatever Baudelaire may have thought of Cousin, these theories could only confirm his own views on the origin and evolution of art.[10] Since art is "un produit naturel, spontané," it may happen to be the creation of an individual, but it retains the universal intelligibility of myth and other products of spontaneous thought.

Baudelaire's understanding of the relationship between myth and art is firmly rooted in personal experiences of the kind that he describes in a fragment of *Fusées*: "Dans certains états de l'âme presque surnaturels, la profondeur de la vie se révèle tout entière dans le spectacle, si ordinaire qu'il soit, qu'on a sous les yeux. Il en devient le symbole" ("In certain almost supernatural states of the soul, the depth of life lies entirely revealed in the spectacle that one has before one's eyes, however ordinary it may be. It becomes its symbol" (*OC*, p. 1257). In experiences of this nature, objective reality appears as a self-evident representation of the structure of Being: the ordinary spectacle of reality becomes its own symbolic representation, its mythic image. This explains why, for Baudelaire, the leap from a psychological to a theological explanation of the universality of myth is so easily made. In *Mon Coeur mis à nu*, Baudelaire lists the fundamental questions that man might ask of himself:

> Où sont nos amis morts?
> Pourquoi sommes-nous ici?
> Venons-nous de quelque part?
> Qu'est-ce que la liberté?
> Peut-elle s'accorder avec la loi providentielle?
>
> > (*OC*, pp. 1275-76)

> Where are our dead friends?
> Why are we here?
> Do we come from somewhere?
> What is freedom?
> Can it be reconciled with a providential law?

He also wonders why men, as far as one can judge from their ordinary behavior, show no concern about these essential problems. Although he offers no explanation for their lack of curiosity, he seems to interpret it as an indication of human mediocrity. In his essay on Hugo, however, another explanation is suggested. When faced with the mystery of life, man does not really ask questions. He does not have to: the secret reveals itself to him. This is, I believe, what is meant by the celebrated stanza of the sonnet "Correspondances" quoted in *Richard Wagner et "Tannhäuser"*:

> La nature est un temple où de vivants piliers
> Laissent parfois sortir de confuses paroles;

L'homme y passe à travers des forêts de symboles
Qui l'observent avec des regards familiers.

Nature is a temple where from living pillars
There come at times confusing words
Man wanders through forests of symbols
Observing him with familiar eyes.

(*OC*, p. 1213).

The essay on Hugo may be read as a development of these lines. Nature presents itself to man under different and simultaneous aspects. Our mind receives from our senses vivid impressions of form and movement, light and color, sound and harmony. What Baudelaire calls "la morale des choses" ("the moral meaning of things") results from this triple impression (*OC*, p. 704). Baudelaire's terminology may make it somewhat difficult to reach a clear understanding of his thought, but his essential point is a fairly simple one: the human mind does not register the impressions made upon the senses like a neutral apparatus. Each object, as it is perceived, makes an emotional as well as a physical impact. We react to what Baudelaire calls its "physionomie," to what might be termed its *Gestalt*. We see its sadness or its sweetness, its magic or its horror. In other words, the human mind spontaneously endows the visible world with meaning.

Baudelaire thus comes quite close to what Bachelard or Sartre have defined as a psychoanalysis of things. When Bachelard and Sartre attempt to establish the objective significance of objects and their qualities, they are indeed attempting to decipher their moral meaning; they are interpreting objects and their qualities as objective representations of Being and the relationships between human reality and the type of Being thus represented. Sartre rightly notes that everything about a lemon is the lemon: the lemon is extended through each of its qualities and each of its qualities extends through the others. Our love or our hate of lemons is not an indifferent matter: we love or we hate lemons because we relate in one way or the other to the objective structure of Being embodied in lemons. Similarly, a man does not learn to hate or to like viscosity. He hates it or he likes it because the experience of viscosity is revealed to him as the possibility of a universal mode of being. This mode of being reveals Being as ambiguous, neither liquid nor solid, both resisting and accepting its absorption by itself. Viscous matter is yielding, but it is impossible to grasp. It is impossible to grasp, but one cannot get rid of it. When dealing with viscous matter, the would-be possessor becomes possessed. Viscosity is thus experienced by Sartre as a threat to human freedom, as a danger to be avoided.[11] For Baudelaire as for Sartre, the moral meaning of things is in the things themselves. For Baudelaire, the poet or the artist is the man most able to decipher these meanings, which they communicate to the reader or the viewer through their work. This type of meaning should not be confused with allegory: it must rather be identified with the indefinable impression made upon us by certain natural objects or phenomena. Sartre might well agree that the poet or the artist is the person most able to *convey* this kind of meaning, but he would probably insist that the person most able to *decipher* or to interpret it would be the critic well versed in existential psychoanalysis.

Baudelaire appears to have been well aware of this difference between the creator and the critic. In the case of Delacroix, for instance, Baudelaire notes that a painting, even when seen at a distance, exudes a magic aura. This impression is completely independent of the subject depicted. The spectator does not enjoy looking at the tortured body of a martyr or at the swooning body of a nymph because he happens to be a sadist or a lecher: he responds to the arabesque that the figures cut in space, to the harmony or the intensity of the colors (*OC*, p. 1125). This response does not take place on the intellectual level. It is a spontaneous reaction, much like Sartre's response to viscosity, and Baudelaire undoubtedly believed that such spontaneous reactions could later be intellectualized or rationalized. The essay on Wagner is indeed an effort to do just so, or, as Baudelaire puts it, to transform the initial shock of pleasure into knowledge ("transformer ma volupté en connaissance") (*OC*, p. 1215). The main difference between Baudelaire and Sartre lies elsewhere. Baudelaire may state that the moral meaning of things is to be found in the things themselves, but he is unable to accept this as a final explanation. His readiness to leap from the psychological to the theological level is quite possibly the fundamental cause of Sartre's annoyance with Baudelaire.

When Baudelaire writes that Hugo makes visible for all men "tout ce qu'il y a de divin, de sacré ou de diabolique" in any existing thing, Baudelaire implies that Hugo, in his capacity of poet, is behaving much like the primitive men who explained the extraordinary character of some nature objects as the result of a supernatural agency (*OC*, p. 704). In describing the worship of sacred stones, Mircea Eliade notes that all stones are not considered sacred. Some stones are held to be sacred only by reason of their shape, their size, or any other distinctive characteristic. Any object or phenomenon with some unusual feature may become an object or phenomenon to be worshiped or religiously avoided.[12] In the essay on Wagner, Baudelaire speaks of the "caractère sacré, divin du mythe," of the "caractère sacré, mystérieux et pourtant universellement intelligible de la légende" (*OC*, pp. 1221, 1227). Myths and legends embody attitudes and feelings experienced by primitive men faced with natural objects and phenomena that they hold sacred. These myths and legends represent

manifestations of mysterious forces to be feared or adored. The intensity of
a passion that can drive the man whom it seizes to self-destructive excesses
is seen as the work of a supernatural and evil power. *Tannhäuser,
Lohengrin,* and *The Flying Dutchman* portray individuals whose fate
cannot be explained in human terms only: Tannhäuser has been enslaved
by the satanic delights of the Venusberg, Elsa has fallen victim to the evil
sorcery of Ortrude, the Flying Dutchman's obstinate pride has delivered
him into the hands of the Devil. The true poets and artists, for Baudelaire,
are those whose works convey the same aura of supernatural magic as
myths and legends. Wagner has succeeded in doing so: his music conveys
the titantic fury of damnation as well as the ecstatic mysticity of redemption. Such art, like myth, brings man into contact with forces whose nature
escapes his intellectual understanding or his rational control. For
Baudelaire, the works of art that affect us most deeply are those in which
the depth of life reveals itself as completely as in those privileged moments
when any spectacle, however ordinary, comes to serve as its symbol. Such
spectacles take on the stature of myths, and, like myths, appear as
persuasive representations of the human condition.

Baudelaire's belief in the intimate connection between art and myth is
most convincingly illustrated in the poem "Le Cygne."[13] The ordinary
spectacle is described as a "mythe étrange et fatal," the only occasion in the
entire volume of *Les Fleurs du Mal* when Baudelaire makes use of the word
myth. In "Le Cygne," the speaker, that is the I-poet, is crossing a section of
Paris which has been marked for urban renewal by the government of the
Second Empire. The ancient buildings that occupied this area have been
razed. New palaces are being erected on the site, which is encumbered
with wooden barracks (presumably used by the working crew), blocks of
stone, columns, and debris. Standing near the Louvre, the poet is
reminded of a scene that he once saw there:

> Là s'étalait jadis une ménagerie;
> Là je vis, un matin, à l'heure où sous les cieux
> Froids et clairs le Travail s'éveille, où la voirie
> Pousse un sombre ouragan dans l'air silencieux,
>
> Un cygne qui s'était échappé de sa cage,
> Et, de ses pieds palmés frottant le pavé sec,
> Sur le sol raboteux traînait son blanc plumage.
> Près d'un ruisseau sans eau la bête ouvrant le bec
>
> Baignait nerveusement ses ailes duns la poudre,
> Et disait, le coeur plein de son beau lac natal:
> "Eau, quand donc pleuvras-tu? quand tonneras-tu, foudre?"
> Je vois ce melheureux, mythe étrange et fatal,

Vers le ciel quelquefois, comme l'homme d'Ovide,
Vers le ciel ironique et cruellement bleu,
Sur son cou convulsif tendant sa tête avide,
Comme s'il adressait des reproches à Dieu!

Long ago, on this spot, there stood a menagerie.
There, one morning, under clear and cold skies,
At the time when Labor awakens, and street cleaners
Drive their darkening storm through the silent air,

I saw a swan escaped from its cage
Rubbing its webbed feet against the dry pavement;
Its white plumage dragged on the rough ground.
Near a dried up stream the beast opened its beak

Nervously bathed its wings in the dust
And said, its heart full of its native lake:
"Rain, when will you fall? Thunder, when will you roar?"
I see this poor creature, strange and fatal myth,

Toward the sky, at times, like the man of Ovid,
Toward the ironic and cruelly blue sky
On its convulsive neck jerking its avid head
As though he were reproaching God!

If the Swan is a myth for Baudelaire, it might not be considered as such by another observer. The mythic dimension of the scene is, at least to some extent, the creation of the poet himself. This mythic dimension, however, is not wholly an arbitrary creation of the poet's imagination. Like the other characters evoked in the poem, Andromache taken captive from her native land and carried off to the kingdom of Pyrrhus or the black woman walking the streets of Paris, the Swan is a figure of exile. All have lost their homeland, all are vainly striving to regain it. The loss which they have suffered is made all the more painful by the contrast between their past life and their present condition. Andromache was the spouse of Hector; she now must share the bed of Helenus, a man who cannot stand comparison with the Trojan hero.

The fate of the black woman is no more favorable: the mud of the city and the all-embracing fog are contrasted with the absent palm trees and the lost splendor of her native Africa. In the case of the Swan, the theme of imprisonment is suggested by the cage of the menagerie from which it managed to escape, but the freedom that it has gained is only an ironic illusion. There is no water for its beak, only a dried up stream, no water for its webbed feet to tread, only the dry pavement, no lake in which to trail its wings, only the rough ground and the dust. The Swan and the women are not only figures of exile; they have also been subjected to degradation. Just as the Swan's plumage is soiled by the dirt, so is Andromache soiled by Helenus's embrace. As to the black woman, the mud of the city appear as a metaphoric representation of prostitution. This interpretation is supported by the parallel situation described in *A une Malabaraise:* prostitution is the only realistic prospect that Paris holds for the East Indian girl who dreams of the big city.

Another figure in the poem serves as a link between the Swan and the two women: the poet himself, or rather the person in the poem who speaks for him and says I. Andromache, the Swan, and the black woman exist only in the mind of this speaker. The poem begins with the words: "Andromaque, je pense à vous!" ("Andromache, I think of you!"), and the words *Je pense* recur when the other two figures are mentioned: "Je pense à mon grand cygne, avec ses gestes fous" ("I think of my great swan, with its mad gestures"), "Je pense à la négresse, amaigrie et phtisique" ("I think of the Negress, wasted and consumptive"). The speaker is their common denominator, and they may be considered as projections or manifestations of his own obsessions. The first line in the last stanza corroborates this identification: "Ainsi dans la forêt où mon esprit s'exile" ("Thus in the forest where my spirit wanders in exile"). "Le Cygne" thus appears as a clear illustration of a mythic pattern: the Fall. There is, however, a significant difference between the figures who appear in the poem and more traditional victims of the Fall. When Icarus dared fly too near to the sun, he fell into the sea and drowned. Bellerophon attempted to fly to heaven on Pegasus, but Zeus caused the horse to throw its rider. Phaëthon proved unequal to the task of driving the Sun's chariot: Zeus hurled a thunderbolt at the presumptuous youth, who fell to earth. Ixion made bold to seduce Hera. As a punishment, in the underworld, he was bound to an ever-turning wheel. Adam and Eve were driven out of Eden. Satan and the rebel Angels were cast into Hell. Ahriman suffered a similar fate when he attempted to conquer Heaven. Adam and Eve, Satan and Ahriman, Icarus and Bellerophon, Phaëthon and Ixion did of course deserve their punishment: all were guilty of presumptuousness, pride, or disobedience. Andromache, the black woman, the Swan (and, presumably, the poet) are presented as innocent victims. If anyone is guilty, it must be the cruel and ironic God who allowed them to be driven into exile, degradation, and despair. The Swan is clearly related to that other winged creature which appears in *Les Fleurs du Mal,* the Albatross captured and tormented by sadistic sailors:

> Le Poëte est semblable au prince des nuées
> Qui hante la tempête et se rit de l'archer;
> Exilé sur le sol au milieu des huées,
> Ses ailes de géant l'empêchent de marcher.

> The Poet is like the Prince of the clouds
> Who haunts the tempest and laughs at the archer;
> Exiled on earth amid the mocking flouts,
> He cannot walk for his giant wings.

The Swan is also like that winged Angel so suddenly trapped in the depths of Hell who appears in another poem, "L'Irrémédiable," a title that might well be translated by the words *Beyond redress*. The reader's attention is thus directed to another significant element of the scene described in "Le Cygne": its location.

"Le Cygne" is the fourth poem in the second section of *Les Fleurs du mal, Tableaux parisiens*. Baudelaire was well aware of the changing nature of Paris during the nineteenth century. He was among the first to recognize that the industrial revolution had created a new environment, the modern metropolis. The City, deprived as it is of all saving water by a cruelly blue sky, which carries its irony so far as to create the illusion of a storm through a cloud of dust, becomes a modern equivalent of Hell. The Swan is indeed a "myth étrange et fatal." It appears to Baudelaire as a paradigmatic representation of the human condition as he describes it in these lines from *Mon Coeur mis à nu:*

> La théologie.
> Qu'est-que la chute?
> Si c'est l'unité devenue dualité, c'est Dieu qui a chuté.
> En d'autres termes, la création ne serait-elle pas la chute
>   de Dieu?
>
> (OC, p. 1283)

> Theology.
> What is the fall?
> If it means unity changed into duality, it is God who fell.
> In other words, would not creation be the fall of God?

If God is considered as the primordial, perfect, and infinite essence that created an imperfect and finite world and made man an imperfect and finite creature without depriving him of his nostalgic desire for the original perfection, then creation was indeed the fall of God, and man the blameless victim of this fall. In his exile, man is condemned to seek forever, but in vain, the original perfection of which he retains the gnawing memory.

One point remains to be considered: the strange behavior of the Swan, Andromache, and the black woman. How does this behavior relate to the poet's activity as a mythmaker? In his *Interpretation of Dreams*, Freud establishes an important distinction between the latent motivation of the dream and its manifest content. The motivation that informs the dream imagery is an instinctive drive, a manifestation of the universal Eros. The manifest content of the dream imagery is conditioned by the dreamer's first mental representations, by his most elementary experiences. At the earliest level of development, the inner needs of the baby create a state of painful excitement. The pain disappears when the need is satisfied:

> The hungry child cries or struggles helplessly. But its situation remains unchanged; for the excitation proceeding from the inner need has not the character of a momentary impact, but of a continuing pressure. A change can occur only if, in some way (in the case of the child by external assistance), there is an *experience of satisfaction,* which puts an end to the internal excitation. An essential constituent of this experience is the appearance of a certain percept (of food in our example), the memory-image of which is henceforth associated with the memory-trace of the excitation arising from the need. Thanks to the established connection, there results, at the next occurrence of this need, a psychic impulse which seeks to revive the memory-image of the former percept, and to re-evoke the former percept itself; that is, it actually seeks to re-establish the situation of the first satisfaction. Such an impulse is what we call a wish; the reappearance of the perception constitutes the wish-fulfillment, and the full cathexis of the perception, by the excitation springing from the need, constitutes the shortest path to the wish-fulfillment. We may assume a primitive state of the psychic apparatus in which this path is actually followed, i.e., in which the wish ends in hallucination. [14]

The human psyche is conditioned by such experiences. Infantile hal-lucinatory images are obviously far simpler than the complex dream imagery of adult life. The original hallucinations are modified by a quantity of analogous sensory images experienced at later times and their memory-traces distort the ones left by the infantile experiences. Through the effect of repression and censorship, a process of condensation and displacement takes place. It causes the original memory-images, already intensified and distorted by the infantile hallucinatory process, to become completely unrecognizable. A trained psychoanalyst is required to decipher the original desire hidden under the imagery of the dream. For Freud, the symbolic imagery of the dream is essentially rooted in the individual's experience. For Jung, the dream images are conditioned by preexisting structures of the human psyche, the archetypes. Hence the recurrent images to be found in myth and folklore as well as in the dreams, visions, and delusions of modern individuals entirely ignorant of all such traditions. Physiology may provide a possible scientific justification for Jung's theories. Some archetypes may be related to the centrencephalic system. Reflexology could support a similar view. The archetypes would be linked to physiological experiences common to all small children: sucking and swallowing, standing and falling, sexual excitement and the release of sexual tension. [15]

In many respects, Baudelaire appears as a forerunner of Freud and Jung. For Baudelaire, the creative energy of genius originates in the depths of the "moi sauvage," the wild self, that is, at the level of the unconscious drives. Any work of art worthy of the name must to some extent be dependent upon the obsessions that haunt the artist's dreams. Baudelaire repeatedly asserts that authentic art is the fatal product of the artist's deepest individuality, that it brings to light the innermost recesses of his soul. This is why the rules that govern the creative process are not and cannot be deliberately chosen by the artist: they escape the control of his conscious will. This is also why the creative imagination obeys identical laws in all men. Baudelaire believes that there are, in any work of art, two separate and distinct elements: one is circumstantial and transitory; the other is eternal and unchangeable. The transitory and circumstantial element is the mark left upon the work of art by such factors as personal experiences, the physical and social environment, the historical conjuncture, or the cultural tradition. The eternal, unchangeable element, the "pure idea," corresponds to the archetypal image. [16]

The preceding considerations suggest another level of relationships between the Swan, Andromache, the black woman, and the poet in whose mind they come to exist. Andromache is acting somewhat like the hungry baby who hallucinates its mother's breast and dreams that it is sucking the nipple. She stands near the stream that had been landscaped for her near Buthrote, the capital of Pyrrhus, an imitation of the Trojan stream Simoïs. This "Simoïs menteur" creates for her the illusion of her homeland. Lost in ecstasy, she leans over an empty tomb in the belief that she is communing with her dead husband. She has lost all contact with her real situation, at least for the moment. The Swan, however, has not reached the stage where a full hallucinatory cathexis of the perceptive system actually overcomes reality. Its need is not satisfied through a complete hallucination: it endures in spite of its mad gestures, which appear as desperate efforts to re-create the hallucinatory percept of its native lake. As to the black woman, her haggard eyes seek "les cocotiers absents de la superbe Afrique / Derrière la muraille immense du brouillard" ("the absent palmtrees of superb Africa / Behind the immense rampart of the fog"). She also seems to be trying to see what is not there as she strains toward a hallucinatory image, but in a more passive way than the Swan. Whatever his creatures are doing, we may infer that, as surrogates of the poet, they reflect what he is doing himself. He says as much in this stanza:

Paris change! mais rien dans ma mélancolie
N'a bougé! palais neufs, échafaudages, blocs,
Vieux faubourgs, tout pour moi devient allégorie,
Et mes chers souvenirs sont plus lourds que des rocs.

Paris changes! but nothing, in my melancholy,
Has budged! new palaces, scaffoldings, stone blocks,
Ancient neighborhoods, for me, everything is but a shadow,
And my treasured memories are heavier than rocks.

The speaker has managed to reach the point where his experience of reality is wavering, where the world of actual experience is fading away and the lost world of the past reasserts itself. The entire poem may thus be considered not only as a symbol of the depth of life, as a paradigm of the human condition as it is lived by the poet, but also as a representation of the various stages in the poet's strategy for dealing with it, from the impulse to overcome the loss of the past typified by the black woman to the fleeting success achieved by Andromache. For her, the "Simoïs menteur" has become, as Cocteau might have expressed it, "a lie that tells the truth."

For Baudelaire, poetry may thus be considered as similar in nature to a cathexis capable of producing hallucinatory images. Its deep purpose is to give man a total victory over the limitations of space and time, over the reality of suffering and death. When it occurs, this victory remains illusory and transient. Andromache's ecstasy does not alter the fact that she is communing with an empty tomb, not with Hector. She is like the buffoon whom Baudelaire describes in the prose poem "Une Mort héroïque" (*A Heroic Death*). The buffoon has been sentenced to death for his part in a plot against the king, but he has been granted a reprieve so that he can give a farewell performance prior to his execution. What he performs is apparently a pantomime, which Baudelaire characterizes as one of "ces drames féeriques dont l'objet est de représenter symboliquement le mystère de la vie." ("these fairyland dramas whose object is to offer a symbolic representation of the mystery of life") (*OC*, p. 271). On the stage, completely lost in the magic world of make-believe, the buffoon is a living proof that "l'ivresse de l'Art est plus apte que toute autre à voiler les terreurs du gouffre; que le génie peut jouer la comédie au bord de la tombe avec une joie qui l'empêche de voir la tombe, perdu, comme il est, dans un paradis excluant toute idée de tombe et de destruction." ("the intoxication of Art is more apt than any other to hide the terrors of the abyss; that genius can play a comedy on the very brink of the grave with the joy that prevents it from seeing the grave, lost as it is in the paradise that excludes any idea of the grave and destruction") (*OC*, p. 271). The king, however, has the final word: he orders one of his pages to hiss the performance. Awakened from his dream by the derisive whistle of the page, the buffoon drops dead. Like

the buffoon, the Swan is mad, ridiculous, and sublime. The artist is mad
and ridiculous, because he is bound to fail. Reality is an absolute monarch
against whose authority it is impossible to revolt. The artist is also sublime:
he bears witness to an injustice from which there is no redress. He gives
voice to a frustration for which there is no cure. Art bears witness to the
human claim, forever doomed to be denied, to a lost paradise: "Tout poëte
lyrique, en vertu de sa nature, opère fatalement un retour vers l'Eden
perdu." ("Every lyric poet, by virtue of his nature, returns fatally to the lost
Eden") (OC, p. 737). This is the lost Eden where, in contrast with the world
in which we live, action was sister to the dream, where desire and reality
were one. It is the magic *illud tempus* of *Märchen* and myth.

Baudelaire's claim to greatness may well lie in his ever-renewed attempt
to achieve a goal similar to that of myth, to overcome an impossible
contradiction, to accomplish the reconciliation of irreconcilable poles.
Faced with an unacceptable reality, the artist seeks through his art to
recapture the lost Eden. He realizes that his efforts are doomed to fail, but
he cannot submit passively to his fate. Andromache may believe in her
vision, but the poet is fully aware of its illusory nature. He knows that the
buffoon, at the height of his performance, remains at the mercy of his
master's whim. The realm of art within which "Tout n'est qu'ordre et
beauté, / Luxe, calme et volupté" (Everything is order and beauty, /
Luxury, peace, and sensuous delight") (OC, pp. 51-52) is only a symbolic
denial of the reality that the artist cannot accept, but from which no real
escape is possible. It does not follow that art must be reduced to mere
wish-fulfillment. "Le Cygne" goes beyond escapism: its denunciation of
reality as essentially evil is simply the only positive act that the poet can
possibly make. The artist's activity must be viewed as the direct result of his
perception of human fate. As a response to this perception, it must appear
at least as reasoned and logical as the ritual behavior commonly found in
certain cultures under circumstances that they consider critical. If a solar
eclipse appears as a threat to the cosmic order, no human action can
actually prevent the eclipse from taking place. Since shouts and noises
can frighten away dangerous animals, it is not unreasonable to hope that
they may have some similar effect against the darkness that threatens
the sun. The poem is equally powerless to bridge the gap between what
is and what should be, but, like the ritual shouts and noises described
by Lévi-Strauss, it points to the existence of this break and it acts, at
least metaphorically, toward its correction.[17]

NOTES

1. Gilbert Durand, *Le Décor mythique de La Chartreuse de Parme* (Paris: Corti, 1961), p. 239.

2. René Galand, *Baudelaire: poétiques et poésie* (Paris: Nizet, 1969), pp. 248-460.

3. "Richard Wagner et *Tannhäuser* à Paris," *Oeuvres complètes* (Paris: Bibliothèque de la Pléïade, 1961), pp. 1208-44, © Editions Gallimard. References to this edition are indicated within the text by the letters *OC*.

4. See Margaret Gilman, *Baudelaire the Critic* (New York: Columbia University Press, 1944), pp. 178-84. Wagner's concerts were given at the Théâtre-Italien on January 25, February 1, and February 8, 1860. The program included fragments from *The Flying Dutchman, Tannhäuser,* and *Lohengrin.* The first performance of *Tannhäuser* at the Paris *Opéra* occurred on March 13, 1861. The English translation of *Oper und Drama* mentioned by Baudelaire has not been identified. Judging from his essay, Baudelaire seems chiefly to have used Liszt's *Lohengrin et Tannhäuser,* which had been published in 1851, in addition to Wagner's *Letter to Berlioz* and *Lettre sur la Musique* (Lettre sur la Musique, à M. F. Villot, traduite par M. Challemel-Lacour, en tête des *Quatre poëmes d'opéra* traduits en prose française, Paris: Librairie nouvelle, 1860). The German version of these two texts is included in Wagner's *Gesammelte Schriften und Dichtungen* (Leipzig: E. W. Fritzsch, 1898), 7:82-86, under the titles: "Ein Brief an Hector Berlioz," and "Zukunftsmusik. An einen französischen Freund (Fr. Villot), als Vorwort zu einer Prosa-Übersetzung meiner Operndichtungen" (pp. 87-137). Quotations from Baudelaire are given in the original French, followed by the English translation. Whenever Baudelaire is quoting Wagner, the German text is given in the appropriate footnote. All English translations are my own.

5. This admission does not appear in Baudelaire's essay on Wagner, but in a letter that he wrote to the artist one year earlier, on February 17, 1860 (*OC*, pp. 1205-7).

6. Baudelaire, *Correspondance générale* (Paris: Conard, 1948), 4:277.

7. "Die Sage, in welche Zeit und welche Nation sie auch fällt, hat den Vorzug, von dieser Zeit und dieser Nation nur den rein menschlichen Inhalt aufzufassen[und diesen Inhalt in einer nur ihr eigenthümlichen, äusserst prägnanten und desshalb schnell verständlichen Form zu geben]." (Wagner, "Zukunftsmusik," *Gesammelte Schriften und Dichtungen* [Leipzig: E. W. Fritsch, 1898], 7:120-21).

8. "[Als den idealen Stoff des Dichters glaubte ich daher] den 'Mythos' bezeichnen zu müssen, dieses ursprünglich namenlos entstandene Gedicht des Volkes, das wir zu allen Zeiten von den grossen Dichter der vollendeten Kulturperioden immer wieder neu behandelt antreffen; denn bei ihm verschwindet die konventionnelle, nur der abstrakten Vernunft erklärliche Form der menschlichen Verhältnisse fast vollständig, um dafür nur das ewig Verständliche, rein Menschliche, aber eben in der unnachahmlichen konkreten Form zu zeigen, welche jedem ächten Mythos seine so schnell erkenntliche individuelle Gestalt verleiht." (Wagner, "Zukunftsmusik," *Gesammelte Schriften und Dichtunger* [Leipzig: E. W. Fritzsch, 1898], 7:104-5).

9. Victor Cousin, *Course of the History of Modern Philosophy*, 2 vols. (New York: D. Appleton and Co., 1854), 1(126-41. (An English translation of Cousin's celebrated *Cours de 1828*.)

10. Baudelaire had but little respect for Cousin, either as a thinker or as a man (*OC*, pp. 683, 798).

11. Jean-Paul Sartre, *L'Être et le néant* (Paris: Gallimard, 1943), pp. 690-708.

12. Mircea Eliade, *Traité d'histoire des religions* (Paris: Payot, 1964), p. 25.

13. The complete text of the poem is given here, followed by my own English translation.

LE CYGNE

I

Andromaque, je pense à vous! Ce petit fleuve,
Pauvre et triste miroir où jadis resplendit
L'immense majesté de vos douleurs de veuve,
Ce Simöis menteur qui par vos pleurs grandit,

A fécondé soudain ma mémoire fertile,
Comme je traversais le nouveau Carrousel.
Le vieux Paris n'est plus (la forme d'une ville
Change plus vite, hélas! que le coeur d'un mortel);

Je ne vois qu'en esprit tout ce camp de báraques,
Ces tas de chapiteaux ébauchés et de fûts,
Les herbes, les gros blocs verdis par l'eau des flaques,
Et, brillant aux carreaux, le bric-à-brac confus.

Là s'étalait jadis une ménagerie;
Là je vis, un matin, à l'heure où sous les cieux
Froids et clairs le Travail s'éveille, où la voirie
Pousse un sombre ouragan dans l'air silencieux,

Un cygne qui s'était évadé de sa cage,
Et, de ses pieds palmés frottant le pavé sec,
Sur le sol raboteux traînait son blanc plumage.
Près d'un ruisseau sans eau le bête ouvrant le bec

Baignait nerveusement ses ailes dans la poudre,
Et disait, le coeur plein de son beau lac natal:
"Eau, quand donc pleuvras-tu? quand tonneras-tu, foudre?"
Je vois ce malheurex, mythe étrange et fatal,

Vers le ciel quelquefois, comme l'homme d'Ovide,
Vers le ciel ironique et cruellement bleu,
Sur son cou convulsif tendant sa tête avide,
Comme s'il adressait das reproches à Dieu!

II

Paris change! mais rien dans me mélancolie
N'a bougé! palais neufs, échafaudages, blocs,
Vieux faubourgs, tout pour moi devient allégorie,
Et mes chers souvenirs sont plus lourds que des rocs.

Aussi devant ce Louvre une image m'opprime:
Je pense à mon grand cygne, avec ses gestes fous,
Comme les exilés, ridicule et sublime,
Et rongé d'un désir sans trêve! et puis à vous,

Andromaque, des bras d'un grand époux tombée,
Vil bétail, sous la main du superbe Pyrrhus,
Auprès d'un tombeau vide en extase courbée;
Veuve d'Hector, hélas! et femme d'Hélénus!

Je pense à la négresse, amaigrie et phtisique,
Piétinant dans la boue, et cherchant, l'oeil hagard,

Les cocotiers absents de la superbe Afrique
Derrière la muraille immense du brouillard;

A quiconque a perdu ce qui ne se retrouve
Jamais, jamais! à ceux qui s'abreuvent de pleurs
Et tettent la Douleur comme une bonne louve!
Aux maigres orphelins séchant comme des fleurs!

Ainsi dans la forêt où mon esprit s'exile
Un vieux Souvenir sonne à plein souffle du cor!
Je pense aux matelots oubliés dans une île,
Aux captifs, aux vaincus! . . . à bien d'autres encor!

THE SWAN

Andromache, I think of you! this narrow stream,
Poor and pitiful mirror which once reflected
The immense majesty of your widow's sorrow,
This lying Simoïs swollen by your tears,

Suddenly stirred my fertile memory,
As I was crossing the new Carrousel.
The Paris of old is no more (the shape of a city
Changes more quickly, alas! than the heart of mortal man);

I see only in my mind's eye all these rows of barracks,
These piles of rough-hewn capitals and columns,
The weeds, the heavy blocks greenish from water puddles,
And, glittering behind window-panes, a jumble of bric-a-brac.

Long ago, on this spot, there stood a menagerie.
There, one morning, under clear and cold skies,
At the time when Labor awakens, and street cleaners
Drive their darkening storm through the silent air,

I saw a swan escaped from its cage
Rubbing its webbed feet against the dry pavement;
Its white plumage dragged on the rough ground.
Near a dried-up stream the beast opened its beak

Nervously bathed its wings in the dust
And said, its heart full of its native lake:
"Rain, when will you fall? Thunder, when will you roar?"
I see this poor creature, strange and fatal myth,

Toward the sky, at times, like the man of Ovid,
Toward the ironic and cruelly blue sky
On its convulsive neck jerking its avid head
As though it were reproaching God!

II

Paris changes! but nothing, in my melancholy,
Has budged! new palaces, scaffoldings, stone blocks,
Ancient neighborhoods, for me, everything is but a shadow,
And my treasured memories are heavier than rocks.

Thus in front of the Louvre an image weighs upon me:
I think of my great swan, with its mad gestures,
Like exiles, ridiculous and sublime,
Tormented by a relentless desire! I think of you,

Andromache, fallen from a hero's arms,
Lowly chattel, under proud Pyrrhus' hand,
Lost in your ecstasy besides an empty tomb,
Hector's widow, alas! and wife to Helenus!

I think of the Negress, wasted and consumptive,
Treading the city's mud, and seeking with her haggard eyes,
The absent palm trees of superb Africa
Behind the immense rampart of the fog.

I think of all who lost what never can be found
Again, not ever! of those whose only drink is their tears,
Suckled by Grief as by a kindly she-wolf!
Of famished orphans withering away like flowers!

Thus in the forest where my spirit wanders in exile
An ancient Memory blows away at its horn!
I think of sailors forsaken on some island,
Of the captives, the vanquished! . . . of so many others!

14. *The Basic Writings of Sigmund Freud* (New York: Random House, Inc., 1938), p. 509.

15. Carl-Gustav Jung, *The Psychogenesis of Mental Diseases* (New York: Pantheon Books, Bollingen Series 20, 1960), p. 254; Gilbert Durand, *Les Structures anthropologiques de l'imaginaire* (Paris: Presses universitaires de France, 1963), pp. 39-56.

16. These considerations represent a brief summary of two previous publications dealing with Baudelaire's views on the unconscious and creative imagination: René Galand, "Baudelaire's Formulary of the True Aesthetics," in *Baudelaire as a Love-Poet and Other Essays*, edited by Lois B. Hyslop (University Park and London: The Pennsylvania State University Press, 1969), pp. 41-64, and "La Vision de l'Inconscient chez Baudelaire," *Symposium* (Spring 1972), pp. 15-23. The emphasis that Baudelaire places upon the unconscious sources of art does not in any way contradict his belief in the essential role of the artist as a conscious and dedicated practitioner of his craft. One fundamental purpose of the work of art is to bring the artist's dream to life. To accomplish this goal, the artist must be in total command of his medium, the complete master of his trade. A few quotations will suffice to illustrate Baudelaire's insistence in this respect: "Delacroix part donc de ce principe, qu'un tableau doit avant tout reproduire la pensée intime de l'artiste . . . il est important que la main rencontre, quand elle se met à la besogne, le moins d'obstacles possible, et accomplisse avec une rapidité servile les ordres divins du cerveau: autrement l'idéal s'envole." ("Delacroix starts from this principle, that a painting must first of all reproduce the intimate thought of the artist. . . . It is essential that the hand, when it starts its work, should encounter as few obstacles as possible, and that it accomplishes with slavish rapidity the divine orders of the mind: otherwise the ideal flies away") (*OC*, p. 891). "Si une exécution très-nette est nécessaire, c'est pour que le rêve soit trè-nettement traduit; qu'elle soit très-rapide, c'est pour que rien ne se perde de l'impression extraordinaire qui accompagnait la conception; que l'attention de l'artiste so porte même sur la propreté matérielle des outils, cela se conçoit sans peine, toutes les précautions devant être prises pour rendre l'exécution agile et décisive." ("If the most precise execution is required, it is in order that the dream be translated with the

utmost precision; if it must be very rapid, it is in order that nothing be lost of the extraordinary impression which accompanied its conception; it is easy to understand why the artist must pay attention even to the material cleanliness of his tools, since every precaution must be taken to make execution prompt and decisive") (*OC*, p. 1120). "Un bon tableau, fidèle et égal au rêve qui l'a enfanté, doit être produit comme un monde. De même que la création telle que nous la voyons est le résultat de plusieurs créations dont les précédentes sont toujours complétées par la suivante, ainsi un tableau, conduit harmonieusement, consiste en une série de tableaux superposés, chaque nouvelle couche donnant au rêve plus de réalité et le faisant monter d'un degré vers la perfection." ("A good painting, faithful and equal to the dream that gave it birth, must be created like a world. Just as creation as we see it is the result of several creations in which the preceding ones are always completed by the one that follows, thus a painting, harmoniously conducted, consists in a series of paintings superimposed upon one another, each new layer endowing the dream with greater reality and bringing it one degree closer to perfection") (*OC*, p. 1121). "Tout poëte, qui ne sait pas au juste combien chaque mot comporte de rimes, est incapable d'exprimer une idée quelconque. . . ." ("Any poet who does not know exactly how many rhymes there are for each word of the language, is unable to express any kind of idea . . .") (*OC*, p. 186). "Il ajouta *que l'écrivain qui ne savait pas tout dire,* celui qu'une idée si étrange, si subtile qu'on la supposât, si imprévue, tombant comme une pierre de la lune, *prenait au dépourvu et sans matériel pour lui donner corps, n'était pas un écrivain.*' " ("He added *'that a writer who did not know how to express everything,* and whom any idea, however strange or subtle one might suppose it to be, however unexpected, falling like a stone from the moon, *would catch unawares and without the necessary material to give it substance, was no writer'* ") (OC, p. 680).

    17. Claude Lévi-Strauss, *Le Cru et le cuit* (Paris: Plon, 1964), pp. 343-44.

SUGGESTED READINGS

Bachelard, Gaston. *L'Air et les songes.* Paris: Corti, 1943.

————. *L'Eau et les rêves.* Paris: Corti, 1942.

————. *La Psychoanalyse du feu.* Paris: Gallimard, 1938.

————. *La Terre et les rêveries de la volonté.* Paris: Corti, 1948.

————. *La Terre et les rêveries du repos.* Paris: Corti. 1948.

Caillois, Roger. *Man and the Sacred.* Glencoe: Free Press, 1960.

————. *Man, Play, and Games.* Glencoe: Free Press, 1961.

Durand, Gilbert. *Le Décor mythique de La Chartreuse de Parme.* Paris: Corti, 1961.

————. *Les Structures anthropologiques de l'imaginaire.* Paris: Presses universitaires de France, 1963.

Eliade, Mircea. *Mythes, rêves et mystères.* Paris: Gallimard, 1957.

————. *Traité d'histoire des religions.* Paris: Payot, 1964.

Huyghe, René. *Dialogue avec le visible.* Paris: Flammarion, 1955.

————. *L'Art et l'âme.* Paris: Flammarion, 1960.

Jung, Carl-Gustav. *Gestaltungen des Unbewussten,* mit einem Beitrag von Aniela Jaffe. Zurich: Rascher 1950.

Lévi-Strauss, Claude. *Mythologiques.* 4 vols. Paris: Plon, 1964-71.

————. *Structural Anthropology.* New York and London: Basic Books, Inc, 1963.

Biographical Note on Lawrence Abler

After earning his B.A. and M.A. degrees at the University of Wisconsin, Lawrence Abler spent a year at the University of Zurich, Switzerland, on a Lafrentz Fellowship in Germanistics. He received his Ph.D. in comparative literature at Occidental College, Los Angeles, in 1958, where he had a Ford Foundation Fellowship. After graduation he taught at Northern Arizona College, Occidental, and Juniata; since 1968 he has taught at Susquehanna University, where he has been chairman of the Department of English.

He served as an editor-translator, Department of the Army, in Frankfurt, Germany, during 1950-51. He has published translations of Rilke's poetry and is preparing a translation of Kleist's *Der zerbrochene Krug*.

From Angel to Orpheus: Mythopoesis in the Late Rilke

LAWRENCE ABLER

In 1923, the year following publication of *Ulysses*, T. S. Eliot praised the effectiveness of Joyce's use of Homeric myth as a narrative structure. "In using the myth," he wrote, "in manipulating a continuous parallel between contemporaneity and antiquity, Mr. Joyce is pursuing a method which others must pursue after him. . . . It is simply a way of controlling, of ordering, of giving shape and significance to the immense panorama of futility and anarchy which is contemporary history. . . . It is, I seriously believe, a step toward making the modern world possible for art." Joyce's method is seen as having "the importance of a scientific discovery."[1]

In the realm of poetry, mythical modes are hardly revolutionary, since they have always offered ready-to-hand allusions, organizing metaphors, or literary ornamentation. Eliot's own *The Waste Land* (also published in 1922) illustrates the advantages of using mythical structures in a longer poem. Mythical modes can fulfill Eliot's intentions for poetry as well as for the novel, for poetry tends to be less linear than narrative, and is more amenable to nondiscursive thought and language. Twentieth-century chaos could then find a parallel in the primordial chaos out of which the poets of antiquity ordered the world, in symbolic groupings of transformations that make up the fund of mythical tradition. "Such groupings of symbols," writes George Whalley, "set up resonances with which to embody a comprehensive view of reality. The relations which induce the resonance are not explicit and logical, but dialectical and in the order of Poetic."[2] The world of myth is "populated" with heroes, demigods, and gods, whose relations to nature are elemental and mysterious; their stories involve change and metamorphosis; further, as Wheelwright notes, such patterns involve physical/moral parallels: nature is a "rhythmically pulsating nature, in which moral finalities, like physical ones, undergo seasonal alteration."[3]

197

THE EARLY WORK: *STUNDENBUCH* AND THE MALTE NOTEBOOKS

The poetry of Rainer Maria Rilke (1875-1926), the subject of this study, was not at first consciously linked to myth traditions, which, as an heir of the Romantic temper, he might well have absorbed. The Romantic Age had represented a great upsurge of interest in protohistorical materials, to which research in the folktale, such as that of the Brothers Grimm, gave impetus. Although Rilke's earliest poetry was self-consciously anti-Philistine and somewhat precious, some awareness of mythical perspectives is shown in his treatment of the familiar landmarks of his Prague birthplace, which achieve a "larean" value similar to the Roman household gods, possessing energies of their own from long use and traditional respect. Although Rilke abandoned the sentimental religiosity of his Roman Catholic boyhood fairly early, the iconography of Christianity, embodied in poems about saints, angels, and madonnas, persists to the end of his career, in his own "groupings of symbols." This circumstance misled many readers and critics of his works to attribute to him an orthodox, "confessional" commitment, which Rilke sought to dispel. The images that characterized the youthful poet's work were often revivified and transfigured into contemporary contexts in later poems.

By temperament, Rilke needed the anchor of a viable metaphysics. While he had lost his belief in a deity, he realized the necessity of positing the dimension of the infinite; when an active faith is lacking, then an infinity must be created. "Wir brauchen die Ewigkeit, denn nur sie gibt unseren Gesten Raum; und doch wissen wir uns in enger Endlichkeit. Wir müssen also innerhalb dieser Schranken eine Unendlichkeit schaffen, da wir an die Grenzenlosigkeit nicht mehr glauben" ("We need eternity, for only it furnishes room for our gestures. Still we find ourselves in narrow finitude. Therefore, within these confines we have to create an infinity, since we no longer believe in the limitless"). With such remarks, Rilke evidently concurs with Nietzsche's clean-sweep assumptions about the death of God. In effect, a return must be made to primitive states, which make possible the new orderings brought about by new myths. Thus, he continues, "Wir sind nicht mehr Naive; aber wir müssen uns befehlen, primitiv zu werden, damit wir bei jenen beginnen können, dies von Herzen waren" ("we are no longer naive ones; but we must command ourselves to become primitive, so that we may be able to begin with those who were so naturally").[4] These journal entries prefigure the development of an aesthetic rooted in basic existence, the cultivation of nondiscursive, evocative, often paradoxical language, the investing of old deity-groups with new, highly idiosyncratic symbolisms: in short, a new mythical creation. Like Nietzsche, Rilke becomes the "begetter of new gods, . . . and a world wholly created by the creator-poet."[5]

To become primitive again presupposes shifts in the time-sense and in the consciousness of man's relations to phenomena. The evocation is not to some remote past, but to the time "behind" all histories; phenomena, the "givens," must be seen anew, in an essentially innocent way. Despite progress, Rilke felt, man had not progressed very much in his "true relations" to others, to objects in the world, to the Cosmos itself. "Doch nun ist die Welt noch nicht über den zweiten Tag hinaus" ("But really the world has not yet come beyond the Second Day"), he once wrote.[6]

For the poet, the new beginnings have to do with transvaluations in the quality of his vision, which asserts the autonomy of the beholder's worldview. "Nichts war noch vollendet, eh ich es erschaut,/ein jedes Werden stand still" ("Nothing was as yet complete before I contemplated it,/and every becoming stood still"), declares the young monk of the *Stundenbuch (Book of Hours)*.[7] There is a basic trust in objects, an entering "into the confidence of" all phenomena. "Ich fing mit den *Dingen* an," Rilke wrote, "die die eigentlichen Vertrauten meiner einsamen Kindheit gewesen sind. . . ." ("I began with *things,* which were the only confidants of my lonely childhood . . .").[8] The phenomena of experience fall under the general rubric of *Dinge,* "things"; the poet seeks to penetrate these objects, not so much to analyze their structure as to discern their intrinsic nature, their "Wesen," their essence, the qualities of their "thing-ness," as if despite Kant's assertion that it was not possible, to realize "das Ding-an-sich" ("the thing in itself"). A Gestalt-aesthetic gradually emerges, which subsumes physical law, modeling, form, surface, and context. "Things" have self-possession, they rest in equilibrium, they have the quality of autonomy. Their "beauty" consists not only in their pleasing form, but also in their impression of having developed from within, and in their "endurance," both qualities more important than mere association. Tranquillity, "resting patiently in gravity," is characteristic of them:

> Wenn etwas mir vom Fenster fällt
> (Und wenn es auch das Kleinste wäre)
> wie stürzt sich das Gesetz der Schwere
> gewaltig wie ein Wind vom Meere
> auf jeden Ball und jede Beere
> und trägt sie in den Kern der Welt.

(320)

> When something falls from a window
> (and even if it were the smallest thing)

> how gravity's law powerfully seizes
> upon it, like a wind from the sea—
> on every ball and every berry
> and carries it to the center of the world.

This "Schwere," "heaviness," or "gravity" achieves a multiple meaning in Rilke's usages, when, in addition to the physical property, the word is considered in a moral sense, as in the Stoic signification of *gravitas*, seriousness; later still, the word will be used in its connotation of "that which is difficult," or in the compound "Schwer-nehmen" "to take life hard," in a slightly pessimistic way. The "gravity" that objects have is what the monk of the *Stundenbuch* believes man lacks: "Eins muß er wieder können: fallen/geduldig in der Schwere ruhn" (321) ("One thing he must know again: to fall,/to rest patiently in gravity").

The poem-cycle of the *Stundenbuch* represents the ruminations and prayers of an Orthodox monk attempting through his craft, which is icon-painting, to capture the lineaments of God on the altar screen that separates the nave from the sanctuary in Orthodox churches. This altar screen comes to signify the gulf between man and God, but also the visual world behind which God obscures Himself. Thus, even though invisible ("dark"), God is manifested in the creation, which embodies His profound conceptions: "Du bist der Dinge tiefer Inbegriff,/der seines Wesens letztes Wort verschweigt" (327) ("You are the profound essence of things,/which keeps the last word of its nature secret").

Deity itself has the qualities of the "things" the young monk gathers as "proofs" for God's presence, however dim His outlines may be. In cataloguing the individual components of the phenomenal world, the supplicant is in effect defining his own nature, by a consciousness of difference to be sure, but also by an acute self-consciousness about his part (and man's generally) in defining the Godhead. Further, the realization enters that man himself has a hand in the building up of God, who is still in the process of "becoming," incomplete. Were He not still "becoming," He would lose all vitality, and remain "clamped up in churches": "Und keine Kirchen, welche Gott umklammern / wie eine Flüchtling und ihn dann bejammern/wie ein gefangenes und wundes Tier" (329) ("And no churches to clamp God inside like a fugitive and then bewail Him/like a captive, wounded animal"). But inconsistently, Rilke used the metaphor of cathedral building to symbolize "building at" the edifice of God: "Wir bauen an dir mit zitternden Händen . . ./Aber wer kann dich vollenden,/du Dom" (261) ("We work at you with trembling hands . . . /But who can complete you,/you cathedral?")

Werkleute sind wir: Knappen, Jünger, Meister,

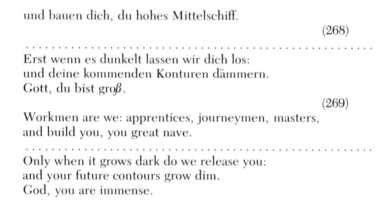

und bauen dich, du hohes Mittelschiff.

(268)

. . . .
Erst wenn es dunkelt lassen wir dich los:
und deine kommenden Konturen dämmern.
Gott, du bist gro*ß*.

(269)

Workmen are we: apprentices, journeymen, masters,
and build you, you great nave.

. . . .
Only when it grows dark do we release you:
and your future contours grow dim.
God, you are immense.

While the medieval craftsman would have been aware that he was building to honor the Deity, he would not have considered God as unfinished, with indefinite contours. Throughout the book, Deity is manifest in manifold ways: as a neighbor ("Du, Nachbar Gott") (255), as an old peasant with a beard ("der Bauer mit dem Barte") (277), as a helpless little bird with yellow claws ("ein junger Vogel mit gelben Krallen") (266). But even though the questionings are an attempt to plumb the nature and origins of the God idea, the search results in vagueness; God is not really amenable to logical proofs, and seems rather a cosmic force, grasped as an intuitively felt relation, but not incompatible with natural law. This primal energy is constantly paid respect in concrete image, behind which the power is sensed, working in invisible, tireless, patient ways. When the monk addresses God, the appeal is not for forgiveness or grace. (Rilke had no patience with the idea of a Fall of Man, and no reference to one appears in the entire poem-cycle.) The prayer is rather for those qualities which "things" (and Nature, and God) possess: patience, stillness, endurance, autonomy.

To symbolize the primordial indefiniteness and ineffability of God most effectively, Rilke uses the adjective *dark*. For this poet, God is not a Heavenly God at all, but a God of Earth, whose organic force operates in hidden ways and manifests itself like a tree:

> Wen soll ich rufen, wenn nicht *den*
> der dunkel ist und nächtiger als Nacht.
>   . . . . von dem ich weiß
> weil er mit Bäumen aus der Erde bricht
> und weil er leis
> als Duft in mein gesenktes Angesicht
> aus Erde steigt.

(310)

> And whom should I call, if not Him,
> who is dark and nightlier than night.
>   . . . . of whom I know
> because he bursts out of the earth
>   with the trees
> and because gently
> as a breeze to my lowered face
> he rises out of earth.

He is the "dark Ground" (296) ("dunkler Grund"), the source.

> Gott aber dunkelt tief.
>
>   (286)
>
> . . . .
> Er, der immer Tiefe war,
> ermüdete des Flugs
> und sich verbarg vor jedem Jahr
> bis ihm sein wurzelhaftes Haar
> durch alle Dinge wuchs.
>
>   (287)
>
> But God darkens deep.
>
> . . . .
> He, who always was depth,
> tired of flight
> and hid Himself from every year,
> until His rootlike hair
> grew through all things.

In this chthonic Deity, exhibiting His power from under the earth, the monk finds a process to emulate: a reciprocity is achieved when the God-seeker follows the patient workings of the earth.

> Aber ich will dich begreifen
> wie dich die Erde begreift;
> mit meinem Reifen
> reift
> dein Reich.
>
>   (319)
>
> But I want to comprehend you
> as the earth comprehends you;
> with my ripening
> your realm
> ripens.

Earlier in the poem, the monk had already discovered some presentiment of a mutal dependence:

Was wirst du tun, Gott, wenn ich sterbe?
Ich bin dein Krug (wenn ich zerscherbe?)
Ich bin dein Trank (wenn ich verderbe?)
Bin dein Gewand und dein Gewerbe,
mit mir verlierst du deinen Sinn.

(274)

What will you do, God, if I die?
I am your vessel (if I should shatter?)
I am your libation (if I should grow sour?)
Am your garment and your occupation,
with me you lose your sense.

Mankind is here seen as a set of artifacts which God uses, the greatest utility of which give Him a reason for existence: "Mit uns *wird* er" ("Through us he comes into being"), as an early diary entry has it.[9] God exists because man seeks. Through the impulse to shape and to question, in the tasks of wielding brushes or sickles or words, man is himself fulfilling age-old laws, valid as natural law itself, thereby "building at" God, and forging qualitative dimensions for his own life.

Fur dich schließen sich die Dichter ein
und sammeln Bilder, rauschende und reiche,
und gehn hinaus und reifen durch Vergleiche. . . .

(315)

For you the poets lock themselves up
and gather images, exuberant and rich,
and go about and ripen through comparisons. . . .

In a sense, the artist's kinship with earth is not dissimilar from God's relation with it; the relation is an essential one: the earth is transformed into landscapes and objects that the poet or painter sees and vivifies and transforms. The Earth-referent remains paramount, as the source of creation/transformation, whether in Nature or in mythopoesis.

While still completing the *Stundenbuch*, Rilke moved to Paris, where his experiences occasioned certain shifts in his aesthetic, especially by a sharpening of his vision, partly under the mentorship of the sculptor Rodin, whose work advanced Rilke's own ideas about the creative animation of phenomena through art. The poems which resulted, the *Neue Gedichte* 1 (1903) and 2 (1907) (*New Poems*) were refinements of his search for the "Wesen" ("intrinsic nature") of objects, whether "things" as such (roses, cathedrals, lace) or whether legendary materials or human fates.

Paris was also the setting for Rilke's major prose work, *Die Aufzeichnungen des Malte Laurids Brigge* (1910) (*The Notebooks of Malte*

Laurids Brigge).[10] The protagonist is a young poet who (like Rilke himself)
sees the harsh life of the metropolis as a challenge, testing his ability to
forge an art in the face of daemonic forces, and, living at the edges of
poverty, to "hold fast," to taste every nuance of the "difficult" ("Schwere").
In this effort to live elementally, Malte forces himself to ask some basic
questions, a series Rilke came to call the *Frage-dynastien* ("Question-
dynasties"), which he later summarized in a letter to a reader.

> Dies, wie ist es möglich zu leben, wenn doch die Elemente dieses
> Leben uns völlig unfaßlich sind? Wenn wir immerfort im Lieben
> unzulänglich, im Entschließen unsicher und dem Tode gegenüber
> unfähig sind, wie ist es möglich da zu sein? . . . Ich bin nicht durch-
> gekommen, in diesem unter der tiefsten Verpflichtung geleisteten
> Buch, mein ganzes Staunen auszuschreiben darüber, daß die Menschen
> seit Jahrtausenden mit Leben umgehen (von Gott gar nicht zu reden)
> und dabei diesen ersten unmittelbarsten, ja genau genommen einzigen
> Aufgaben (denn was haben wir anderes zu tun, noch heute und wie lange
> noch?) so neulinghaft ratlos, so zwischen Schrecken und Ausrede, so
> armsälig gegenüberstehen.[11]
>
> This: how is it possible to live, when the elements of this life are
> completely incomprehensible to us? When we are always inadequate,
> uncertain in decision, unready in the face of death, how is it possible to
> exist? . . . I have not succeeded, in this book written under cir-
> cumstances of the profoundest obligation, in delineating my total
> astonishment that for millennia men have trafficked with life (much less
> to speak of God) and all the while confront this first, most incommensur-
> able, yes, truly understood, only task (for what have we really to do but
> this, today still and for how long?), so amateurishly helpless, somewhat
> between horror and evasion, so pathetically.

With such questions, the young Malte seeks to revert to essential values,
stripped of comfort and facile "happiness." Any "bliss" he would have felt
would consist in the consciousness of the intensity with which he was
experiencing life, even in the presence of abysmal despair. Such a life by its
nature demanded "being humble like a thing" ("demütig sein wie ein
Ding") (306). Such a paradoxical "bliss" would fortify Rilke's principle of
conversion, *Umschlag:* literally, "turning over," or "reversal," the circumstance of events converting into their opposites. Hence Malte's
abysses could convert into paradises, for, as Rilke said, an abyss is filled
with the dark mystery of God: "Dieser Abgrund ist voll vom Dunkel Gottes,
und wo ihn einer erfährt, so steige er hinab und heule darin, das ist nötiger
als ihn überschreiten" ("This abyss is full of God's darkness, and whenever
one discovers it, he should descend into it and howl, that is more needful
than stepping across"). "Erst zu dem, dem auch der Abgrund ein Wohnort

war, kehren die vorausgeschickten Himmel um"[12] ("Only to him, for whom the abyss has also been a dwelling place, will the prophesied Heaven be revealed").

Like the *Stundenbuch* monk, Malte's quest for integrity in his craft parallels a developing God-idea; in neither quest is success achieved, which is to say that the redeeming *Umschlag* does not occur; the stamina and forbearance that a difficult life demands are beyond his power. His God has retreated further "behind things," as if intimidated by the stark outlines of urban life. His craft's greatest need, continuous work, eludes him also. Rilke saw Malte's fate as a salutary example of an artist's travail; despite failure, the process of living as an artist is embodied in the notebooks, and Malte never loses his integrity.

The creation of the *Stundenbuch* God has represented the earliest example of a "God-begetting" in a major Rilke work. The Malte God complements that one in the emphasis on the "wrestling" ("ringen," as Rilke often called it) with God; like the earlier conception, He remains dark, elusive, unapproachable; the monk's effusions give way to Malte's subdued, sometimes bitter, questionings. He is still a "forest of contradictions" ("ein Wald der Widersprüche") (283). Although not often personified as "God" in later works, His cosmic force is metaphorically transformed into the stern Angel-figure of the *Duino Elegies*, and, using the classical tradition, becomes the Singer-god of the *Sonnets to Orpheus*.

THE ANGEL OF THE ELEGIES

The *Duino Elegien* (1922) (*Duino Elegies*) are a lament for the human condition. In the *Stundenbuch* Rilke had posited a God as the "Other" in his solitude; in the Elegies he uses the figure of the Angel as the symbol of the gulf between man and the infinite. Compared with other angels in the Rilke canon, the Elegies angel is "schrecklich," "terrible," in the sense of "evoking terror"; the *Stundenbuch*-angel had been "das letzte Wehn / an seines (Gottes) Wipfels Saum" (287) ("the last zephyr at the edges of God's treetop"). Typically, earlier angels were languorous creatures, "bright souls without a seam" ("helle Seelen ohne Saum") (380), in the conventional roles of guardians, angels-in-waiting, or messengers.

The background of the plaintive laments in the ten elegies is still that of Malte's metropolis, and like Malte, Rilke wishes to assess human destiny according to its "proper value"; "Jenes Schwer-nehmen des Lebens, von dem meine Bücher erfüllt sind . . . will ja nichts sein . . . als ein Nehmen nach dem wahren Gewicht, also ein Wahrnehmen; ein Versuch, die Dinge mit dem Karat des Herzens zu wägen, statt mit Verdacht, Glück, oder Zufall . . . Keine Absage! . . oh, im Gegenteil, wieviel unendliche Zustimmung und immer noch Zustimmung zum Da-Sein!"[13] ("This taking life seriously with which my books are filled . . . wants to be nothing . . . but measuring according to proper weight, therefore a perception: an attempt to weigh things according to the carat-value of the heart, instead of suspicion, happiness, or coincidence. No refusal! oh, on the contrary, how much infinite agreement and still more assent to existence!").

Such affirmation is also arrived at in the Elegies, but in the context of a long examination of man's place in the Cosmos. The Angel has become the "Other" whom the poet addresses. Who are we? he asks the Angel. Where can we turn for answers? Throughout, the Angels do not deign to answer. It is one of their attributes that they seem concerned only with themselves, as a rather narcissistic mirror-image suggests: "*Spiegel:* die die entströmte eigene Schönheit wiederschöpfen zurück in das eigene Antlitz" (i,689) ("mirrors: which reflect back to each, into his own visage, his flowing, individual beauty").

Are such beings approachable by man? "Wer, wenn ich schriee, hörte mich denn aus der Engel/Ordnungen?" ("Who, if I cried out, would hear me among the angelic/orders?") the poet asks, "und gesetzt selbst, es nähme/einer mich plötzlich ans Herz: ich verginge von seinem/stärkeren Dasein" ("and even assuming one would take me to his breast: I would vanish in his more powerful presence") (i,685). "Nicht Engel, nicht Menschen/ . . . und die findigen Tiere merken es schon daß wir nicht sehr verlässlich zu Hause sind in der gedeuteten Welt" (i.685) ("Not Angels, not men/ . . . and the clever animals note only too well that we are not at home in our classified world"). The poet then turns to such human beings as might have been characterized by the patience and endurance that mark a mastery over fate: the lovers, the heroes, the dead, who are now "Sein" ("Being"). "Liebende, euch . . . frag ich nach uns" (i,691) (Lovers, you . . . you I ask about us"). But most lovers are consumed by their famed emotions. They should model themselves on the hero, who withstands: "selbst der Untergang war ihm nur Vorwand zu sein: seine letzte Geburt" (i,686) ("even downfall was for him only a pretext to be: his last birth"). Do the dead point the way to a more worthy life? It is possible that man has never attempted to range that side "turned away from us"[14] into his realm of experience, a component to be embraced?

> Aber Lebendige machen
> alle den Fehler, daß sie zu stark unterscheiden.
> Engel (sagt man) wüßten oft nicht, ob sie unter
> Lebenden gehen oder Toten. Die ewige Strömung
> reisst durch beide Bereiche aller Alter
> immer mit sich und übertönt sie in beiden.
>
> (i,688)

> But the living all
> make the mistake of differentiating too rigidly.
> Angels (they say) often don't know, whether they
> move among the living or the dead. Through both realms
> the eternal stream tears all ages along
> with itself and drowns out their sound in both.

The "eternal stream" subsumes both realms. Even our time-sense is misplaced. "O Bäume Lebens, o wann winterlich?/Wir sind *nicht* einig" (iv,697) (O Tree of Life, when is your winter?/We are *not* in agreement"). Our orientation in the world is missing; we are always in opposition, with no affinities to the rest of creation. We are only spectators: "Zuschauer, immer, überall,/dem allen zugewandt und nie hinaus!" (viii,716) ("And we: spectators, always, everywhere,/ever looking *at* everything and never from!") It is as if we were watching a puppet play, at which we sit before the "Herzens Vorhang" (iv,697) ("curtain of our heart"). The curtain is raised. "Die Szenerie war Abschied" (iv,697) ("The scenery was departure"). It is the theater of our alienation. Only when an angel intervenes, does our time-sense alter itself:

> Engel und Puppe: dann ist endlich Schauspiel.
> Dann kommt zusammen, was wir immerfort
> entzwein, indem wir da sind. Dann entsteht
> aus unseren Jahreszeiten erst der Umkreis
> des ganzen Wandelns. Über ans hinüber
> spielt dann der Engel.
>
> (iv,699)

> Angel and puppet: then we finally have a show.
> Then comes together, what we always
> divide by our being here. Only then, out
> of our seasons the cycle of all
> our change comes into being. Above, beyond us
> the angel acts.

The angel "reißt die Bälge hoch" (iv,699) ("lifts the puppets high"), taking the puppets from the stage altogether. This highly ambiguous metaphor can be unraveled if Rilke's emphasis on "things" is recalled: puppets (man-made) bear a relation to man himself; they have the appearance of men, but also the self-containment of objects, which are pulled up, taken out of the realm of the transient into the angel's, which is an invisible one. The puppet-theater hence becomes a symbol for an angel's function, which is being. While puppets are not "actual" men, they represent men. In being raised up, they are transformed into *being* themselves.

The theatrical imagery is echoed in the Fifth Elegy, which deals with a troupe of traveling jugglers, whose performances, done with great skill, evoke admiration but also seem too effortless. Here the poet senses a certain emptiness suggested by the rather smug smiles the tumblers and acrobats wear, as a sign of their "Können" ("know-how," "skill"). If only such skills could be applied to the difficult tasks of life! the poet exclaims; if love could be mastered, relation to other beings achieved, death understood, then skill would have meaning, and smiles would have content. Speaking specifically of the lovers, he asks where there might be a show-place where such skills as transcendence could be demonstrated, where the lovers would pass far beyond the erotic into the infinite. "Wo, o *wo* ist der Ort?" (v,705) ("Where, *o where* is there such a place?").

Gradually, amidst the complaining tones, a note of acceptance, at first subdued, is heard. There are moments of perception, presentiments of verities, which, despite their transitory aspects, achieve endurance in memory, enabling us to anticipate and foresee: seasons, for example, which become "Tempel der Zukunft" (vii,709) ("temples of the future"). As the invisible Angel animates the puppet-play, so man can animate through art by transforming the visible world into an interior one (memory, image). The "Weltinnenraum" "world-space within" is the place where the world is really brought into being.

> Nirgends, Geliebte, wird Welt sein, als innen. Unser
> Leben geht hin mit Verwandlung. Und immer geringer
> schwindet das Außen. Wo einmal ein dauerndes Haus war,
> schlägt sich erdachtes Gebild vor, quer, zu Erdenklichem
> völlig gehörig, als stand es noch ganz im Gehirne.
>
> (vii,711)
> Nowhere, beloved, will world come into being, except
>   inside us. Our
> life goes on in transformation. And what is outside
> dwindles more and more. Where once there was an
>   enduring house,
> imagined image imposes itself, squarely, belonging
> entirely to the conceivable, as if it still stood
>   wholly in the mind.

The Angel, whose gaze encompasses past, present, and future, is admonished to remember the achievements of man:

> —Dies *stand* einmal unter Menschen,
> mitten im Schicksal stands, im vernichtenden, mitten
> im Nichtwissen-Wohin stand es, wie seiend, und bog

Sterne zu sich aus gesicherten Himmeln. Engel,
dir noch zeig ich es, *da!* In deinem Anschaun
steh es gerettet zuletzt, nun endlich aufrecht.
Säulen, Pylone, der Sphinx, das strebende Stemmen
grau aus vergehender Stadt oder aus fremder, des Doms.
War es nicht Wunder? O staune, Engel, denn *wir* sinds,
wir, o du Großer, erzähls, daß wir solches vermochten,
                    mein Atem
reicht fur die Rühmung nicht aus.

                                        (vii,712)

              This once stood among men,
amidst fate it stood, in nihilistic fate, in the midst
of Not-Knowing-Whereto it stood, as if being, and curved
to itself the stars from sheltered heavens. Angel,
even *you* I show it, *there!* In your gaze
it stands redeemed now, finally upright.
Pillars, pylons, the Sphinx, the straining buttresses
of the cathedral, rising out of a decaying city, or
                    a foreign one.
Wasn't it a miracle? O be astonished, Angel, for
              it is *we*,
we, o you great one, relate that we dared such;
                    my breath
is inadequate for praise.

Show the angel, too, the poet exclaims, how "selbst das klagende Lied rein
zur Gestalt sich entschließt, / dient als ein Ding, oder stribt in ein Ding—,
und jenseits / selig der Geige entgeht" (ix,719) ("even the lamenting song
forms itself into a pure shape, / serves as a thing, or dies in a thing—, and
beyond, ecstatically transcends the violin").

   In this apology for the human with which the poet confronts the Angel,
language itself is seen as a paramount achievement, furnishing value,
investing the world with meaning:

         . . . Sind wir vielleicht *hier*, um zu sagen: Haus,
         Brücke, Brunnen, Tor, Krug, Obstbaum, Fenster,—
         höchstens: Säule, Turm . . . aber zu *sagen*, verstehs,
         oh zu sagen *so*, wie selber die Dinge niemals
         innig meinten zu sein.

                                        (ix,718)

         . . . Are we perhaps *here*, to say: house,
         bridge, fountain, gate, jug, fruit tree, window—
         at most: pillar, tower . . . but to *say*, understand,
         oh to say in *such a way*, as the things themselves
         never in themselves meant to be.

This animating force, this ability to "indicate" the things of the world, to "give names to" phenomena, objectifies them and makes them live in our hearts. Affinities are sensed akin to those of ancient animistic religions in endowing certain trees or stones or fetishes with divine energy. For man nowadays to say "tree" may not portend the presence of indwelling dryads, but the naming power still confers a value beyond denotation. We note that the catalogue in the passage consists almost entirely of the artifacts of human culture, a way, the poet-persona infers, of putting a human imprint upon the cosmos. Although words may pass away in a breath, they are nevertheless more durable than monuments; themselves "invisible," they aid in the process of "turning over" the tangible and transient Earth into the invisible realm of Being.

> —Und diese, von Hingang
> lebenden Dinge verstehn, daß du sie rühmst; vergänglich,
> traun sie ein Rettendes uns, den Vergänglichsten, zu.
> Wollen, wir sollen sie ganz im unsichtbarn Herzen
> verwandeln
> in—o unendlich—in uns! Wer wir am Ende auch seien.
>
> (ix, 719)
>
> Erde, ist es nicht dies, was ou willst: *unsichtbar*
> in uns erstehn?—Ist es dein Traum nicht,
> einmal unsichtbar zu sein?—Erde! unsichtbar!
> Was, wenn Verwandlung nicht, ist dein drängender
> Auftrag?
> Erde, du liebe, ich will.
>
> (ix, 720)
>
> —And these things,
> perishable, mortal, know that you praise them;
> transitory,
> they wish us to redeem them, we, the most perishable.
> Wish, that we change them completely in our invisible
> hearts
> O eternally—in ourselves! Whoever we may finally be.
> Earth, isn't it this, which you want: to resurrect
> in us invisibly?—Is it not your dream
> once to be invisible?—Earth, invisible!
> What is your urgent task, if not transformation?
> Beloved earth, I wish it!

In the yea-saying to the task of transformation, the supplicant can find a measure of self-justification for a while. Because of his transitory nature, he can never exist in simultaneous time, as can the Angel; his creativity must take place *in* time, using tangible means. The Angel-mentor, on the other hand, can be serene in his power, for all possible transformations have already occurred for him. "Für den Engel der Elegien sind all vergangenen Türme und Paläste existent, weil längst unsichtbar, und die noch bestehenden Türme und Brücken unseres Dasein schon unsichtbar, obwohl noch (für uns) körperhaft dauernd" (Hu900) ("For the Angel of the Elegies all past towers and palaces are existent, because long since invisible, and those towers and bridges still standing in our existences already invisible, even though [for us] still materially enduring"). "Der Engel der Elegien ist dasjenige Geschöpf, in dem die Verwandlung des Sichtbaren in Unsichtbares, die wir leisten, schon vollzogen erscheint" (Hu900). ("The Angel of the Elegies is that being, in whom the transformation of the visible into the invisible, which we achieve, has already taken place".) These achievements have a cosmic import:

> Die Elegien zeigen uns . . . am Werke dieser fortwährenden Umsetzungen des geliebten Sichtbaren und Greifbaren in die unsichbare Schwingung und Erregtheit unserer Natur, die neue Schwingungszahlen einführt in die Schwingungs-Sphären des Universums. (Da die verschiedenen Stoffe im Weltall nur verschiedene Schwingungsexponenten sind, so bereiten wir, in dieser Weise, nicht nur Intensitäten geistiger Art vor, sondern wer weiß, neue Körper, Metalle, Sternnebel und Gestirne.) (Hu898)
>
> The Elegies show us . . . at the work of these continual transpositions of the beloved visible and tangible into the invisible vibrations and pulsations of our nature, which introduced new frequency rates into the oscillation-spheres of the universe. (Since the various elements of the cosmos consist only of varying oscillation-series, we prepare, in our way, not only intensities of a spiritual sort, but who knows? new substances, metals, nebulae, and stars.)

The Angel's function, as Rilke conceives it, is to admonish man to perform tasks that give life meaning. Although the word is hardly used, it is a spiritualizing function, or a way for man to have a presentiment of Being itself. The Angel cannot really impart the "know-how" of this process: it can only be an intuitive relation, since the Angel never acts as a mediator; at best, he is a model, an "ought." The power he possesses is never manifested; we know only that he is "above," as a Taskmaster. With the exception of the metaphorical puppet-play passage, the Angel is never seen to intervene in the lives of men. As the poet's laments make clear, there is no real relation to him, no reciprocity and, as Lou Salomé points out, it is exactly this "totally Other" character that is important. The Angel's force cannot be that of "Eins-Sein mit dem Anbetenden, sondern aus dem Anders-Sein; das Entzücken, daß er erregt, ist nicht brüderlich beantwortend"[15] ("being-at-one with the petitioner, but his being-other; the enchantment which is aroused is not answerable in a fraternal way"). Much earlier, in a letter to his wife, Clara, Rilke had characterized angels as rather strict guardians of duty; he suggested playfully that he never needed any police to suggest order: "haben nicht Engel uns schon dazu angehalten mit der tiefen, überzeugten Unerbittlichkeit, die Engeln gegeben ist?"[16] ("haven't angels held us to it with the persuasive harshness that angels possess?").

The formidable symbol of the Angel is an intensification of the attributes of the *Stundenbuch* God, with some of the "distance" of Malte's. The monk-supplicant of the *Stundenbuch* had reminded Him of His dependence upon man. From that God to the Elegies Angel is a shift of function; God is mentioned very seldom in the Elegies, where He seems to represent the All. As a challenge to man, the Angel presents an "eternal consciousness" ("unendliches Bewußtsein") (Hu900), a symbol of spiritual dimension that is Pure Being. Although invisible, he moves with ease through the All without affecting anything directly. His seems to be a "steady-state" being, much like the "Inbegriff" ("essence") of the *Stundenbuch* God. Commentators have compared him to a Nietzschean Superman, combining Nietzsche's "Power" with Rilke's "Inwardness";[17] as an "Artist-God";[18] or as a "working hypothesis" for the possibilities of transcendence.[19] In any case, as Rilke makes clear, the Angel is not a Christian angel. "Der Engel der *Elegien* hat nichts mit dem Engel des christlichen Himmels zu tun" (Hu899-900) ("The angel of the *Elegies* has nothing to do with the angel of the Christian Heaven").

In his Angel-myth, Rilke has created an effective "Other" whose spheres of Being include not only those spaces through which angels have conventionally been believed to move, but (what may seem surprising to the modern age) the physical and psychical landscapes of contemporary life. The Christian mediator between heaven and earth has undergone a transvaluation into the symbol for Pure Being, and to a certain extent, symbol for essence, potentiality, form, and energy of a primal kind. His connection with man is tenuous, but as the later elegies show, man's realm is really Earth, *his* sphere of creation, and there is even great value in being able to proclaim that "Hiersein ist herrlich!" (vii,710) ("Being here is splendid!"). Rilke's interest remains rooted in Earth, the mysterious primordial.

ORPHEUS

Language is a perpetual Orphic song
Which rules with daedal harmony a throng

Of thoughts and forms, which else senseless
and shapeless were.
(Shelley, *Prometheus Unbound.* IV, 413-15)

In both the literal and figurative sense, the *Sonette an Orpheus* (1922) (*Sonnets to Orpheus*) form a frame for the *Duino Elegies*. The Elegies, begun in 1912 in Duino, were not completed until Rilke's Swiss sojourn, after the first group of sonnets was written; after the Elegies were finished, a second group of sonnets was "dictated," as Rilke put it. The Elegies hence found their final form in the context of praise. "Nur im Raum der Rühmung/darf die Klage gehn" (l,vii,735) ("Only in the realm of praise/may lament be heard"), one sonnet begins. As Rilke asserts, the two great works "unterstützen sich einander beständig" (Hu900) ("mutually support each other constantly"). A long period of drought in poetic activity was broken, "umgeschlagen" ("reversed").

Two circumstances furnished the inspiration for the sonnet sequences. One was the death of a young girl, Wera Ouckama Knoop, of leukemia; the other was a chance glimpse into a shop window, where the poet saw a gravure print depicting Orpheus with his lyre. The occasion of Wera's death accounts for the preoccupation with death and mutability in the poems; the choice of the controlling symbol was fortuitous and apt, since Orpheus was one of the few mythological figures ever to have penetrated the realm of death and returned to earth. In the sonnets, he moves invisibly through the double realm of death and life, which Rilke sees as a whole, "die große Einheit" (Hu897) ("the great unity"), or as "das Ganze" (Hu898) ("the totality").

Orpheus was reputedly the most famous singer of classical times before Homer. He played the lyre and sang with such mastery that mountains were moved, rivers ceased to flow, and animals were enchanted. When his wife, Eurydice, was killed by an asp, Orpheus charmed the guardians of Hades and Pluto himself into allowing Eurydice's shade to return to earth with him. In leading her out of Hades, he broke the promise not to look at her until they had returned to the light. He lost her forever, and spent the rest of his days in wandering, lamenting her loss to the accompaniment of his lyre. He met his death in Thrace, where maenads, incensed at his refusal to do them honor, stoned and dismembered him, casting the remains into a stream, where, from his severed head, his singing continued. His lyre was translated into a constellation.

Rilke's principal interest in the myth is Orpheus as Singer. Eurydice's fate is not emphasized, although she is not completely effaced by the fate of Wera Ouckama Knoop, who is usually addressed directly by the poet Rilke, with little affinity to Orpheus himself. Wera, whose chosen profession (dance) was not incompatible with Orphic song, affected Rilke deeply, as did her young age.

In the first of the sonnets, Orpheus is compared to a tree, one of Rilke's favorite symbols; but synaesthetically, he also becomes a "temple in the ear":

> Da stieg ein Baum. O reine Übersteigung!
> O Orpheus singt! O hoher Baum im Ohr!
> Und alles schwieg. Doch selbst in der Verschweigung
> ging neuer Anfang, Wink und Wandlung vor.
>
> Tiere aus Stille drangen aus dem klaren
> gelösten Wald von Lager und Genist;
> Und da ergab sich, daß sie nicht aus List
> und nicht aus Angst in sich so leise waren,
>
> sondern aus Hören. Brüllen, Schrei, Geröhr
> schien klein in ihren Herzen. Und wo eben
> kaum eine Hütte war, dies zu empfangen,
>
> ein Unterschlupf aus dunkelstem Verlangen
> mit einem Zugang, dessen Pfosten beben,—
> da schufst du ihnen Tempel im Gehör.

(1, i, 731)

> There soared a tree. O pure overreaching!
> O Orpheus sings! O mighty tree in the ear!
> And all was silent. Yet even in silencing went
> new beginning, beckoning, and change.
>
> Out of the stillness, animals crowded out of
> newly cleared forest glade from lair and nest;
> and it came about that not out of fear and
> not out of guile were they so gentle,
>
> but because of listening. Bellowing, roar,
> and cry seemed tiny in their breasts. And
> where before there was hardly a hut to receive
> such sounds,
>
> In a hiding place of darkest yearning
> with an entrance-way whose pillars tremble,
> there you built temples for them in their hearing.

When Orpheus enters the world of men, the charm of his song has edges of poignancy, for Rilke believed that beasts had an affinity with Being, which

Orpheus, like the Angel, symbolizes. In the Elegies Rilke had held that animals have no consciousness of death. In his comings and goings in the world, in the embrace of the death/life unity, Orpheus celebrates all losses, all mutability, by singing hymns to entropy, converting all into song; he will energize stasis, and be the instrument of all metamorphosis. As one who has known abysses, he can sing eternal praise. "Nur wer die Leier schon hob/auch unter Schatten/darf das unendliche Lob/ahnend erstatten" (l,ix,736) ("Only he who has raised the lyre/also among the shades/may with foreboding, render eternal praise"). "Rühmen, das ists!" (1,vii,735) ("Praising, that's it!")

The range of subjects praised is very wide: poems that explore the relevance of roses (2,vi,754), poems that puzzle over the enigmatic nature of mirrors (2,iii,752), unicorns (2,iv,753), or vital energies (2,1,751), all placed in the All and, except for their transitory nature, "pleasant" subjects. As a foil to these are the praises of what seem to Rilke to be ugly subjects, or at least associated with "petty" fates, dailiness: banks (2,xix,763), aircraft (1,xxii,745), or machines (1,xviii,742). Rilke realized that a comprehensive view of reality had to include such artifacts, for they too are subject to eventual change. But praise them: "Sieh, die Maschine:/wie sie sich wälzt und racht/und uns entstellt und schwacht. . . . Hat sie aus uns auch Kraft, sie, ohne Leidenschaft/treibe und diene" (2,xviii,742) ("See, the machine:/ how it reverses and revenges,/displaces and weakens us. . . . Even if it gets its power from us,/without passion/it pulses and serves"). In the poem immediately following, retrogression is a force, for which all things, even machines, return to a primal source: "Wandelt sich auch die Welt/wie Wolkengestalten/alles Vollendete fällt/heim zur Uralten" (1,xix,743) ("Though the world changes swiftly/like cloud formations/everything completed falls/back home to the primordial").

Some of the sonnets raise doubts as to man's ability to emulate Orpheus's singing, although one senses that Rilke sees all poets as Orpheus. There is only the consciousness that the song is different: that of Orpheus sings of reality; by comparison, man's song is a soundless breath: "Gesang ist Dasein. Fur den Gott ein leichtes. . . . In Wahrheit singen, ist ein andrer Hauch./Ein Hauch im nichts./Ein Wehn in Gott./Ein Wind" (l,iii,732) ("Song is Existence. For the god something easy. . . . To sing in truth, is another kind of breath./A whiff about nothing./A zephyr in God./A wind"). The plaintive note of the Elegies enters again. Existence is not reality; man is a dual creature still. But in another poem, an affinity, or "relation," can be intimated:

> Ohne unsern wahren Platz zu kennen,
> handeln wir aus wirklichem Bezug.

Die Antennen fühlen die Antennen,
und die leere Ferne trug . . .

(l,xii,738)

Without knowing our true place
We deal out of actual relation.
Antennae sense antennae,
and the empty distance bore . . .

At times, not only can a "relation" be sensed, but an experience of "being" itself, in a profoundly earthly sense, can be experienced:

Voller Apfel, Birne und Banane,
Stachelbeere . . . Alles dieses spricht
Tod und Leben in den Mund . . . Ich ahne . . .
Lest es einem Kind vom Angesicht,

wenn es sie erschmeckt. Dies kommt von weit.
Wird euch langsam namenlos im Munde?
Wo sonst Worte waren, fließen Funde,
aus dem Fruchtfleisch überrascht befreit.

Wagt zu sagen, was ihr Apfel nennt.
Diese Süße, die sich erst verdichtet,
um, im Schmecken leise aufgerichtet,

klar zu werden, wach und transparent,
doppeldeutig, sonnig, erdig, hiesig—:
O Erfahrung, Fühlung, Freude—, riesig!

(1,xiii,739)

Pithy apple, pear, and banana,
gooseberry . . . all these bespeak
death and life in one's mouth . . .
Read it in the face of a child

tasting them. This comes from afar.
Does it slowly become nameless in the mouth?
Where words once were, flow discoveries,
released from fleshy fruit surprisingly.

Hard to say, what one calls apple.
This sweetness, compressed at first,
gently to mount in the tasting,

becomes clear, aware, transparent,

> double-sensed, earthy, sunny, here and now—
> O experience, connection, joy—immense!

The Sonnets are a colorful fabric of such celebrations, joyful poems occasionally counterpointed by somber ones reminiscent of the Elegies: "Nicht sind die Leiden erkannt, /nicht ist die Liebe gelernt, /und was im Tod uns entfernt, /ist nicht entschleiert" (1,xix,743) ("Sufferings have not been recognized, /love has not been mastered, /and what distances us in death /is not unveiled"). But such plaints are followed (in the same verse) by "Einzig das Lied überm Land /heiligt und feiert" (1,xix,743) ("Only your song o'er the land /blesses and praises").

If the Elegies Angel represents a Power in which transformation is complete, and True Being has been achieved, why could he not have served as the transformer as well? The answer may well rest in Rilke's Earth-orientation, and the somewhat forbidding mien the Angel presents. The Angel has nothing "Erdenhaft" ("earthly") about him; he is not a participator *in* life. As a symbolic abstraction he is not able even to suffer, which may seem like a singular advantage, but following Rilke's *Umschlag*-principle, he cannot experience transformations materially. For earthbound creatures, and for the transformers of earth, whether seekers of the invisible or not, the anthropomorphic figure of Orpheus is a more concrete, more organic mythical reanimation. Though a partaker of the double-realm of death /life and "invisible" himself, he comes to stand for the things of earth, where, in a continuous contemporaneity, transformations occur under his aegis. In his human aspect, he experienced suffering, alienation, and loss, which prepares him well to sing the losses that human beings understand. In his way, he is as effective a mentor as is the Angel, for he shows the ways of song and the "naming" power. In the Sonnets "wird das menschliche Wort das magische Organ der Verwandlung, es hebt sich zur göttlichen Schöpferkraft des Logos" ("human speech becomes the magical organ of transformation; it raises it up to the divine creativity of the Logos").[20]

The language in the Sonnets is often paradoxical. But "Umschlag" is itself paradoxical, as anyone who understands peripeteia or irony knows; it is paradoxical, but "true," and, to a great extent, organic. It is also a component of the language associated with myth. "The language of primitives tends to employ paradox freely," says Wheelwright, "for the Mystery which it tries to express cannot be narrowed down to logical categories.[21]

Without consciously trying to emulate the language of myth, Rilke constantly indulged in verbal paradox; it did not seem incongruous to him to have abysses "turn over into" Paradises, an example of what Heller calls "affirming from negation, and creating from denial."[22] For Rilke, empty space can become fruitful (1,xii,738); or, "Ist dir Trinken bitter, werde Wein" (2,xxix,770) ("If drinking is bitter for you, become wine").

In both the Elegies and the Sonnets, man is conscious of his duality. But in Orpheus there is duality too, a paradoxical nature. He is half-man/half-god; he moves in the "double realm" of life/death. Yet he becomes the apotheosis of the Poet. "Song is Being. " When the maenads slew the god and dismembered him, the mangled parts fructified the earth, where his song lingered in lions and rocks, and from his severed head floating in a stream, the singing continued (1,xxvi,747). This singing is Orpheus's immortality.

In Rilke's appropriation of myth, Orpheus's transformational song, like the transfigured God's primal power and the Angel's invisible force, brings immortality into an eternal present. In each, the Earth is the ultimate referent, as that Ground which is symbolically transformed, "not in some Beyond," as Rilke wrote (Hu898), ". . . but in a profoundly earthy, a blessed earthly consciousness . . . into a whole, into *the* Whole."

NOTES

1. T. S. Eliot, "Ulysses, Order, and Myth," *The Dial* 75, London (November 1923), as excerpted in Richard Ellmann and Charles Feidelson, Jr., *The Modern Tradition* (New York: Oxford University Press, 1965), p. 681.

2. George Whalley, *Poetic Process: An Essay in Poetics* (Cleveland: World Publishing Co., 1967), p. 181.

3. Philip Wheelwright, "Poetry, Myth, and Reality," in *The Language of Poetry*, ed. Allen Tate (New York: Russell and Russell, 1960), p. 25.

4. Rainer Maria Rilke, *Tagebücher aus der Frühzeit* (Frankfurt: Insel, 1973), p. 62. All translations from Rilke are by Lawrence Abler.

5. Erich Heller, "Rilke and Nietzsche," *The Disinherited Mind* (Cambridge and New York: Cambridge University Press, 1952), p. 135.

6. To Hugo von Salis, 7 May 1899. Rainer Maria Rilke, *Briefe und Tagebücher aus der Frühzeit 1899 bis 1902* (Leipzig: Insel, 1931), p. 13.

7. Rainer Maria Rilke, *Sämtliche Werke*, ed. E. Zinn (Frankfurt: Insel, 1955), 1:320. This volume contains all the poetry from which quotations appear in this paper. Citations appear in the text as follows: Arabic single-digit numbers refer to parts of works; lower-case roman, to Rilke's numbering of poems; three-digit Arabic, to pages. Translations by Lawrence Abler.

8. To Ilse Jahr, 22 February 1923. Rainer Maria Rilke, *Briefe* (Wiesbaden: Insel, 1950), p. 819.

9. *Tagebücher*, p. 295.

10. *Sämtliche Werke*, vol. 6, ed. E. Zinn (Frankfurt: Insel, 1966).

11. To Lotte Hepner, 8 November 1915. *Briefe*, p. 510.

12. To Ilse Jahr, 22 February 1923. *Briefe*, p. 820.

13. To Rudolf Bodländer, 13 March 1922. *Briefe*, p. 765.

14. To Withold Hulewicz, n.d. (Postmark: 13 November 1925) *Briefe*, p. 896. Further reference to this "letter of explication" of Rilke's will be signaled in the text as "Hu."

15. Lou Andreas-Salomé, *Rainer Maria Rilke* (Lepizig: Insel, 1929), p. 44.

16. To Clara Rilke, 17 December 1906. *Briefe*, p. 144.

17. Heller, "Rilke and Nietzsche," p. 128.

18. Eliza Butler, *Rilke* (Cambridge and New York: Cambridge University Press, 1941), p. 246 passim.

19. Dieter Bassermann, *Der späte Rilke* (Munich: Leibnitz, 1947), p. 181.

20. Erich Hofacker, "Rilke und Morgenstern," PMLA 48 (1933): 814.

21. Wheelwright, "Poetry, Myth, and Reality," p. 15.

22. Heller, "Rilke and Nietzsche," p. 127.

SUGGESTED READINGS

Andreas-Salomé, Lou. *Rainer Maria Rilke*. Leipsig: Insel, 1929.

Basserman, Dieter. *Der späte Rilke*. Munich: Leibnitz, 1947.

Betz, Maurice. *Rilke à Paris & les Cahiers de Malte Laurids Brigge*. Paris: Editions Emile-Paul frères, 1941.

Faesi, Robert. *Rainer Maria Rilke*. Zurich: Amalthea, 1919.

Guardini, Romano. *Rainer Maria Rilkes Deutung des Daseins: Eine Interpretation*. Munich: Kösel, 1953.

Heidegger, Martin. "Wozu Dichter?" *Holzwege*. Frankfurt: V. Klostermann, 1950. Pp. 248-95.

Heller, Erich. *The Disinherited Mind*. Cambridge and New York: Cambridge University Press, 1952.

Kassner, Rudolf. "Erinnerungen an RMR." *Inselschiff*, vol. 8. Leipsig: Insel, 1937. Pp. 119-25.

Kippenberg, Katharina. *Rainer Maria Rilke, Ein Beitrag*. Leipsig: Insel, 1935.

Mandel, Siegfried. *Rainer Maria Rilke: The Poetic Instinct*. Carbondale and Edwardsville: Southern Illinois University Press, 1965.

v. Thurn u Taxis-Hohenlohe, Marie. *Erinnerungen an Rainer Maria Rilke*. Munich and Berlin: Oldenbourg, 1937

Wood, Frank. *Rainer Maria Rilke: The Ring of Forms*. Minneapolis: University of Minnesota Press, 1958.

Biographical Note on Ronald L. Dotterer

Ronald L. Dotterer is a graduate of Bucknell University (1970) and received his M.A. (1971) and M. Phil. (1972) from Columbia, where he is presently completing his work for his doctorate. He is assistant professor of English at Susquehanna University, where he has taught since 1972. He was co-chairman of the 1975 Bucknell-Susquehanna Colloquium on "The Nature and Functions of Literature" and presented a paper at the Northeast Modern Language Association Annual Meeting in 1974 on "Illusory Form in Wallace Stevens' 'The Comedian as the Letter C.' "

The Fictive and the Real: Myth and Form in the Poetry of Wallace Stevens and William Carlos Williams

RONALD L. DOTTERER

Discussing William Blake in this volume, Deborah Austin refers to artists as makers of forms, and the artistic process as "to cause to come into being."[1] The linking of these two aspects is appropriate to a discussion of William Carlos Williams and Wallace Stevens, since Austin's association points simultaneously to the act of creating and to the evolution of a distinct form for that creation. I have chosen to examine the two most influential American poets of their day because their careers, despite endless differences of style, subject, and temperament, show at least one similar progression: the gradual evolution of a long poem that served as the arena and the achievement of the poet's struggle with word and world. A study of the ways in which these poets caused their most important poems "to come into being" points to at least one common element within the diversity of modern American poetry: the centrality of the poem itself in giving order to life.

Specifically, I shall examine what Williams called "the clouds resolved in a sandy sluice,"[2] that is, the five books of *Paterson;* and Stevens's "abstraction blooded,"[3] his *Notes Toward a Supreme Fiction.* In a larger sense, I shall refer also to the gradual complication, expansion, and elucidation of two poetic theories. Both Williams and Stevens sought formal poetic structures that could surpass earlier, more fragmentary visions and could suggest an order that is at once without and within poetry. That ambitious search for a poem with such a structural unity, an essential part of mythopoesis, depends on the making of fictions. For Williams and Stevens, these fictions became respectively the all-inclusive figure of Paterson and the metaphysical figure of a supreme fiction.

Although these poems may appear at first to contrast as markedly as the

221

diction of their creators, they bear strong similarities in form and substance that illustrate complementary views concerning the relationship of the imagination to the world at large. And although the attitudes and lives of Williams and Stevens may differ, an overriding similarity linking their careers is that the evolution of their literary forms is both a private and an isolating process. The making of these extended poems involves for the authors a distancing not only from earlier poets but from culture in general—even if there is no permanent rejection of these traditions. Such making, I shall argue, depends upon an intentional avoidance of other men's fictions, of setting out to make or reinterpret societal myths; it relies instead upon a search for what Stevens at one point calls a "mythology of self" (*CP*, 28)—a fiction that arises from the self yet ultimately can exist without the self.

I

Form and fiction—like myth—have as many meanings as interpreters. In "What is Art?", his influential essay on the visual arts, Clive Bell uses the term *significant form* to refer to "lines and colours combined in a particular way, certain forms and relations of forms [that] stir our aesthetic emotions."[4] Kenneth Burke, in "Lexicon Rhetoricae," his "judgment machine for criticism,"[5] has chosen this same slippery term to reinterpret Pope's insistence that "the sound must seem an echo to the sense" ("An Essay on Criticism," l. 385). Illustrating from Wilde, Wordsworth, and Racine, Burke suggests that language is not simply an echo of meaning. In "significant" form, he argues, sound and sense are one and the same. Form-making here presents a central paradox of mimetic art: if artifice is used to convey the unartificial state of reality, "significant" form is at once fact and fiction. My reading of Williams and Stevens adds another element to this paradox of significant form: an augmentation of style and rhythm that not only creates an appearance of reality, but also captures within the poem a form of the creative process itself. In other words, a truly significant form will represent in a particular poem the process of creation itself. The ultimate poem, at least as seen by Williams and Stevens, must not only present a universe but present that universe being created. The making of significant form is, therefore, both result and process.

The achievement of significant form in the modern world has been made increasingly difficult not only by political, social, and cultural events, but also by an avoidance of what Burke calls syllogistic and conventional forms. The poet who rejects logical narrative and conventional genres as he begins to shape his poem must not only create forms to replace them but also prove to us that what he is substituting is both "better" structure and "better" art.

Consequently, the poet becomes increasingly his own interpreter and aesthetician. Stevens, for example, begins his *Notes* with an evaluation of the role of his supreme fiction, the role of "you":

> And for what, except for you, do I feel love?
> Do I press the extremest book of the wisest man
> Close to me, hidden in me day and night?
> In the uncertain light of single, certain truth,
> Equal in living changingness to the light
> In which I meet you, in which we sit at rest,
> For a moment in the central of our being,
> The vivid transparence that you bring is peace.
>
> (*CP*, 380)

For Stevens, the gift of the Muse is transparence and peace. Williams introduces his poem by citing a similarly resolute though less stable transformation that he has experienced in fashioning his *Paterson:*

> a local pride; spring, summer, fall and the sea; a confession; a basket; a column; a reply to Greek and Latin with the bare hands; a gathering up; a celebration; . . .
> hard put to it; an identification and a plan for action to supplant a plan for action; a taking up of slack; a dispersal and a metamorphosis. (*P*, 10)

Stevens's tranquil "living changingness" and Williams's volatile "metamorphosis" suggest mutually reinforcing perspectives on the difficult yet necessary task of writing the modern long poem. Each poet challenged himself to compose that great poem which the poet is never able to write, the final form upon which the reality of his imagination is based. The writing of Stevens's notes and Williams's books was designed to ease the pursuit of those unwritten poems. An equally important intention of each poet was, however, the invention and achievement of the form of that quest.

The second term that requires definition is *fiction*. As I have indicated earlier, my readings of Williams and Stevens see them concerned with a process that precedes the formulation of myth: that is, the crafting of imaginary, personal realms of fiction. The figure of Paterson and the notion of a supreme fiction are extended, disembodied falsifications. Williams's giant lying under the Passaic Falls embraces the imaginative possibilities of a small-town doctor's mind far more than the geographical reality of a New Jersey landscape. Stevens's terrestrial vision that had stopped revolving "except in crystal" (*CP*, 407) is even more of a mental fabrication, yet the invention of a Hartford insuranceman and lawyer. These men of fantasy, at home with, yet not limited by the practical considerations of their day-to-day careers, based the making of their poems of reality on abstractions and distortions of that reality. "The multiple seed," said Williams, "packed tight with detail, soured, / is lost in the flux and the mind" (P, 12). The imagination's activities are at once clarification and obfuscation, personal truth and lie. Fiction-making simultaneously orders and distorts.

In these two poems, Stevens and Williams launch this contradictory process with a rejection of all previous fictions, a rejection that parallels the prisoners' rejection of the shadows in Plato's cave. In the fictions of all three writers, there is a return to the sighting of truth (the sun) as a way of understanding the real and a means of stripping away appearance. Here is Stevens's use of that process at the opening of *Notes:*

> Begin, ephebe, by perceiving the idea
> Of this invention, this invented world,
> The inconceivable idea of the sun.
>
> You must become an ignorant man again
> And see the sun again with an ignorant eye
> And see it clearly in the idea of it.
>
> Never suppose an inventing mind as the source
> Of this idea nor for that mind compose
> A voluminous master folded in his fire.
>
> How clean the sun when seen in its idea,
> Washed in the remotest cleanliness of a heaven
> That has excelled us and our images . . .
>
> (*CP*, 380-81)

Plato presented men trapped in a world of appearances and seemings; Stevens draws his ephebe as an equally fettered man. Here, however, newly freed, that young figure must not only "see the sun again" but see it with an ignorant eye. For Stevens, like Plato before him, truth can be approached only by seeing clearly not the shadows on the wall, not even the sun as divinity or source of this world, but simply the "idea of the sun" cleansed of any images, purposes, or shadows.

Williams's use of that return to ignorance yet truth at the start of Book 1 of *Paterson* adds the turbulence and contradictions of the Passaic River to the viewing of reality:

> Yet there is
> no return: rolling up out of chaos,
> a nine months' wonder, the city

the man, an identity—it can't be
otherwise—an
interpenetration, both ways. Rolling
up! observe, reverse;
the drunk the sober; the illustrious
the gross; one. In ignorance
a certain knowledge and knowledge,
undispersed, its own undoing.

. . . .

It is the ignorant sun
rising in the slot of
hollow suns risen, so that never in this
world will a man live well in his body
save dying—and not know himself
dying; yet that is
the design. Renews himself
thereby, in addition and subtraction,
walking up and down.

(*P*, 12-13)

Here the emerging sun is partly Plato's ever-present fact but also a "rolling up out of chaos." This sun-reality, this embryonic vision, is vexing to its subjective observer for it points to man's mortality and to the fact that at this moment truth is seen by itself. Not only do no preconceived ideas exist at this point, but here exist no ideas at all. This is the moment of no fictions (what later in *Paterson* is expanded into the recurring motif of "no ideas but in things"). Williams ends up sighting that sun as empty death, the blankness of objects that surround our dying. With a somewhat different tone the poetic voice of Stevens's "Sunday Morning" announces a similar credo: "Death is the mother of beauty; hence from her, / Alone, shall come fulfillment to our dreams / And our desires" (*CP*, 68-69). All of these returns to ignorance involve a recognition of the truth upon which all of the poet's fictions are predicated. For Stevens that truth is majestically imageless and stark; for Williams that stark imagelessness is tragic, since it reveals man's mortality. One thread links both visions: the poet's metaphors, his "as ifs," cannot cover completely the harsh fact that all myths and beliefs are dispelled at the outset in the creation of these fictive forms. Despite their varied tones, both poets see a world free of images as they are about to begin their own image-making.

Why should not such an awe-inspiring vision lead to the abandonment of the making of poems? How can it instead serve as the motivation for the most ambitious poem of each man's career? One way to answer these difficult questions is to insist on a distinction between poetry and truth. Both of these poets recognize their fictions as false from their inception;

neither poem is an attempt to embody either truth or an invention of belief—two traditional contexts for myth. Poetry, for Stevens and Williams, is descriptive *and* false, not one or the other. The sun-reality needs to be described even if that description must distort it, even if descriptive images are inherently defective and destroy the sun's perfection. Reality can be seen again, this theory says; return to ignorance will be possible again. However, ignorance is not an end in itself but a beginning. For Stevens, the poet therefore must create a fiction to cover the stone of reality. His poem is a "rolling up" that cloaks the "hermit in the poet's metaphors" (*CP*, 381), that hides and distorts what it is also revealing. For Williams, the poem is a "flickering green/ inspiring terror . . . [shrouding] earth, the chatterer, father of all/ speech" (*P*, 52). The difficulties of achieving such a productive fiction in the industrially ravished city of Paterson or the suburban sprawl that Stevens in *The Man with the Blue Guitar* calls Oxidia evokes the evolution of both poems. But these chattering landscapes also challenge these two poets to create significant forms and fictions through what each sees as his ultimate poem: synthetic glimpses of reality itself—fictions that both illustrate and transform their imaginations and their worlds.

In order not to confuse one man's fiction with another, I should like to examine each of these two poems independently; my aim is not to provide exhaustive analysis of either poem but to offer illustrations of the forms of these two fictions.

II

Williams made his own observations about the original four books of *Paterson*, stating what he saw as the poem's "Argument":

> Paterson is a long poem in four parts—that a man in himself is a city, beginning, seeking, achieving and concluding his life in ways which the various aspects of a city may embody—if imaginatively conceived—any city, all the details of which may be made to voice his most intimate convictions. Part One introduces the elemental character of the place. The Second Part comprises the modern replicas. Three will seek a language to make them vocal, and Four, the river below the falls, will be reminiscent of episodes—all that any one man may achieve in a lifetime. (*P*, 7)

There are interesting equations here. Book 1: beginning/ elemental character; Book 2: seeking/modern replicas; Book 3: achieving/language; Book 4: concluding/reminiscences of a lifetime. Williams's plan reflects not only an equation of the aging of man and city but also an equation of the history of civilization and the history of the imagination. Historical Paterson, the city closest to Williams's life, is wedded in one direction to the world that surrounds it and in another to the imagined Paterson of his mind. For Williams, the process of willing that union into being was not a rapid one; there is some evidence that he was at work on the poem as early as 1928.[6] All of the patients whom he saw and all of the other poems that he wrote during the twelve years from the publication of Book 1 in 1946 to the appearance of Book 5 in 1958 did not dilute the need to continue his ultimate poetic undertaking. Book 6 was in its earliest stages when Williams died in 1961.

The first four books follow the figure of Paterson through the falls, then the park, the library, and finally from his home to the sea. Book 5 deals with a Paterson wedded to that sea, a figure slowly voyaging through the world of art, a figure at once individual and representative of all of reality itself. As Williams's experiments with the form of his poem grew, so did the consciousness of his mythic character until, in Book 5, it almost becomes antithetical to his earthly beginning.

The preface of the work suggests the sort of oppositions Williams felt compelled to wed; the quest of beauty is begun by "defective means":

> Sniffing the trees,
> just another dog
> among a lot of dogs.
>
> (*P*, 11)

Though the rest of the dogs are chasing rabbits, this lame dog sniffs out beauty. The simple and the complex must be held as one, even in metaphors such as this one. The "craft" of poetry (vessel and talent) that links the ordinary and the beautiful must be washed clean by a disintegrating stream:

> divided as the dew,
> floating mists, to be rained down and
> regathered into a river that flows
> and encircles. . . .
>
> (*P*, 13)

The form and the substance that can encircle reality, a significant form, requires the inclusion of more than the structure seems prepared to hold. Overcrowding of the lines must occur to avoid the writing of what Williams repeatedly called "stale" poems.

"A false language," "a/language (misunderstood) pouring (misinterpreted) without / dignity, without minister, crashing upon a stone ear" (*P*,

24), the estrangement of men and women from each other and their world:
these inefficacies dominate the disintegrating stream of Book I of *Paterson*.
Images of divorce and separation also appear: the thunder of the Passaic
Falls; daredevil Sam Patch's suicidal leap into the Genesee River; Mrs.
Cummings's antithetically silent slip into the Passaic River; the insular
university and its "clerks" (an institution Williams also named Jacques
Barzun). These figures, alienated from their world, are "rolled up" into

> a bud forever green,
> tight-curled, upon the pavement, perfect
> in juice and substance but divorced, divorced
> from its fellow, fallen low—
>
> (*P*, 28)

The modulating roar of Williams's long poem seeks to connect these
disparate figures. Historical figures are thrown together, drawn from
newspaper accounts, from local gossip, from Williams's correspondence
with persons whose names we sometimes do and sometimes do not know
(names that include Edward Dahlberg, Allen Ginsberg, and Ezra Pound).
Yet the most important source for these figures remains Williams's own
imagination; even actual characters are "fleshed out" by the poet. This
conglomeration of things inside and outside himself produces an atypical
mix; mundane elements are given the irridescent serenity of the ordinary
world that surrounds us:

> Things, things unmentionable,
> the sink with the waste farina in it and
> lumps of rancid meat, milk-bottle-tops: have
> here a tranquility and loveliness
> Have here (in his thoughts)
> a complement tranquil and chaste.
>
> (*P*, 51)

Poets want an aesthetic order in the ordinary, in things themselves, yet the
order that assembles their "things unmentionable" is given form and
substance in the tropicality of the poet's shaping mind:

> Thought clambers up,
> snail like, upon the wet rocks
> hidden from sun and sight—
>   hedged in by the pouring torrent—
> and has its birth and death there
> in that moist chamber, shut from

the world—and unknown to the world,
cloaks itself in mystery—

(P, 51-2)

This initial, fertile stability of thought wedded to thing, both cut off from the world, soon starts to split apart. As Eliot observed in "Burnt Norton," describing a similar stage in the poetic process:

> Words strain,
> Crack and sometimes break, under the burden,
> Under the tension, slip, slide, perish,
> Decay with imprecision, will not stay in place,
> Will not stay still.

For the poet, the failures of wedding thing to thing and word to word are often the same problem.

These linguistic movements were a continual problem for Williams. Such a dissolving force appears at the opening of Book 2 as the chief sense of the world outside the poet. The divorce of thing from thing, thought from thought, becomes for Paterson a self-inflicted malady, a "kind of blockage, exiling one's self from one's self" (*P*, 59). Walking alone through a park on a Sunday afternoon, he sees a more communicative "ceremonial of love" (*P*, 63), "Love/combating sleep" (*P*, 64). Paterson, the poet-freak in this world of workers released from work who are free now to manifest their love, sees them face to face, sees them "mottled by the shadow of the leaves/upon them, unannoyed" (*P*, 67). But Paterson cannot write his praise of those simple figures who are "not undignified," for he refuses to borrow from erudition in describing them and his own language is "worn out" (*P*, 103); he is

> —saying over to himself a song written
> previously   .   inclines to believe
> he sees, in the structure, something
>   of interest. . . .

(P, 105)

The form of Paterson's fiction-within-this-fiction, though churning, will not come out.

Gradually Paterson's repetitions build their own rhythm, a rhythm that swells into an Aeolian wind that blows through Book 3. The leitmotif "Beautiful thing," as it runs through the books, libraries, newspaper files in which Paterson now rummages, suggests that external reality and the fiction world of the poem are beginning to fuse:

> The province of the poem is the world.
> When the sun rises, it rises in the poem
> and when it sets darkness comes down
> and the poem is dark
>
> (*P,* 122)

The "Beautiful thing" of Book 3 as a "dark flame/a wind, a flood" is a "counter to all staleness" (*P,* 123). Even though the poet apprehends beauty, the reality that creates that beauty still goes unheeded in the world. The fusion of fiction and reality that is present within Paterson is counterbalanced by a despair he finds in a skeptical world outside:

> Give up
> the poem. Give up the shilly-
> shally of art.
>
> What can you, what
> can YOU hope to conclude—
> on a heap of dirty linen?
> —you
> a poet (ridded) from Paradise?
>
> (*P,* 132)

In this despair, the wind turns to fire, the fire consumes the library, and the ashes of the library are carried by the wind. The force that destroys art is very similar to that which creates it. The dissolution of "Beautiful thing" resembles its growth. First it is transformed into "Persephone/gone to hell" (*P,* 151).[7] Persephone—for a moment, a feminine counterpart to Paterson's inclusiveness—turns rapidly into the tapestry of a dying unicorn, a figure that becomes important later in Book 5. These pronounced metamorphoses of Book 3 usher in the most chaotic section of *Paterson:* scrawlings of diary notes, fragments from news clippings, abbreviations introduced with the warning "It is dangerous to leave written that which is badly written. A chance word, upon paper, may destroy the world" (*P,* 155). Williams's solution to the consuming fluid processes that he cannot control becomes: "write carelessly so that nothing that is/not green will survive" (*P,* 155). That assessment is an accurate evaluation of what is found in the third section of Book 3, even if it was meant as an ironic statement of intent. These Poundian poetic imitations are concrete yet isolated signs of the "roar of the present." Nonetheless, in that roar and its chaotic disorder a new creation of fictional form becomes possible, for language itself here is finally heeding the injunction of the poem's beginning: seeing the sun, becoming ignorant again. Books 1 through 3 have meant the breaking of not only cultural myth and poetic tradition, but language itself.

The flow of the river has subsided; the sludge remains:

> When the water has receded most things have lost
> their form. They lean in the direction the current
> went. Mud covers them
>   —fertile (?) mud.
>   (P, 167)

What is now necessary is a reconstruction of language, the river, the giant that sleeps beneath the falls, the form of poetic speech. That task seems beyond human capacity:

> The words will have to be rebricked up, the
> —what? What am I coming to   .
>   pouring down?
>   (P, 170)

Like the Passaic's heroic washing of great Paterson's hair, the making of proper speech becomes an heroic cleansing:

> the future's no answer. I must
> find my meaning and lay it, white,
> beside the sliding water: myself—
> comb out the language—or succumb
>   (P, 173)

World and word have now been washed clean.

The fictions that are constructed in Book 4 become a blend of past and imagination; discontinuity now is minimal. The pastoral figures of Corydon and Phyllis speak with contemporary Bergen County speech; biographical material concerning Williams, his wife, Flossie, and their son mix in the second section of Book 4 with economic theories and iconoclastic scientific advice. We are being led to the point at which the river actually opens into the sea. Old Man Paterson, although approaching death, remembers the women he has known and the babies he has seen born; he still stands with an assurance worthy of Tennyson's Ulysses, who stood "strong in will/To strive, to seek, to find, and not to yield." This analogy to Odysseus is suggested by Williams himself. The sea waits and the image of Odysseus-in-Paterson becomes manifest as the Sirens call (cf.P, 234-36). Aged Paterson, released to the "nostalgic sea," finds himself and his language "afloat with weeds, bearing seeds" (P, 234) yet rejecting warnings to turn back, warnings that say that "the sea is not our home" (P, 235). His search for language and the arrangement of those words have marked his own pursuit of fame, have demanded that the sea be his home. His seeds link him to previous generations, as his analogous relation to Odysseus links him to an earlier world. But those seeds reflect new life, not an earlier one, something yet to be achieved, a potentiality.

On the mariner's return to the shores of the modern Ithaca, Paterson receives no welcome but that of a yawning and stretching she-dog who takes us back to the sniffing dog of the start of this quest for beauty. She greets him "frisking/her rump awkwardly" (P, 237). Here is the ironic reception of the returning modern hero. Paterson, having ended his pursuit, heads inland, followed by that faithful dog, his only fanfare the spitting out of a plum seed, his colony built with poetry:

> This is the blast
> the eternal close
> the spiral
> the final somersault
> the end.
>
> (P, 238)

This evocation of the world of "The Hollow Men" is not the end, however, despite the emphasis on termination here. Seven years separate the completion of Books 4 and 5. In that time the bare rock of the figure of Paterson as common city, man, and river was wrapped more and more by a muse that has spun earlier artists' fictive coverings, particularly the dancing peasants of Peter Brueghel the Elder's paintings and the many medieval unicorn tapestries. Williams, however, sees the unicorn and Brueghel's peasants not as artistic creations with cultural significance, but simply as things, things that are of a kind with that waste farina in the sink. All are tranquil, lovely, and finally chaste. As it ages, Paterson's eye accepts more and more things into its field of sight. Consequently, his vision is also improving.

The America of Paterson is diverse enough to combine the generating plants of the Passaic with the Cloisters of the Hudson and is paralleled in Book 5 by the metaphor of the whore and the virgin as an inseparable identity. The "Beautiful thing" is simultaneously soiled and inviolate. Finally, it is death that becomes the ultimate "beautiful thing"; its nature is equally contradictory, escape yet defeat. Death stalks the still dying Paterson as it stalks the unicorn; the only escape is a "hole in the bottom of the bag":

> It is through this hole
> we escape
> . . . .
> Through this hole
> at the bottom of the cavern

of death, the imagination
escapes intact.

                                                          (*P*, 247)

Gradually evolving an image of whore-virgin, the poet confesses that she
has been his driving force, the source as well as example of his "Beautiful
thing," even the raison d'être of the imagination itself:

                intelligent woman
                have you read anything that I have written
        It is all for you
                                                          (*P*, 257)

With this confession begins the dance of Paterson the satyr and his virginal
whore. It is the same dance that was launched in the hunt of the unicorn
and the making of a poem: the pursuit of a being at once spirit and matter.
The most important tapestries of that hunt are not those found within the
Cloisters; rather, they are woven by Williams in his poem. That dance
continues through the section of Paterson in which Williams experiments
with his three-part "variable foot," a combination of separation and
connection that attempts to capture stasis and change simultaneously. That
dance draws into its circle such fellow satyrs as Paul Klee, Dürer,
Leonardo, Bosch, Picasso, Juan Gris and, curiously, Freud.

   After an interruption for an interview in which the poet is asked, "can
you tell me, simply, what poetry is?" (*P*, 261), the dance returns,
subsuming the double vision of Brueghel in a final "rolling up." Here we
get the answer to that amateur's question. In the works of this Flemish
painter as Paterson sees them, is hard reality, a hard reality covered with
the fictions of the imagination. For "the/suits of his [Brueghel's] peasants
were of better stuff, hand woven, than we/can boast" (*P*, 265). Brueghel's
peasants and the unicorn tapestries must still become one with Paterson
himself; the final fiction-making of *Paterson* is the creation of Williams's
own peasant tapestry which he calls

                . . . the living fiction
                    a tapestry
        silk and wool shot with silver threads
                                                          (*P*, 272)

The poem—at least the poem as we have it—ends on the dance made
possible by the making of a form, the only weaving of the tapestry that is
possible. It is a tragic rhythm that suggests the fate of the dying Paterson,
yet a rhythm of significant form:

We know nothing and can know nothing
                    but
the dance, to dance to a measure
contrapuntally,
                    Satyrically, the tragic foot.

                                        (*P*, 278)

The "living fiction" of that contrapuntal music has made vivid fiction and
vivid fact inseparable partners in this formal dance. The dance has resulted
in weaving the fictive form of Paterson as a "tapestry [of] silk and wool shot
with silver threads," a tapestry woven so well that we can't know which
is which. "How can we know the dancer from the dance?" asked Yeats in
"Among School Children." Williams here becomes both; Paterson is finally
both poet and poem.

                                III

    The irregularity and constant movement of *Paterson's* open, accumula-
tive form contrasts sharply with the measured regularity of the thirty
strophes of tercets that comprise the body of *Notes Toward a Supreme
Fiction.* While the contemplative tone of Stevens's poem may seem less
inclusive than the constantly modulating voices of *Paterson*, each poem
deals with the possibility of poetry itself. The poet, simultaneously a
craftsman, an aesthetician, and a model for the abstract character in the
poem, has set out to understand his own metaphysic of poetry and reality.
Through an act of mind the poet wills the form of that metaphysic into
being.
    Stevens's poem, framed by a dedicatory prologue and an epilogue, is
divided into three groupings of ten strophes each: "It Must Be Abstract,"
"It Must Change," and "It Must Give Pleasure." The three divisions share
a syllogistic form that previous critics, as far as I know, fail to note. The first
three strophes of each division present the difficulties of achieving
abstraction, change, and pleasure in terms of thesis, antithesis, and
elaboration; the fourth strophe asserts a new proposition as a resolution of
the conflict presented in 1 through 3. Strophes 5 to 9 move through positive
and negative variations on the proposition, a movement into the final
strophe 10, which acts as a synthesis and conclusion for each division. The
result of this reassertion of syllogistic form—a form implied, not stated—is
the cohesion of a series of parts brought together. That cohesion not only
seeks to present the poetic mind at work but also sets out to capture the
dialectical nature of thought itself in the poem's ultimate "idea": any
supreme fiction (1) must be abstract so that a union may be produced

between the particular and the general; (2) must neither retain an imposed rigidity nor adhere to constant, unordered change; and (3) must not impose a covering denying reality, but through fiction discover and portray an integral order relating that covering and reality.

As early as *Harmonium*, his first volume of poetry, Stevens announced to a "High-Toned Old Christian Woman" that "Poetry is the supreme fiction, madame" (*CP*, 59). Bernard Heringman has convincingly pointed to another poem of that same volume, "To the One of Fictive Music," as an early example of poetry of synthesis that attempts to reveal itself as a supreme fiction.[8] In *Notes*, a supreme fiction is the culminating intention and major achievement of the poem. The poet of *Notes* insists on an unrelenting return to the "rock," strips away all fictions but one—the fiction of the real. The dedication of *Notes* refers to such a fiction as "the central of our being" and in "An Ordinary Evening in New Haven" that fiction becomes a search for

> The poem of pure reality, untouched
> By trope or deviation, straight to the word,
> Straight to the transfixing object, to the object
>
> At the exactest point at which it is itself,
> Transfixing by being purely what it is. . . .
>
> (*CP*, 471)

1. "IT MUST BE ABSTRACT"

The source of the "poem of pure reality" is the sun itself. It is the thesis of strophe 1 of "It Must Be Abstract" that all fictive coverings, human and divine, must be stripped away by the ephebic artist if he is to see the sun. An antithesis, however, appears directly in 2: reality seen clearly is blinding, "so poisonous/Are the ravishments of truth, so fatal to/The truth itself" (CP, 381). The third strophe presents examples of the contradictory propositions of 1 and 2; it establishes tension between the poem's "ever-early candor" and "its late plural" (*CP*, 382), our points of departure and our ultimate results. In strophe 3 polarities abound: feel-think, one-many, reason-emotion, night-day, wild-gentle, peculiar-ordinary, even the hoobla-hoobla-hoobla-how of an exotic Arabian's song (his way of giving meaning to the moon[9]) against the hoobla-how of the wood dove's natural song.

The reader's task of making sense of this polar world mirrors the task of the poet in 4 to transform the dialectic of the first three strophes into a suitable proposition. If we are to find the "central of our being," we must return to a state that predates man, one that may predate paradise:

> The first idea was not our own. Adam
> In Eden was the father of Descartes
> And Eve made air the mirror of herself,
>
> Of her sons and of her daughters. They found themselves
> In heaven as in a glass; a second earth;
> And in the earth itself they found a green—
>
> The inhabitants of a very varnished green.
>
> (*CP*, 383)

Descartes and even prelapsarian man gave order to existence, creating for themselves a mythic heaven that, like a mirror, served as a reflection of the earth they saw ("a second earth"). Yet this heaven-as-second-earth is imperfect even in Eden (a "very varnished green"). Stevens insists on a myth before that myth of heaven began, a "muddy centre."[10] For Stevens the confirmed agnostic, our origins are cloudy, indefinable, but "venerable and articulate and complete." By returning to this origin and not that which follows, the poem's growth imitates that of the world and of man:

> From this the poem springs: that we live in a place
> That is not our own and, much more, not ourselves
> And hard it is in spite of blazoned days.
>
> (*CP*, 383)

That the artist has essential links to what has preceded him is here denied. Like Williams's necessary escape from a present in which language is dead, divorced from itself, Stevens's insistence on a primal state that transcends tradition places him in the only adequate world for poets.

The variations now begin. Can we create a somewhat permanent system (a "castle-fortress-home"), a system in which to preserve that vision of the primal state, that "muddy centre"? Can we link a mythic "giant" of the weather to the literal weather we can see (the "mere air")? Attempts at answers appear: (1) the "first idea is an imagined thing" (*CP*, 387); (2) the "giant of the weather" may be the heroic figure for man (the "MacCullough" as Stevens calls him); and (3) the MacCullough remains MacCullough—that is, any man might become the hero, yet every man is not by definition this heroic "major man." The search in *Notes* for a man-hero, a "major man," to replace a divine hero does not lead to every man. The rejection at the outset of the poem of the ephebic artist as model has shown that "It does not follow that major man is man" (*CP*, 387). The ephebe has not yet sighted that "muddy centre." If one opens oneself to an experience of reality, like the mystic receiving his enlightenment, if one then can imagine and accept a "blooding" of the "first idea," one *may* become major man. Poetic speech may then be possible:

> As if the waves at last were never broken,
> As if the language suddenly, with ease,
> Said things it had laboriously spoken.
>
> (*CP*, 387)

We are now ready for the clarifying summation of strophe 10. The "idea of man" is close to that "muddy centre"; major man's duty is to that idea and not himself alone. Man is "abler/In the abstract than in his singular" (*CP*, 388); the "idea of man" exceeds any one man. The poet can and must demonstrate the capacity of man, the "final elegance."

Stevens's advice to the ephebic artist becomes clear: he must accept himself neither as a victim ("to console") nor as one of the chosen ("to sanctify"). Instead, the poet must "plainly propound" that the capacity of man, his "final elegance," is based on what man actually is "in his old coat, his slouching pantaloons" (*CP*, 389). Poetry as a supreme fiction must be abstract, but it must be an "abstraction blooded." The ordinary man is the source of major man, for he is at once man in the abstract and in the specific.

2. "IT MUST CHANGE"

It is as an attempt "plainly to propound" that the poem continues into its second major division, "It Must Change." In the initial strophe, an old seraph, an apotheosis of the romantic self, seeks an immutable world. He chooses only what he wishes to see as suitable reality, secluding himself from all but a self-reinforcing world. His imagination chooses, among other things, Italian girls with jonquils in their hair. Stevens's word choice is not haphazard, for jonquils are of the species *Narcissus*. The world of self-reinforcement that Stevens playfully presents is broken by the bees who "came booming/As if they had never gone." (*CP*, 390). The order of the seraph's selected objects-in-reality is explored by the natural world's demand for change just as Paterson's desire to control was destroyed early in Williams's poem. Romantic choice cannot control time's flux; the imagination, even of that old seraph, must choose "inconstant objects of inconstant cause/In a universe of inconstancy" (*CP*, 389).

A self-focused imagination like the seraph's is destroyed by such inconstancy. Here booming bees herald clattering pigeons, as "casual flocks" of pigeons intrude at the conclusion of "Sunday Morning." According to Stevens, the difficulty here is not that the seraph's world changes, but that the seraph has created a "withered scene" that "has not changed enough" (*CP*, 390). It is not just that change cannot be prevented; it must be fostered. Here, then, is our initial assertion of "It Must Change."

The selective seraph, however, is not the worst offender; he has an antithesis in the impositions of the President in strophe 2. A comic representative for political man in general, the President "ordains the bee to be/Immortal" (*CP*, 390) and orders his aides to adjust the curtains to a "metaphysical t." Both the President and his ordered world are indicted by the "everloudening" bee:.

> This warmth is for lovers at last accomplishing
> Their love, this beginning, not resuming, this
> Booming and booming of the new-come bee.
>
> (*CP*, 391)

Time and love have eroded the fixed order of the President's world.

Both of these distortions of the mutable world are presented in strophe 3, specifically in the equestrian statue of General Du Puy. This memorial to an insignificant man is an empty show of form. What was "true flesh" is no more than "inhuman bronze"; there is an absence of the imagination in the General's life and in the statue's sculptor. Not only is it an unimaginative fiction, but it also resists change and movement, cut off and silent in its own "empty heaven." Art in general, like a supreme fiction here, creates no permanence. If any optimism exists in "It Must Change," it lies in an endurance outside individual artistic durability. In Yeats's "Lapis Lazuli,"

> All things fall and are built again
> And those that build them again are gay.

In *Notes*, Yeats's cycle is paralleled by the "intrinsic couples" of polar opposites wedded in strophe 4, opposites that depend upon and embrace each other: the imagined-the real, music-silence, feeling-understanding. From their tension, change is born:

> The partaker partakes of that which changes him.
> The child that touches takes character from the thing,
> The body, it touches. The captain and his men
>
> Are one and the sailor and the sea are one.
> Follow after, O my companion, my fellow, my self,
> Sister and solace, brother and delight.
>
> (*CP*, 392)

Viewing the "muddy centre" results in change for the viewer, change that strengthens and delights. The song of the man of imagination is forming.

But his inevitable testing must follow such a successful wedding of "the sailor and the sea."

As the variations begin in 5, the Southern island-mountain-pineapple-great banana tree that was the poet's reflection of his actual landscape appears as vivid and as "real" as the world before him. The "he" of this passage calls to mind many of Stevens's earlier characters, such as Crispin in "The Comedian as the Letter C," Hoon from "Tea at the Palaz at Hoon," and, most notably, the blue guitarist; each contemplated his origins and his creations (Crispin's "idea of a colony," Hoon's desire for self-sufficiency, the song played upon a pale blue guitar). Even as "he" dies, "sighing that he should leave the banjo's twang" (*CP*, 393), he still affirms the power of the imagination to transform reality even as the imagination and that reality are both changing themselves:

> He thought often of the land from which he came,
> How that whole country was a melon, pink
> If seen rightly and yet a possible red.
>
> (*CP*, 393)

After this positive variation on the theme of change, negative versions appear in strophe 6. A chorus of birds, an "idiot minstrelsy," sing rigid songs of vanity ("Bethou me") or of dogma ("Bethou him") in a droning note, their "ké-ké." These songs, like the "men of one idea," produce a world of one particular, a world "Of stone, that never changes" (*CP*, 394). "It will end," Stevens says; change must and will occur. The response of 7 suggests that after experiencing the brilliance of the imagination, "the lustre of the moon," man has no need of any divinity—either of the self or of any external locus. It is the "easy passion, the ever-ready love/Of the lover" magnified by the natural world ("the lilacs") that allows a sighting of the real; it is a love

> Which he can take within him on his breath,
> Possess in his heart, conceal and nothing known.
>
> (*CP*, 395)

But the moment of bliss inevitably fades; it cannot be held for long, even by the poet. With a warning that should humble all of his interpreters, Stevens writes of the poet as an "ignorant man"

> Who chants by book, in the heat of the scholar, who writes

> The book, hot for another accessible bliss:
> The fluctuations of certainty, the change
> Of degrees of perception in the scholar's dark.
>
> (*CP*, 395)

In strophe 8, Nanzia Nunzio stands in a similar "dark" before Shelley's inflexible Ozymandias and offers herself as spouse to his "noble majesty." She performs the only stripping away of coverings that she comprehends and asks him to array her with "the spirit's diamond coronal." She seeks a transcendent moment by wedding her sensuality to his rigidity. But the egocentric imagination cannot escape itself by surrendering to strict order. Even Ozymandias, inflexible though he is, has heard the "booming of the bees" and seen those immortal sands. Nanzia Nunzio's belief that she is the "woman stripped more nakedly than nakedness" (*CP*, 296) is another example of idiot minstrelsy. Ozymandias realizes that "the spouse, the bride is never naked" (*CP*, 396). Her desire for a perfect coupling denies the fact that a "fictive covering/Weaves always glistening from the heart and mind." The imagination and reality continue their harmonious conflict. Art—and in turn a supreme fiction—that achieves such a harmonious conflict can transcend itself, existing as it does at the very "origin of change." Dialectical movement, not permanent polarity, is Stevens's way of producing a significant form of that fiction in the poem:

> The poem goes from the poet's gibberish to
> The gibberish of the vulgate and back again.
>
> (*CP*, 396)

While it is common speech that the poet seeks, he must "compound the imagination's Latin with/The lingua franca et jocundissima" (*CP*, 397), combining vision with the language of things themselves.

In strophe 10 of "It Must Change," the poet (the major man of "It Must Be Abstract") sits on a park bench and looks out on a lake "full of artificial things" (*CP*, 397). Metamorphosis occurs; swans become seraphs, saints, and "changing essences." The literal swan of beauty, through the imagination's language (the "Theatre of Trope") undergoes a "will to change" that makes it a source rather than an ending. Through many variations, like those metamorphosing swans, "It Must Change" has led to its summation, its ultimate moment:

> The freshness of transformation is
>
> The freshness of a world. It is our own,
> It is ourselves, the freshness of ourselves,
> And that necessity and that presentation
>
> Are rubbings of a glass in which we peer.
>
> (*CP*, 397-98)

Change in the world of poetry is not a permanent end, but a permanent beginning that offers the ultimate transcendence of our ignorant blindness, gives us our first sight through that impenetrable glass of the "muddy centre."

3. "IT MUST GIVE PLEASURE"

The pleasure of such a beginning ("To speak of joy and to sing it" [*CP*, 398]) organizes the third division of the fugal song of *Notes*, "It Must Give Pleasure." The thesis of strophe 1 deals with three degrees of the song of art: singing the love of humans; transferring that "joyful love" to a spiritual dimension, "more than sensual" (CP, 398); finally, singing of that "difficultest rigor," the immediate perception of total experience. Not surprisingly, the highest form of pleasure for Stevens involves a vision of the sun:

> On the image of what we see, to catch from that
>
> Irrational moment its unreasoning,
> As when the sun comes rising, when the sea
> Clears deeply, when the moon hangs on the wall
>
> Of heaven-haven. These are not things transformed.
> (*CP*, 398-99)

This assertion of the first strophe is balanced by the example of the second: the "blue woman." She rejects the concealing silver-coatings ("feathery argentines," which disguise the real). It is sufficient for her to remember the highest moment of pleasure, the "corals of dogwood, cold and clear" (*CP*, 400), even if she cannot now experience them. What was, need not be what is, for autumn follows summer's heat. That moment is "real, / Clear and except for the eye, without intrusion." We see here an affirmation of the untransformed moment, but also an admission of the fictive covering that perception and memory must bring (the "intrusion" of the eye).

Between the theoretical affirmation of strophe 1 and the actual example of the blue woman of 2 lies an experiential gap, like the gulf between the first two stages of pleasure and the "difficultest rigor" in 1. The achievement of that third state is the concern of the remainder of "It Must Give Pleasure." The "lasting visage" in the burning bush of 3 illustrates the tension mentioned above, a face that suggests the metamorphic qualities that Ozymandias's inflexible order cannot:

> A lasting visage in a lasting bush,
> A face of stone in an unending red,
> Red-emerald, red-slitted blue, a face of slate . . .
> (*CP*, 400)

The burning image of "red-in-red repetitions never going/Away" accrues more and more intensity as the strophe develops. Yet its reality is predicated on what "might and might have been." Although this sort of god is the vivid creation of an imaginative man, perhaps Moses' vision of Yahweh as told by an Orphic poet, this image's reality is less than the precise memory of the blue woman. Her vision "was"; this image "might and might have been" (*CP*, 400).

With an echo of the last line of 1, the opening of 4 returns us to "what we see clearly/And have seen." In Catawba, a land seen clearly, a "great captain and the Maiden Bawda" enter a "mystic marriage." This is the marriage that Ozymandias and Nanzia Nunzio could not make, a marriage of an imaginative man and his earth as "love's characters come face to face" (*CP*, 401).

Distortions of this sort of marriage dominate the next three strophes. In 5, 6, and 7, the allegorical figure of Canon Aspirin, the curer of spiritual headaches, tells a tale of his sister and her daughters at a posh dinner. These children are transformed by their mother into tragic extensions of herself—drab, motley, forbidden to dream. She thinks that she is achieving a perfect childhood for them; instead, what she is producing are images of herself, a song of "Bethou me."

Ironically, the Canon does not reflect upon these consequences until in the starkness of his own sleep: "normal things had yawned themselves away" (*CP*, 402). In a harsh "nothingness [that] was a nakedness," his dreaming imagination forces him to construct a way to deal with not only the events of the day but "the very material of this mind." He becomes his own angelic guide, flies to the children's bed and confronts a choice between descending to their inflicted drabness or ascending to a heaven of his dreams in which these children are what he makes of them. His choice is not to choose, but to include

> things
> That in each other are included, the whole,
> The complicate, the amassing harmony.
>
> (*CP*, 403)

His choice, as the opening lines of 7 indicate, is a rational imposition and not a discovery of order. The shortcomings of those idiot minstrelsies of General Du Puy and Nanzia Nunzio are still present. The Canon cannot allow himself to discover; he must rather compose an order.

A more positive alternative to an imposition of eternal summer is drawn; discovery is and must be possible:

> To discover an order as of
> A season, to discover summer and know it,

To discover winter and know it well, to find
Not to impose, not to have reasoned at all,
Out of nothing to have come on major weather,

It is possible, possible, possible. It must
Be possible. It must be that in time
The real will from its crude compoundings come. . . .

(*CP*, 403-4)

These forceful injunctions are the result of sightings and resightings of the real that occur during "major weather," since they are the moments of triumph for "major man." The poet insists here on the highest form of pleasure: the real emerging and developing from its dark, elemental origin:

To find the real,
To be stripped of every fiction except one,

The fiction of an absolute—Angel
Be silent in your luminous cloud and hear
The luminous melody of proper sound.

(*CP*, 404)

The "absolute" is an absolute reality; the only pleasure or fiction tolerable is the supreme variety. Here, too, is the source of the only acceptable language.

Yet the failure of the Canon Aspirin to recognize the "golden centre, the golden destiny," to see the sun, needs to be reconciled with this theoretical success. In 8, the poet asks himself if, in imagining this angel, he has perhaps imagined only himself:

Is it he or is it I that experience this?
Is it I then that keep saying there is an hour
Filled with expressible bliss, in which I have

No need, am happy, forget need's golden hand,
Am satisfied without solacing majesty . . . ?

(*CP*, 404-5)

By demanding his own flight to the "nothingness that was a nakedness," Stevens admits that the heroic major man as well as the orders imposed by the President General Du Puy and the Canon Aspirin, are all reflections of the self. Even his insistence that there must be an "expressible bliss" is a distortion of the real (although he calls it the "fiction of an absolute"). Any answer to "Bethou me" songs must be an imaginative expansion of the self, based not upon what that self desires or ought to be, but "as I am, I am"

(*CP*, 405). The poet's language must be based on what is; the injunction "plainly to propound" has not been forgotten.

In that expansive state, the poet then (9) can "do all that angels can," or ever could. As that supreme state becomes more visible, as the poet-major man "turns the thought round and round," and participates in the act of creating a universe, he becomes his own divinity, his own hero, his own imitation of reality. He does not attempt to limit or to define his own self, reality, or the major weather appropriate for his major man, but offers only that result of imaginative creation which allows him to see and know: a fictive covering for the real. The ephebe has given way to the developed poet; tortured impotence has become fruitful growth.

Even as the poet recognizes and addresses the result of that development (his vision of the earth, his "fat girl,") and even as he weaves his fiction, the substance of his poetry, the earth, what is, is changing:

> How is it I find you in difference, see you there
> In a moving contour, a change not quite completed?
>
> You are familiar yet an aberration.
>
> > (*CP*, 406)

The "universe of constancy" shifts even as the poet is in the midst of crafting his vision of it. Here is the ultimate reason why the poet must cloak his reality with a fiction: to stop the spinning of a "fluent mundo" in the delicate craftsmanship of the poem. In the synthesizing conclusion of "It Must Give Pleasure" is, as well, the awaited moment of *Notes Toward a Supreme Fiction*, a moment like that foreshadowed in the "vivid transparence" of the poem's dedication:

> They will get it straight one day at the Sorbonne
> We shall return at twilight from the lecture
> Pleased that the irrational is rational,
>
> Until flicked by feeling, in a gildered street,
> I call you by name, my green, my fluent mundo,
> You will have stopped revolving except in crystal.
>
> > (*CP*, 406-7)

That nearly perfect moment is at once recognition and naming, vision and achievement. The crystal clarity of Stevens's vision is not static but motion perceived and given form.

Finally, the epilogue to Notes demonstrates the inseparability of these three aspects of a supreme fiction and the inseparability of poetic form and theory. Both the soldier to whom the epilogue is addressed (the poem was written during World War II) and the poet fight interdependent battles. The war between the real and the imagined depends upon "changing" without falsifying the real. In the necessary shifting of reality, the poet must face his antithesis—the contemplative man must meet the man of action. The real war, says Stevens, ends, while the imaginative man's struggle between sun and moon goes on:

> How simply the fictive hero becomes the real;
> How gladly with proper words the soldier dies,
> If he must, or lives on the bread of faithful speech.
> (CP, 408)

In *The Necessary Angel*, his series of essays on the imagination, Stevens says that the imagination pressing back against the pressure of reality "seems in the last analysis, to have something to do with self-preservation; and that, no doubt, is why the expression of it, the sound of its words, helps us to live our lives."[11] The artist is literally, therefore, not only a soldier of the imagination but also a soldier of reality, of life itself. Art's debts to experience and the effect of art upon future happenings are only corollaries to the conviction that the "theory of poetry" is the "theory of life." In "An Ordinary Evening in New Haven," that equation becomes the "life of poetry":

> This endlessly elaborating poem
> Displays the theory of poetry,
> As the life of poetry. A more severe,
>
> More harassing master would extemporize
> Subtler, more urgent proof that the theory
> Of poetry is the theory of life,
>
> As it is, in the intricate evasions of as,
> In things seen and unseen, created from nothingness,
> The heavens, the hells, the worlds, the longed-for lands.
> (*CP*, 486)

The "Bread of faithful speech" that closes *Notes Toward a Supreme Fiction* is both the only Host possible in this poem and the only form appropriate to the clearest sighting we have of that "endlessly elaborating poem" that for Stevens was the life of a poetry of a supreme fiction.

IV

My illustrations and interpretations are offered with the consoling words of Frank Kermode in mind:

It is not expected of critics as it is of poets that they should help us to make sense of our lives; they are bound only to attempt the lesser feat of making sense of the ways we try to make sense of our lives.[12]

The task of the critic, while "lesser," is often as elusive as making sense of life. Yet it should be clear by now that even this secondary role is cloaked in suggestions of the fictive, particularly in that phrase *the ways we try*. Conclusions of the critic are therefore unavoidable fictions, even if they make sense.

The significant fiction, its form and the source of new life rested for Wallace Stevens and William Carlos Williams in their pursuit of the long, synthetic poem. Stevens's abstractions had to be "blooded" on the rock he called the real; Williams, who rummaged, borrowed, and collected, demanded "no ideas but in things." For both of these poets, the fictive and the real were joined only in the making of poetry, in making *the* poem about the making of poetry itself. This form-making became for each of them a dependence upon a mythology that arises through the single imagination observing objects-in-reality, through wedding the imaginative self and the outside world in the poem being formed. For each poet, such a fictive form could become the ground of his being while simultaneously transcending that being. While Williams's vision of fictive and real enlarged the personal imagination and expanded the self to an inclusive abstraction he called Paterson, his unifying force remained the physical reality of "things" controlling the imagination. On the other hand, while Stevens's wedding of reality and imagination began with the "muddy centre" preliminary to all fictions, a self stripped to a nakedness that he cloaked with an abstraction called a supreme fiction, his unifying force remained his liberated imagination ordering that concrete reality.

Here are two final examples of the results of these parallel processes. Each points to the moment when fictive and real become indistinguishable. First, the pungent asphodel that is Williams's "greeny flower":

> Asphodel
>> has no odor
>>> save to the imagination
>
> but it too
>> celebrates the light.
>>> It is late
> But an odor as from our wedding
>> has revived for me
> and begun again to penetrate
>> into all crevices
>>> of my world.[13]

That medicinal process has a counterpart in the reddening rubies that define Stevens's "Description without Place":

> In a description hollowed out of hollow-bright,
> The artificer of subjects still half night.
>
> It matters, because everything we say
> Of the past is description without place, a cast
>
> Of the imagination, made in sound;
> And because what we say of the future must portend,
>
> Be alive with its own seemings, seeming to be
> Like rubies reddened by rubies reddening.
>
> (CP, 345-54)

While the shapes, tones, and details of their poems differ, Williams the physician and Stevens the insurance man share something crucial: the voice of the poet speaking not only of his world but of how it can be formed, of the moment of making as well as the creation itself, that point at which the making of our myths may yet begin.

NOTES

1. Cf. p. 85.

2. William Carlos Williams, *Paterson* (New York: New Directions, 1963), p. 10. All subsequent references to *Paterson* are from this edition and will be abbreviated throughout as *P* plus the appropriate page number (s).

3. Wallace Stevens, *The Collected Poems* (New York: Knopf, 1954), p. 385. All subsequent references to Stevens's collected poetry are from this edition and will be abbreviated as *CP* plus the appropriate page number(s).

4. Clive Bell, *Art* (London: Chatto and Windus, 1913), p. 8.

4. Kenneth Burke, *Counter-Statement*, 2d ed. (Los Altos: Hermes Publ., 1953), p. ix.

6. John C. Thirlwall, "The Genesis of the Epic *Paterson*," *Today's Japan* 4 (March 1959): 65.

7. A later use of Williams's 1920 improvisation *Kora in Hell*, written to the actual figure of Flossie, his wife, as well as the Kora of the poet's imagination. This motif also appears in "Asphodel, That Greeny Flower" and, of course, figures prominently in Ezra Pound's early cantos.

8. Cf. Bernard Heringman, "Wallace Stevens: The Reality of Poetry" (Ph. D. dissertation, Columbia University, 1955), p. 149.

9. The identification of the Arabian with the moon is made explicit in a letter Stevens sent to Hi Simon on 12 January 1943, which is collected in *Letters of Wallace Stevens*, selected and edited by Holly Stevens (New York: Knopf, 1966), and appears there on p. 434.

10. This "muddy centre" seems to echo a concept suggested several centuries earlier by the

German mystic Jacob Boehme. For Boehme, God was the *Ungrund*, the indefinable matter of the universe, not an anthropomorphic or external being.

11. Wallace Stevens, *The Necessary Angel* (New York: Knopf, 1951), p. 36.

12. Frank Kermode, *The Sense of an Ending: Studies in the Theory of Fiction* (New York: Oxford University Press, 1967), p. 3.

13. William Carlos Williams, "Asphodel, That Greeny Flower," *Pictures from Brueghel and Other Poems: Collected Poems 1950-1962* (New York: New Directions, 1962), p. 182.

SUGGESTED READINGS

Conarroe, Joel. *William Carlos Williams' 'Paterson': Language and Landscape*. Philadelphia: University of Pennsylvania Press, 1970.

Kermode, Frank. *Wallace Stevens*. New York: Grove Press, 1960.

Litz, A. Walton. *Introspective Voyager: The Poetic Development of Wallace Stevens*. New York: Oxford University Press, 1972.

Mazzaro, Jerome. *William Carlos Williams: The Later Poems*. Ithaca, N. Y.: Cornell University Press, 1973.

Miller, J. Hillis. *Poets of Reality: Six Twentieth-Century Writers*. Cambridge, Mass.: Harvard University Press, 1966.

Pearce, Roy Harvey. *The Continuity of American Poetry*. Princeton, N. J.: Princeton University Press, 1961.

Riddell, Joseph N. *The Clairvoyant Eye*. Baton Rouge: Louisiana University Press, 1965.

Spender, Stephen. *The Struggle of the Modern*. Berkeley: University of California Press, 1963.

Stevens, Wallace. *The Necessary Angel*. New York: Knopf, 1951.

Thirlwall, John C. "William Carlos Williams' *Paterson:* The Search for the Redeeming Language—A Personal Epic in Five Parts," *New Directions 17* (1961): 252-310.

Vendler, Helen Hennessy. *On Extended Wings: Wallace Stevens' Longer Poems*. Cambridge, Mass.: Harvard University Press, 1969.

Williams, William Carlos. *I Wanted to Write a Poem*. Boston: Beacon Press, 1958.

Section IV

Mythic Thought as Archetypal Patterns

SECTION PREFACE

The essays in the preceding section deal with poetry as mythic process in the sense that through such a process poetry creates an appropriate truth. In Section IV, the interest in process reappears in the essays dealing with plays and films, but this time the interest concerns process as ritual.

All the essays deal with archetypes, and the combined papers demonstrate the breadth and richness of this mythic approach to literature. For example, the first two, those of Catherine Smith and John Vickery, explore different archetypes, showing how they pervade and shape specific works and even whole cultures. In doing so, the authors manage to survey a large range of literature as well as supplying illuminating commentary on individual authors. On the other hand, the essays by Tucker Orbison, Louis Casimir, and William Arrowsmith, dealing with single works and responding to the temporal nature of their genre, display particular interest in process as ritual. They show basically how the play or film constitutes for the audience a vicarious ritual through which the author can modify the spectator's sensibility—a notion related to Aristotelian catharsis.

In the first paper, Catherine Smith demonstrates how the archetypes of sex were essentially created by literature and the mythic faculty, and how normal sexual attributes were eventually displaced to the wrong sex, thus wrenching the psyche into employing otherwise inexplicable symbols. In this way literature and mythos gave us great works, but at the same time gave us hobbled poets and humiliated women.

John Vickery explores the archetype of the scapegoat in its remarkable range of manifestations in the literature of many times and genres. He finds the source of the scapegoat in Jung's "shadow," and he discusses the complicated strategies that authors have worked out for this protean figure.

Vickery allows us to perceive once again literature's role in helping us understand ourselves through a distanced experience of life, thus, it is hoped, mitigating the terrible necessity for scapegoats in political and social reality.

Tucker Orbison, in his discussion of a particular production of Arrabal's *The Solemn Communion,* shows first how it is constructed around the initiatory rituals of communion and marriage and around the archetype of the terrible mother. Second, by examining the details of the performance, he shows us how it effectively functions as an initiation ritual for empathetic audiences.

Louis Casimir, dealing with the film and play *Dutchman,* explores the techniques by which LeRoi Jones consciously employs the elements of ancient myth to construct a modern myth and an ancient ritual. The play has, in addition, an overt political dimension emerging from the author's intention to alert and change his audience in highly specific ways.

The last paper of Section IV and of the volume is William Arrowsmith's analysis of Antonioni's film *Red Desert.* His exploration differs from those of Orbison and Casimir in that Arrowsmith shows us how Antonioni so constructs his film as to take his audience through a repetition of the same psychological process of painful growth into life and awareness as that of his heroine, intending thus to affect his audience in a similar way. Again the emphasis is on art and myth as process and ritual.

Biographical Note on Catherine Smith

Following receipt of her doctorate from the University of North Carolina in 1972, Catherine F. Smith worked with Ralph Nader as an editor and writer of *Citizens Look at Congress* (Washington, D.C.: Grossman, 1972), and wrote a filmscript on technology and human values for a movie made by WPSX-TV under a grant from the Pennsylvania Department of Education. She has taught at Pennsylvania State University and is currently assistant professor of English at Bucknell University. She has published in *Women's Studies: An Interdisciplinary Journal* and teaches courses in women's literature and the Victorian period. At present she is working on the relation of Jacob Boehme to the intellectual history of the imagery of androgeny as used by the Romantic poets and modern feminist critics.

The Invention of Sex in Myth and Literature

CATHERINE SMITH

Tributes to *la différence* are hoary and honored. Celebrating what is woman and what is man has traditionally seemed satisfying, probably because experiencing the difference is often not. Since the possibilities are diverse, the only clarifying aids may be preconceived notions of ideal duality or simple urges for order. Certainly sexual differences are easier to imagine than to define reliably. *Feminine* and *masculine* are matters of cultural style, varying sharply within and between groups. Even the biological definition of female and male has been shown to be problematic over evolutionary history, and its description has been as relativistic in scientific theory as in social commentary. In medieval science, for example, woman was viewed primarily within traditional associations of femaleness with evil materiality and multiplicity. In nineteenth-century biological and medical terms, she was often a portrait drawn from Darwinian theories of sexual selection.

La différence, then, is significantly more idealization than representation. A premise in this study is that imagination, independent of observation, impels and preserves the notion of two sexes with separate, fixed, and constant traits. As a heightened, preferred reality, two sexes map relationships in theoretical or imaginative universes, whether they are scientific, poetic, or individual. Leslie Fiedler, in *Love and Death in the American Novel,* develops the idea that love is an invention and the poets its inventors.[1] But love is only the foreground in a field of sexual metaphor. From a wider perspective, an elaborate sexual cosmos appears, with the poets and mythmakers as its principal inventors.

Yet the poetic invention of sex has been curiously narrow in its development. Derived from the apparent biology of human procreation, sexual imagery has traditionally imposed that model on every idea it touched. Mythic activities carried out by males evoke phallic images. The female's symbolic expressiveness is fundamentally marked by her body type and supposed procreative capacities. Imagination operates deterministically in the subject of sex, but we require a form of cultural debriefing to allow us to recognize the limitations that such determinism imposes. C. S. Lewis in *The Allegory of Love* asks the reader to imagine literature without romantic love, as a way of perceiving the impact of its introduction into medieval poetry. I am suggesting a more difficult adjustment of consciousness: the attempt to imagine myth and literature without sex.

Making the attempt calls for comprehending paradises, wildernesses, or new worlds without describing them as virginal; comprehending primordial loneliness without visualizing a lone man or woman; union without copulation or marriage; conflict without rape; new life without pregnancy or the birth of a baby; solipsism or wasteland without whores, hermaphrodites, incest, or homosexuality. Models for the epic could not depend on the sexual politics of hero and queenly prize, or man and lesser mate, or monster and vengeful mother. Muses and artists would not appear as we commonly objectify them. Clearly, the implications of sexual analogy in art are many, and the work of considering them is large.

The principal effort here will be to show the spectrum of sexual metaphor in occidental mythology. More pointedly, I will examine the sexual symbolism in William Blake's poetry. Blake, one of the major inventive poets in English literature, creates his own myth in his later, long poems. Sex is a central mode of expression in that myth.

For many mythmakers, including Blake, the states of existence are four: precreation, creation, experience, and apocalypse. Collections of myth such as Joseph Campbell's *The Masks of God* and *The Hero with a Thousand Faces* show that all four stages are principally described through sexual imagery.[2] Each of those stages is associated with a different aspect of human sexuality. Precreation is imaged as a void of potentiality prior to sexual division. During the next phases of creation and the period of experience, sexes are the chief binary contrast. Sexual relationship becomes the basic dynamic of experience, symbolizing dualistic existence. In apocalyptic transformation, the image of ideal reunification is one of sexual merging.

Looking at these mythic stages individually, we can see the development or invention of sexual symbolism. Frequently in Eastern myth and in the more heterodox Western myths, the precreation stage is represented by an androgynous Being of beings. This primal Being transcends pairs of opposites. It is described as both female and male, but is objectively neither.[3] Orthodox Western myth, on the other hand, usually designates a sex-dominant creator. Perceived as either female or male, this deity creates the world out of itself or through sexual activity with a created Other. In the older myths, the creator is often female; in later ones, such as the Judeo-Christian, the creator is male. Campbell has shown the profound effect on consciousness of the Western Bronze Age cultural revolution from goddess worship to god worship.[4] The imaginative reversal from viewing the source of things as female to viewing it as male must have wrenched minds in ways that scientific revolutions can only approximate. Copernicus, Darwin, and Einstein have had their effect on poetic metaphor, but they are shadows beside the first makers of patriarchal creation myths.

It is perhaps easy to understand why the second mythic stage, creation, might be depicted in its earliest forms as a female maker, a great mother. For early peoples or for a child any time, primitive observation of menstruation, pregnancy, birth, and suckling is powerful. Without knowledge of male functions in reproduction, the observer may perceive woman's swelling belly and regular emissions of blood, babies, and milk as self-generated events. Thus understood, woman provides a store of images by which to express creation. At any rate, her biological liquidity as a context for birth seems to have marked the human psyche. The emergence of life from a fluid medium seems to be one law of imagination.

The shift in creation stories from female to male creators poses obvious problems for imagery drawn from human reproduction. Campbell suggests that patriarchal myth accommodates this shift by agency of a psychic dynamic that Freud calls "displacement of accent." Referring to censorship in dreams, Freud discusses the substitution of a distracting secondary theme in manifest dream content, around which the elements of the latent situation are regrouped, omitted, or reinterpreted. A feeling of indefinable difference, "a sense of something far more deeply interfused," then permeates the whole.[5] In dreamlike mythic displacement, male creativity is the manifest content masking a latent female model for creation. The regrouping of elements calls for new hierarchies of deity. The former goddess is devalued or reexplained. She becomes sister, daughter, mate, or mother of the new god. Her names are sometimes masculinized to name him.[6] Most important, her principal functions and images are transferred to him.

In patriarchal creation, then, divine motherhood becomes divine fatherhood. Through complicated sublimation, birth function shifts, illogically, to male bodies and activities. Campbell cites the example in India of the World Tree growing from the navel of the reclining god Vishnu; before, it had more logically represented the umbilical cord connecting the world of things with the goddess Padma, whose body was the universe. Similarly, Zeus bears Athene from his brain in what Freud termed "transference upward." As the woman gives birth from the womb, so the man from his brain. In Genesis, Eve emerges from Adam's side. The Shaping Spirit in that account creates by the power of the word: the mind the male womb, the mouth the vagina, and the word the birth.[7]

This transference of birth function from goddess to god has been noted and certain of its image displacements pointed out by Campbell and others. Another striking pattern of imagery should also be explored: the imagery of blood. In patriarchal myth, with masculine deities and predominantly male heroes, blood is primarily associated with wound and injury. Bleeding seems especially honorable if caused by traumatic injury in quests, battles, or other extreme efforts to bring about change, and to give birth to new worlds. That imagery may well be another sublimation of earlier myth, a displacement of female menstrual blood and the placental blood that accompanies birth. It may be an imaginative corollary to primitive initiatory rites for males. In those rites, mutilation to emulate female menstrual bleeding, mock childbirth, and the like, illogically express the transition to active manhood. In its original female circumstances, mythic or actual, procreative bleeding is unconnected with wounds or injury. To accommodate male creativity within biological metaphor, the necessary blood must be expressed in ways that males bleed.

Male activity in literature, even at its most constructive, is often objectified as violent bloodiness. Reasons for the bloodiness have been suggested here. The violence may be expression of the shock of displacement. In a universe where life must be viewed as either female or male, and where creativity is understood in female terms yet imaged in male experience, psychic conflict is predictable. It is likely, also, to be terrible. The mythic male may express unconscious envy of femaleness, which for him is the deep structure of creativity. He may resent the necessity to become femalelike, to bleed, in order to create. That ambivalence may result in omnipresent violence. For the mythic female, life may be unending dissociation. A profoundly dispossessed figure, she commonly comes to represent eternal woe, loss, or revenge.

The second mythic stage, creation, is marked by the separation of the sexes. In Western myth, a female emerges from an original androgyne (who is nevertheless usually described as *he*) or from a primal male. She is born only by a split or loss in the previously autonomous male, or by introduction of foreign substance into his environment. In either case, she exists solely in relation to him. He begins to function as perceiving Self; she is objective Other.[8] A goal of existence then becomes reintegration. The original male reachieves autonomy by absorbing his splintered or alien part, the female.

By this sexual dynamic, female symbolism in the third mythic stage, experience, expresses two main areas: all things that are not Self and all unknown parts of Self. She is both phenomena and the unconscious. She also bears the anger and anxiety resulting from fragmentation. As poet Carolyn Kizer has put it, females become

> . . . custodians of the world's best kept secret:
> Merely the private lives of one half of humanity.[9]

Woman objectifies all the enigmatic, paradoxical, unpredictable elements of Self and world for patriarchal man. In a male-centered universe the most exasperating dizzy dame of television comedy is on the same image frequency with the Sphinx of Greek myth. They each suggest to men the terrible otherness of knowledge.

Woman's liquidity serves as image for both her symbolic roles, as fluid phenomena and mercurial perception. Her imagery, in this third stage of experience, depends upon liquidity as it did in the creation stage. Because she flows, she develops a nearly universal association with water. It is the female in myth who inhabits or guards sacred wells; cries floods of tears; ascends from, lives in, or bathes in rivers; is born of sea foam; throws water into male eyes and brutalizes their owner; lures him to destruction or inspires him to new tasks from the rivers, lakes, pools, meres, or seas she inhabits. She suggests the medium, not only of his birth, but also of the existence he stares into, sinks into, sails across, or is engulfed by. Her blood may well be the primary perception underlying that medium. That blood may be the wine-dark sea whose storms and currents he must understand to get himself home again.

At the mythic fourth stage of existence, apocalypse, female physical characteristics and functions are again significant. As the virginal female images new worlds and the procreative female suggests actualized ones, the barren woman chiefly depicts dying ones. The most common examples are the old woman or the whore. In conventional thought, the crone or hag is biology exhausted and the whore is biology wasted. They are opposite sides of the same perception of female as biological functionalism. The biblical description of apocalypse stresses that pregnant or lactating women are inappropriate presences when all is collapsing. One prediction is that it will be "woe to them that are with child and to them that give suck in those days" (Matt. 24:19). On the other hand, a central sign of the coming end is a woman dressed in purple and scarlet, sitting on a scarlet beast "near waters" with the name written on her forehead "MYSTERY, BABYLON THE GREAT, THE MOTHER OF HARLOTS AND ABOMINATIONS OF THE EARTH" (Rev. 17:4-5, 15). Christ's mother and the whore Mary Magdalene are the most significant observers at the crucifixion and the burial, and they are given the first revelation of the ascension (Matt. 28; Mark 16; Luke 24, John 20). The Edda of Northern mythology visualizes the final cataclysm as a breakdown of social and sexual organization:

> Brothers shall fight and fell each other
> And sisters' sons shall kinship stain
> Hard it is on earth with mighty whoredom.[10]

In her final guise as life-destroyer, the symbolic female becomes definite and solid. She completes her earlier elusive fluidity as life-creator and embodier. If engulfment is the way things end, she is its medium. In the Mayan myth of world destruction, for example, the old goddess, patroness of floods and cloudbursts, her head crowned by a writhing snake, overturns the bowls of heavenly waters.[11] The image of the serpent is another sign of the apocalyptic whore, possibly related to the folds of fat that often encircle her body in iconography. A world annihilator who is both woman *and* snake is seen in the lamia and the medusa. Capable of engulfing or absorbing the perceiving mind, the apocalyptic female suggests experience out of control by that mind imaged as male. In patriarchal myth committed to human reproductive metaphor, when the female cannot or will not function, the world ends.

Or, her refusal may signal transformation of the mythic universe. When former sexual patterns are depleted, they may be revitalized in several ways. The whore or hag may be revealed to have been a disguised maiden all along. The aged hero may be made youthful again and the same round can begin once more. Transcendant beings, androgynous or epicene, may emerge to suggest yet another possibility, that of moving beyond sexually determined imagery.

The full mythic round from precreation through apocalypse is scattered over various myths. It appears as a unique whole in William Blake's long poems *The Four Zoas*, *Milton*, and *Jerusalem*. Blake's intent included the construction of his own "system," a comprehensive myth of existence that would be explicable on both social and psychological levels. Sexual imagery systematically expresses much of that myth.

Blake calls the preexistent state Eternity, representing fullest imaginative potential. Creation is the fall from Eternity, a regrettable but necessary event that gives substance to potential. Experience, called Generation in Blake's myth, is the world in which substance actively strives to become form. Failure means lapsing into either the blissful or the brooding passive worlds of blind acceptance that Blake calls Beulah and Ulro. Apocalypse is the return via experience to eternal imagination. The voyage through all these stages is traced by Blake's figure of universal Man, Albion. This primal Man is constituted by four principles called Zoas, each with a panoply of associations and modes of being.

In Blake, as in myth generally, sexual process symbolizes each stage of existence. Blake's Eternity has no sexes; Creation brings them into being. At Creation the Zoas split into male personages with female projections called Emanations. The appearance of Zoas separated from their Emanations suggests all formal conditions placed on previously undivided existence. In Generation, the strife and relationship among the divided Zoas denote all experiential struggles. When their struggle relaxes into acceptance, or tenses into opposition, they are an image for experience at its most reductive. When the sexes become effective contraries, apocalyptic breakthrough is made possible.

Blake takes this conventional, mythical, sexual structure, exploits it gloriously, and then turns it into a comment on itself. His states of eternity, precreation, creation, and apocalypse are themselves metaphors for states of understanding. They are perspectives, not stages of time; mental events, rather than historical ones. Each mind is continually in process through all of them. The cycle to and from Eternity expresses infinite possibility of change as it continually moves through finite stages. Forms of being, such as the sexes, are also only stages along the way. Male and female in Blake are, like all of his contraries, alternative perspectives through which to view existence. They do not exhaust the possible modes. Specific imagery such as associations of female and water thus are subject to the state of the perceiving mind. In creation, life becomes manifold and is imaged by the binary unit of twofold sex. Los, one of the fallen Zoas, is Blake's symbolic male personage. Los's female Emanation, called Enitharmon, appears to him alienated, elusive, and perhaps illusionary after his fall from Eternity. Hence she is described as watery and vague of outline. Her substance depends on Los's perspective. In Generation he actively tries to hammer existence, including his own, into some form of order. Enitharmon then gains more substance in his eyes. Since she is his unconscious energy and his projections, she materializes and begins occasionally to glow. Her changes, subject to Los's efforts, are a little like the effect on the fairy Tinkerbell in *Peter Pan* when believers clap their hands. Enitharmon's sinister weaving of nets, veils, and webs, in Los's more optimistic perspective, appears to be a necessary complement to his own hammering. This relativity of Los and Enitharmon continues throughout Blake's mythic stages.

To become locked into any one perspective or mode of being on this mythic round is to fall asleep. It is to accept a single condition of existence. Exclusively male or female perspective rejects the balance of contraries and limits the mind. To remind us that perspective must continually battle subject/object divisions, Blake calls for androgynous outlooks. He tells us that in the new Jerusalem, his image for Eternity, the sexes must vanish and cease to be.

Yet Blake, for all his insight into the reductiveness of polarizing experience, limits his art by his use of sexual symbolism. In spite of his cabalistic insistence on removing sexes from thought and art, he is orthodox and patriarchal in much of his symbolism. His personifications of time, the artist, the powers of abstraction, feeling, memory—in short, all the major components of the perceiving mind and the active imagination—are male. His figure for the universe itself, Albion, is also male. Characterization of space, materiality, nature, fragmentation, and projectiveness—the obstacles and materials the mind works with—are female. Northrop Frye in *Fearful Symmetry* effectively paraphrases this imagery.

> The material world is in a way feminine to the perceiver; it is the body which receives the seed of his imagination, and the works of the imagination which are the artist's children are drawn from that body. We think of Nature as feminine, and so she is. But as the artist develops he becomes more and more interested in the art and more and more impatient of the help he receives from nature. . . .
>
> The worship of a female principle, therefore, specifically a maternal principle, is not imaginative and is only possible to natural religion.[12]

Frye's comment demonstrates the tendency of criticism to echo traditional sexual symbolism without analyzing it. He does not mention, if he is aware, that Blake's symbolism does not allow for an active, autonomous artist figure who is female, for example.

Blake does offer certain restrictions on this conventionally patriarchal symbolism. His sexes are theoretically contraries, or aspects of wholeness, and not absolutes in themselves. He also suggests, by naming his male artist figure Los, for example, the losses sustained by a purely androcentric imagination.

Yet male and female in Blake's poetic practice typically *are* single conditions. The artist or struggling subject in the long poems is always male, and his emanated energy, vision, and achievements are nearly always female. Male Emanations, or even the advocated androgynous ones, are extremely rare, occurring unambiguously only twice in Blake's poetry.[13] Female exists to mark male incompleteness. Her substance and form are dependent on his perspective at any given point. Her highest realization is to embody his vision.

Blake's sexual imagery that expresses this symbolism is also in many ways orthodox. The splitting of Enitharmon from the male figure Los is visualized as a roiling cataclysm of "blood, milk & tears" that sends a shriek through all Eternity, which "shuddered at sight/Of the first female form now separate" (*The First Book of Urizen*). Throughout experience, Enitharmon and other female Emanations that image the state of separateness are described as wateriness, showers of rain, tears, blood. They may also be fading or dawning light. Slightly more substantial as beautiful young weavers, they draw milky fibers from male loins to make veils, nets, and webs. They trail these over the face of creation, deceptively disguising the eternal forms their male contraries seek. When apocalypse approaches, the females consolidate into the obscenely pleased and plump whore of Babylon, or into a bright, jeweled serpent-dragon. These images are a taunting last view of earthy materiality. At apocalypse itself, the whore of Babylon is transformed into a glowing bride. Called Jerusalem, she is the redeemed energy of Blake's primal male, Albion.

Blake, then, is a tantalizing case study of mythic sex in literature. His achievement tempts us to ask what can be inadequate in so rich an expressive device. Certainly much of modern literature has extended it. The notion that female means fluid experience and male means comprehension of experience is important to Joyce's novels. For Yeats, Hemingway, and T. S. Eliot, whores and hags express life-in-death just as they do for makers of apocalypse myths. Chekhov, in a statement about the genesis of fiction, says, "The centre of gravity must be in two persons: him and her. . . ."[14] Yet for all their persuasive power, Blake and these others demonstrate the confinements that traditional concepts of him and her have placed on imagination.

Sexual imagery in mythology and literature reveals a deep confusion of potential form with apparent function. Our objectified images of transition, as shown in mythic stages of existence, are relentlessly tied to narrow notions of human sexuality. In an unbroken link with life, imaginative sexes are perceived in a profoundly physical mode. Regardless of the circumstances symbolized by sex, the patterning of the imagery usually evokes on some level a mental picture of wiggling sperm and waiting egg. It is a case of physicality not quite transformed as art. The limits placed by this configuration on both male and female characterization are stringent.

Perhaps a need to idealize simpler forms of experience is apparent in the sexual symbolism discussed here. We anachronistically employ the terms *candlepower* and *horsepower* to measure complex technologies that have developed far beyond their original form. Names from older orders somehow control anxiety in stressful new conditions. It is not surprising, then, that we nostalgically attempt to contain discontinuous, increasingly inorganic experience in the familiar organic rhythm of female and male.

The image of woman is particularly limited to her body type and biological role. Stephen Dedalus in Joyce's *A Portrait of the Artist as a Young Man* observes this circumstance, labeling it a confusion of aesthetics and eugenics. Stephen suggests to his friend Lynch, in their discussion of the nature of the beautiful, that every physical quality admired by men in women is in direct connection with the manifold functions of women for the propagation of the species. . . . The world, it seems, is drearier than even you, Lynch, imagined.[15]

This primitive linkage of art and life suggests a conservatism, a time-lag, in metaphor. Even while culture at large moves beyond biological functionalism, as ours is moving, artists still objectify the sexes primarily in those terms. As if there were no new ways to perceive human sexuality, or to understand the condition of duality itself, we have gone on counting up to two: him and her.

It is time for another revolution in the poetics of sex. Goddesses have for too long been unconvincing, and unconvinced, as gods. Revolutions express crises in imagination. They occur when conceptual centers will not hold. When the individual's position relative to God, the king, the sun, the ape, and the atom came into question, the matter and metaphors available to artists changed. Now the female's relativity to the male is altering and art must change again. Masculine and feminine, like the great chain of being, divine right, and the clockwork cosmos, are no longer metaphysical certainties. It is time for imagination, if it can, to create anew the universe.

NOTES

1. Leslie Fiedler, *Love and Death in the American Novel,* rev. ed. (New York: Stein and Day, 1960; 1966), preface, p. 13.

2. Joseph Campbell, *The Hero with a Thousand Faces* (Cleveland: The World Publishing Company, Meridian Books, 1965; first published 1949), p. 273.

3. Ibid., pp. 151-52.

4. Joseph Campbell, *The Masks of God: Occidental Mythology* (New York: The Viking Press, 1964), pp. 1-17.

5. Ibid., pp. 157-58.

6. Robert Graves, *The White Goddess: A Historical Grammar of Poetic Myth* (Farrar, Straus and Cudahy, 1948), p. 47.

7. Campbell, *Occidental Mythology,* p. 157.

8. Simone de Beauvoir discusses this male/female dynamic in chapter 9, "Myths: Dreams, Fears, Idols," of *The Second Sex,* trans. H. M. Parshley (New York: Knopf, 1953).

9. Carolyn Kizer, "Three" from "Pro Femina," in *No More Masks! An Anthology of Poems by Women,* ed. Florence Howe and Ellen Bass (Garden City, N. Y.: Doubleday Anchor Books, 1973), p. 175.

10. Campbell, *Hero,* pp. 375-76.

11. Ibid.

12. Northrop Frye, *Fearful Symmetry: A Study of William Blake* (Boston: Beacon Press, 1962; first published 1947), pp. 74-75.

13. *Jerusalem,* Pl. 49, 1. 47; Pl. 88, 1. ll, in David V. Erdman and Harold Bloom, *The Poetry and Prose of William Blake* (Garden City, N.Y.: Doubleday, 1965).

14. Anton Chekhov, *Letters on the Short Story, the Drama, and Other Literary Topics*, ed. Louis S. Friedland, trans. Constance Garnett (New York: Minton, Balch, 1924), p. 71.

15. James Joyce, *A Portrait of the Artist as a Young Man* (New York: The Viking Press, 1966; first published 1916), p. 208.

SUGGESTED READINGS

Abrams, M. H. *Natural Supernaturalism: Tradition and Revolution in Romantic Literature.* New York: Norton Library, 1971.

Davis, Elizabeth Gould. *The First Sex.* Baltimore, Md.: Penguin Books, 1971.

Ellmann, Mary. *Thinking About Women.* New York: Harcourt Brace Jovanovich, 1968.

Heilbrun, Carolyn G. *Toward a Recognition of Androgyny.* New York: Alfred A. Knopf, 1973.

Hirst, Désirée. *Hidden Riches: Traditional Symbolism from the Renaissance to Blake.* New York: Barnes & Noble, 1964.

Raine, Kathleen. *Blake and Tradition.* London: Routledge & Kegan Paul, 1968.

Secor, Cynthia. Guest ed., "The Androgyny Papers," *Women's Studies: An Interdisciplinary Journal* 2, no. 2 (September 1974).

Biographical Note on John B. Vickery

John B. Vickery, a Canadian, received his doctorate from the University of Wisconsin, where he held an ACIS Advanced Graduate Fellowship. Since then, he has taught at Tennessee, Northwestern, Purdue, and the University of California at Riverside, where he is presently professor of English. In 1975 he was awarded a Guggenheim Fellowship to work on myth and philosophical fiction in the nineteenth and twentieth centuries.

In addition to numerous articles, he has published *Robert Graves and the White Goddess* (Lincoln: University of Nebraska, 1972) and *The Literary Impact of "The Golden Bough"* (Princeton, N. J.: Princeton University Press, 1973). He has edited several collections of essays, notably *Myth and Literature* (Lincoln: University of Nebraska, 1966) and with J. M. Sellery *The Scapegoat: Ritual and Literature* (New York: Houghton Mifflin, 1971). His major interest is modern literature and its anthropological, philosophical, and psychological implications.

The Scapegoat in Literature: Some Kinds and Uses

JOHN B. VICKERY

To the twentieth century the figure and rituals of the scapegoat constitute a peculiarly vital cultural phenomenon. From Watergate to Auschwitz, from assassinations to urban riots, from the Depression of the 30s to royal abdications, from the Moscow trials to World War I munitions kings, the image of the scapegoat in all its enigmatic ambiguity is reflected in a variety of guises. And whether we accept or reject Oscar Wilde's witty dictum about art and life, it remains true that an equally rich efflorescence of the figure marks the literature as well as the history of the century. Modern writers have seized eagerly upon the paradoxical possibilities inherent in the scapegoat and exploited them with subtlety and originality. Cruelty, desire, self-preservation, witting and unwitting sacrifice, jealousy, hope, and fear all help to shape the scapegoat as he appears both in reality and in imagination.

Yet the modern writer is far from unique, for the concept of the scapegoat is found in many cultures and times. From earliest times it has traditionally been one of the chief means by which men have sought the preservation of society, the honoring of the gods, and their own psychic release. The paradox that a figure destined for punishment and sacrifice should also be honored and even worshiped is fraught with tragic, ironic, and even comic possibilities. Before, however, considering some of the specific ways in which writers throughout history have realized these possibilities, I want to look at some general features of the scapegoat. The sources of information concerning this figure are essentially threefold. Even today the most familiar tradition of the scapegoat is probably that of the Judeo-Christian as presented in the Bible. Leviticus XVI recounts the gradually evolving customs in the ritual of atonement, but for our purposes it is enough to note that a live goat selected by lot had the sins, crimes, and general iniquities of Israel ritually transferred to it by the high priest and then was sent out into the wilderness as a religious presentation to Azazel, the demon of the desert. Apart from the fact that in postexilic times the general sacrificial system of the temple, including the scapegoat ritual, was abandoned, leaving remission of sins to be achieved solely through genuine repentance of the heart, the most interesting thing about the custom was the restricting of the sacrifice of a sin-receiver to an animal.

When we move to the classical world, we find that though animals still figure prominently in such rituals, the scapegoat may often also be human. As Jane Harrison, Gilbert Murray, and others have pointed out, the festival of Thargelia, celebrating the offering of firstfruits at harvest time, was dominated by the ceremony of the *pharmakos* or scapegoat. Two individuals—sometimes two men, other times a man and a woman—one representing the men of the community, the other the women, were led out of the city, ceremonially beaten to the sound of music, and then either expelled or stoned to death. Versions of this human sacrifice were also performed at other times and places, in Greece as well as in Rome. In the latter, Mamurius Veturius, Mars as god of the old vegetative year, suffered a similar ritual expulsion.

Finally, when we step back even further, into the world of primitive cultures via the richly detailed pages of *The Golden Bough* and related works, we encounter an even broader handling of the scapegoat. Sticks, stones, trees, and images of all sorts are used to effect the transference of evils, sins, and misfortunes of every kind from the individual, family, or dwelling suffering the affliction. However diverse and however random or infrequent in occurrence, the operative factor is constant: the principle of vicarious suffering dictates the impulse and the action.

Out of the dense welter of instances before him, Frazer draws four main conclusions, which have certain implications for the interpretation of scapegoat motifs in literary texts. First, he suggests that regardless of the nature of the evil afflicting the individual or the community, whether intangible or material, the ritual intent is to achieve a complete removal and clearance of all the evils and ills besetting the individuals involved. In short, the focus is upon what Jane Harrison calls riddance or rituals of aversion, upon purification through vicarious suffering. Second, while the practice may be either occasional or periodic, the latter is increasingly common but usually on an annual basis that is correlated with a major seasonal change, which in turn is equated with the beginning of a new year. Here the aim is to effect a new lease on life for the individual and the community. Third, the scapegoat ritual itself is preceded or followed by a saturnalian interval in which social hierarchies are inverted, carnival revelry and hedonistic feasts enjoyed, and sexual profligacy and promiscuity practiced. Depending on when it occurs in relation to the scapegoat sacrifice, the saturnalian experience is either a final plunge into evil before purification or else a brief and clearly delimited expression of relief at the removal of all those things afflicting and oppressing man's spirit. And finally, the scapegoat includes among its candidates the divine man or king-god whose ritual death at the hands of his subjects originally formed a separate and distinct ritual from that of the scapegoat. The chief points involved in this elision are the increased probability of misinterpretation as a result of the loss of the sense of divinity and the replacement of it with a notion of mere, ordinary, human victimhood.

For interpretation of the scapegoat and his rituals we are essentially indebted to the disciplines of anthropology and psychology. Classical representatives of the former, like Frazer, Jane Harrison, and others, suggest that the scapegoat is the community's religious attempt to free itself of everything that it takes to be maleficent, corrupting, and painful. This attempt is based on what Frazer calls a mistaken association of ideas and what Freud labels a species of magical thinking. Both agree that this mode of reasoning derives from an early, primitive, almost precivilized state of man's development. But both also make it quite clear that this method of thinking and responding to threats to survival does not disappear with the advent of civilization and rational approaches to human misfortune and error. It continues to lurk just below the surface of man's civilized veneer and to haunt the not-so-distant recesses of his mind as a result either of the residue of religious superstitions (Frazer) or of the propensity for regression (Freud).

The fullest attempt to interpret the personal and cultural significance of the scapegoat occurs, however, neither in Frazer nor in Freud but in Jung and depth psychology. Briefly put, this view holds that in the process of ego development a part of the personality, called the shadow, is repressed for the sake of the ego ideal.[1] The shadow is the negative part of the psyche, consisting of all those qualities, values, and attitudes which the persona finds most despicable, unbearable, and hateful. These elements generate a powerful, though largely unconscious, guilt-feeling in the individual and the group. Freedom from the distress of this feeling, from this unconscious conflict, is achieved by the activity known as projection, whereby the negative qualities resident in the psyche are projected or transferred to the external world and experienced not as something within but as something outside and alien to one. So seen, this entity, individual, type, or group is blamed, attacked, punished, and otherwise eliminated; for it is literally the stranger, the enemy, the personification of evil. By instituting such a scapegoat and performing the ritual expulsion, the individual and group discharge their own repressed negative drives and behavior impulses. In this way, the mind eliminates, at least for a time, those feelings of guilt, inadequacy, and insecurity that inevitably haunt the psyche that refuses to face its shadow. Such a psychological interpretation, as opposed to the anthropological description, fulfills two functions. It explains the perdurability of the scapegoat and it also suggests that adaptations of the ritual are constantly being made in order to conform to the prevailing values and norms of social structures, which are subject to the endless dynamics of nature as well as history.

When we turn to literature, we find that the twin foci of anthropology and psychology, of the primitive and the civilized, of the ancient and the contemporary converge in a number of texts that both recapitulate and extrapolate from the forms of the scapegoat in their respective cultures and times. Indeed, one modern writer and critic, who began by examining the scapegoat role in a single author and then was impelled on to a number of other authors, ultimately was led to a highly radical conclusion. Rayner Heppenstall remarked:

> After a while it began to seem to me that all the key characters in fiction were scapegoats in one sense or another. Indeed, I began to wonder whether the whole of our narrative and dramatic literature were not a concerted effort to find and employ scapegoats.[2]

Doubtless a speculation of such universal scope is ultimately indefensible as well as programmatically pointless. Nevertheless, it does serve to call attention to the wide variety of uses to which the scapegoat and his rituals can be put by the resourceful creative imagination. One can scarcely declare with any confidence that all literary ways of handling the scapegoat have been classified, but it is certainly possible to identify some of the major aspects that come readily to mind. And it is to these that I wish to turn now, considering them in terms of two central categories: formal structures or strategies, and types of scapegoat.

The first of these is in many ways the most difficult to assess and describe, for it involves authorial attitudes that determine the shape and design of the text and these are notoriously slippery matters to pin down. Any sustained examination of the sort mentioned by Heppenstall quickly makes us aware that there is a significant difference in texture and structure between works whose authors are conscious and those who are unconscious of the scapegoat and his tradition. Immediately, however, one recognizes that precisely what a writer has conscious knowledge of at a particular moment of creation is an extremely murky and problematic issue in the majority of instances, so that it is better perhaps to couch the difference in formal terms and to say that some writers make an overt use of the traditions of the scapegoat while others deploy a more covert strategy. Novelists like

Strindberg and Jocelyn Brooke and short-story writers like V. S. Pritchett title certain of their works "The Scapegoat." From this it is obvious that they recognize the concept and that they wish their readers' response to be structured by the awareness that the concept is being utilized. In Strindberg's novella *The Scapegoat*, the shaping force in the tale is largely the Christian notion of the figure, wherein it is merged with the biblical image of the suffering servant. After enduring enormous vicissitudes at the hands of parents, teachers, his beloved, the courts, the police, and society generally, the attorney Libotz prepares to leave the remote Swedish town where the aged come to "prepare themselves for the final journey." He hears two inhabitants jestingly refer to him as the scapegoat. Quietly he contemplates the image and finds in it his salvation:

> . . . he recalled to his mind the Feast of the Atonement of the Old Testament, at which a goat, loaded down with the sins of all the people, was driven out into the desert, consecrated to Azazel, or in other words, the Evil One. . . . This role was neither a grateful one nor an honorable one. But had not Christ carried the same burden of disgrace and dishonor? . . .
>
> The outcast, also, felt some of the sting of this, the onus of bearing the hatred of others. . . .
>
> Could it be that he was the serum animal, who had within him the virus of poison and ills, which through him was to be transmuted, transubstantiated into the curing remedy? As long as he did not return hatred with hatred, he was out of reach of their power. But the moment he let himself be influenced and was roused to anger, he felt the poison.[3]

In Brooke's case, however, his novel is shaped not by a Christian perspective on the scapegoat but by a pagan and primitive one. The thirteen-year-old boy who ultimately assumes the scapegoat role is redheaded, presented with mistletoe by his uncle who finally performs the sacrifice, psychologically compelled to become a thief and criminal, indulged with festivities and fireworks, and finally slain on a stone altar that reminds him of Stonehenge. It is clear that Brooke means these details from primitive rites and customs to open up to us the awesome and psychologically disturbing prospect of the ancient ritual's being performed in a modern, ostensibly civilized setting under a compulsion that is partly unconscious wish and partly tragic necessity spiritually ordained.

The conscious deployment of scapegoat images and actions in both cases is central to the narrative thrust and thematic design. But the choice of quite different source materials and traditions markedly differentiates the results. For Strindberg the scapegoat is a paradigm of suffering who ultimately achieves a contemplative and compassionate perspective on his fate through the apprehension of his divine affiliations. As a result the novel ends on a note of transcendence and acceptance: "And Libotz trudged forward again toward the highroad, and went to face new experiences—which he could not help but foresee, but no longer had any fear of. . . ."[4] For Brooke, on the other hand, the scapegoat is a victim created at the moment of his entry into a world that sees him as an alien and ethical inferior with pathological qualities. Consequently, Brooke's narrative and the psychic disintegration of his characters move inexorably toward the final tragic fatality in which the participants regress in trancelike acquiescence to primal emotions acted upon but scarcely understood. In the final pages pity and terror converge in a vision of human waste and failure constrained by a necessity beyond the bounds of comprehension:

> Wearily, he stooped over the prostrate body, and shifted it into a more decent position. Bending lower, he gently kissed the pale, dawn-chilled face; then, unhurriedly, laid his hand on the smooth flesh above the heart: knowing, before he did so, that it had already ceased to beat.
>
> From far away, at the barracks over toward Glamber, came the faint nostalgic note of a bugle, sounding reveille. Gerald turned away, seeing everything clearly at last: knowing that the long initiation was over; the rites observed, the cycle completed.[5]

When literary texts employ a more covert use of the scapegoat, not only is there a subtle alteration in the reader's response but there is also a functional change in the scapegoat's part in the formal economy of the work. This can be seen in a work such as Hawthorne's "My Kinsman, Major Molyneux," where the scapegoat proper appears only in the final pages of the story, utters no words, and disappears as part of a local tar-and-feathering. Daniel Hoffman has shown beyond question that Robin's kinsman is an American Colonial scapegoat king.[6] But this fact is revealed only at the end of the story, so that the scapegoat motif is not part of the conscious shaping forces that make up the bulk of the reading experience, which instead revolves primarily around the issues of search or quest, mystery or puzzle, and transformation. In such a work the function of the scapegoat is not so much actively structural as it is revelatory. Robin's confrontation with his uncle occurs precisely at the point when he is ready to perceive the infantile inadequacy and stultifying consequences of his original dependence on the sustaining support of another. The "overwhelming humiliation" and "foul disgrace" he sees visited upon his kinsman are prophetic of the fate that awaits his own humorless obsession with social and economic advancement and cultural dependence. Thus, his joining in the saturnalian laughter of the community signals his emancipation and the demise of an inadequate because external authority figure. The two coalesce in Robin's objectively realized perception that with the end of a sentimental and selfish attachment to familial authority there comes also a genuine feeling and regard for the ultimate paternal force or factor in one's existence:

> On they went, like fiends that throng in mockery around some dead potentate, mighty no more, but majestic still in his agony. On they went, in counterfeited pomp, in senseless uproar, in frenzied merriment, trampling all on an old man's heart.[7]

In short, the scapegoat is in this instance the dramatic means by which the youth's initiation into maturity is effected. It is a beneficent trauma that catalytically alters and deepens the mystery of the narrative rather than, as is the case in Jocelyn Brooke's novel, a ritual paradigm forecasting the story's action.

Hawthorne's story suggests another pair of formal strategies that condition the use of the scapegoat in literature. When one studies the anthropological material dealing with the communal reliance on the scapegoat and his rituals, one is struck by the necessary discrepancy between the purpose and the possible achievement. That is to say, one may taunt, revile, and humiliate selected individuals, and one may even expel or sacrifice them in order to purge a community of plague, pollution, and evil as energetically as one can manage without effecting the desired result. And yet this does not seem to have materially altered the enthusiasm with which societies have pursued the goal of, as Frazer remarks, "a fresh start in life, happy and innocent."[8] In a remarkable way, the scapegoat ritual, like many primitive rituals, resembles the belief in apocalypse, which, as Frank Kermode has remarked, "can be disconfirmed without being discredited."[9] In actual societies, in other words, the lack of social, agricultural, medical, and military efficacy in no way invalidates the ritual in the minds of its adherents. In short, anthropologically and sociologically, the scapegoat ritual is necessarily efficient and perpetually successful.

When one turns, however, to its literary expressions, it is a far different matter. Most works concentrate upon inefficient or unsuccessful instances of the ritual, and when they do dramatize successful rites, as in *Lord of the Flies* or James Baldwin's "Going to Meet the Man," they do so with such an ironic inflection that the efficacy is called in question. One might, of course, attribute this to the fact that literature is a relatively recent human mode and so may have a more skeptical view of the practicality of ancient rituals. Yet even when one goes back to classical times, a tragedian such as Euripides in a play like *The Bacchae* reveals a profoundly ironic perspective on the scapegoat. Pentheus, the king of Thebes and the antagonist of

Dionysus, in the course of the play clearly becomes the scapegoat chosen by the god, transformed into a new mode of life by impersonating a woman, and subjected to ritual dismemberment at the hands of an inflamed mob led by his mother. From one standpoint, the ritual sacrifice is efficient and successful: the victim is sacrificed, the city of Thebes is brought to a proper appreciation of Dionysus, and the impious pollutants of the city are expelled. But, concomitantly, Euripides shows that the god's assertion of his divinity results in his own assumption of the mantle of the scapegoat. Pentheus, the epitome of the rational mind devoid of feeling, is driven to assume the role of the scapegoat by Dionysus, functioning as an articulation of the demands of feeling and emotion and of wholeness of being and psychic integration. The culpability of Pentheus and so the warrant for his becoming a scapegoat in the course of the play lies in his psychological incompleteness and moral rigidity. And yet in the course of this, Dionysus becomes the victim of an equally inflexible power, that of his own tyrannical will and drive for justification. In the end he emerges as the victim of the same straitened lack of self-knowledge that led Pentheus to his destruction. As William Arrowsmith has remarked, "there, . . . the god and his victim meet."[10] The religious success of Dionysus's invoking the scapegoat ritual—his vindication as a deity and his purification of the community—is balanced by the failure of the ritual and its perpetrator to invest the consequences with humanity and the saving grace of self-awareness. As a result, Euripides simultaneously celebrates the efficacy of the scapegoat pattern and reveals its sinister psychological and moral limitations.

Though Euripides' skepticism and irony concerning the scapegoat are fully as profound as those of modern writers like William Faulkner and James Baldwin, he also shows us one of the central mysteries that may surround the figure, and he does so by choosing the king as his ritual protagonist. From the available anthropological material it is clear that there have been three main types of scapegoat: the hero or king, the criminal or knave or slave, and the fool or clown. As *The Golden Bough* makes clear, the use of the hero or king as the scapegoat is the result of fusing the periodic ritual slaying of the king as a representative of the dying and reviving god with the sacrifice of a scapegoat for the benefit of the society at large. Frazer rationally but implausibly suggests that this fusion is the result of forgetfulness as to the meaning of the king's sacrifice, coupled with an impulse to economy of ritual and manpower. Literature provides both more varied and subtle answers, though all seem to devolve into a watchful tentativeness before the awesome contradiction inherent in sacrificing one's touchstone against death and guardian of fertility in order to escape material and spiritual evils. Thus, Euripides makes Pentheus, the

king and linchpin of communal order and stability, suffer the fate of the
scapegoat; but this exercise of divine justice concludes with the community
bereft of its traditional source of authority and exposed to the terrors of
potentially radical change. The authentication of Dionysus's divinity is
achieved but at a cost that appears to presage spiritual, moral, and political
bankruptcy.

If Euripides is concerned with the terrible power of the god and the loss
of the city's central symbol of order, centuries later D. H. Lawrence limns
in the portrait of an individual who driven by his own personal anguish and
demoniac autonomy grows into something like heroic stature. His assumption of the scapegoat's role becomes a savagely ironic acquiescence in the
nullity of modern society and his participation in world combat the chief
emblem of psychic fissure. In "England, My England" Egbert begins as a
rather ineffectual aesthete and "epicurean hermit" redeemed only by "a
delightful spontaneous passion."[11] With his eldest daughter's maiming and
his own exclusion from his family, he contracts into "the triumphant
loneliness, the Ishmael quality" in which nevertheless he is "an erect,
supple symbol of life," one dedicated to "the mystery of blood-sacrifices, all
the lost, intense sensations of the primeval people of the place."[12] And with
the advent of war he emerges as the soldier who grimly accepts "his own
degradation" at the hands of his spiritual inferiors in the army.[13] By
exercising his belatedly discovered capacity for tragic choice, he becomes
enough of a hero to endure all the rites of the scapegoat. Through these he
achieves a feeling of participation in an inescapable experience that sustains
him through even his death agonies. Yet the culminating irony is that the
experience is one of dissolution and total forgetfulness eagerly sought in
preference to a life of will and memory and communion with others.

In general, the hero cast as a scapegoat seems to have to be something of
a manqué figure, something less than the full-blown tragic or epic hero.
Even Dr. Stockmann in Ibsen's *An Enemy of the People* is marked by an
ingenuousness that encourages his impulsiveness. He becomes a scapegoat
not so much as a result of making tragic choices quite deliberately but by
following out in doggedly determined fashion the increasingly sinister
consequences of purely rational decisions and responses. It is this fact,
realized in the course of the play with impressively cumulative power, that
makes his final discovery that "the strongest man in the world is he who
stands most alone"[14] such a profoundly ironic and poignantly pitying
epitaph for the hero as scapegoat.

This mystery of the sensitive, perceptive, powerful individual plunging
relentlessly forward to assume the mantle of the unaware, helpless victim
makes of those works which contain it haunting forays into the depths of
emotional disquietude. When, however, the scapegoat is not the hero-king

but the criminal or slave, the character of the work takes a quite different turn. Those two brilliant companion stories, William Faulkner's "Dry September" and James Baldwin's "Going to Meet the Man" take a more programmatic and unequivocal stance concerning the scapegoat, one in which dramatic refutation and frustration replace contemplative awe. Both are lynch tales with a helpless black man as scapegoat and both are dedicated to showing the irrationality and psychological abnormality of the ritual. Faulkner concentrates on presenting the arbitrariness of the selection of Will Mayes as scapegoat through the eyes of Hawkshaw, the barber and epitome of the ordinary rational mind investigating the mare's nests of rumor and violent impulse. Baldwin, on the other hand, shows the subtle and far-reaching personal and social consequences for an impressionable white child of witnessing the brutal burning, mutilation, and slaying of a nameless, silent, black stranger. Jesse's vague perception of his parents' sexual excitement at the emasculation of the victim, his own desire to be identified with the emasculator, and his sense of supreme joy as "he watched the hanging, gleaming body, the most beautiful and terrible object he had ever seen till then," all combine to make him feel that he had survived a fundamental initiation experience that "had revealed to him a great secret which would be the key to his life forever."[15] This acceptance of a world and life that creates scapegoats is, Baldwin shows, absolutely fatal to Jesse. Later in life, as deputy sheriff, his casual, dehumanized miscegenation, his brutality with local civil rights leaders, his impotence with his wife, his secret terror of being involved in an incipient and incomprehensible race war, all follow from that initial experience. The terrible irony resident in man's passionate acquiescence to bloodlust, wherein sexuality and death feed upon and demean one another, is that it affords man a parody of revelation, a mock integration of selfhood. The "key" to Jesse's life is not the means to enter into a larger, richer, more meaningful region of existence. Instead it forever locks him into a constricted, blind round of callous insensitivity that he slowly and dimly realizes to be genuine hell, a place rooted in and ringed round by black hatred. It is as if Baldwin has taken Eliot's image of *Dayadhvam* and pulled it inside out so that cultural solipsism effectively debars forever the restoration of the waste land. In "Going to Meet the Man" Baldwin's injunction is not "Sympathize" but "Recognize" even as the spiritual and psychological setting mirrors Eliot's Dantean inferno:

> . . . I have heard the key
> Turn in the door once and turn once only
> We think of the key, each in his prison
> Thinking of the key, each confirms a prison.[16]

Faulkner and Baldwin focus on the means and consequences of society's criminalization of an ordinary individual as a way of rationalizing the ritual of the scapegoat. For them, the criminal, like the hero, is manqué, a pseudo- or institutional criminal whose chief lack is inherent or actual criminality. But for others, from Dostoevski to Genet, from the amoral rogue of the picaresque to the deformed sadistic killers of Graham Greene, the genuine criminal is a much more primitive, less displaced form of the scapegoat. In some cases the criminal's role is explained by a naturalistic sociological interpretation, as when Popeye in Faulkner's *Sanctuary* has his sadism and impotent sterility attributed to heredity. Yet in the majority of instances the criminal-scapegoat in modern literature serves to dramatize religious motifs and themes. Thus Dostoevski grapples with the antithetical notions that Mochulsky calls the "idea of Rastignac" and the "idea of Napoleon," the image of the altruistic murderer who is essentially a Christian humanist and that of the demoniac atheistic superman beyond redemption.[17] Out of his struggles emerges the central contention of *Crime and Punishment*, namely, that Raskolnikov ultimately stands forth as a religious scapegoat. He carries into the Siberian wastes the infinite spiritual freedom of the irreligious, which blights man's personal and communal life by subjecting him to the blind forces of an imperturbable and relentless fate.

Almost a century later Jean Genet in works like *Our Lady of the Flowers* and *Miracle of the Rose* evokes the criminal as a scapegoat for almost diametrically opposite purposes. For him crime is a potential source of spiritual wonderment and worship, as Richard Coe has observed.[18] To come into contact with the sacred through transgression is necessarily to suffer the scapegoat's punishment, isolation, and death ordained by a society and religion striving for a rational existence. By having his characters violate virtually all of man's multifarious taboos, Genet simultaneously invests them with the roles of criminal and scapegoat in a radical transformation of society's judgment and the prevailing anthropological pattern. Instead of receiving the multiple sins of others and suffering death in order to ensure the perpetuation of the world of others. Genet's characters perform the violations and evils repressed by most people precisely in order to become scapegoats. For Genet that is the route into isolation, solitude, and the realm of the sacred, which embraces the infinitude of mystery and the suprarational. In short, Genet becomes a criminal in order to become a scapegoat, for that is the point of contact with the sacred and the moment of escape from the profane. Where Dostoevski celebrates the scapegoat ritual as an exercise in spiritual transcendence, Genet ceaselessly performs, both actually and imaginatively, that ritual as a declaration of divine immanence.

The final major form of the scapegoat is the fool or clown who is allowed to play the absolute monarch as a temporary substitute for the actual ruler. Anthropologically and existentially, the fool's lot is scarcely more palatable than that of other types of scapegoat. Yet in literature a broader range of associations and significance accrues around the figure of the fool. He is not only the knockabout burlesque figure of Roman comedy and the astringent wit and honest touchstone of reality and truth associated with the Shakespearean clown; he is also the harmless dunce, the gentle prey of retardation, and the guileless possessor of ultimate good fortune and luck. In virtually all of the subforms, however, there is a basic incapacity for the simple habits and quotidian rituals of ordinary existence. When this quality is associated with the Christian tradition, as in Dostoevski's *The Idiot* and Strindberg's *The Scapegoat*, the scapegoat assumes in greater or lesser measure a kind of helpless sacrificial sanctity. Prince Myshkin is in virtually every conceivable respect resident in a world he neither is part of, comprehends, nor even recognizes. Yet what Aglaya intuitively calls the Prince's "essential mind" grasps the spiritual purpose and achievement of the scapegoat. His alienation's impact on others makes him a stranger and outcast to everything. Paradoxically enough, this effects the novel's vision of Paradise in which sin and evil vanish. The smiles, the rueful shakes of the head at Prince Myshkin's aberrations, confusions, and faux pas are replaced in Strindberg, however, by incredulity, mockery, and hatred issuing from Libotz's incapacity to function effectively without eliciting the shadow qualities of others.

So long as the individual's incapacity is rooted in congenital mental limitations of one sort or another, modern writers are inclined to treat him more as a victim and less as a scapegoat unless, as in Dostoevski's case, he can also be invested with some sort of supernatural or sacred associations. Thus, Faulkner's Benjy in *The Sound and the Fury* or Darl in *As I Lay Dying* or Ike in *The Hamlet* and Steinbeck's Lennie in *Of Mice and Men* are basically moral victims of an individual or group self-regard that leads to callous and dehumanized indifference. Whatever aspects of the scapegoat may envelop them are more a function of psychological dynamics than of anthropological ritual and symbolism. More fully developed scapegoat figures appear with characters whose foollike nature is the result of a touching but appalling inexperience—as with Melville's Billy Budd—or of a suspicious and fearful lack of familiarity with another race, as with Bernard Malamud's Yakov Bok in *The Fixer*. In the former case, the scapegoat is cast in his role partly by his own naive nature and partly by society's efforts to teach him the secret truth about himself and so to redeem him.

Malamud's novel takes the opposite course. Yakov, all too aware of his ignorance before the mysteries of the gentile world, apprehensively struggles to conform to the mores of its inhabitants. Yet unerringly he always does or says precisely that which leads him to become a national scapegoat to Czarist anti-Semitism. Harrowing though *The Fixer* is in its slow-motion enactment of authoritarian and judicial ritual, Yakov transforms the scapegoat role from one of helpless sacrificial victim to that of legally accused prisoner whose crimes, sins, and guilt must be proved. Despite appalling physical and mental torture, threats, temptations, and appeals from guards, judicial officials, fellow prisoners, friends, and relatives including his wife, Yakov continues to make the apparent blunder or mistake that threatens his very existence. Yet by doing so, he makes his scapegoathood into both a weapon for his liberation and a refutation of the rationale for the use of scapegoats. His apparent folly in insisting on a thorough legal disposition and conclusion of his case is a brilliant comic transcendence of the tragic necessities ordained by the invoking of the scapegoat ritual. We are simultaneously appalled and convulsed by the dogged effrontery with which Yakov thwarts society's ritual as he responds to his visitor's good news that the Tsar planned to include him in a general amnesty:

> Then he asked, Pardoned as a criminal or pardoned as innocent? The former jurist testily said what difference did it make so long as he was let out of prison. . . . Yakov said he wanted a fair trial, not a pardon. If they ordered him to leave the prison without a trial they would have to shoot him first.[19]

The scapegoat as fool finds in his own folly the only certain means of assuring his release from his role; by insisting on a trial, Yakov destroys the ritual as a viable communal response. William Blake once observed that if a fool will persist in his folly, he will become wise. Yakov Bok persists relentlessly in the folly of his innocence and emerges with a deeply integrated conviction born of experience that explodes the underlying premise of the scapegoat and his ritual. At the end of the novel he has a hallucinatory conversation with Nicholas II in the course of which he totally undercuts the attitudes that insistently generate scapegoats:

> Excuse me, Your Majesty, but what suffering has taught me is the uselessness of suffering, if you don't mind my saying so. Anyway, there's enough of that to live with naturally without piling a mountain of injustice on top. . . . In other words, you've made out of this country a valley of bones. You had your chances and pissed them away. . . . You say you are kind and prove it with pogroms.[20]

The principle of vicarious suffering that Frazer finds animating the concept of the scapegoat is denied by its moral and psychological antithesis, the principle of individual human responsibility whose ultimate form rests in Yakov's final recognition that "You can't sit still and see yourself destroyed."[21]

With this we see that the only admissible place for the scapegoat and his rituals is in the imaginative world of literature, where the destruction is solely linguistic. This fact is brilliantly and uniquely dramatized in *Finnegans Wake*, where the scapegoat ritual is celebrated in song and in fact while itself being comically mutilated in a verbal reenactment of man's immemorial penchant for irresponsibility. Thus Joyce has the scapegoat ballad accompanied by "the flute, that onecrooned king in inscrewments." And the victim's death is reported in accents that merge the archetypal and the comic in a linguistic displacement that affords a responsible place for irresponsibility in the human economy:

> As holly day in his house so was he priest and king to that: ulvy came, envy saw, ivy conquered. Lou! Lou! They have waved his green boughs o'er him as they have torn him limb from lamb. For his muertification and uxpiration and dumnation and annuhulation.[22]

But the fascinating implications of this prospect are the material for another day and another paper.

NOTES

1. For a succinct discussion of this concept, see Edward C. Whitmont, *The Symbolic Quest* (New York: G. P. Putnam & Sons, 1969), pp. 160-69.

2. Rayner Heppenstall, "Bernanos: The Priest as Scapegoat," *Partisan Review* 13 (1946): 499.

3. August Strindberg, *The Scapegoat*, trans. A. Paulson (New York: P. S. Eriksson, 1967), pp. 169-70.

4. Ibid., p. 175.

5. Jocelyn Brooke, *The Scapegoat* (New York: Harper, 1949), p. 209.

6. Daniel G. Hoffman, *Form and Fable in American Fiction* (New York: Oxford University Press, 1961), pp. 113-25.

7. Nathaniel Hawthorne, *Selected Tales and Sketches*, ed. H. H. Waggoner (New York: Holt, Rinehart & Winston, 1962), pp. 32-33.

8. Sir James G. Frazer, *The Golden Bough* (London: Macmillan & Co., 1913), 9:73.

9. Frank Kermode, *The Sense of an Ending* (New York: Oxford University Press, 1967), p. 8.

10. William Arrowsmith, "Introduction, 'The Bacchae,'" in *The Complete Greek Tragedies*, ed. D. Grene and R. Lattimore (Chicago: University of Chicago Press, 1960), 4: 534.

11. D. H. Lawrence, *The Tales* (London: William Heinemann, 1948), pp. 208, 205.

12. Ibid., pp. 223, 222.

13. Ibid., p. 226.

14. Henrik Ibsen, *Eleven Plays* (New York: Random House, n.d.), p. 288.

15. James Baldwin, *Going to Meet the Man* (New York: Dial Press, 1965), pp. 247, 248.

16. T. S. Eliot, "The Waste Land," *Collected Poems, 1909-1962* (New York: Harcourt, Brace & World, 1963), p. 69.

17. K. Mochulsky, *Dostoevski*, trans. M. A. Minihan (Princeton N. J.: Princeton University Press, 1967), pp. 282-83.

18. Richard N. Coe, *The Vision of Jean Genet* (New York: Grove, 1969), p. 38.

19. B. Malamud, *The Fixer* (New York: Farrar, Straus & Giroux, 1966), p. 294.

20. Ibid., p. 333.

21. Ibid., p. 335.

22. James Joyce, *Finnegans Wake* (New York: Viking, 1947), p. 58.

SUGGESTED READINGS

Bronowski, Jacob. *The Face of Violence*, "The Scapegoat King." New York: G. Braziller, 1955.

Elliott, Robert C. *The Power of Satire: Magic, Ritual, Art*. Princeton, N.J.: Princeton University Press, 1960.

Frazer, Sir James. *The Golden Bough*. 3d ed., vol. 9, "The Scapegoat." London: Macmillan, 1907-15.

Harrison, Jane. "The Pharmakos" in *Prolegomena to the Study of Greek Religion*. Cambridge: Cambridge University Press, 1903.

Neumann, Erich. *Depth Psychology and a New Ethic*. New York: G. P. Putnam's Sons, 1969.

Radin, Paul. *The Trickster*. New York: Philosophical Library, 1956.

Vickery, John B. *The Literary Impact of "The Golden Bough,"* chap. 13, "James Joyce: Ulysses and the Human Scapegoat." Princeton, N.J.: Princeton University Press, 1973.

——, and Sellery, J. M., eds. *The Scapegoat: Ritual and Literature*. Boston: Houghton Mifflin, 1971: 1972.

Biographical Note on Tucker Orbison

After receiving his lower degrees from Yale and Trinity, Tucker Orbison taught as a teaching fellow and lecturer at Boston University, where his doctorate was awarded in 1963. He is now associate professor of English at Bucknell University. In 1975 he received a Folger Library Fellowship and a grant-in-aid from the American Philosophical Society. In addition to *The Tragic Vision of John Ford* (Salzburg: Institut für englische Sprache und Literatur, University of Salzburg, 1974) he has written on Renaissance drama in such journals as *Studies in Philology* and *Yearbook of English Studies*. Two of these articles are a Jungian study of *Hamlet* and a collaboration on a description of a Young Vic performance of *The Taming of the Shrew*. Currently he is working on an edition of Middle Temple documents for the Malone Society. Among his interests are Renaissance and modern drama and the relation between myth and literature. He is an editor of the present volume.

Arrabal's *The Solemn Communion* as Ritual Drama

TUCKER ORBISON

The *return of the repressed* makes up the tabooed and subterranean history of civilization.

—Herbert Marcuse

The theater will never find itself again . . . except by furnishing the spectator with the truthful precipitates of dreams.

—Antonin Artaud

The spectator enters a small, windowless room called "the cave." Coming in as he does from the bright light of the hall, he feels disoriented in the semi-darkness. He must be led to his seat. The row of candles that sets off the acting space enables him to perceive shadowy figures standing motionless at the right. Against the wall in front of him is a giant brass rubbing of a bishop. He is about to witness an enactment of Fernando Arrabal's *The Solemn Communion*, directed by John Vaccaro.

I

This production, which took place at Bucknell University on 2 May 1974 affected its audience in powerful and subtle ways.[1] To account for the effectiveness of this twenty-minute presentation, one may find a clue in Arrabal's statement that "c'est en se déroulant sur les trois modes du grotesque, du sublime et du rite que le théâtre peut jeter une certain clarté sur nos interrogations."[2] ("It is in unfolding itself under the three modes of the grotesque, the sublime, and the rite that the theater can throw a certain light on our questions.") By using the example of this production, I propose to examine the relation between drama and ritual, my ultimate aim being to describe the ways in which the ritual nature of this play affected its

280

audience. The place to begin such an investigation, properly enough, is to raise the question of origin.

I do not mean to broach once more the problem of the relation between drama and ancient ritual that was brought to our attention by Jane Harrison, Gilbert Murray, and F. M. Cornford. Nor is it material to the present essay whether English drama rose from the liturgical plays of the Church or from the mummers' plays of St. George. Northrop Frye has asserted that the critical problem to address is the presence of ritual patterns in the work at hand: "The *literary* relation of ritual to drama, like that of any other aspect of human action to drama, is a relation of content to form only, not one of source to derivation."[3] The source of a ritual pattern in a work of literature is the same as the source of almost everything else in the work, namely, the conscious patterns and unconscious material in the mind of the creator. Thus, this essay assumes that the playwright consciously uses ritual patterns as he sees them in the world around him, and that the playwright projects onto the screen of the play, so to speak, a film composed of selected contents from his unconscious. Eugène Ionesco, one of the figures who form Arrabal's unacknowledged paternity, puts the idea this way: "The unseen presence of our inner fears can . . . be materialised. So the author is not only allowed, but recommended to make actors of his props, to bring objects to life, to animate the scenery and give symbols concrete form."[4] The play, then, functions doubly as a mirror, for it reflects certain ritual structures in the world around the playwright, and it reproduces, as a kind of secondary reflection, the unconscious anxieties and desires that result from the playwright's internalization of the rites and ceremonies of his society. If these assumptions hold true, one should be able to show that ritual is fundamental to the structure of *The Solemn Communion*. Indeed, if one accepts the notion that man's desires and anxieties are given objective form in ritual, one sees the close relation ritual bears to drama. In short, one way to justify Vaccaro's deliberately ritualistic *mise en scène* is for us to discover a pattern that corresponds both to a conscious, social rite and to an unconscious design of repressed material that is externalized in ritual and mythic patterns in the drama.

A second way in which to validate Vaccaro's staging is to investigate the relation between the play and the audience. In this perspective a play differs from a ritual in that the spectators of drama are physically separated from the action on the stage, whereas in a ritual no psychic distance separates the participants from the enactment. But the fact is that most drama, even that of Brecht, involves the audience to some extent. John Holloway has written that, like the ritual, the enacted play has a psychological effect on both actors and audience, which in both cases is a "sustained, renewed or enhanced vitality."[5] Now which of the many forms of ritual gives to the participant that sense of renewal? Probably the one that produces most directly the kind of power that would renew the psyche is the initiation. In describing the essential nature of this pattern, Mircea Eliade explains that "the term initiation in the most general sense denotes a body of rites and oral teachings whose purpose is to produce a decisive alteration in the religious and social status of the person to be initiated. In philosophical terms, initiation is equivalent to a basic change in existential condition; the novice emerges from his ordeal with a totally different being from that which he possessed before his initiation; he has become *another*."[6] Eliade adds the important idea that "the majority of initiatory ordeals more or less clearly implies a ritual death followed by a resurrection or a new birth. The central moment of every initiation is represented by the ceremony symbolizing the death of the novice and his return to the fellowship of the living" (p. xii). In the same way a spectator at a play may undergo an alteration in his psyche, greater or lesser depending upon the psychic distance between himself and the action on the stage.

Describing the relation between the play and the audience offers considerable difficulty, since spectators vary in their responses. Perhaps it is worth pointing out, however, that such an effort is not merely the whim of the academic critic of drama. It is indeed an increasingly important element in current dramatic theory.[7] Furthermore, the avowed goal of certain modern directors is to invade the mind of the spectator with the intent of forcing the same sort of change that ritual creates. Writing of the Polish Theatre Laboratory, for example, Eugenio Barba points out that Grotowski "wished to create a modern secular ritual, knowing that primitive rituals are the first form of drama. Through their total participation, primitive men were liberated from accumulated unconscious material. . . . Grotowski preserves the essence of primitive theatre by making the audience participate, but he leaves out the religious elements and substitutes secular 'stimuli' for them. Grotowski uses archetypal images and actions to unleash his attack on the audience. He breaks through the defenses of the spectator's mind and forces him to react to what is going on in the theatre."[8] Grotowski himself describes his technique as "a sort of ritual through which the actors and spectators free themselves from their own demons."[9]

The second way in which we can investigate drama as ritual, then, is to ask how it invades the unconscious of the audience and how it creates a radical change within. *The Solemn Communion* will be a particularly interesting example because the two approaches are related by the same rite: the play embodies as one of its structures the initiation pattern, and in performance the pattern moves the audience toward the same kind of psychic transformation as would an initiation ritual. A study of the Calder text used by Vaccaro will establish the way in which the pattern makes its appearance, and a description of the performance by the Theater of the Ridiculous, directed by Vaccaro, will help us to see how, as ritual, the play may free the spectator of some of his demons.

I I

The Solemn Communion is a short, one-act play by Fernando Arrabal, the Spanish-born dramatist who now makes Paris his home. It was first staged at the Théâtre de Poche-Montparnasse in Paris on 8 July 1966, by Jorge Lavelli,[10] and has since been produced in England and America. A brief description of the plot will explain why, as Arrabal himself said, it "created a scandal" in Paris,[11] and will provide a basis for interpretation. According to John Calder's translation,[12] the play takes place at night. On the stage are an empty coffin, lighted candles, an iron cross, and a bench on which a girl's communion dress is laid out. The play begins with a dumb show. Two men carry in the nude corpse of a woman, place it in the coffin, and kneel at prayer. At the approach of a necrophile (named only that in the text), they pick up the coffin and hurry out, closely pursued by him. Twice more during the action the pallbearers return with the coffin and begin their prayers, only to flee at the approach of the necrophile. Meanwhile, a partially dressed young girl and her grandmother have entered (they are called simply Girl and Grandmother). While explaining the proper behavior for a good Christian and a good wife, the Grandmother dresses the Girl for her first communion. Each time the necrophile enters, his state of sexual arousal is more apparent. Each time, the Girl questions her Grandmother about the necrophile's aroused condition, but is turned away by a laconic answer, and the catechism about Christianity and marriage continues in an unabated torrent. The last entry of the pallbearers with the coffin finds the necrophile in such close pursuit that they drop the coffin and run out. The necrophile undresses and gets into the coffin. For a time the Girl and her Grandmother watch the young man's movements, then leave, the Grandmother intoning her instructions about becoming a "proper little woman." The last sentence the audience hears is the Grandmother's "The Good Lord will come down into your heart and purify you of all sin. . . ." After a pause, the Girl returns and stabs the necrophile repeatedly, bloodying her communion dress. She laughs, and red balloons rise from the coffin.

From this plot summary it is clear that the play dramatizes two parallel initiatory actions: the Grandmother's oral instruction ostensibly prepares the Girl to participate in the spiritual life of the Church, and at the same time the girl is made aware of her sexual nature. Mircea Eliade's discussion of "Women's Mysteries" suggests that the simultaneous appearance of these two motifs is not accidental. According to him, in many societies the girl's initiation into the sacred characteristically takes place at the first menstruation, that is, "upon [her] assuming the condition of woman."[13] She is instructed "under the admonition of old women," and in the course of this instruction the old women teach "the feminine ritual songs and dances, most of them erotic or even obscene" (pp. 210-11). Thus, while providing, in Eliade's terms, "the *access to the sacred*" (p. 209), the Grandmother reveals that her true intent is the preparation of the Girl for marriage. She gives lip service to the importance of the first communion, but devotes most of her instruction to the proper behavior of a wife:

> Yes, my child, one day you'll be married and you'll be the pride of your husband. There's nothing a man appreciates so much as a good house-keeper like yourself. You'll be a real jewel for any man. Because it's very important that you should know, when a man gets up in the morning, he likes to put on a very white, very well ironed shirt, and socks without holes in them and beautifully pressed trousers. You'll be a real jewel to your husband. Because you know how to iron, how to mend socks and even how to cook. And now that you're about to receive communion, you'll become a perfect Christian. I know that you're going to be a model housewife, aren't you, my child? (p. 222)

The constant theme is care of house and husband. But even this motive is deceptive, for as the play nears its conclusion, it becomes apparent that the Grandmother is instructing the Girl in methods for controlling her future husband: "A man who finds a good meal waiting for him when he gets home will do everything his wife wants him to" (p. 225). Instead of enslaving herself to her husband, the Girl is taught that she must enslave *him*. Finally, we realize that even this motive is subordinate to a compulsive desire for cleanliness, order, and a fear of social disapproval:

> Believe me, there's no excuse for sloppy women. Of course we don't have fancy furniture because it's so dear, especially just now; but I can't tolerate furniture that's dirty and covered with dust. It costs nothing to be clean. But some women are so dirty and lazy. I don't see why they aren't red with shame. If I were them, I'd never let anyone visit me. . . . The dining room should remain impeccable to receive visitors on Sunday. (pp. 225-26)

The most important thing is that the dining room be impeccable, the kitchen clean smelling, and the curtains white, so that the Sunday visitors will approve. The husband is to be secondary, a mere adjunct.

The Grandmother functions, then, as the transmitter of the traditional mythology of an authoritarian culture, Christian in its religion and matriarchal in its social organization. When one is aware that Arrabal was born and grew up in Spain and has now rejected the religious and political conditions of life in his homeland to live in France, it is possible to see suggested in the figure of the Grandmother Arrabal's notion of the enslaving character of Spanish Catholicism and fascism.[14] Indeed, the tyrannical mother (or here, grandmother) is a recurring character in Arrabal's plays. *The Solemn Communion* is, accordingly, centrally concerned with the insidious, emotionally exhausting indoctrination of a young girl into the mores, values, and attitudes of a narrow, repressive older generation. (The generalized nature of the theme is suggested by Arrabal's refusal to provide any of the characters with proper names.) The transmission of cultural values is often thought of as a force for social unity and cohesion and as a sustainer of the individual psyche,[15] but this play represents a perverted initiation ritual that is demeaning, dehumanizing, and psychically destructive.

The second initiation theme—the young Girl's sexual awakening—is horrifically dramatized in the concurrent action of the necrophile and the pallbearers. What can the appearance of the necrophile in pursuit of the corpse mean? It precedes the entrance of the Girl and her Grandmother. This indicates that the vision does not arise from the personal unconscious of either the Girl or the Grandmother; rather, coming out of the night, a figure inducing anxiety and creating scandal, it suggests a collective representation of that sexual perversion in which the life instinct is directed toward death. In myth, perhaps the closest archetypal pattern is that of the young girls who were sacrificed to a beast or a dragon, such as the Minotaur, in order to preserve a city or appease a sense of guilt; the necrophile suggests the monstrous death figure that dominates the young female—here represented by the nude corpse. The act of necrophilia about to take place on stage, has, in the Girl's initial view, nothing to do with her. Only later does she begin to identify, as we do, the corpse and herself. From a psychological point of view, the necrophile is an image of domination by the Great Mother (the Grandmother). As Erich Neumann explains, "Many [psychic] contents which, in 'perversion,' come to be dominants of sexual life have their prototypes in [the] mythological stage of dominance by the Great Mother. As mythological facts they are transpersonal, i.e., beyond and outside personality. . . . Only when they intrude into the narrow personalistic sphere do they become 'perverted' . . . [and] hamper individual development."[16] What has happened, then, is that the domineering Grandmother has forced the Girl to repress her normal sexual feelings; but these feelings require projection into the conscious when the

Girl becomes aware of her sexual nature. The only way they can take conscious form is to adopt the necrophilic, perverted shape approved by the Grandmother, who, it now becomes clear, disapproves of Eros. This explains her repressive attitude toward her own husband and her grand-daughter's future husband. Society (here the Grandmother) has always repressed Eros,[17] and in the play the Girl reenacts her racial history, as the repressed instincts return in a form acceptable to her society. Thus, the ordeal that constitutes the Girl's initiation into the sexual life consists of finding a way to escape her Grandmother's sexual attitude toward men, namely that because men—husbands in particular—are necrophiles in treating women as sex objects (corpses), women should treat men in kind, as objects to be controlled. The Girl can survive only by seeing that normal sexual desire has been perverted by society and that she is about to become one of its victims, a future corpse. How can she prevent Eros from becoming Thanatos?[18] Only by acting, when she perceives that she also will be a violated corpse in the coffin of marriage and home, to destroy the necrophile, who represents the perversion of the sexual impulse. The play ends with her victory over death, her successful rebirth from the state of innocence into that of the condition of woman, fully possessed of the secret of her femininity. She is liberated into the world of experience and knowledge, just as the red balloons are released from the coffin into the free reaches of the upper atmosphere. *The Solemn Communion* accords with Benjamin Hunningher's notion of ritual drama in that, like ritual drama in all times and places, it "centers on the burial of winter [Thanatos] and the resurrection of life [Eros]."[19]

Arrabal's play, then, juxtaposes two parallel rituals: the preparation for the Girl's communion, a ceremony that in Arrabal's view has become desacralized by the despotic Grandmother's oppressive and obsessive concern with the Girl's future place in social rather than in sacred life; and the rite of passage, in which the Girl awakens to the secret of her sexuality and fertility. The first initiation is essentially a conscious one, the second an unconscious one that rises to consciousness at the end of the play. Both are perverted from their normal purpose, and both are united by the Girl's rejection of enslavement by either. Marcuse's statement in my epigraph is borne out here: "Art is perhaps the most visible 'return of the repressed,' not only on the individual but also on the generic-historical level. . . . Since the awakening of the consciousness of freedom, there is no genuine work of art that does not reveal the archetypal content: the negation of unfree-dom."[20] The downward sweep of the Girl's knife and her laughter reveal exactly this.

In presenting the play as ritual, John Vaccaro was responding to the structures he perceived in the play. He was also acting in accord with

Arrabal's own instruction to any director of his plays: "I tell him that he must create an extraordinary theatrical event, a magnificent ceremony, a real theatre of panic with its rituals and its rites, its initiations and sacrifices."[21]

I I I

It is clear that *The Solemn Communion* embodies in its structure a ritual content. But, to take up our second approach, does the play itself function as a ritual? Certainly Arrabal intends his plays to act as such: "For me the theatre remains a ceremony: it's a feast both sacrilegious and sacred, erotic and mystic, which would encompass all facets of life, including death, where 'humor' and poetry, fascination and panic would be one. The theatrical rite then would be changed into an 'opera mundi,' like the phantasies of Don Quixote and the nightmares of Alice in Wonderland" (Knapp, p. 201). Just as Artaud wrote that he wanted to "attack the spectator's sensibility on all sides,"[22] Arrabal has been quoted as saying that "the poet must—and this is inherent in his art—provoke all kinds of reactions."[23] How are these effects to be achieved? By revealing to the spectator the contents of his unconscious. Artaud wrote that "the theatre will never find itself again—that is, constitute a means of true illusion—except by furnishing the spectator with the truthful precipitates of dreams, in which his taste for crime, his erotic obsessions, his savagery, his chimeras, his utopian sense of life and matter, even his cannibalism, pour out, on a level not counterfeit and illusory, but interior."[24] This is precisely the sort of theater demanded by Arrabal: "Si une pièce est conçue comme une fête démesurée, le spectateur peut recevoir des lumières sur la part la plus mystérieuse ou la moins accessible de lui-même, grâce aux rites grotesques et sublimes, sordides et poétiques qui se déroulent sous ses yeux."[25] ("If a play is conceived of as an unrestrained festivity, the spectator can receive insights into the most mysterious or least accessible part of himself, thanks to the grotesque and sublime, sordid and poetic rites that take place before his eyes.") In short, by presenting man's fantasies and obsessions in a ceremonial or ritual form, Arrabal wishes to reveal to the members of the audience their unconscious fears and desires and, in so doing, to provoke a basic change or reaction in the psyche. Did this in fact occur in the production by John Vaccaro?

Vaccaro's central conception of the play was governed by his decision to enact it as a manifestation of the impulse toward women's liberation. To emphasize the liberating effect at the close, Vaccaro underscored the sense of enclosure at the outset. In addition to being small and windowless, the "cave" at Bucknell University is walled around by a brown, ruglike material that deadens sound and absorbs light. The sense of ritual that Peter Brook requires for what he calls "the Holy Theatre" (or "The Theatre of the Invisible-Made-Visible")[26] was fully suggested by the religious connotations of the props: a row of candles that set off the acting area, the outline of the mitered bishop against the far wall, and the powerful odor of incense that pervaded the room. As soon as the audience was seated, the chorus of fourteen masked figures against the right wall began chanting. "Today is . . . today is . . . *descendit deo*. . . ." The spectators were thus included as participants in a religious ceremony. Psychically, the empty space became a mental or spiritual region where the invisible (the unconscious) could become visible (conscious) on stage. Vaccaro transported the spectators from the external world of routine activity to an internal, essentially unconscious, childhood world of the nurturing, primordial mother and soothing religion.[27] Perhaps some spectators even felt that sense of oneness of self and nonself that Freud labeled "the oceanic sense." As the play began, then, the audience, though partially expectant, was to some extent lulled by the protective "cave" and the religious atmosphere into a secure state of mind, untroubled by problems.

Into this situation of paradisal innocence broke the pallbearers with their coffin, closely pursued by the demonic necrophile. Eden was shattered by death and evil. Many in the audience no doubt underwent momentary anxiety as mythic timelessness gave way to mortality, but a second look revealed that, under Vaccaro's direction, the necrophile, dressed in black cape and leering in a grotesquely evil way, conjured up nothing so much as a character from the Grand Guignol or Bela Lugosi as vampire.[28] The spectators relaxed in amused reassurance that they need not begin to set up defenses against being drawn into sympathetic identification with a necrophile: the action onstage was only a parody. The audience's initiation had, however, begun for they had been prepared for the psychic danger shortly to be represented by the Grandmother.

The macabre humor of the necrophile was immediately counterpointed by the entrance of the Girl and Grandmother, who formed their own contrast—the Girl an archetype of innocence in her pink communion dress, the Grandmother an archetypal authority figure with priest's cowl, cassock, and silver cross. In accordance with Vaccaro's notion that this was to be a play about women's liberation, the Girl was fully dressed, as was the corpse in the coffin. (During rehearsal Arrabal, who was present not only for much of the rehearsal time but also for the first of the two performances, questioned Vaccaro's decision, because earlier productions, in conformity with the text, had presented the Girl as partially nude and the corpse as totally nude. Vaccaro was able to convince Arrabal, however, that such staging would run counter to his conception, of which Arrabal approved.) The Girl's gradual psychic imprisonment was fully presented on stage by a metaphor not in the text: as the Grandmother's relentless catechism wore on, a young man representing the Girl's future husband approached and began to wrap the Girl in chains.[29] The Grandmother's authoritarianism, symbolized by this encasing process, was also brought home to the audience by Vaccaro's choice of the bearded William Duff-Griffin as the Grandmother. Not only did the actor give the appearance of an Old Testament ecclesiastic, but he also read his catechism from a book as though it were the lesson for the day.

As the spectator watched the slow, relentless encasement of the Girl and listened to the indoctrination by the Grandmother, the "cave" became a kind of crypt, in which the Girl was about to be buried alive. By internalizing the play, the spectator became subject to claustrophobic anxieties, which were not relieved (or were so only momentarily) until the knife made its arc into the body of the necrophile. The black comedy of the necrophile's repeated appearances failed to provide a sufficient defense against these fears, for the apparent lack of connection between the action of the necrophile and the pallbearers on the one hand and the action of the Girl and her Grandmother on the other created further uncertainty. This second source of anxiety was, however, reduced as the spectator began to understand the way in which the two separate actions related to each other and formed meaning: the Grandmother's lessons instilled in the Girl the sense that as wife she will become a mere sex object in the eyes of the husband-to-be—a corpse to be ravished.

Vaccaro established the Grandmother as the perverse guide—the destructive Terrible Mother of Jung—in two ways. Each time the Girl referred to the necrophile's state of tumescence, the Grandmother, contrary to Arrabal's stage directions, responded in a tone of anger and outrage that clearly indicated her rejection of the life force and her desire to communicate the attitude that sex is dehumanizing. Second, Vaccaro substituted a corpse dressed in a wedding gown for the nude body in the coffin, and just before the necrophile got into the coffin, the "corpse" sat up brightly and sang in a bouncy, musical-comedy style:

> Come into my kitchen, it's very clean,
> Come into my bathroom, it's very clean,
> Yes, yes, yes . . . Oh,
>
> No nasty smells to worry about (sniffs) phew!
> No dirty panes so you can look out,
> No, no, no . . .

> Come into my coffin, it's very clean,
> I mean, it's *very* clean
> And that's the most important thing,
> And that's the most important thing,
> And that's the most important thing!
>   (Unpublished lyrics by Richard Weinstock)

The identification of kitchen and coffin, presented in this hilarious way, revealed clearly the destructive effect of the Grandmother's indoctrination, and also relieved the sense of claustrophobic anxiety by allowing the release of liberating laughter.

But at this point the granddaughter was still there on the stage. She had left with the old woman and then returned to watch the necrophile in action. The response of the audience was now exceedingly complex, varying of course from one spectator to another. It is possible to say, though, that many spectators empathized consciously with the Girl in her plight, calling forth their unconscious desire for free sexual expression and their fear of the Grandmother's tyranny. At the same time many, no doubt, felt both the power of the Grandmother's authority as a surrogate mother and the need to submit to her. Admixed with these affects perhaps was an unacknowledged pleasure in watching the Grandmother aggressively bend the Girl to her wishes and in experiencing her subservience. As the spectator observed the Girl to see what she would do, he had to undergo the conflict of these fears and desires on both the conscious and unconscious level. For the Girl to do nothing would be to submit to her superego, to accept a death-wish, and consequently to fail to move through the initiatory process into adulthood. For her, Eros would become Thanatos.[30] In order to indicate the sense of joy, relief, and deliverance with which the Girl succeeds in passing the ordeal and in order to release the spectator from his psychic conflict, Vaccaro directed the actress who played the Girl to burst out in a wild, uncontrollable, maniacal laughter as she repeatedly stabbed the necrophile. This cathartic paroxysm was accompanied by the visual metaphor of her violently throwing off the incarcerating chains and, as a result, the spectator experienced the exhilarating sense of freedom that accompanies the defeat of Thanatos and the resurgence of Eros. The triumph of the life force signaled the ego's ability to resist the death instinct symbolized by the Grandmother. The excessive restrictiveness of society and conscience had been objectified on the stage and made subservient to Eros. To the extent that the Girl is representative of the race and to the extent that what happens to her recapitulates the history of man, the spectator perhaps sensed the truth that Freud stated in *Civilization and Its Discontents*: "The meaning of the evolution of culture is no longer a riddle to us. It must present to us the struggle between Eros and Death, between the instincts of life and the instincts of destruction, as it works itself out in the human species."[31] If, as Freud said, civilization is a process "in the service of Eros" (p. 102), the spectator might well have sensed the importance of the Girl's victory.[32] Freed by the erotic instinct, the ego—both the Girl's and the spectator's—survived the aggressive attack by the super-ego. According to Norman O. Brown, the function of art is to liberate us from our repressions by representing "an irruption from the unconscious into the conscious."[33] By this standard, the Bucknell production of *The Solemn Communion*, under the direction of John Vaccaro, succeeded.

If it is an exaggeration to describe the spectator at this performance as reborn, it is not too much to say that he was in some sense renewed. He introjected the action of the play, he experienced that action internally, he watched the projection of his inner fears and repressions in the mirror of the stage, and by understanding and coming to terms with them, he was initiated into a revived desire "to regain lost liberties" (in Brown's words) and was awakened to a livelier sense of the need for sexual freedom. Neumann puts it succinctly: "Consciousness = deliverance: that is the watchword inscribed above all man's efforts to deliver himself from the embrace of the primordial uroboric dragon."[34] The draconic Grandmother has attempted to devour the Girl, and, in the process, what the Grandmother represents—repression, the Terrible Mother, aggression, the punishing super-ego, authoritarian social and religious structures—has revealed itself to the spectator's consciousness. The audience's response destroyed the danger that threatened by making the antagonist conscious, that is, by allowing the ego to assimilate it.

Though one can say, because the spectators of a play maintain varying degrees of aesthetic distance, that they are not the full participants required by ritual, nevertheless plays like *The Solemn Communion* create affects in the audience similar to those created by ritual.[35] To the extent that this was true of the members of the Bucknell audience who experienced the production of Arrabal's play just described, the play functioned as a ritual ceremony of just the kind that Arrabal has called for, and for at least some spectators it produced the effects he desires:

Je ne désire pas un monde de victimes. Au contraire. Je voudrais un monde très libéré. . . . Mes personnages ne connaissent pas les lois. Ils essayent de comprendre des lois qui ne servent à rien. Même dans les cas extrêmes, ils ne sont pas coupables. Ce ne sont pas mes personnages qu'il faut changer, mais la société.[36]

I do not desire a world of victims. On the contrary. I would like a very liberated world. . . . My characters do not know laws. They try to understand laws that are useless. Even in extreme cases, they are not guilty. It is not my characters but society that must change.

And how does he expect his audience to change? In his usual symbolic and poetic fashion, he writes with approval of the ways in which spectators react to productions directed by the three Argentinians who have been responsible for some of his own plays, Victor Garcia, Jerome Savary, and Jorge Lavelli: "les spectateurs, prisonniers d'un enclos pour tentations de saint Antoine, se métamorphosent en mages, victimes et prestidigitateurs, vêtus de désespoir et de félicité" (*Théâtre panique*, p. 9). (". . . the spectators, prisoners of an enclosure for the temptations of St. Anthony, are transformed into magi, victims and jugglers, dressed in despair and bliss.") A metamorphosis takes place that is produced from a spiritual, psychic ordeal, and though it may result in paradoxical emotions, the spectator is wiser for the experience. I suggest that *The Solemn Communion* reawakens an awareness of the need for and the difficulty of attaining freedom, and in doing so, it recovers for us what Marcuse says any true work of art does, namely, "the archetypal content: the negation of unfreedom."[37]

Arrabal has written that "the work of art bursts forth from the author's own confused innards with all of its fascination and terror."[38] He, like the rest of us, has lived through the initiatory ordeals that structure one of the rites of passage, and these have then become elements in the structure of *The Solemn Communion*. We who go through the experience of a play like this one must face some of the demons within ourselves, and the fact is that, as Arrabal wrote of Toulouse-Lautrec's experiences, "Vivre la nuit peut être dangereux. C'est regarder un peu l'abîme. C'est se rapprocher des forces maléfiques" (*Théâtre III*, p. 10). ("Living at night can be dangerous, something like looking into the abyss. It is an approach to evil forces.") By raising these demons and fears to consciousness, we find an accommodation with them and can achieve thereby an identity that is to some extent new. We recognize that we are not alone in wrestling with the terrors of the night, for we have in Arrabal (and his play) a guiding spirit who will lead us to a fuller sense of community with all men. Because we have the feeling that "l'ère de la bureaucratie religieuse est terminée," and that we are entering into a period "de la connaissance, de l'énergie sexuelle, de l'imagination" (*Théâtre III*, p. 17), we leave the theater, as John Holloway said, with a renewed power and vitality.

NOTES

1. This production of *The Solemn Communion* was staged under the aegis of Ellen Stewart and The Playhouse of the Ridiculous, one of the companies that comprise La Mama Experimental Theater Club. It was the culmination of both a year-long program on myth and literature at Bucknell University and a four-day workshop, directed by John Vaccaro. Ellen Stewart oversaw the production as a whole, and William Duff-Griffin played the part of the Grandmother. Gordon Bressac the part of the necrophile, and Betty Moses the part of the Girl. A Bucknell student, Jane Curry, took the part of the singing corpse. Twenty-three other Bucknell students either sang in the chorus or played the music. The music and lyrics were composed and arranged by La Mama's Richard Weinstock. The workshop and production coincided with a visit to the campus by Fernando Arrabal, who saw the first of the two performances of the play.

2. Alain Schifres, *Entretiens avec Arrabal* (Paris: Pierre Belfond, 1969), p. 114. This and all subsequent translations from the French are my own.

3. Northrop Frye, *Anatomy of Criticism: Four Essays* (Princeton, N.J.: Princeton University Press, 1957), p. 109.

4. Eugène Ionesco, *Notes and Counter-Notes*, trans. Donald Watson (New York: Grove Press, 1964), p. 29.

5. John Holloway, *The Story of the Night: Studies in Shakespeare's Major Tragedies* (London: Routledge and Kegan Paul, 1961), p. 178.

6. Mircea Eliade, *Birth and Rebirth: Religious Meanings of Initiation in Human Culture*, trans. Willard Trask (New York: Harper, 1958), p. x.

7. See, for example, Norman Rabkin, ed., *Reinterpretations of Elizabethan Drama* (New York: Columbia University Press, 1969) and Bernard Beckerman, *Dynamics of Drama: Theory and Method of Analysis* (New York: Knopf, 1970).

8. Eugenio Barba, "Theatre Laboratory 13 Rzedow," *TDR* 9, no. 3 (Spring 1965): 154-55.

9. Jerzy Grotowski, *Journal de Genève*, Geneva, 26 April 1962, quoted in Eugenio Barba and Ludwik Flaszen, "A Theatre of Magic and Sacrilege," trans. Simone Sanzenbach, *TDR* 9, no. 3 (Spring 1965): 186.

10. "*Solemn Communion: Panic Ceremony*," trans. Bettina L. Knapp, *TDR* 13, no. 1 (Fall 1968): 77. In 1970 *The Solemn Communion* was produced by the Stables Theatre Club in Manchester, England, and at the Soho Lunchtime Theatre in London.

11. Bettina L. Knapp, "Interview with Fernando Arrabal," *First Stage* 6 (1967-68): 200.

12. Calder's translation can be found in *Arrabal: Plays Volume 3*, trans. Jean Benedetti and John Calder (London: Calder and Boyars, 1970), pp. 217-27. All quotations from the play are from this text.

13. Mircea Eliade, *Myths, Dreams, and Mysteries: The Encounter Between Contemporary Faiths and Archaic Realities*, trans. Philip Mairet (New York: Harper, 1960), p. 209.

14. Knapp, "Interview with Fernando Arrabal," p. 199, quotes Arrabal as follows: "I was brought up in the Catholic faith. This has stamped me for life. I am very hostile, however, toward Catholicism. I blame Catholicism to a great extent for having made my life such an excruciatingly unhappy one. I am haunted as a result of my Catholic instruction by the idea of hell, of sin, of torture. I try to rationalize, to tell myself that these things are really impossible, a figment of the imagination; and yet, these fearful ideas return time and time again to haunt me." Arrabal's anti-Fascism is indicated in the same interview when he describes the bad son in *Les Deux Bourreaux* as modeled on his brother, "who is an aviator in Franco's army. He's very reactionary, very devout and represents all those forces that I despise" (p. 199).

15. On these two functions of myth, see Joseph Campbell, "Mythological Themes in Creative Literature and Art," in *Myths, Dreams, and Religion*, ed. Joseph Campbell (New York: Dutton, 1970), pp. 140-41.

16. Erich Neumann, *The Origins and History of Consciousness*, trans. R. F. C. Hull (Princeton, N.J.: Princeton University Press, 1954), p. 308, no. 40.

17. See Wayland Young, *Eros Denied: Sex in Western Society* (New York: Grove, 1964).

18. Herbert Marcuse, *Eros and Civilization: A Philosophical Inquiry into Freud* (Boston: Beacon Press, 1966), p. 51: "The perversions suggest the ultimate identity of Eros and death instinct, or the submission of Eros to the death instinct. . . . Civilization has acknowledged and sanctioned this supreme danger: it . . . outlaw[s] the . . . expressions of Eros as an end in itself."

19. Benjamin Hunningher, *The Origin of the Theater* (New York: Hill and Wang, 1961), p. 103.

20. Marcuse, *Eros and Civilization*, p. 144.

21. Knapp, "Interview with Fernando Arrabal," p. 201.

22. Antonin Artaud, *The Theater and Its Double*, trans. Mary Caroline Richards (New York: Grove, 1958), p. 86.

23. "*Arrabal: Auto-Interview*," trans. Bettina L. Knapp and ed. Kelly Morris, *TDR* 13, no. 1 (Fall 1968): 74. For discussions of the relationship between Artaud and Arrabal, see, for example, John Fletcher, *New Directions in Criticism: Critical Approaches to a Contemporary Phenomenon* (London: Calder and Boyars, 1968), pp. 29-31, and John Killinger, "Arrabal and Surrealism," *Modern Drama* 14 (1971): 223.

24. Artaud, *The Theater and Its Double*, p. 92.

25. Quoted by Christian Bourgois on the back cover of *Théâtre III* (n.p.: Christian Bourgois, 1969). Knapp, "Interview with Fernando Arrabal," p. 200, quotes Arrabal as saying, "If my plays were to be produced in Spain—and I'd love this—it would probably cause a trauma in the heart beat of that country."

26. Peter Brook, *The Empty Space* (New York: Atheneum, 1968), p. 42.

27. Neumann, *Origins and History*, p. 14, writes, "Anything deep—abyss, valley, ground, also the sea and the bottom of the sea, fountains, lakes and pools, the earth . . . , the underworld, *the cave*, the house, and the city—all are parts of [the primordial womb] archetype. Anything big and embracing which contains, surrounds, enwraps, shelters, and nourishes anything small belongs to the primordial matriarchal realm" (italics mine).

28. In "Stage: Puerto Rican Travel Theater," *New York Times*, February 24, 1975, p. 32, Clive Barnes indicates his awareness of this humorously grotesque element in Arrabal: "Arrabal's plays—particularly his early ones—are difficult to deal with. They tend toward an absurdist Grand Guignol, with something of the mood of Samuel Beckett mixed with the theories of Artaud." That Vaccaro was justified in so treating the necrophile is indicated in Arrabal's own words: he describes his 'panic' theater as composed of the most widely disparate elements: "La tragédie et le guignol, la poésie et la vulgarité, la comédie et le mélodrame, l'amour et l'erotisme, le happening et la théorie des ensembles, le mauvais goût et le raffinement esthétique, le sacrilège et le sacré, la mise à mort et l'exaltation de la vie, le sordide et le sublime s'insèrent tout naturellement dans cette fête, cette cérémonie 'panique.' " ("Tragedy and guignol, poetry and vulgarity, comedy and melodrama, love and eroticism, the happening and set theory, bad taste and aesthetic refinement, the sacrilegious and the sacred, putting to death and exaltation of life, the sordid and the sublime are inserted quite naturally in this festival, this 'panic' ceremony.") This statement is found in Arrabal's essay titled "Le Théâtre comme cérémonie 'panic,' " *Théâtre panique: l'architecte et l'empereur d'assyrie*, ed. Christian Bourgois (n.p.: Christian Bourgois, 1967), p. 8.

29. This stage metaphor echoed that used by Victor Garcia in his production of the play as

part of *Cimetière des voitures* (1967), in which the Girl is caged in an iron yoke. This performance is described by Renée Saurel in "Les Fils de Brecht et les fils d'Artaud," *Les Temps Modernes,* no. 260 (January 1968), pp. 1318-19.

30. Robert Abirached, "Au théâtre: irréguliers et francs-tireurs," *La Nouvelle Revue Française,* no. 183 (March 1968), p. 496, has also noticed the alliance of Eros and Thanatos in this play.

31. Sigmund Freud, *Civilization and Its Discontents,* trans. Joan Riviere (Chicago: University of Chicago Press, [1930]), p. 103.

32. In ibid. Freud describes how aggressiveness is converted into the super-ego as follows: "What happens in [the individual] to render his craving for aggression innocuous? Something very curious, that we should never have guessed and that yet seems simple enough. The aggressiveness is introjected, 'internalized'; in fact, it is sent back where it came from, i.e., directed against the ego. It is there taken over by a part of the ego that distinguishes itself from the rest as a super-ego, and now, in the form of 'conscience,' exercises the same propensity to harsh aggressiveness against the ego that the ego would have liked to enjoy against others" (p. 105).

33. Norman O. Brown, *Life Against Death: The Psychoanalytic Meaning of History* (Middletown, Conn.: Wesleyan University Press, 1959), p. 62.

34. Neumann, *Origins and History,* p. 105.

35. The characteristic production by La Mama E.T.C. is ritualistic. Mario Fratti, in "An Interview with Ellen Stewart," *Drama and Theatre* 8 (Winter 1969-70): 89, asked her, "What's theatre, in your own words? What should it be to excite and survive?" Stewart answered, "An emotional experience. A celebration. A ritual. It must strike not only the intellect but the heart, the guts." For a description of some ritual effects in a New York La Mama production, see Bill Eddy, "The Trojan Women at La Mama," *TDR* 18, no. 4 (1974): 112-13.

In the course of a symposium at Bucknell University on 1 May 1974, Fernando Arrabal defined the function of ritual and the significance of the Playhouse of the Ridiculous in the following way: "What is a ceremony? A ceremony is a rite by which a group of people gathered together in a church try to communicate with Someone Whose dialogue is unknown; that is, God. What happens to us, the group of poets, artists who live in our society? We are men directed by madmen. What do we try to do? Communicate with the people around us; but the language of the people around us is unknown to us. That's where ceremony and rite come in: they are an attempt to communicate with this bestial surrounding. In La Mama's Playhouse of the Ridiculous we find one of the most interesting phenomena of this sort. . . . Vaccaro, since he is a poet, is a mirror for society" (translated from the Spanish by Mills F. Edgerton, Jr.).

36. "Entretien avec Arrabal," ed. Françoise Espinasse, in *Théâtre III,* p. 20.

37. In the Bucknell symposium on 1 May 1974 (see n. 35), Arrabal said that La Mama creates "a freedom of body and soul that is going to change American society. . . . La Mama is like a seed from which flowers spring in many different places" (translated from the Spanish by Mills F. Edgerton, Jr.).

38. "Auto-Interview," p. 75.

SUGGESTED READINGS

Anderson, Michael. "Dionysus and the Cultured Policeman," *TDR* 11, no. 4 (Summer 1967): 99-104.

Díaz, Janet Winecoff. "Theater and Theories of Fernando Arrabal," *Kentucky Romance Quarterly* 16 (1969): 143-54.

Farmer, R. L. "Fernando Arrabal's Guerrilla Theatre," *Yale French Studies* 46 (1971): 154-66.

Gille, Bernard. *Fernando Arrabal.* Paris: Seghers, 1970.

Highsmith, James Milton. "Drama-As-Ritual: Antonin Artaud and the Cambridge Anthropologists," *Drama and Theatre* 2, no. 1 (Fall 1972): 7-11.

Hinden, Michael. "Ritual and Tragic Action: A Synthesis of Current Theory," *JAAC* 32 (1974): 357-73.

Holland, Norman. *The Dynamics of Literary Response.* New York: Oxford University Press, 1968.

Killinger, John. "Arrabal and Surrealism," *Modern Drama* 14 (1971): 210-23.

Schifres, Alain. *Entretiens avec Arrabal.* Paris: Pierre Belfond, 1969.

Thiher, Allen. "Fernando Arrabal and the New Theater of Obsession," *Modern Drama* 13 (1970): 174-83.

Walls, Vivian R. V. "Arrabal and Ionesco—A Study in the Theatre of the Absurd," *Pacific Northwest Conference on Foreign Languages: Proceedings* 21 (1970): 263-70.

Biographical Note on Louis J. Casimir, Jr.

Louis J. Casimir, Jr., earned a B.S. in Agriculture from the A & M College of Texas and a Ph.D. from the University of Texas. He has taught at Texas and Oklahoma, and currently is associate professor of English at Bucknell University, where he teaches courses in American literature and film. As the essay below gives evidence, he has had a continuing interest in black literature.

Dutchman: The Price of Culture Is a Lie

LOUIS J. CASIMIR, JR.

Dutchman is a one-act play by Imamu Amiri Baraka, who was known as LeRoi Jones at the time of its publication. Because the play is copyrighted under the latter name, I shall refer to its author as LeRoi Jones. Moreover, if I understand correctly the significance of his change of name, my remarks on *Dutchman* may have little relevance to most of the subsequent work of Baraka.[1]

The play was published almost fourteen years ago. Its first production opened at the Cherry Lane Theater in New York City on 24 March 1964, and won the Obie Award for that year, the same year that the Free Speech Movement erupted at Berkeley and Lyndon Johnson was elected 36th President of the United States, the year after the assassination of John F. Kennedy and the year before the assassination of Malcolm X. A film version of *Dutchman* went into production in England under the direction of Anthony Harvey shortly after its stage success, and was released in 1966, with Al Freeman, Jr., and Shirley Knight in the leading roles. Because the running time of the film is a little less than an hour, it has not received wide commercial distribution in the United States, but a 16mm version has reached many college and film society audiences across the country.[2] In addition to being anthologized in many recent collections of American literature and drama, *Dutchman* is in print in an Apollo paperback, with a companion piece entitled *The Slave*.[3] My comments will refer both to the script of the Apollo edition and to the film, noting the few instances where discrepancies between the two exist.

All the action of the play occurs on one set, the interior of a New York City subway car, and the plot can be summarized very quickly. As the lights come up, Clay Williams, a "twenty-year-old Negro," is the sole occupant of the car. He is neatly dressed in a conservative suit and necktie, and he is reading. Gradually be becomes aware that Lula, a "thirty-year-old white woman" who is "tall, slender, beautiful," dressed in "bright, skimpy summer clothes," and wearing "loud lipstick in somebody's good taste," is

298

staring, and then smiling, at him through the window. He returns her smile
and the train begins to move. Shortly thereafter, Lula enters the car from
behind Clay, stops by his seat, and announces her intention to sit beside
him. She is eating an apple, and throughout the play she continues to eat
apples produced from her large handbag.

Every bit of ensuing action and dialogue is initiated by Lula, who is
alternately seductive and cold, affectionate and belligerent, but always the
aggressor. As time elapses, the subway car takes on more passengers, both
black and white. They studiously ignore Clay and Lula, whose conduct
becomes more and more overtly erotic and, at the same time, raucously
combative. Clay, as his name suggests, is malleable to Lula's every whim;
her attraction for him outweighs his embarrassment at her vulgarity and the
sting of her insulting comments on his race and virility. He is on his way to a
party; Lula tells him that she entered the car only because of his presence,
even though it was not going in the direction she intended to take. Through
a series of events, Lula appears to be alternately seducing and assaulting
Clay, until she finally goads him to strike back at her, physically as well as
verbally, whereupon she at once cringes and cowers before his anger. At
this point Clay delivers an impassioned, angry, eloquent speech, a
powerful verbal attack, not only upon Lula, but also upon the other
occupants of the car and, by implication, upon the audience and the whole
Western European cultural tradition it assumes. Clay's speech is a scathing
denunciation of cultural arrogance that refers to the origins of our history,
our religions, our philosophies, and even our arts, and it is the dramatic
high point of the play, the moment toward which all the preceding action
has been leading. Clay says,

> Let me be who I feel like being. Uncle Tom. Thomas. Whoever. It's
> none of your business. You don't know anything except what's there for
> you to see. An act. Lies. Device. Not the pure heart, the pumping black
> heart. You don't ever know that. And I sit here in this buttoned-up suit,
> to keep myself from cutting all your throats. I mean wantonly. You great
> liberated whore! You fuck some black man, and right away you're an
> expert on black people. What a lotta shit that is. The only thing you know
> is that you come if he bangs you hard enough. And that's all. The belly
> rub? You wanted to do the belly rub? Shit, you don't even know how.
> You don't know how. That ol' dipty-dip shit you do, rolling your ass like
> an elephant. That's not my kind of belly rub. Belly rub is not Queens.
> Belly rub is dark places, with big hats and overcoats held up with one
> arm. Belly rub hates you. Old baldheaded four-eyed ofays popping their
> fingers . . . and don't know yet what they are doing. They say, "I love
> Bessie Smith." And don't even understand that Bessie Smith is saying,
> "Kiss my ass, kiss my black unruly ass." Before love, suffering, desire,

anything you can explain, she's saying, and very plainly, "Kiss my black ass." And if you don't know that, it's you that's doing the kissing.

Charlie Parker? Charlie Parker. All the hip white boys scream for Bird. And Bird saying, "Up your ass, feebleminded ofay! Up your ass." And they sit there talking about the tortured genius of Charlie Parker. Bird would've played not a note of music if he just walked up to East Sixty-seventh Street and killed the first ten white people he saw. Not a note! And I'm the great would-be poet. Yes. That's right! Poet. Some kind of bastard literature . . . all it needs is a simple knife thrust. Just let me bleed you, you loud whore, and one poem vanished. A whole people of neurotics, struggling to keep from being sane. And the only thing that would cure the neurosis would be your murder. Simple as that. I mean if I murdered you, then other white people would begin to understand me. You understand? No. I guess not. If Bessie Smith had killed some white people she wouldn't have needed that music. She could have talked very plain and straight about the world. No metaphors. No grunts. No wiggles in the dark of her soul. Just straight two and two are four. Money. Power. Luxury. Like that. All of them. Crazy niggers turning their backs on sanity. When all it needs is that simple act. Murder. Just murder! Would make us all sane.
    (suddenly weary)
Ahhh. Shit. But who needs it? I'd rather be a fool. Insane. Safe with words, and no deaths, and clean, hard thoughts, urging me to new conquests. My people's madness. Hah! That's a laugh. My people. They don't need me to claim them. They got legs and arms of their own. Personal insanities. Mirrors. They don't need all those words. They don't need any defense. But listen, though, one more thing. And you tell this to your father, who's probably the kind of man who needs to know at once. So he can plan ahead. Tell him not to preach so much rationalism and cold logic to these niggers. Let them alone. Let them sing curses at you in code and see your filth as simple lack of style. Don't make the mistake, through some irresponsible surge of Christian charity, of talking too much about the advantages of Western rationalism, or the great intellectual legacy of the white man, or maybe they'll begin to listen. And then, maybe one day, you'll find they actually do understand exactly what you're talking about, all these fantasy people. All these blues people. And on that day, as sure as shit, when you really believe you can "accept" them into your fold, as half-white trusties late of the subject peoples. With no more blues, except the very old ones, and not a watermelon in sight, the great missionary heart will have triumphed, and all those ex-coons will be stand-up Western men, with eyes for clean hard useful lives, sober, pious and sane, and they'll murder you. They'll murder you, and have very rational explanations. Very much like your own. They'll cut your throats, and drag you out to the edge of your cities so the flesh can fall away from your bones, in sanitary isolation.[4]

The eloquence of this speech is due, in large measure, to the diction, the cadences, the unique felicities of phrasing that Afro-Americans have contributed to the English language, as well as to the power of its themes. Those themes are concerned with interrelationships between murder and creation, with the paradox that great art can arise from the great pain of cruelty, oppression, and injustice, and with a notion of sanity as being no more than willing acquiescence to a culture that has become as vicious as it is decadent, as hell-bent upon self-destruction as upon obliteration of everything not itself.

At the conclusion of his speech, Clay picks up his books and prepares to leave, but Lula suddenly drives a knife into his body and, as Clay dies, he falls onto her body in a parody of a lover's embrace. Moments later she shouts, "Get this man off me!" The other occupants of the car respond like robots or soldiers to her command, and remove Clay's body from the car.[5] Up to this point in the action, no one has exited from the car, and all the entrances have been unobtrusive.[6] Until this moment the other passengers have been more a part of the set than actors in the drama. But the action is not quite completed. There is one more scene, in which Lula, alone, writes briefly in a notebook, takes an apple from her bag, and moves down the aisle of an apparently empty car, only to stop by the seat of its sole occupant, another young black man almost identical to Clay, equally surprised to discover this stranger interrupting his reading and invading his solitude. He smiles questioningly at Lula as the final blackout of the play occurs, and whether or not a given audience is immediately aware that the play has ended, the inescapable conclusion is that what has been witnessed is a ritual murder performed by Lula and her cohorts.

If ritual precedes myth, as some scholars have maintained, then *Dutchman* presents a ritual whose myth must be inferred. If, on the other hand, ritual is the performance of myth, as a play is a performance of a script, then the ritual of *Dutchman* is a manifestation of preexistent myth, myth that already exists, however dimly and unfocused, in the consciousness of those who participate in or observe the ritual. The latter approach is the one I intend to pursue, even though the former might at some future time result in a more coherent comprehension of the play as prophecy.

What I intend to explore, however, is the existence in the play of at least three myths that are part of our common heritage and consciousness. They are not *concealed* underneath or within or between the action and dialogue, but are, instead, *manifest* for anyone who is willing and able to perceive them. *Dutchman* is not a vehicle for moral commonplaces, but it does reveal aspects of our condition, and its initial stage directions refer to the scene as "heaped in modern myth." The three specific myths with which I am concerned have to do with the relationship of the protagonist and antagonist (Clay and Lula), the immediate setting of the agon (the subway car), and the larger context in which they exist (the subway *system* as it is represented in the play).

If "a myth is a large controlling image that gives philosophical meaning to the facts of life," as Mark Schorer has said,[8] then one of the most widespread myths in the modern history of European peoples has evoked an image of a dark male exercising brutal or hypnotic power over a pale woman, ravishing her mind and body for reasons that are horrifying in their inscrutability, but nearly always under the shared assumption that such is the nature of the beast. Iago's challenge to Brabantio that "an old black ram is tupping your white ewe" is the image that begins and sustains one of Shakespeare's greatest tragedies, but it is also significant that the popular stage of the nineteenth century included heroines such as that pale virgin Trilby, enslaved by the malign darkness of Svengali. Herman Melville also evoked this image,[9] and Robert Lowell elaborated on it,[10] in their dramatizations of an incident from American history, both entitled *Benito Cereno*. In this tale, a ship's sternpiece portrays a dark satyr with his foot on the neck of a prostrate white goddess as an unheeded warning to the *innocent* American, whose inability or unwillingness to acknowledge any image other than the abstraction of a flag, any myth save that of an ideal democracy, saves his life, but only at the cost of his soul. For that matter, it is unlikely that King Kong would have retained the fascination of a popular audience for more than three decades without the delicate vulnerable blonde whom he menaces, and relinquishes only when his doom is inevitable.

The tale of Beauty and the Beast is one of the best-known narrative embodiments of this image but, as an affective story, its outcome has become uncertain if not equivocal. Rather than the Beast's succumbing to Beauty, contemporary versions have tended more and more to emphasize the possibility that Beauty may be reduced to Beastliness. That the titillating horror of such a myth might have a special attraction for a people engaged in the systematic exploitation of the darker-skinned inhabitants of three continents to the consequent destruction of dozens of ancient cultures is not difficult to comprehend. The ambivalent attitudes of "white" residents of the United States toward native Americans is a case in point. Nor should it be surprising for a young, black, male American writer to reverse the conventional roles of popular fiction by creating a beastly blond female as the ravisher of a younger, darker, more innocent male. "Beast," like "ofay" (pig Latin for foe), is one of the less complimentary terms that black ghetto dwellers in New York have applied to whites for a good many years.[11]

However, that revisionist image, the rape and murder of Othello by Desdemona, or King Kong's demise as the helpless captive of Fay Wray, is only a starting point for reflection upon *Dutchman*, which addresses itself to a racially mixed audience, if not to a racially integrated public. The play does much more than merely invert the usual figures of the image to attack white arrogance and reinforce black resentment. Clay's name indicates not only his malleability, the tolerant good humor that renders him helpless on the potter's wheel of Lula's obsessions, but it also evokes the origin myths in which mankind was originally formed of clay, or mud, or dust, or earth, by gods or a God who then breathed life and spirit into the inanimate matter. Clay is not only a young, male Afro-American, but he is also revealed to be the representative of all humanity, and not only that portion of it that is black *or* male.

Lula, on the other hand, first identifies herself to Clay as "Lena the Hyena," a comic-strip character created by Al Capp a quarter-century ago; this is an image from the playwright's childhood, an image that epitomized physical ugliness and repulsion to the point that one glimpse of Lena's awful countenance would flatten an ox. That is to say that she is inhumanly, if not supernaturally, repulsive. This Medusa-like creature appears in many variations in world literature, of which the Loathly Lady who is central to Chaucer's Wife of Bath's Tale is only one example. While Lula almost immediately disavows the name Lena, she retains the descriptive part of her appellation, and she is hyenalike in character. She behaves like a malevolent creature of the night—if not a hyena, then a vampire or a succubus. But Lula, who appears to be condemned to haunt the subway and to embody the repulsive, antihuman forces in the play, is also a Siren who beckons the hero to his doom. She is Eve as the temptress, and Clay's acceptance of an apple from her early in the action signals the beginning of his end, even though she asserts that the Savior, not the Serpent, is her master. Or, more accurately perhaps, her servant: "My *Christ, my* Christ,"[12] she exclaims in frustration at Clay's amiability. However, the possibility that Clay's demise may be a fall into knowledge, even a fortunate fall, is another theme to which I shall return.

Beyond these references to myth and literature, folklore and fairytale, popular culture and the past, Clay confesses to Lula that he had at one time fancied himself a black Baudelaire. His own self-mockery, however, indicates that he will produce no flowers of evil, or flowers of any kind, having settled for the barren grayness of conventional wisdom, as Lula derisively taunts him. In fact, Lula, who is a self-proclaimed actress and liar, not only tells the truth, but contains most of the explicit truth in the play. She lies a lot, she says, because it helps her control the world, and she does control the world of the play. Not only Clay, but also every other occupant of the car, is subject to her will. Even Clay's eloquent outburst, quoted above, is not of his own volition, and, in asserting himself, he does exactly what Lula has been goading him toward almost from the beginning of their dialogue. *Almost* what she has been goading him toward, since he stops short of committing murder, just as, by his own account, Bessie Smith and Charlie Parker stopped short of the murders that would have liberated them from the sources of the pain that they converted into art. This is the point to which I must finally return.

But first, I want to consider the immediate surroundings in which the action occurs. The stage directions, unlike the location of the film version, do not insist upon the authenticity of the setting, but they do insist upon conveying the sense of speed as the subway car hurtles through the night. The word *flying* occurs in the first sentence of the written description of the setting, and in the film the title "*Dutchman*" appears to "fly" toward the audience out of the lights of an approaching train, seen from its exterior. There can be little doubt, then, that one referent of the title is the Flying Dutchman. Another may be the stagecraft device known as a dutchman, a covering of the seam where two flats are joined; the term, like many others used in scenic design, appears to have been derived from the technical jargon of sailors. It is also true that the first Africans introduced against their will into what later became the United States were disembarked from a Dutch ship at Jamestown, Virginia, in 1619; this bit of historical information may intensify meaning, but it may also limit the play's significance rather than extending it, since such historical detail is probably no more widely known than is the jargon of set construction. The legend of the Flying Dutchman is, however, like the story of Beauty and the Beast, the common property of most heirs of European culture.

Most of us are likely to know very little of that legend beyond its reference to a sailing ship condemned to sail the seas forever without rest or respite. However, it was said to be visible in stormy weather off the Cape of Good Hope at the southern tip of Africa, and the sight of it was believed to be an omen of ill fortune. The legend dates from sometime since the fifteenth century, but it has also been seen as derived from the legend of the Wandering Jew, which is, of course, much older. But however slight our knowledge of the Flying Dutchman, the image helps to account for the final scene of the play, in which Lula approaches her next victim. It is Lula who is identified with the legend, and that identification should result in further awareness of the resonance of the play beyond its specific geographic and historic setting. Not, of course, that racial conflict in the United States in the second half of the twentieth century is unimportant to the play's meaning, but that it also reverberates back into history and across the earth to the origins, and perhaps the destinies as well, of Clay and Lula and all their kind.

I have used the word *legend* to refer to the image of the Flying Dutchman because it has relatively clear historical origins; however, in the simple sense of an image by which man makes sense of his world, its effect is the reverse of the image of Blond Beauty and the Black Beast. The Flying Dutchman is not a myth of justification, but a myth of guilt without atonement. "All stories are whole stories," Lula remarks toward the end of *Dutchman*, and for those with eyes to see them, all images that enable us to make sense of the world contain the whole stories of their meanings. Sir Walter Scott recorded one version of the Flying Dutchman in which the ship was carrying a precious cargo, a horrible crime was committed, plague broke out among the crew, and thus no port would allow the vessel to land. From the perspective of LeRoi Jones's play, the precious cargo consisted of the human beings who were kidnapped from their homes in Africa to be treated as beasts of burden in the New World; the horrible crime was the systematic destruction of their culture by their captors; and the plague that broke out among the crew is racism, the curse that William Faulkner believed lay over his land and his people, a curse brought down by the sins of human ancestors, but a curse that could be lifted only by the hand of God. That Faulkner's land and his people extend beyond the borders of Mississippi and outside the American South is unquestionable today. And the plague of racism that has cursed English-speaking people in the twentieth century is not a purely modern phenomenon; it extends back in time before the Renaissance to Roman Imperialism and even to Greek civilization.

Recent advances in anthropology have clarified some of the ways in which the detribalization that resulted in the power and glory of civilization also entailed demythification and consequent dehumanization, insofar as human beings require images that enable them to make sense of the world. "Be as we are, speak as we speak, think and act as we do," say the civilized to the tribal, "and you need no longer be a savage, a barbarian, and a slave to supernatural forces or to mere human institutions." That is the glowing promise of evangelical civilization, and the response that has become widespread among enslaved and colonized peoples is the bitter joke that before the Europeans came the natives had the land and the whites had the Bible, while afterwards the Bible belonged to the natives and the land to the whites. Whether or not they always recognized it, the sight of any European ship in any weather was a bad omen, for Polynesians as well as Africans, for Asians as well as Azetcs. Clay Williams is as civilized as he knows how to be; it is Lula who insists upon his ancestry and his social identity, not as an American man, but as a black boy. And she is a prophet who fulfills her own prophecy: neither Clay's civilization nor his education nor his cultural aspirations prevent her from killing him, any more than the achievements of Bessie Smith or Charlie Parker prevented their premature deaths.

Richard Wagner's operatic version of the Flying Dutchman legend may throw additional light on Jones's play. Wagner's opera presents the origin of the curse as the hubris of the ship's captain, who, like Melville's captain Ahab, swore an oath, in defiance of powers greater than himself, to round the Cape of Good Hope even if it took eternity to do it. The curse he brought down upon himself could be lifted only if he found a woman willing to lay down her life for his love. Perhaps, then, Lula is searching for the man who will release her from an endless voyage, not by sacrificing his own life, but by taking hers. She raises the question of murder early in her taunting of Clay; she accuses him of being a murderer, and murder is the controlling image of his final speech. But Clay's violence ends with his speech. His words do not lead to action, and into the vacuum of his inaction Lula plunges her knife. She has told him earlier that he will say he loves her in order to keep her alive, but it is Clay's civilization, his acculturation, and not love, that stays his hand. He recognizes what would free him, and all those like him, from her dominance, her ability to humiliate and tyrannize; it is called that simple act of sanity: murder. Lula's action, then, may be the ritualized bloodletting of an execution or a human sacrifice, Clay having failed to fulfill his potential role by sacrificing her to preserve his own life and the lives of those to follow him, like the young man in the last scene.

However, I do not mean to suggest that Clay's speech is simply a program for action, or that his angry denunciation of what Lula represents is the simplistic "message" of the author of the play. There is the inescapable paradox (referred to by Clay's mention of "some kind of bastard literature" that he might produce) that Clay, and his creator, LeRoi Jones, had no myth, no language, no frame of reference, through which to make sense of the world other than the myth, the language, the frame of reference, of the culture that created them. Killing Lula would not be equivalent to destroying (or sacrificing) the insanity of Western culture and history. Such an action could not be a genocidal one directed against every subway rider whose ancestors came from Northern Europe rather than Africa. It might be, however, a beginning of the end of that myopic vision of no greater values than, as Clay enumerates them, "money, power, and luxury." Nor is there any suggestion that Clay's murder of Lula would have resulted in his taking her place, endlessly flying before the wind. Her death might have been a sacrifice of atonement, but it does not occur, and the play itself is not so much a call to action of the oppressed peoples of the world as it is a revelation to their oppressors.

Few of us seek to know the painful truths that Lula forces upon us through her attack on Clay and that are found in his response to her assault, any more than Clay initiates the scenario that he and Lula enact. And most of us who have any choice in the matter would prefer to avoid what Jones, in his stage directions, refers to as the "underbelly of the city," the entrails of civilization, the bowels of those monuments that may well become our tombstones. Clay, the city-bred, civilized man, is an archetypal minder of his own business but, once tempted, he is susceptible to all that Lula represents. As a would-be poet, he is her potential nemesis, who would free the minds of his fellow travelers. But he does not do that by walking away from Lula. She, in turn, may be a white goddess or a pale demon or somehow both but, whatever she is, poets keep her alive, poets resurrect her when she seems to have died, poets die in her embrace.

The dilemma of *Dutchman* is insoluble except through the death of its hero. However much we desire to awaken from the nightmare of history, however much murder might free us to create, we honor the art of Bessie Smith and Charlie Parker, art that Clay has portrayed as an alternative to, a substitute for, murder and sanity. What begins in the play within the confines of racial and sexual strife in a specific time and place becomes a timeless image of the artist's mission. Pastless himself, Clay's personal acculturation is as superficial as his conservative suit and as deep as his inability to carry through his murder threat; his medium is only a variant dialect of the language of his oppressor but, at the same time, the unique vehicle of genuine poetry. This is the only culture, the only language, that Clay knows; "some kind of bastard literature" may partake of what geneticists call hybrid vigor, whether Clay or Lula or the witnesses of their struggle recognize it or not. Decadent for at least a century, European art has looked westward for revitalization for some time now, but Clay's response is of little aid or comfort to those who would preserve those myths which, whatever their past glory, have become murderous.

Lula is not a woman, but a personification of an idea; not a human being, but an inhuman or supernatural force, amoral rather than immoral. She acts whether wittingly or not, as a muse to Clay, interrupting the passivity of his reading to goad him to eloquence, to become the poet that he is when his speech dominates the stage. Clay's art, like that of Bessie Smith and Charlie Parker, is an alternative to murder, rather than either's being the precondition to the other, as is true for Bigger Thomas in Richard Wright's *Native Son*.[13] Clay's monologue is, in fact, similar to that of J. Alfred Prufrock, who paradoxically makes poetry of his inability to murder *or* create. What is miscalled culture, the veneer of Clay's bank-clerkly exterior, is, as W. E. B. Du Bois wrote at the turn of the century, achieved only at the price of a lie that denies the self, "the pure black heart" that Clay refers to, and his self-denial has made him a walking corpse until he is possessed by Lula and momentarily brought to life as a poet, if not a prophet. It has been said that the first requirement for a poet is discontent, and Lula forces Clay's latent discontent to become manifest for our enlightenment. Clay becomes a light-bringer, a modern Prometheus. His death from the wound in his side does not bring salvation, but revelation, the secular revelation of art before it becomes ossified into religious or other institutions. And without the "color" contrast between Clay and Lula, there would be nothing to see on the speeding subway car except the ghostly gray faces of the passengers in their isolation from one another and from life itself.

The subway system itself, as an image, is one of our modern myths, similar to ancient ones such as the system of Dante's Hell, which is the title of Jones's first novel, published the year after *Dutchman*.[14] Because of its size and complexity, the subway system, like Dante's Hell, is more difficult to visualize than any version of Beauty and the Beast or any vision of the Flying Dutchman. A chart or diagram of it may be read, but even then what is perceived is an abstraction from the actual. Yet, as abstract as it is, such an image enables us to assume, without necessarily comprehending, an interconnecting pattern below the surface of our great cities and civilizations, which may otherwise appear to us as chaotic tangles of unrelated phenomena. Such a system serves as an image of order underlying the perceptible disorder of contemporary urban life. But the subway of *Dutchman* runs according to no apparent schedule and reaches no destination; it merely fills and then empties, with obvious physiological analogies. The subway setting of the drama, whether it is an obvious mock-up, as in the stage directions of the script, or completely authentic, as in the film, does not meet our expectations, does not enable us to continue to assume a rational system underlying perceptible chaos. Instead, it has become a purely symbolic setting, perhaps even the ghost of a previously shared conventional image.

I have already implied this third image, the third myth the play invokes, and it is stated in one word set apart at the opening of the stage directions in the script, as well as in the title shot of the film. Before we know that the specific location is the subway, we know that it is *underground.* The underworld of the subway only gradually becomes perceptible as a mythic Hades or Hell or Purgatory. Clay, like Orpheus, may be said to have sung his way out of it. If it is Hell, then Hell is not "other people," as in Sartre's *No Exit,* but rather the absence of any *people* at all in a world of ghosts. Clay's forced expulsion from that world may be a final recognition of his humanity, an acknowledgment of his vitality, his refusal to remain a shade in a world of shadows, or a "spook," as Ralph Ellison plays upon that word at the opening of *Invisible Man.*[15] As the Flying Dutchman is a floating Hell populated by the damned, so the subway car is a speeding one.

Norman Mailer wrote recently that a revolution in the consciousness of Americans would result if the President of the United States were capable of speaking in public some of Marlon Brando's lines concerning love in death in *Last Tango in Paris*.[16] It is such a revolution in consciousness, rather than in social institutions, that *Dutchman* directly addresses, which may explain why lines from it were submitted to a court of law as evidence of its author's subversive intentions. Only a revolution in consciousness could result in the democratic elevation to political power of a person who could speak with candor and eloquence of love and death, as heretofore only poets have, through their creation of the images that enable us to make sense of the world we actually experience, as opposed to the world of official explanations. Four years before *Dutchman* was published, Leslie Fiedler, following D. H. Lawrence, wrote that "American literature is distinguished by the number of dangerous and disturbing books in its canon— and American scholarship by its ability to conceal this fact."[17] "Fact" or not, *Dutchman* is more dangerous, more disturbing, the more its mythic resonance is perceived.

Consider, finally, the complete first paragraph of the stage directions that define the world of the play. Heretofore, I have referred to fragments of it; complete, it constitutes both prologue and epilogue to this drama.

In the flying underbelly of the city. Steaming hot, and summer on top, outside. Underground. The subway heaped in modern myth.[18]

NOTES

1. Even in the unlikely event that the author of *Dutchman* could have been unfamiliar with *Up from Slavery* and *The Souls of Black Folk*, what I see as constituting the major theme of the play is implicit in Booker T. Washington's famous autobiography and explicit in W. E. B. Du Bois's collection of autobiographical essays, especially in the essay entitled "Of the Faith of the Fathers," printed as chapter 10 of the *Souls of Black Folk*, from which the second half of my title is derived. The specific quotation can be found in *Three Negro Classics*, ed. John Hope Franklin (New York: Avon, 1965), p. 348.

2. The 16mm film version is distributed by Walter Reade 16, 241 East 34th Street, New York, New York 10016.

3. *Dutchman* and *The Slave* (New York: William Morrow, 1964).

4. *Dutchman*, pp. 34-36.

5. In the script, Lula orders the other passengers to throw Clay's body off the train, and then to get off at the next stop. They do so. The second young man then enters the car and sits a few seats in back of Lula. In the film the same actions occur with fewer words and the use of fadeouts, so that the final scene, fading in as it does on the second young man already seated, even more closely resembles the introduction of Clay.

6. Again, through the use of fades in the film, no one is ever seen entering or leaving the

car, so that it seems to fill gradually and empty suddenly; the passengers are as immobile and passive as statues until Lula, and then Clay, insist upon their attention.

7. As ceremonial forms, rituals are nearly always performed repeatedly, so that any behavior that is formally consistent and performed repeatedly may take on the aspect of ritual, especially if it has supernatural overtones.

8. From *William Blake* (New York: Vintage Books, 1959), p. 25.

9. *Melville's Benito Cereno,* ed. John P. Runden (Boston: D. C. Heath, 1965).

10. Robert Lowell, *The Old Glory* (New York: Farrar, Straus & Giroux, 1965).

11. My sources for this information are purely literary, but these words, and other comparable terms, occur repeatedly in the writing of black New Yorkers such as James Baldwin and Adrienne Kennedy.

12. *Dutchman,* p. 20. Neither word is italicized in the script, but my italics reflect the stress that Shirley Knight gives each of them in the film.

13. *Native Son* (New York: Harper & Brothers, 1940). Book 3 begins and ends with the reflections of the protagonist on this theme.

14. *The System of Dante's Hell* (New York: Grove, 1965).

15. *Invisible Man* (New York: Random House, 1952), p. 7.

16. "A Transit to Narcissus," *N.Y. Review of Books,* 17 May 1973, p. 7.

17. *Love and Death in the American Novel* (New York: World, 1960), p. ix.

18. *Dutchman,* p. 3.

SUGGESTED READINGS

Baldwin, James. *Notes of a Native Son.* Boston: Beacon Press, 1955.

Cruse, Harold. *The Crisis of the Negro Intellectual.* New York: W. Morrow, 1967.

Dillard, J. L. *Black English.* New York: Random House, 1972.

Herskovits, Melville. *The Myth of the Negro Past.* Boston: Beacon Press, 1958.

Jones, LeRoi. *Blues People.* New York: W. Morrow, 1963.

Reck, Tom S. "Archetypes in LeRoi Jones' *Dutchman,*" *Studies in Black Literature* 1, no. 1 (1970): 66-68.

Roemer, Michael. "The Surfaces of Reality," *Film Quarterly* 18, no. 1 (Fall 1964): 15-22.

Warren, Robert Penn. *Who Speaks for the Negro?* New York: Random House, 1965.

Biographical Note on William Arrowsmith

William Arrowsmith has had a distinguished career as a scholar and an educator. While receiving his degrees from Princeton, he was a Woodrow Wilson Fellow, and in succeeding years he won a Rhodes Scholarship and Bollingen and Guggenheim Fellowships. Recipient of numerous honorary degrees, he has taught at Princeton, Wesleyan, the University of California at Riverside, Texas, and Boston University, where he is currently a University Professor and professor of classics.

As well as articles on education, particularly graduate schools, and on Greek drama, his publications include a translation of *The Satyricon* (Ann Arbor, Mich.: University of Michigan Press, 1959), *The Image of Italy* (Austin: University of Texas, 1961), and a translation in progress of *The Complete Greek Comedies* (Ann Arbor: University of Michigan Press, 1960-). During his career he has acted as an editor of *Chimera, Hudson Review, Tulane Drama Review, Arion, Delos,* and *Mosaic.* At present he is translating the poetry of Cesare Pavese, and is working on translations of American Indian speeches, some of which have appeared in *American Poetry Review.* Also in progress are studies of Euripides and Antonioni, and in progress is *The New Greek Tragedy* (1973-), of which Professor Arrowsmith is general editor.

Antonioni's "Red Desert"
Myth and Fantasy

WILLIAM ARROWSMITH

Q: *Comment expliquez-vous ce titre: "Le Désert rouge"?*

A: *Ce n'est pas un titre symbolique. Les titres de ce genre ont un cordon ombilical avec l'oeuvre . . . "Désert" peut-être parce qu'il n'y a plus beaucoup d'oasis, "rouge" parce que c'est le sang. Le désert saignant, plein de la chair des hommes. . . .* (From an interview with Michelangelo Antonioni by Michele Manceaux)[1]

First, a few cautionary remarks. The literary reader unfamiliar with film criticism should perhaps know that, with a few notable exceptions, *Red Desert* has had a "bad press." Admired for its virtuoso camera work and remarkable technical use of color, it has otherwise been treated as an unsatisfactory clinical account, psychologically inept, of a woman's neurosis. The artistic problem here, however, lies not with the film but with audience expectations. With depressing regularity audiences and critics alike demand that films should satisfy their expectations of conventional narrative realism, perhaps because so few films require or suggest anything else. In the circumstances, a kind of lazy McLuhanite consensus that film is a serial "throwaway" medium has come to prevail. It is a rare director indeed who dares to challenge this consensus, as Antonioni has done. He, by the precision and complexity of his composition, the coherence of his structure implicit in every scene, the functional beauty of his detail, and his unmistakable effort to think and feel in genuinely cinematic terms, has taken the great risk of demanding from his audience the kind of intellectual respect or attention it would willingly give to a

This paper was presented after a screening of Michelangelo Antonioni's *La notte, Deserto rosso,* and *Blow-up,* and it therefore assumes an audience that had recently seen three films and could be expected to recall scenes and incidents with some degree of vividness.

312

poem, a play, or a painting. But not, it would seem, to a film. In this we have tangible evidence of the cultural lag that still separates film from the other arts. Equally revealing, I think, is the fact that the audience for films still demands from directors the "solutions" to the problems they analyze[2]—a demand that audiences have long ceased to make of poets, dramatists, or even novelists.

Antonioni literally compels his audience to see his works again and again (and they will more than repay, as I hope to show, such reseeing). Needless to say, such compulsion is resented by those who prefer staged "happenings" or mere technical bravura; and it is this resentment that is at work in the constant "under-reading" of Antonioni's films. Simply stated, it is dangerous, very dangerous indeed, for a director to ask his audience to think and feel in new ways, to treat them with real artistic respect.

But the respect is *there*—visible, audible, demonstrable. Each frame, each scene, I have suggested, contains the pressure and sense of the whole. If this is so, it means that, in critical discussion, we can begin literally anywhere and be certain of discussing, by implication, almost everything. What is needed is simply to choose the best *point d'appui*—not the scene that best illustrates the critic's reading, but the one that best gives, to audiences in any way tainted by naturalistic expectations, access to the film as a whole, to the director's characteristic *tematica*, that is, his "thematic repertory."

At its simplest, *Red Desert* is not a story of neurosis, but an account of individuation; a story of the emergence of the psyche in a time when individuation has become exceptionally difficult. This story is, for Antonioni, inherently tragic; any discrete gain in human awareness, any progress in becoming or remaining human, is won at the cost of very considerable pain. Pain can kill a man, or it can make him human. In different ways, from *Il grido* to *Zabriskie Point*, this is Antonioni's most persistent and obsessive subject: small, discrete advances in awareness; the acceptance of tragic loneliness and pain as the price of human existence; becoming, remaining (or trying to remain) human in a world so unbalanced and strange that it means literally improvising, from day to day, one's own humanity. Again and again the protagonists of these films must discover their humanity by improvising the courage to accept their necessary loneliness (or, like Aldo in *Il grido*, "lose their balance" and die precisely because they cannot accept it).

In *Red Desert* all of these themes, explicit or implicit, are involved in, and developed by, the scene of the sad, abortive "orgy" in Max's shack by the sea. Near the close of that sequence Giuliana (Monica Vitti) stands alone on the mole in the dense fog; the others stand around her in a mute, staring semicircle. One by one their individual faces appear, each shrouded in his private envelope, before being obliterated by the swirling fog. Only Corrado, defined by Giuliana's need, stands out, nearer and clearer, a little less blurred than the others. Each character is now seen as Giuliana for the first time sees them, not huddling together in a warm, sleep-blurred group in the red-walled shack, but suddenly *there*, seized in individual isolation before dissolving into the anonymous fog. For the first time she sees them alone and then as a group, "alone" together, discretely, in their separation from each other and from her; then she sees them together, linked by a common extinction, all slowly folded in the fog. It is the fact of *visible* separateness that suddenly overwhelms her. She feels the separation as pain, a pain so intolerable that she frantically drives her car toward the end of the mole, away from the ship, away from the land and the others, toward the fog and the sea. "I didn't see the ship, Ugo," she tries to explain. "I wasn't thinking about it." "I wanted to go home, just to go home . . . the fog confused me." By "home" here she means the sea that we see surfacing in her Sardinian fantasy—that blue expanse of maternal water whose blue, sheeted water is fitted to the girl's brown adolescent body like a glove, containing and enclosing, the same sea that she earlier says she fears "drowning in." The sea is "home," the only refuge from the unbearable loneliness she has come to feel in Max's hut and outside on the mole, a loneliness heightened now by the felt loneliness of the others, and her new perception of human isolation generally.

But if we note Giuliana's regressiveness, we are also meant to observe her progress: the gradual emergence of that consciousness toward which, blindly and doggedly, something slowly drives her. More than anything else she fears separateness, both because it hurts and because it is the way she must, against her wishes, go. But again and again she falters, and the to-and-fro pattern of her progress and regression is presented in a severely stylized form, quite as though the director wanted, even at the cost of static naturalism, to divert attention from clinical report of neurosis to the general existential and cultural *malaise* of which it is a symptom. Giuliana's neurosis, that is, is a story about *us*, and the director's generic and metaphysical ambitions lead him to a psychology that is overtly modal—that is, generic and ontological—rather than clinical and individual.

In sum, Giuliana's illness is presented as a generic disease of contemporary human nature; a tension of polar opposites between which she (and we) must somehow learn to live, and thus resolve. Both poles are rooted in her nature, though the pole toward which she is fatally attracted is what looms largest in her nature: her femininity, her instinctual life, her desperate need of others, and her hunger to be contained by a natural world of which she is an unseparated part, protected against any intrusion into her "oceanic feeling." Something in her (as in us all, though it is perhaps less repressed, more dramatically visible, in her) wants desperately to remain what and where it is, not to change, to be a natural, unthinking, passive part of the season, the winds, and the waters, to "be" and not "to know," to be spared the anguish of "becoming." Her profoundest instinct is to build an unbreachable wall against everything that might change her world. This is why she tells Corrado that she would like to have "everybody who has ever loved me . . . here around me, like a wall"; why she instinctively closes doors and cupboards, protecting herself against what might emerge from them; why she persistently seeks the shelter of walls, crouching against them to screen herself from exposure. Thus, when she and Corrado visit the worker's house in Ferrara, she huddles in the couch as though trying to lose herself in the leaves and branches figured in the slipcover, or to camouflage herself by finding a background into which she can merge and disappear. In the first scene, when she goes off to eat her roll, she instinctively screens herself behind the trees, trying to evade the reality that threatens her in the industrial landscape of Ravenna. But reality breaks through her screen; the smokestack emits its poisonous yellow vapor, while a few feet away, to her horror, the waste smokes and steams. The same need for shelter later drives her to her shop in Via Alighieri, out of the painful present into the dead past, a timeless street where today intrudes only as a torn newspaper floating down, and she can surround herself with the blues and greens of her own psyche. But despite her defenses, reality keeps intruding. No shelter is proof against it. Underfoot, the pollution spreads; a boat breaches the privacy of that island where she peers out with fear and wonder; industrial wastes poison the marshes so that even the eels taste of crude oil; epidemic arrives in the shack by the sea; paralysis finally seeps into her own home—a contagion she cannot seal off or expel.[3]

But with another part of herself, with the incipient consciousness of her newborn eyes, she resists her instinct to find shelter—an instinct that, in her more conscious moments, compares to drowning, to sliding down a slope, or sleeping on quicksand. Offered the containment of physical love, she instinctively, with one part of herself, resists, even while she hungers for it too. She is virtually torn to pieces, her psyche partly rooted in the old world of instinct and "oceanic feeling," partly straining to remain loyal to a vague but insistent sense of dawning selfhood. Whether she is with Ugo or Corrado, she responds to physical love with desperate need but equally desperate fear—fear of somehow losing herself in *their* need, of *becoming* them, at the same time that she wants nothing more than the warmth and security of their being, to be part of them fused in a single identity. Giuliana's problem here is like that of almost all of Antonioni's protagonists:[4] the tragic pain of those who, in order to become themselves, must suffer the loneliness of an individual destiny. The pain is intensified by the psyche's knowledge of how it was with it before it suffered separation, before it was expelled from the garden and entered time and history—before it became human. This primal knowledge is the content of the personal and collective fantasy that, in Antonioni, each carries about with him, the ground of his being, like Giuliana's fantasy of the girl on the beach. But the fantasy periodically irrupts into ordinary life, transforming it as it does everywhere in Antonioni's films—in the wrapping-paper sequence of *Blow-Up;* in the sudden summer cloudburst in *La notte* that sends the party into the swimming pool and Lidia and Roberto into the magic carapace of the car moving slowly through the rain; in the African sequence of *L'eclisse*. The effect of such irruptions is always to intensify, by contrast, the loneliness of those cut off from a felicity of an eternal moment they can remember but cannot re-create. It is the desire to recover that same felicity that drives them to drink or drugs or aphrodisiacs or frantic amusement or simple somnambulism—to anything that might assuage the pain of consciousness and restore them their lost paradise.

Obsessively, in film after film, Antonioni explores this perennial fantasy of the paradisal world,[5] which contains so much of us that we are constantly in danger of thinking it our true selves, what we once were before being expelled from the bright garden of Being. Philosophically, its power and appeal are in our bones as the old human hunger of "Becoming" for "Being." It is Plato's sun, Spinoza's God, or Heidegger's *Dasein*. Erotically, it is Freud's "oceanic feeling," the warmth and security of the womb. Culturally, it is animistic feeling—the individual's absolute "oneness" with nature and society, so irresistible to those who fear that they have fallen out of culture into mere fragmentary existence,[6] that nature and the "gods" are dead. Politically, it is the appeal of millennialism in any form, the ideal past projected as the future. Wherever we turn, we find it subtly, often grossly, shaping us, "living" us. But whether "archetype," "oceanic feeling," or *participation mystique*,[7] its tyrannical control can be challenged only by confrontation: by articulating it and "bringing its contents to the light." Even this is not enough, for nothing necessarily follows from perception and clarity.[8] The crucial task, for individuals and cultures alike, is to transform *fantasy* into *myth*, making myth conform wherever possible to the vectors of unconscious energy, even though this may mean correcting fantasy with consciously *lived* patterns, often of great difficulty and complexity. The alternative is bad faith: to remain less than human, to deny responsibility for oneself and the world.

The essential content of this primal fantasy is childhood and love. For obvious reasons. The child has no memory; he lives like a god in the eternity of the moment; he is wholly one with his world; his rapport with "things" is total. Indeed, he and his world are a single-sheeted, continuous "being." In love it is the same, since love transcends the person and makes of two lovers a single, all-contained world. "When a love-relationship is at its height," says Freud,[9] "there is no room left for any interest in the environment; a pair of lovers are sufficient to themselves, and do not even need the child they have in common to make them happy. In no other case does Eros so clearly betray the core of his being, his purpose of making one out of more than one." In Giuliana's fantasy—the Sardinian beach sequence—love and childhood are fused in the figure of the adolescent girl on her island. Dark, gawky, browned by the sun, she is both the adolescent and the primitive, standing on the edge of childhood as on the verge of consciousness; and the innocence and primordial coherence of her world are suggested in those Gauguin-like frames in which she peers out at the strange boat making its appearance in her Eden. With the arrival of the romantic invader, she senses for the first time the mysterious allure of "the other" in a world until now wholly bounded by her own being. Something new "swims into her ken," and she swims out to meet it, when it suddenly veers and vanishes. But then a second "mystery" follows the first—that high, sweet, singing voice that leads her out where she has never been before, around the promontory of golden rock, into a new inlet where the rocks are like "flesh" and where, in a stonescape of pinkish-golden torsos and buttocks, she sees what looks like two human figures lying side by side, and "at that point the voice was especially sweet." Thus upon the primal landscape of childhood Antonioni imposes the landscape of love, or its erotic anticipation. We see a child's self-contained world complicated and extended by the arrival of the "other"; and then the same world enhanced and transformed again by the anticipation of love. As the sequence closes, everything, even the rocks, are singing to her, embracing her, everything united in one ecstatic voice, in which nothing is missing, nothing separated. Blue sky, blue water, the singing voice, everything combined in the single intensity of the primal fantasy as remembered or colored by the yearning unconscious—and the whole screen goes blue blue blue.

Unless we feel the intense, vital coherence of this world where individual loneliness is annulled in universal community—this timeless, paradisal landscape of Chaos and "the eternal moment," alive with divinity—it is, I believe, quite impossible to make sense of the film or, I would add, of art generally. For fantasy and "ordinary reality" constantly inflect each other; neither can be understood without the other. Thus when the fantasy reaches peak intensity, ordinary reality is demoted and degraded; the quotidian becomes, as here, in Giuliana's neurotic vision, the nightmare: dingy or frightening or boring; oppressive and intolerable.

And the fantasy reaches peak intensity precisely in times of great change, and therefore of great pain; for change *is* pain—expulsion from old and familiar things. It is the crucial fact of change in modern man's condition that makes this fantasy of such obsessive power and allure. Change is now so violent, swift, and brutal that the fantasy becomes nearly omnipotent; the enhancement of fantasy leads to the further demotion of reality and the attenuation of responsibility. Men are literally estranged from themselves—from place, community, even their own humanity; and this estrangement makes them increasingly vulnerable to *possession* by fantasy in all its many forms, but by Eros in particular. As the old institutions of culture disappear one after another—family, church, the web of environing "ways," that is, of common culture—individuals are more and more tempted to imagine that Eros can perform all the tasks of the failed institutions of the culture. "Eros is sick," wrote Antonioni some fifteen years ago at Cannes. "Something is bothering man. And whenever something bothers him, man reacts badly, only on erotic impulse, and he is unhappy." From the erotic misery that afflicts Aldo in *Il grido*, to the compulsive eroticism exhibited by almost everyone in *L'avventura*, to Giuliana's neurosis in *Red Desert*, to *Zabriskie Point*, with its stylized ballet of copulating dancers in Death Valley, the theme is obsessively and searchingly employed.

But the crucial irritants are uncertainty and change. By estranging men from themselves, they endow the primal fantasy with quite demonic powers of possession. Thus to the old human anguish of expulsion from the garden there is added the unbearable pain imposed by the change in man's very condition, with all its attendant uncertainty. "For the first million years of human history," says Toynbee, "the rate of change that man's science produced in his environment was still so slow that it was not perceptible within the span of a single lifetime. No psychological adjustment, or at most only an infinitesimally small one was required during those first million years. In our time, the amount of change in the environment to which an individual has to keep on readjusting himself psychologically is so great, and the pace of this change so rapid that the demand is straining the human psyche's capacity to adapt. . . . Here the human spirit must fight its own battle, spiritually naked."[10] The point is perhaps familiar, but it has real weight and force. From *Il grido* to *Zabriskie Point*, quite without exception, Antonioni has insisted that modern life has added to the ancient problem of human tragedy the ultimate demand—that the human psyche itself should change.

He shows us this above all through the situation of a woman. He prefers, as he has said, to put women at the center of his films because "they are more realistic, closer to nature."[11] But also, because cultural change touches them first, men are insulated from change by activity, by fate, by profession—like Corrado and Max—and are therefore less "open." Women are also more rooted, at least in Italian culture, in nature, more bound to place and time, than men. Giuliana, of course, is a neurotic exaggeration. For her the central problem, both psychologically and culturally, is how to endure the separation imposed upon her—separation from the old cosmos, the old social order, from childhood and her own nature. Her nature is rooted in a sense of life that is everywhere opposed by an alien mode that she feels as a universal and invisible pollution. And her own hunger for "life," her submission to the fantasy that "lives" her (as opposed to living her own authentic "myth"), leads her to act in ways that inevitably sap her power of adapting or resisting. So she regresses, irresistibly drawn to those experiences which promise to end her separation by giving her security and love. Her plight in this respect is common, indeed nearly universal, and Antonioni intends that we should observe its pervasiveness, its application to *us*. This is why, I think, he shows us in the first scene the long, massed parade of striking workers and, contrasted with them, the lonely scab who dares to resist the coercion of the group and to act on his own—much as Giuliana will later emerge from the group in Max's shack, defining herself in contrast to them.

Antonioni's point here is Jung's: "All mass movements, as one might expect, slip with the greatest ease down an inclined plane made up of large numbers. Where the many are, there is security; what the many believe must of course be true; what the many want must be worth striving for. . . . In the clamour of the many resides the power to snatch wish-fulfillments by force; sweetest of all, however, is that gentle and painless slipping back into the kingdom of childhood, into the paradise of parental care, into happy-go-luckiness and irresponsibility."[12] Giuliana's dangerous regressing, her instinctive need for the security of physical love, is thus paralleled by the situation of the strikers, who take comfort in anonymity and numbers. It is first the scab and then the individual workman—that isolated but healthy young man, seen in clear focus, eating his sandwich—who interest Giuliana because she unknowingly desires what they have—the courage to be themselves, to accept separation, against the coercion or comfort of the crowd. Finally, in the faces of the workmen whom Corrado has enlisted for his Argentine expedition, we see the general social equivalent of Giuliana's terror, the fear of the new world to which she must adapt, and her hunger for security—all those superbly troubled faces over which the camera moves, peasant faces with the color of the Italian earth, lined and stacked like so many baskets and bottles for export, while their voices tensely, anxiously, ask whether they will be supplied with the old familiar things—newspapers, journals, TV, and wives—in the strange world into which they are being expelled. Like Giuliana, they too want to protect themselves with a wall of the familiar against the terrors of the new. Nomadism, of course, is a persistent theme in Antonioni; in one way or another every film employs it. But Antonioni's point is not Eliot's—the image of an atomized, polyglot society, without roots and traditions—but is rather designed to give the *sense* and *degree*, the universality, of modern mobility. Mobility here is such that it makes all ages and cultures simultaneously contemporary—American blacks in Italy (*L'eclisse*), Italian smugglers in Australia (*L'avventura*), Italian workers in Argentina (*Il grido*), and so on—and thereby fatally disorients the psyche. It paralyzes it, stupefies it, drugs it, or forces it to dangerous forms of compensation and, by nullifying its possibility of making its own myth, cuts it away from nature and the earth, imposing a new, "man-made" reality upon it.

This is surely why Ugo everywhere uses engineering and electronic metaphors for what, in Giuliana's world, are essentially psychical operations. Moral and physical equilibrium becomes gyroscopic; adjustment to reality is a form of "shifting gears."[13] His new reality is, like ours, technological, and we and the world must adapt to it. Antonioni has repeatedly said that he does not regard technology as baleful in itself, and that this film is not anti-technological.[14] But this is quite compatible with a fear that something indisputably human or animal or natural in us will be ignored or scanted by the frequently stunted engineers of our fate; the scanted element may be crucial to our lives and humanity. In Antonioni, this scanted element is precisely that instinctive part of the psyche which the modern world so elaborately represses, which Giuliana and Vittoria in *L'eclisse* are attuned to and live by. I mean the natural, the primitive, the animal—whatever it is in us that is still, despite all our sophistication, bound to the natural world. This is their value and allure—and their most immediate danger: their "red desert."

Giuliana's plight then is her fear of separation—of being cut away from a landscape, from the past, from the "ground" of her own being. In the deepest part of herself (as opposed to the woman who wants to escape what is intolerable in reality) she does not want to embark on one of those ships whose sudden looming and passing suggest man's contemporary condition—a passenger on a voyage somewhere, God knows where, ripped from the harbor of our past and nature, and therefore terribly uncertain and anxious, confused in our very natures, forced to consent to adaptations and permutations whose terminus we cannot begin to guess, toward an unknown destination. For some, like Corrado, the voyaging is an activity that prevents self-exploration, a deliberately chosen "busyness." For others, like Giuliana, the voyage is ultimately inward bound, like Thoreau's, to an unknown landfall, the slow, courageous exploration of a new or altered place, a new psychic geography. And her characteristic danger is to refuse identity, loneliness, and consciousness. She cannot bear to part from others, because they are part of her. Thus she tells Corrado that he is a "part of her" and that, if she went away, she would take him with her. If she loved him, she would eat him; she would somehow, anyhow, assimilate him, make him "hers." Typically, her own situation is revealed by her son. "Mommy," he asks, "how much is one and one?" "Two," she answers. "No," he says, and shows her that two blue drops coalesce on his microscopic slide into a single blue drop. "One and one is one," he says, at which she says, "You're right. One," and bends down to kiss him. And for a brief instant we see the two heads together, mother and son, as though it were one head of tangled, orange-reddish curls. Then, suddenly, Giuliana's eyes ("two little black points") open, as she peers anxiously toward the other room, where Ugo is packing for his trip to London. One and one, seen as two, but then, miraculously, one again—and then, separated, again two. It is an extraordinarily condensed scene, which succeeds in stating with remarkable clarity the whole emotional situation: Giuliana's intellectual knowledge that one and one are two suddenly confronted with her emotional conviction that they are one, child and mother alike, at a single stage in their psychic histories; then, like a knife, the thought of separation makes her open her eyes, and we see that one has become two, that her "separation" has begun. Her own separation of course influences her son's, Valerio's, for his feigned paralysis is his way of compelling his mother to give him the affection she herself so desperately craves. Because of Giuliana's new closeness to Corrado, Valerio unconsciously feels abandoned and so resorts to a trick to compel his mother to return. Valerio's trick in turn frees Giuliana from her dependence on Valerio, pushing her toward her last "defense," Corrado.

All this, and perhaps more, is contained in this extraordinary sequence, whose thematic import is revealed in the penultimate scene of the film. Standing on the loading dock at night, talking to a Turkish sailor who cannot understand a word she is saying—that is, in absolute loneliness—she struggles to "communicate" her new knowledge, the fact of the adult calculus—that one and one are two. *Participation mystique* is no longer possible. "I'm not a woman alone . . . although at times . . . it's as though I were . . . separated. No, not separated from my husband. . . . The bodies are . . . separate. If you prick me, you don't hurt. . . ." Here, stated with the compelling slowness of conscious realization and pained understanding, is the adult recognition of separateness and loneliness, which divides child from woman, neurotic from healthy, each from each. In one way or another, everything in the film has been a preparation for this scene.

As so commonly in Antonioni's work, then, Giuliana's predicament is "explained" by a series of pervasive polarities between which she must somehow live, resisting both her own nature and the unnatural world in which she lives. To assent fully to either—the "red desert" or the technological desert (represented by the poisoned marshland of the Ravenna coast) is death. On one side lies the primitive, instinctive, unconscious sea, that "oceanic feeling" toward which her nature and needs constantly push her, a sense-world of touch and sound where the eyes are of no earthly use, since nothing is really distinguishable; on the other side is the bright, divisive, fractured, thing-cluttered world of the eye and daily reality, of technologically manipulated nature, where human touch and sound become vestigial through disuse. "What," says Giuliana, "am I supposed to do with my eyes? What should I look at?" and Corrado answers, "You say 'What should I look at,' and I say 'How should I live?' " "It's the same thing." It is the uselessness of her new-found eyes that Giuliana is protesting, so she "looks" at the restless sea ("Non è mai ferma. Mai, mai. . .") and says "I think my eyes are wet," meaning, "What good are eyes except for crying, since seeing is unbearable?" Unconscious sea, then, against conscious land; conscious eye pitted against the other repressed senses; sea-fog as against industrial steam, technological death, and polluted air; dark against light; natural greens at war with sulphuric and lethal yellows; female versus male, and so on. Between these polar extremes lies a spectrum along which the characters are placed so that they constantly define one another. The interaction is too chromatically complex for close scrutiny here, but one example may suffice to illustrate the technique.

Time and again throughout his oeuvre, Antonioni depicts the sense of human loneliness by hinting at the envelope each character carries about with him, and the way in which it literally seals him off from others, cutting off his access to a common world. He also shows us the revealing reverse of this encapsulation—the rapturous, miraculous feeling, so close to religious transcendence, that explodes when an individual breaks out of, or momentarily penetrates into, another's Umwelt. The theme of communication, which critics have so persistently said is Antonioni's only theme, is merely, I think, a function of his insistence on this subjective reality, and what happens when these individual worlds do, or do not, intersect. But he is above all fascinated by the typical difference of Umwelt in man and woman, extrovert and introvert, conscious and unconscious. A central theme in L'eclisse, for instance, is that of psychological independence and subjection: how far can either Piero or Vittoria enter each other's world without sacrificing his own individuality? How much sacrifice of one's own nature can erotic dependence exact? How can one love and still remain himself unless he can resist this very appropriation of his soul, this merging with the person he loves, which is the very purpose of eros?

In *L'eclisse*, for instance, this theme is stated visually, through an exquisitely rich and functional use of black and white. Thematically opposed throughout, these blacks and whites attract to themselves subclusters of associated images and ideas (e.g., night and day; country and city; nature and man-made artifice, or technology; silence and sound), constantly complicating as the film progresses. Only at the end, in the final shot, do these accumulated inflections reveal their summary meaning, as a streetlight suddenly goes on, flares in the gathering darkness, "eclipsing" the night and driving the natural blacks to the fringes of the frame; on the soundtrack, a blaring, ominous, electronic crescendo. So, in human terms, we watch as Piero's artificial and cerebral world increasingly threatens to "eclipse" and extinguish Vittoria's more natural world and her precarious psychic balance. On one side is the "blackout" world of pure sensation (the "erotic desert," *plein de la chair des hommes*, of *Red Desert*, even more vividly depicted in *Zabriskie Point*), with its chaos of the instincts and passions, without individuation, moral distinction, or tragedy (we recall the dark pool in which the drunkard dies; the dogs running loose in the black freedom of the park at night; the sudden murk of the cloud that envelops the airplane on its way to Verona). On the other side is the harsh Apollonian noise-and-light-world of the city, the stock market, and manipulative mind, represented by the pure abstraction of money, figures uprooted from the context of natural things and moving down the "big board" and then reaching out, across the *geographical* frame, for the provinces, for Verona, Milano, and the world. Vittoria, unlike Giuliana, is not neurotic, and her psychic balance is expressed in *L'eclisse* by her ability to find a visual "mean" between the lethal extremes of black and white; an emotional *chiaroscuro* whose varying inflections, now dark, now light, chart the rise and fall of her feelings, her lapses and achievements, as she struggles to find and keep her balance in a world constantly shifting underfoot and tilting toward disaster. This striving for balance is the reason why, for instance, she feels so much at home on the airport terrace at Verona, poised happily but briefly and precariously between old and new, country and city, plant and machine, between one "affair" and another. The mean she barely succeeds in finding is her existential ambience; and in its fused or interwoven whites and blacks, depicted as latticed light or zebra stripes, in that afternoon aura she carries around with her, and in her lovely mesh of feeling and thought, we come to recognize her personal, visual "music." Her whole effort is devoted to avoiding Giuliana's plight, to avoid falling into "oceanic feeling," and losing balance before her lover's needs and erotic invasion. Both health and balance, as Antonioni ominously observes, are increasingly difficult in a world already desperately unbalanced.

But whereas in *L'eclisse* (1961) Antonioni had only black and white at his disposal, in *Red Desert* (1964) he has the whole chromatic scale, with all its possibilities of shade and intensity. And his craftsman's pleasure in the expansion of his technical means is no less apparent than Uccello's delight in perspective. But despite the stylized exuberance of these chromatic experiments, Antonioni's use of color here is wholly in keeping with his artistic purpose in black and white. Color may make for greater complexity, but it still serves the same obsessive themes, the same mode of seeing and thinking, and the same persistent ordering of reality in terms of polar opposites. Color provides, that is, a richer spectrum, in which individuals can be chromatically "placed" and defined; but the spectrum is essentially that which we see in *La notte* and *L'eclisse*. (*Il grido* and *L'avventura* are clearly marked by a more naturalistic idiom.) Thus Giuliana temperamentally inhabits a world of earth-colors, above all dark blue, vegetation-greens, mauves, and ochers, more or less matte and pastel in tone, while Ugo's technological world is defined by bright, mechanical, sometimes strident yellows, blues, reds, and whites (corresponding to the functional colors of the refinery), without subtlety or depth. And just as the artificial streetlight of *L'eclisse* invades and usurps the natural night, so here the refinery spills over into green nature, seeping like a poison into the lagoons and estuaries (all deliberately painted a dreary dun color to give the sense of a literal *nature morte*). But Antonioni's point is not ecology or a conventional anti-industrial idyll. Nature and technology are here opposed, not as sentimental opposites, but rather as the framing facts of life on this earth, the essential terms of his artistic geography of the human spirit. The point here is not the imbalance (which, Antonioni seems to suggest, may be inevitable), but rather the human *perception* of the imbalance and responsible reaction to it. It is *clarity* that counts, for the characters and the audience whose fantasy and myth the characters enact, and, ultimately, for the sake of the action to which clarity must finally lead.

Consider Corrado, for instance, his "chromatic" character. The romantic engineer *par excellence*, he occupies a point midway between Giuliana and Ugo, modulating easily between their poles just as he moves, chameleonlike, changing color as he passes, between the violent noise and bright colors of the refinery to the secretive silence and the ochers and gray-greens of Giuliana's hideaway on Via Alighieri. Color, that is, provides immediate psychic definition, which in turn guides and explains affinities, sympathy, antipathy, and affection. Corrado, with his reddish hair and pastel greens, his shades of straw and stone, is immediately admissible into Giuliana's world, without jar, as Ugo is not. Color declares him *simpatico*, just as his emotional and erotic coarseness link him to the vulgar Max, to the world of money-making and mere "busyness." What is suggested by color is confirmed by his psychic geography: the wanderer and escapist, lured constantly seawards and away, moving back and forth between sea and land, a peregrine and nomad, between one adventure and another, a mining engineer who, instead of going down, as he says, went up; a mobile and transitional man, always in flight.

In her relation to Corrado, Giuliana finds, as she comes to learn, a projection of her own psychic world and a sea-sympathy, that regressiveness toward the unconscious and the erotic which is her special danger. What finally saves her is her confrontation with her own most personal peril—the appeal of the "red desert"—represented in the film by Corrado and her brief affair with him. For unlike him, the perpetual escapist, she has the courage to confront her fears. In his own words, "One goes round and round and ends up finding himself just where he was. That's what happened to me. I'm no different now from what I was six years ago. But I don't know whether that's what makes me leave or stay." Antonioni has commented on Corrado's role, and his words deserve attention: "The character played by Richard Harris is almost a Romantic, who thinks about fleeing to Patagonia and has no idea at all about what he must do. He is taking flight and believes that he is resolving, in this way, the problems of his life. But this problem is inside him, not outside. All the more true is it that he has only to meet a woman to provoke a crisis, and he no longer knows whether he will leave or not. . . . When, at the breaking point, the woman needs someone to help her, she finds a man who takes advantage of her and her crisis. She finds herself face-to-face with old things, and it is these old things that shake her and sweep her off her feet. Had she met someone like her husband, he would have acted differently. . . ."[15] It is Corrado's evasion—his flight to the sea, his casual, nomadic existence, erotic and peregrine—that Giuliana confronts in the penultimate scene, when in desperation she seeks passage on a Turkish tramp steamer. Here colors, symbols, and themes converge. The blaze of the ship's red hull below the waterline as the scene opens, the piles of industrial materiel, the derelict and foreboding steamer, with its suggestions of death and eros—all these things reveal the real meaning of the romantic sailboat in the Sardinian fantasy and make possible Giuliana's recognition of the tragic tension to which her individuation has finally led her.

It is herself she now confronts, as she confronts the colors that are, no less than the romantic colors of her Sardinian fantasy, her real world. Deep reds, blues, greens, and the rusting hull of the sinister ship—everything in the scene corresponds to, has its equivalent in, her Sardinian paradise, but it is now revealed in another aspect. What the unconscious once presented in the intense colors and delicate pastels of fantasy now suffers a conscious translation, as the erotic and paradisal dream is revealed as the nightmare. Soft pinks are intensified to violent reds; the blaze of red bulwarks and red hull recalls the start of the scene in Max's shack—that blurred, pullulating pink, a rosy chaos of red coals not recognized as coals until a foot suddenly emerges from them. The focus widens to show a stockinged curve of leg. From the rosy coals to the pink legs to the girl stretched out languorously before the fire, and then to the plank walls, the same bright red as the coals from which the camera began its journey: here, in one brief sequence, we are given the whole intricate scale of colors that set the scene and declare its nature. Rose and red breeds a pink, a sinuous curve of flesh; out of rosy nothing a pink leg constructs the bright red walls that frame and define it.

In this way, by accumulation and echo, Antonioni inflects his chromatic scale. In the rusty hull and the red bulwarks on the waterfront later, we know through the scene in the red-walled shack by the sea what Antonioni intends: the erotic "signature" of red, attached now, for the first time, to a ship, a ship no less sinister than the fever-ship by the shack, but with suggestions of the boat that, like Corrado, breaches Giuliana's island-world, and then mysteriously veers away. Red too is what the whole scene in the shack *aims* at—at the ruddy passion, the red desert, which the group wants somehow, by drugs, by wine, by aphrodisiacs, to compel into existence. But here everything is abortive, turns into mere words, as the worker's girl disgustedly observes. Only Giuliana genuinely feels anything resembling passion. The aphrodisiacs touch her, work on her, because of her participation in the same organic nature from which they derive; no aphrodisiac really works unless, like a true animist or primitive, one accepts the world as one continuous living whole, so that you and it—whether quail eggs or ground rhinocerous horn—are really one thing, fused in *participation mystique*. The others must artificially construct the red feelings that come naturally, instinctively, to Giuliana; it is consciousness she lacks and for which she must struggle. Red is her peril. Hence we are meant to understand the danger implied in those red bulwarks, but also Giuliana's courage in what she here confronts at its peak intensity. The pale pinks in the curving sands of Giuliana's fantasy island reappear with ruddier force in the pink-suffused room of Corrado's hotel after their love-making; and these romantic and rosy pinks are then subsumed in the red blaze of the hull, against which she stands, alone with her particular peril. Here, in short, is the "red desert," a pink from which all white has vanished; pink darkened into unconsciousness, into instinctive blood-red. So too the romantic sailboat of the Sardinian island is transmogrified into a Turkish tramp, and the sense of mystery surrounding the yawl earlier, becomes the deathlike quality of this sinister steamer.

Giuliana's world, then, is wholly defined by color; we know who she is from what she sees, the colors she chooses to wear and also be worn by, just as we know the others from what they see and cannot see, from the colors of their world. The same is no less true of the other senses. It is Giuliana, for instance, who hears, with certainty, the cry—*il grido*—from outside the shack: a cry that sounds, in fact, very much like the cry of a baby. The other women clearly hear it too—and so does Ugo, if the spectator is attending closely, even though Ugo consciously is unaware that he has heard it. But the other women are quickly persuaded to deny what they have heard. And the reason is not only the authority of male consensus, but the women's habitual deference to this authority. They are *accustomed* to deny the reality of their own perceptions, to disbelieve and even disown their own senses (or at least to act as though they did). Their very disbelief or denial is evidence of Antonioni's thesis of the one-sided domination of the conscious over the unconscious, to which the women have readier access than the men. Here too, then, the director provides a spectrum consisting of different responses to reality. At one end is Giuliana, who is so close to the unconscious, to "others," that she is in danger of drowning in them; to her the cry is unmistakable. The other women have heard it, but less distinctly. Ugo has unconsciously heard it, but denies it. The gross Max and the others have heard nothing; in them the unconscious, the other senses, are deaf or dormant. This is why the compensatory power of the unconscious is so strong in them; why they project their libido in aphrodisiacs and sexual innuendo; why they want to drown their individual "identities" in a collective "life." It explains their moods of childish "play" and the weight of "adult" propriety (the sudden hilarious tearing down of the plank walls to feed the dying fire, followed by that sad, embarrassed, individuated silence). And so they act like unhappy somnambulists, determined not to waken and to punish, through the coercion of consensus, anyone who, like Giuliana, brings the contents of the unconscious to consciousness, or succeeds in achieving a childishness and primitivism they envy but cannot create for themselves. Thus each character defines the other. Giuliana, isolated by her illness, is terrified of being thought mad if she contradicts the male consensus; the alternative is to deny her own senses, to disavow reality. When she resists the group, she inevitably separates herself from it; resistance individuates her. The sudden pain of finding herself separated from the others, of finding herself alone, drives her *seawards,* toward the fantasy-world—those blue maternal waters of her island-world—to annul the unbearable pain of her sudden loneliness and "difference." Yet this same sense of "difference" is also crucial to her individuation.

Separation and containment: between these polar psychological worlds the film moves. Just as the beauty and clarity of Giuliana's fantasy-world are our best evidence of her "neurotic" hunger for containment and her immersion in it, so the final scene unmistakably reveals her separation from it, her *conscious* decision to accept the tension and live it. She is "separated" but also "not separated"; she is still pained and surprised by the *discontinuity* of pain: "When you prick me, you don't hurt" (*Quando lei me punge, lei non soffre*). And she realizes, sadly, at the moment of articulate decision, that her life is what "happens to her"; that is, that she is responsible for her own life—as she has not been until now.[16] This is the moment of conscious wakening toward which her life and her neurosis have steadily, despite constant regressions, been driving her. One after another, Antonioni deprives her of all emotional support—first her husband, then her child, then her lover. All in some sense desert her or fail her. With each fresh abandonment she feels a wound, a hurt like death; yet each desertion drives her toward her own identity, away from fantasy and toward a myth of her own. Almost at the end of the film, back in her shop on Via Alighieri, she can respond to Corrado's advice not to worry about infidelity by saying scornfully, "Just don't think about it! A fine solution!" Here moral consciousness, the sense of duties, the sense of *others* supervenes. And it is the consequence of this decision, combined with her recognition of her own loneliness in her "conversation" with the Turkish sailor, that finally brings her to her true human "home."

A word about structure. *Red Desert*, like all of Antonioni's films, is very tightly composed, but the structure is based upon a complex criss-cross of correspondence and echo whose matrix is the fantasy of the Sardinian island. It should be stressed that this is a genuine psychological fantasy, the emergence, at a moment of diminished consciousness, of the contents of the unconscious. What has been repressed suddenly surfaces, and the power, beauty, and intensity of the fantasy unmistakably declare its unconscious origins. This, I am certain, is how we are meant to see it; not as a lyrical flashback intruded as a fairy-tale to beguile a sick child, but a genuine fantasy, rich with unconscious life. In harmony with psychoanalytical theory, it looks both backward and forward; it is at once an ordering of past experience and a guide to future action. Thus it controls the film throughout, gathering up earlier themes and visual images, transmuting them according to the new experience and psychic needs of the dreamer, and thereby giving fresh meaning to the "manifest material." By so doing, it also anticipates the dreamer's future behavior, projecting the structure of past and present on the future. The "meaning" of the dream ultimately depends upon what the dreamer does with it. He can actively transmute his fantasy into conscious myth by understanding and, to some degree, controlling its patterns; or he can remain the passive victim of the recurrence imposed by old behavior and personal need, doomed to perpetual repetition. The difference is that which divides adult from child, health from neurosis, purposive behavior from mere somnambulism. What matters for the dreamer is his perception of the pattern and his courage in confronting its hold on his life.

Structurally, the film depends upon *our* perception of the pattern—a pattern that makes its full epiphany only in the Sardinian fantasy, that is, when the film is two-thirds over. Only then do we see how firmly the fantasy echoes, with the skeletal clarity of fable, earlier scenes. Only then do we see that earlier events are nothing but the manifest material of the fantasy; that *it* explains *them* as much as they explain it; that repetition is precisely the artistic and psychological point. The reader need merely recall the fantasy's chief features: a lonely, adolescent girl, at one with the landscape, then hiding behind the branch of a tree (a repeated *motif*); the arrival of the mysterious boat (in the distance, a glimpse of fabulous landfalls); and, finally, the girl's discovery of an erotic landscape in the rocks at a point where everything is fused, singing in a single ecstatic voice.

Formally, however, reduced to its simplest terms, this fantasy is not new, but a repetition that has been radiantly transformed by the unconscious. Its "everyday" source or "manifest material" lies above all in the earlier scene in Giuliana's "shop" in Via Alighieri. We see a timeless street, deserted, all leached greens, grays, and ochers, and the room where Giuliana, like a lonely child, "plays" shopkeeper, sheltered from reality by the comforting blues and greens of her amniotic world. Into this street, as dead as the past, where nobody lives, slides the car of Corrado, the curious and mysterious invader. He gently pushes her door open, then retreats as she anxiously peers out to see who has broken into her isolation. They talk of boats, of Corrado's comings and goings. He is attentive, and this makes an impression, for she abruptly asks, *à propos* of nothing except the fact of his *arrival* in *her* world, "When did you arrive?" (*Quando sei arrivato?*"—with the stress on *arrivato*). The scene closes, like the fantasy, on a note of romantic anticipation. And the high, singing voice of the fantasy has, as its visual precursor, the incipient love we see blooming—a pink carnation in soft focus—between Giuliana and Corrado in Ferrara.

Even Giuliana's "island" is more than a metaphor of isolation. It too has its own manifest material in the floating oil depot (*isola della Sarom*, in the Italian) where Giuliana and Corrado, alone together, surrounded by waves and gulls, talk of love and Corrado's imminent departure (each mention of departure visually stressed by shots of struts, spars, and bars between them). But this scene tells us why, in Giuliana's fantasy later, the invading boat suddenly veers away, off toward the fabulous world it brings with it. Indeed, throughout the film boats and ships are images of transient, nomadic life, cut away from all locality and home—visible emblems of the possibility of flight and the hope of "getting away from it all." In the scene on the floating depot and in the Sardinian fantasy, boats also acquire an aura of erotic hope, of flight *from* loneliness. Thus, after Giuliana recognizes Corrado's coarseness and irresponsibility, she runs, in sudden regressiveness, desperate to escape her loneliness by taking passage on the Turkish tramp (just as earlier she drove her car suicidally toward the sea in which she sees the shining blue "home" of her fantasy-lagoon). It is in her confrontation with the Turkish sailor, her halting, desperate recognition, as she is confronted by his utter incomprehension, that she knows what evasion means—not annulment of loneliness, but simply a repetition of the pattern; that, for better or worse, she is on her own. Knowing this, she can at last return, for the first time, truly home.

The correspondences between Giuliana's fantasy and her behavior before and after are too complex for full discussion here. But the schematic intricacy with which they are developed, thematically, visually, and aurally, leaves no doubt about the director's strategy. A brief glance at one scene—the "seduction" in Corrado's hotel room—is enough to suggest the meticulous craftsmanship of Antonioni's texture. For instance, immediately after the seduction, the bedroom is suddenly suffused in pink—the same tonal pink we see in the curving sands of Giuliana's Sardinian beach. And in the writhing bodies of the lovers Antonioni clearly *requires* his audience to see again those twisted torsos and buttocks discernible in the island's rocks (rocks that "seemed to be made of human flesh," as the subtitle says), and thus to recognize the actualization in the bedroom of the erotic suggestions so vivid in the fantasy. To reinforce the point, the sound of the lovers' bodies moving in the sheets is made to echo that gentle plash of the small surf on the pink beach. Indeed, only an audience completely inured to the narrative conventions of conventional realism, blinded and deafened by its own expectations, could possibly miss the fineness and complexity and power of Antonioni's *poetic* composition. For *poetry* is precisely what it is, sustained poetry at that, and one of the very few valid cinematic poetries yet created.[17]

Finally, a word about neurosis. It is important if we are to recognize in *Red Desert* something more than an essay in neurotic psychology, that we should understand what is involved in Guiliana's illness and the victory of individual courage, however hesitant and faltering, that Antonioni intends. We need go no further than Jung (though Freud or indeed almost any eclectic psychiatry would do equally well). By citing Jung I am not suggesting that this film is a doctrinaire or even consistent application of Jungian theories of neurosis; I mean merely that the neurosis depicted here follows the general lines of humanistic therapy in the twentieth century. For the film's "subject" is neurosis only insofar as it is a film about man's contemporary neurosis, the "diseased Eros" (the phrase is Antonioni's, not mine) from which he suffers, its cultural origins and universal pervasiveness. On Antonioni's view (as on Mann's or Eliot's) we can speak of individual neurosis only if we are prepared to view the world itself as a great sanatorium or hospital, of which we are all inmates, and the sickest of all may be those who think themselves most sane. In Jung's judgment, the courageous neurotic is the patient who copes creatively with his own life, who comes to terms with himself by confronting the reality of his own nature and his responsibility for his illness or health. The neurotic in this sense is of course only the classical hero in disguise; his antagonist is his illness, and his illness is ultimately himself. But in Jung's words:

> The neurotic has no need to feel himself beaten; he has merely misjudged his necessary adversary, thinking that he could give him the slip. The whole task of his personality lies in the very thing he sought to avoid. Any doctor who deludes him on that score is doing him a disservice. *The patient has not to learn how to get rid of his neurosis, but how to bear it.* His illness is not a gratuitous and therefore meaningless burden; it is *his own self,* the "other" whom, from childish laziness or fear, or for some other reason, he was always seeking to exclude from his life. . . .
>
> We should not try to "get rid" of a neurosis, but rather to experience what it means, what it has to teach, what its purpose is. We should even learn to be thankful for it, otherwise we pass it by and miss the opportunity of getting to know ourselves as we really are. A neurosis is truly removed only when it has removed the false attitude of the ego. We do not cure it—it cures us. A man is ill, but the illness is nature's attempt to heal him. From the illness itself we can learn so much for our recovery, and what the neurotic flings away as absolutely worthless contains the true gold we should never have found elsewhere.[18]

Jung insists in volume after volume that Western man's reason has long since outrun his instinct. The result has been to develop an overly rational, overly technical civilization that has conquered much of the organic world at the cost of contact with its own soul. Only by drawing on our unconscious creative powers can we hope to redress the balance. Such a restoration, Jung argues, can begin only with the creative and resistant individual. The value and allure of Giuliana for our one-sided and over-rationalized civilization is clearly exemplary. She is, after all, the one genuine "individual" in the film, that is, the only one who accepts tragic loneliness as the normal condition of existence and who asserts responsibility for her own life. Even more important perhaps is what she (like each of the four women played by Monica Vitti in these films) contributes to the culture and to others: that is, her own irreducible femininity, still integral, still "unassimilated" by masculine modes, rich with the mystery and complex appeal of what Jungians call the "anima."[19] She and she alone provides access to an unknown world, a world so strange that others can scarcely acknowledge its reality or its power, which, undetected and repressed, deforms them, turning them into mere sleepwalkers or claiming them in compensatory violence. She is the taproot to the past, the primitive and natural, recognizable by her affinity with old, forgotten things, with trees and plants, with her earthy aura of blue and green. Like Vittoria in *L'eclisse* or Valentina and Lidia in *La notte,* she reveals what would otherwise remain concealed: dormant sense and instincts, eclipsed feelings, all the layered humus of the unconscious world. When she appears, we are meant to glimpse, if only for an instant, the presence of the eternal rhizome buried in the earth, informing the ephemeral leaves with their seasonal continuity, and giving life to "the great-rooted blossomer."[20]

The beauty of Giuliana's individuation is that she achieves it without loss of what she represents to others. She no more loses her aura and appeal than she surrenders her nature. And even though she may succeed in transforming her personal fantasy into myth, she can do so only by retaining access to her own internal landscape. She acquires a psychic balance by mapping and exploring, not obliterating or abandoning, the ground of her being. Admittedly, her balance is precarious, her consciousness tentative and insecure. Yet, at least for now, for the finale, the psychic pressures are under control, as the visual metaphor (underground pipes, their valves periodically venting and liberating the violent pressures they contain) and the last line of the script clearly declare. What counts here is the *discrete* achievement, the *incremental* but crucial advance, which, as so often, contains the hint, the arc, of the completed circle. These discrete advances are of course typical of Antonioni's endings: small, revealing clarities; a gesture of compassion; minute but significant distinctions of awareness. This preference for hints and tentative gestures lies partly in the director's notorious, even fastidious, disdain for heroics; but also, more to the point, in his clear-sighted, scrupulous concern for contemporary reality. This concern precludes the splendid quantum-leap of the classical hero. Advances in Antonioni's world are discrete because he postulates a world of total and universal uncertainty, whose violence of change and flux means that any significant advance is a step into the moral unknown, a new human condition, not the courageous assertion of an old *arête*. And, as in *Red Desert,* the protagonist's advance is more difficult and painful because it is invariably made in a world almost paralyzed by fear of the new—that is, in opposition to the intimidated many and the conformist crowd.

It is above all Corrado's evasion and cowardice that give us the measure of Giuliana's achievement (just as in *La notte* Lidia's clarity in confronting the death of love is meant to be measured against her husband's effort, by physical love, to pull her back into a world she no longer emotionally inhabits). With Ugo, it is harder to say how she stands, since we see him almost entirely through her neurotically needful eyes. Considerate, even kind, but also flat, one-dimensional, and uninteresting, perhaps because his adaptation is so effortless and perfect. Thus he lives in his formidable technological world with the same practiced ease and assurance of habit as the young girl in Giuliana's fantasy fits her blue lagoon. This may, in fact, be all that can be said of him. Yet I think Antonioni expects us, out of a humanity closer to Giuliana's than his, to find him dull, a man so assimilated by the technological world around him that he functions like a well-mannered robot. An engineer, a cerebral product of a pure Apollonian world, he lacks both psychic energy and depth. And, even from him, the unconscious exerts a kind of compensation that visibly affects his behavior. Not all of his nature is expressed by the conventionally purposive life he leads; he hears, after all, sounds that he will not let himself hear. And this tells us that he has driven a part of himself underground where it waits its chance to claim him in neurosis or violence (image: the refinery boilers erupting, with a hideous roar, into great clouds of steam, curling around Ugo and Corrado until, like an explosion, they nearly obliterate the screen—which is to say, the world). It is a dangerous condition. "Whoever protects himself," warns Jung, "against what is new and strange and regresses to the past falls into the same neurotic condition as the man who identifies himself with the new and runs away from the past. The only difference is that one has estranged himself from the past and the other from the future. In principle both are doing the same thing; they are reinforcing the narrow range of consciousness instead of shattering it in the tension of opposites and building a wider consciousness."

That this is Antonioni's view of the matter seems to me to be confirmed by *Blow-Up*, that remarkable study of a one-dimensional man, far friskier and livelier than Ugo here, but unmistakably of the same mold. And the whole purpose of *Blow-Up* is surely to subject that restless, shallow, one-dimensional photographer, with his easy adaptation and his utter unwisdom, to a sudden, overwhelming involvement in mortality, an experience of death that leaves him shaken to the depths of his being, by the things he can no longer shut out, so that the photographer uses his human eyes for the first time, to cry at the transience and brief bravery of the flesh, made clear in the green grass, the omnivorous natural world that alone survives.

NOTES

1. Cf. *L'Express* (Paris, 16 January 1964). Reprinted in its entirety in *Il deserto rosso di Michelangelo Antonioni*, ed. Carlo di Carlo (Bologna, Cappelli, 1964).

2. See Antonioni's pertinent comments in "Michelangelo Antonioni: Two Statements,"*Film Culture*, no. 22-23 (Summer 1961): "Lucretius, who was certainly one of the greatest poets who ever lived, once said, 'Nothing appears as it should in a world where nothing is certain. The only thing certain is the existence of a secret violence that makes everything uncertain.' Think about this for a moment. What Lucretius said of his time is still a disturbing reality, for it seems to me that this uncertainty is very much part of our own time. But this is unquestionably a philosophical matter. Now you really don't expect me to resolve such problems or propose any solutions? Inasmuch as I am the product of a middle-class society, and am preoccupied with making middle-class drama, I am not equipped to do so. The middle class doesn't give me the means with which to resolve any middle-class problems. That's why I confine myself to pointing out existing problems without proposing any solutions. I think it is equally [as] important to point out the problems as it is to propose solutions."

3. Antonioni's remarks on the causes and nature of Giuliana's neurosis make quite clear that the sense in which "reality" is portrayed as a pollution goes far beyond ecological sentiment; indeed, it extends directly to that unconscious and apparently uncontrollable *hubris*, which is the chronic malaise of our Faustian world: "I want to underline the fact that it isn't the milieu that gives birth to the breakdown: it only makes it show. One may think that outside of this milieu, there is no breakdown. But that's not true. Our life, even if we don't take account of it, is dominated by 'industry.' And 'industry' shouldn't be understood to mean factories only, but also and above all, products. These products are everywhere, they enter our homes, made of plastics and other materials unknown barely a few years ago; they overtake us wherever we may be. With the help of advertising, which considers our psychology and our subconscious more and more carefully, they obsess us. I can say this: by situating the story of *Red Desert* in the world of factories, I have gone back to the source of that sort of crisis which, like a torrential river, swells a thousand tributaries, divides into a thousand branches in order, finally, to submerge everything and spread everywhere." From "An Interview with Michelangelo Antonioni by Jean-Luc Godard." *Cahiers du cinéma* (November 1964).

4. Consider, for instance, Aldo in *Il grido*: a man whose entire world is destroyed when his common-law marriage breaks up and he is expelled from the enclosing comfort of his *paese*, out of the "magic circle" of familiar faces and things, into the increasingly desolate and boundless landscape of the lower Po, whose yearly floods, sweeping everything before them, stand as an image of a world in change, in which Aldo, having lost a crucial part of himself, can no longer keep his "psychic balance." His situation is mirrored by that of his daughter Rosina (just as the little boy's "paralysis" in *Red Desert* mirrors and informs Giuliana's neurosis), who stands at her father's side, looking longingly from the street into the comforting enclosure of a schoolyard. In *L'avventura* the intensity of love fuses the two lovers into a single being, an erotic *participation mystique* so total that Claudia can say to Sandro: "When you go out without me, it will be like losing a leg; you'll be lame." In *La notte* Valentina—alert to the dangers of the "red desert"—refuses her lover by saying, "Love's a bit of a fraud. It makes an emptiness all around you." The idea is visually expressed in the magnificent sequence of the magic bubble of the car containing Lidia and Roberto moving, sealed away from the world, through the rain; finally, it is confirmed by the love letter that Lidia reads to Giovanni, and that culminates in the evocation of that night "which I felt would never end, but would go on

forever; that you were not only mine, but even more, *a part of me.* . . . ." Finally, in *Zabriskie Point* the erotic intensity hitherto expressed as metaphor or fantasy surfaces as film *action*, as love-making in the *desert* that the love-making, by its intensity, creates.

5. Ultimately, of course, the reasons for this are personal, a matter of artistic vision. But we should not ignore the great *visual* potential of paradisal imagery. Bergman, for instance, returns as obsessively as Antonioni to imagery and evocations of "earthly paradise" (wild strawberries; shots of the midnight sun and Swedish island summers, etc.). *Summer Interlude* depends almost wholly upon our perception that the ballerina is unable to develop and grow because she has been paralyzed by a remembrance of paradise lost; the protagonist of *Monika* remains a vulgarly erotic child because she cannot accept her expulsion from her summer Eden. The same imagery persists through the exquisite comedy of *Smiles of a Summer Night*, to *Wild Strawberries*, and *Virgin Spring*. In the "trilogy" we recognize it by its absence, articulated as "God's silence." Finally it appears, this time blended with apocalyptic imagery and themes (compare Antonioni's blend of "erotic desert" and nuclear apocalypse in *Zabriskie Point*) in *Shame* and *Passion of Anna*.

6. A paraphrase of a passage in Edward Sapir's remarkable essay "Culture, Genuine and Spurious." Cf. *Culture, Language and Personality* (Berkeley: University of California Press, 1970), p. 97.

7. Cf. Lucien Lévy-Bruhl, *Primitive Mentality* (London: George Allen and Unwin, 1923); and also *The "Soul" of the Primitive* (London: George Allen and Unwin, 1928).

8. An echo of Antonioni's remarks in the famous Cannes statement at the exhibition of *L'avventura*: "To be critically aware . . . is not enough or serves no purpose. And here we witness the crumbling of a myth, which proclaims it is enough for us to know, to be critically conscious of ourselves, to analyze ourselves in all our complexities. . . . The fact of the matter is that such an examination is not enough. It is only a preliminary step."

9. *Civilization and Its Discontents*, trans. James Strachey (New York: W. W. Norton, 1962), p. 55.

10. As quoted in the *New York Times* (2 April 1969) in an interview on his eightieth birthday.

11. Cf. Melton S. Davis, "Most Controversial Director," *New York Times* (15 November 1964): "Antonioni has explained his interest in women, through whose eyes he has progressively portrayed his personal vision of life and love ('doomed to failure'), as follows: 'With so many changes—social, political, moral—happening so quickly, we can't help but see that the rules we were taught as youngsters have become outdated. For me women can best portray this; they provide such a subtle and delicate measure. They are stronger, more realistic, closer to nature, the first to adapt themselves to changing times.' "

12. C. G. Jung, *Collected Works*, trans. R. F. C. Hull, *Civilization in Transition* (New York: Pantheon Books, 1964), 10:277.

13. In the Italian, *ingranare*. The point has been obscured by insensitive subtitling; thus the technological metaphor used here by Ugo to describe his wife's illness is blandly ignored (even though Ugo visibly searches for the right phrase—that is, the director as it were italicized Ugo's language). Gone too is Ugo's reference to some of his workers as *ottimi elementi* ("splendid elements"), as though they were so many transistors—a use of language wholly in accord with the scene that shows us anxious workers stacked in rows for export like bottles. Perhaps the worst failure, however, occurs in the first scene, when the soundtruck reproaches the "scab": "Romeo Salviati . . . tu sei uno che lavora per dare *mangiare* ai tuoi figli" (literally: "Romeo Salviati . . . you're a man who works to give *food* [*eating*] to your children." It is the word *mangiare* ("to eat") that provides the *klang*-association that sends Giuliana in pursuit of the young workman eating his roll. The subtitler, by rendering *mangiare* as "support," manages to strip the scene of its motivating cue.

14. "My intention . . . was to express the beauty of this world where even the factories can be very beautiful. . . . The line, the curves of the factories and their chimneys are perhaps much more beautiful than a line of tree, of which the eye has already seen too much. It is a rich world, lively, useful. For my part, I say that the sort of neurosis one sees in *Red Desert* is entirely a question of adaptability. There are some people who adapt themselves and others who have not been able to do so, for they are too tied to the structures or rhythms of life which are now obsolete. This is the case with Giuliana. . . . If I had chosen a normally adaptable woman, there would have been no drama. . . ." "Interview with Jean-Luc Godard," *Cahiers du cinéma* (November 1964).

15. Ibid.

16. Cf., for instance, J. P. Sartre: "Absolute responsibility is not resignation; it is simply the logical requirement of the consequences of our freedom. What happens to me happens through me, and I can neither affect myself with it nor revolt against it nor resign myself to it. Moreover, *everything which happens to me is mine*. . . . The most terrible situations of war, the worst tortures do not create a non-human state of things; there is no non-human situation. It is only through fear, flight, and recourse to magical types of conduct that I shall decide on the non-human. . . . Thus there are no *accidents* in a life. . . . The one who realizes in anguish his condition as *being* thrown into a responsibility which extends to his very abandonment has no longer either remorse or regret or excuse; he is no longer anything but a freedom which perfectly reveals itself and whose being resides in this very revelation. But . . . most of the time we flee anguish in bad faith." *Existentialism and Human Emotions* (New York: Philosophical Library, 1958), pp. 53 ff.

17. "I think it is important at this time," wrote Antonioni a few years before *Red Desert*, "for cinema to turn towards an internal form of film-making, towards ways of expression that are absolutely free, as free as those of literature, as free as those of painting which has reached abstraction. Perhaps one day cinema will also achieve the heights of abstraction; perhaps *cinema will even construct poetry*, a cinematic poem in rhyme. Today this will seem absolutely unthinkable, and yet little by little, perhaps even the public will come to accept this kind of cinema." From "Michelangelo Antonioni: Two Statements," *Film Culture* (Summer 1961), nn. 22-23.

18. C. G. Jung, *Civilization in Transition, Collected Works*, trans. R. F. C. Hull (New York, 1964), 10:169-70 ff.

Despite the numerous citations of Jung and my persistent use of Jungian terms, I must insist that I have no intention of suggesting that *Red Desert* is a Jungian account of neurosis. There seems to me not the slightest doubt that Antonioni has been much influenced by Jung; but there is also a clear debt to Freud (and to the existentialists; to Spengler; to Gaston Bachelard; perhaps to the phenomenologists; to Leopardi, F. Scott Fitzgerald, Musil, Joyce, Rilke etc.). Antonioni is a widely read director (as even the most cursory survey of his interviews and statements demonstrates), but he is as eclectic as most European intellectuals. All that one can say of *Red Desert* is that the account of neurosis is not sufficiently clinical to indicate any particular school of therapy; besides, its intentions are more metaphysical and cultural than they are clinical (which is perhaps why Jung, with his broad humanistic interests, above all in the phenomena of consciousness, seems more pertinent than Freud—though Freud's theory of regression as the organism's effort, by reverting to a prior existential state, to avoid the pain of change, is wholly appropriate here). But only damage is done by interpreting Antonioni as anything but an artist, visibly influenced by the major thinkers of the age. To paraphrase Italo Svevo, artists have a habit of playing with ideas without really being in a position to expound them. They falsify them, but they also humanize them.

19. Cf., for instance, Jung's account in *Two Essays on Analytical Psychology*, in *Collected Works*, 7:188, 206. "Woman," he observes, "with her very dissimilar psychology, is and

always has been a source of information about things for which a man has no eyes. She can be his inspiration; her intuitive capacity, often superior to man's, can give him timely warning, and her feeling, always directed toward the personal, can show him ways which his own less personally accented feeling would never have discovered. . . . An inferior consciousness cannot *eo ipso* be ascribed to women; it is merely different from masculine consciousness. But, just as a woman is often clearly conscious of things which a man is still groping for in the dark, so there are naturally fields of experience in a man which, for woman, are still wrapped in the shadows of non-differentiation. . . . The wide fields of commerce, politics, technology, and science, the whole realm of the applied masculine mind, she relegates to the penumbra of consciousness; while, on the other hand, she develops a minute consciousness of personal relationships, the infinite nuances of which usually escape the man entirely."

But, for a quite different account, see Freud's essay "On Narcissism: an Introduction," in *General Psychological Theory*, ed. P. Rieff (New York: Crowell-Collier, 1963), pp. 69 ff: "The importance of this [narcissistic] type of woman for the erotic life of mankind must be recognized as very great. Such women have the greatest fascination for men, not only for aesthetic reasons . . . but also because of interesting psychological constellations. . . ."

20. Examples of this identity—or rather affinity—between woman and the life of plants are innumerable. One thinks immediately of: Vittoria, walking with Piero, caressing a branch; of her fossil plant, the constant framing of her against trees, among vegetable, fibrous textures; the shot of a tree, shuddering in the dawn breeze, at which Claudia looks, in the coda of *L'avventura*; Lidia in *La notte* leaning fondly against a tree, and Valentina, later, reading on a tape-recorder: "Put your ear against the trunk of a tree and if you wait long enough, you'll hear a sound. Maybe it comes from inside us, but I like to think it's the tree." Or Giuliana's affinity for vegetation-greens, and her fantasy's integration of the girl with the plants, rocks, and life of her island. So too in *Blow-Up*, it is the green silence and mystery of the park that so attract the restless Thomas, that provide him with the psychic peace that also attracts him to Patricia.

The metaphor of the "rhizome" is Jung's. In the introduction to his autobiography Jung writes: "Life has always seemed to me like a plant that lives in its rhizome. Its true life is invisible, hidden in the rhizome. The part that appears above ground lasts only a single summer. Then it withers away—an ephemeral apparition. When we think of the unending growth and decay of life and civilizations, we cannot escape the impression of absolute nullity. Yet I have never·lost a sense of something that lives and endures beneath the eternal flux. What we see is the blossom, which passes. The rhizome remains" (*Memories, Dreams, Reflections* [New York: Pantheon Books, 1961], p. 4).

SUGGESTED READINGS

Antonioni, Michelangelo. *Sei Film*. Torino: Einaudi, 1964.

Carlo, Carlo di, ed. *Il deserto rosso di Michelangelo Antonioni*. Bologna: Cappelli, 1964.

Lane, John Francis, ed. *L'Eclisse di Michelangelo Antonioni*. Bologna: Cappelli, 1962.

Selected Bibliography

With occasional exceptions this bibliography is limited to works published between 1966 and 1976. It is designed to supplement the earlier bibliography given in John Vickery, ed., *Myth and Literature: Contemporary Theory and Practice* (Lincoln: University of Nebraska Press, 1966).

Abrams, M. H. *Natural Supernaturalism: Tradition and Revolution in Romantic Literature.* New York: W. W. Norton and Co., 1971.

Ackerman, Robert. "Frazer on Myth and Ritual." *Journal of the History of Ideas* 36 (1975):115-34.

Adams, Richard. *Faulkner: Myth and Motion.* Princeton, N.J.: Princeton University Press, 1968.

Allen, Donald Cameron. *Mysteriously Meant.* Baltimore, Md.: Johns Hopkins University Press, 1970.

Altizer, Thomas J. J. "William Blake and the Role of Myth in the Radical Christian Vision." *Centennial Review* 9 (1965): 461-82.

Armens, Sven. *Archetypes of the Family in Literature.* Seattle: University of Washington Press, 1967.

Armstrong, John. *The Paradise Myth.* London: Oxford University Press, 1969.

Aronson, Alex. *Psyche and Symbol in Shakespeare.* Bloomington: Indiana University Press, 1972.

Babb, Terry A. "*Beowulf*: Myth and Meaning." *Arlington Quarterly* 2, no. 4 (1970):15-28.

Bachelard, Gaston. *On Poetic Imagination and Reverie.* New York: Bobbs-Merrill Co. Inc., 1971.

Bachofen, J. J. *Myth, Religion, and Mother Right.* Princeton, N.J.: Princeton University Press, 1967.

Barnard, Mary. *The Mythmakers.* Athens: Ohio University Press, 1967.

Barthes, Roland. *Critical Essays.* Evanston, Ill.: Northwestern University Press, 1972.

———. *Mythologies.* Translated by Annette Lavers. New York: Hill and Wang, 1972.

338

————. *Writing Degree Zero*. New York: Hill and Wang, 1968.

Belli, Angela. *Ancient Greek Myths and Modern Drama: A Study in Continuity*. New York: New York University Press, 1969.

Bloch, R. Howard. "Tristan, the Myth of the State and the Language of the Self." *Yale French Studies* 51 (1974):61-81.

Broembsen, F. von. "Mythic Identification and Spatial Inscendence: The Cosmic Vision of D. H. Lawrence." *Western Humanities Review* 29 (1975):137-54.

Brown, Daniel Russell. "A Look at Archetypal Criticism." *Journal of Aesthetics and Arts Criticism* 28 (1970):465-72.

Bruns, Gerald L. "Poetry as Reality: The Orpheus Myth and its Modern Counterparts." *Journal of English Literary History* 37 (1970):263-86.

Brylowski, Walter. *Faulkner's Olympian Laugh: Myth in the Novels*. Detroit, Mich.: Wayne State University Press, 1968.

Budick, Sanford. *Poetry of Civilization: Mythopoetic Displacement in the Verse of Milton, Dryden, Pope and Johnson*. New Haven, Conn.: Yale University Press, 1974.

Burnham, Jack. *The Structure of Art*. New York: Braziller, 1971.

Bush, Douglas. *Pagan Myth and Christian Tradition in English Poetry*. Memoirs of the American Philosophical Society 72. Philadelphia: American Philosophical Society, 1968.

Caillois, Noyer. *Man, Play and Games*. Glencoe, Ill.: Free Press, 1961.

Campbell, Joseph. *The Flight of the Wild Gander*. New York: Viking Press, 1969.

————. *The Masks of God*. 4 Vols. New York: Viking Press. *Primitive Mythology* 1959; Compass ed. 1970. *Oriental Mythology* 1962; Compass ed. 1970. *Occidental Mythology* 1964; Compass ed. 1970. *Creative Mythology* 1968; Compass ed. 1970.

————, and Abodie, M.J. *The Mythic Image*. Princeton, N.J.: Princeton University Press, 1974.

————, ed. *Myths, Dreams, and Religion*. New York: E. P. Dutton and Co., 1970.

Carson, Joan. "Visionary Experience in *Wuthering Heights*." *Psychoanalytic Review* 62 (1975):131-51.

Chabrowe, Leonard. *Ritual and Pathos—the Theater of O'Neill*. Lewisburg, Pa.: Bucknell University Press, 1976.

Cherpack, Clifton. "*Paul et Virginie* and the Myths of Death." *PMLA* 90 (1975):247-55.

Chomsky, Noam. *Language and Mind*. New York: Harcourt & Brace, Jovanovich, 1972.

Comito, Terry. "Exile and Return in the Greek Romances." *Arion*, n.s. 2 (1975):58-80.

Crowley, Francis E. "Henry James' *The Beast in the Jungle* and *The Ambassadors*." *Psychoanalytic Review* 62 (1975):153-63.

Dalziel, Margaret, ed. *Myth and the Modern Imagination*. Dunedin, New Zealand: University of Otago Press, 1967.

Dickinson, Hugh. *Myth on the Modern Stage*. Urbana: University of Illinois Press, 1969.

Ehrmann, Jacques, ed. *Structuralism*. Garden City, N.Y.: Anchor Original, Doubleday & Co., 1970.

Eisenstein, Samuel. "Literature and Myth." *College English* 29 (1967-68):369-73.

Eliade, Mircea. *Cosmos and History: The Myth of the Eternal Return*. Translated by Willard R. Trask. New York: Harper and Row, Inc. 1959.

———. *Mephistopheles and the Androgyne: Studies in Religious Myth and Symbol*. New York: Sheed and Ward, 1965.

———. *Myth and Reality*. New York: Harper and Row, Inc., 1963.

———. *Myths, Dreams, and Mysteries: The Encounter Between Contemporary Faiths and Archaic Realities*. New York: Harper and Brothers, 1960.

———. *Rites and Symbols of Initiation: The Mysteries of Birth and Rebirth*. New York: Harper and Row, 1965.

———. *The Sacred and the Profane: The Nature of Religion*. Translated by Willard R. Trask. New York: Harcourt, Brace, and World, Inc., 1959.

Evett, David. " 'Paradise's Only Map': The *Topos* of the *Locus Amoenus* and the Structure of Marvell's *Upon Appleton House*." *PMLA* 85 (1970):504-13.

Feder, Lillian. *Ancient Myth in Modern Poetry*. Princeton, N.J.: Princeton University Press, 1971.

Feldman, Burton, and Richardson, Robert D., eds. *The Rise of Modern Mythology: 1680-1960*. Bloomington: Indiana University Press, 1972.

Fletcher, Angus. *Allegory: The Theory of a Symbolic Mode*. Ithaca, N.Y.: Cornell University Press, 1964.

Fitzpatrick, William P. "The Myth of Creation: Joyce, Jung, and *Ulysses*." *James Joyce Quarterly* 11 (1974):123-44.

Fontenrose, J. E. *The Ritual Theory of Myth*. Berkeley: University of California Press, 1966.

Frye, Northrop. *Fables of Identity: Studies in Poetic Mythology*. New York: Harcourt, Brace, and World, Inc., 1963.

———. *Fools of Time: Studies in Shakespearean Tragedy*. Toronto: University of Toronto Press, 1967.

————. *The Critical Path: An Essay on the Social Context of Literary Criticism.* Bloomington: Indiana University Press, 1971.

Fuller, Edmund, et al., eds. *Myth, Allegory and Gospel: An Interpretation of J. R. R. Tolkien, C. S. Lewis, G. K. Chesterton, and Charles Williams.* Minneapolis, Minn.: Bethany Fellowship, 1974.

Fyler, Anson C., Jr. "Self-Unification: An Archetypal Analysis of Prospero in Shakespeare's *The Tempest.*" *Hartford Studies in Literature* 3 (1971):45-50.

Geeriz, Clifford, ed. *Myth, Symbol and Culture.* New York: Norton, 1974.

Gelfant, Blanche. "Residence Underground: Recent Fictions of the Subterranean City." *Sewanee Review* 83 (1975):406-38.

Giamatti, A. Bartlett. *The Earthly Paradise and the Renaissance Epic.* Princeton, N.J.: Princeton University Press, 1966.

Gillett, Peter J. "O'Neill and the Racial Myths." *Twentieth Century Literature* 18 (1972):111-20.

Girard, René. "Lévi-Strauss, Frye, Derrida and Shakespearean Criticism." *Diacritics* 3:34-38.

Goens, Mary B. " 'The Mysterious and Effective Star': The Mythic World View in Conrad's *Victory.*" *Modern Fiction Studies* 13 (1967):455-63.

Goode, William O. "Hand, Heart, and Mind: The Complexity of the Heroic Quest in *Le Cid.*" *PMLA* 91 (1976):44-53.

Gyurko, Lanin A. "Self, Double, and Mask in Faustes' *La Muerte de Artemio Cruz.*" *Texas Studies in Literature and Language* 16 (1974):363-84.

Hapgood, Robert. "Shakespeare's Maimed Rites: The Early Tragedies." *Centennial Review* 9 (1965):494-508.

Harder, Bernard D. "Cradle of the Gods: The Birth of the Hero in Medieval Narrative." *University of Windsor Review* 10 (1974):45-54.

Hardison, Osborne Bennett. *Christian Rite and Christian Drama in the Middle Ages.* Baltimore, Md.: Johns Hopkins University Press, 1965.

Hartles, Robert A. "The Uroboros in Shelley's Poetry." *Journal of English and German Philology* 73 (1974):524-42.

Hatfield, H. C. *Clashing Myths in German Literature from Heine to Rilke.* Cambridge, Mass.: Harvard University Press, 1974.

Herd, Eric V. "Myth Criticism: Limitations and Possibilities." *Mosaic* 2 (1969):69-77.

Higdon, David L. "Conrad's *The Rover:* The Grammar of Myth." *Studies in the Novel* (1965):17-26.

Hirst, Désirée. *Hidden Rites: Traditional Symbolism from the Renaissance to Blake.* New York: Barnes and Noble, 1964.

Hoffman, Daniel. *Barbarous Knowledge: Myth in the Poetry of Yeats, Graves, and Muir.* New York: Oxford Press, 1967.

Holtan, Orley I. *Mythic Patterns in Ibsen's Last Plays.* Minneapolis: University of Minnesota Press, 1970.

Huberman, Elizabeth. "Initiation and Tragedy: A New Look at Edwin Muir's 'The Gate.' " *PMLA* 87 (1972):75-79.

Hughes, Catharine R. "New Ritual and New Theater." *Arts in Society* 7 (1970):62-68.

Jackson, Mary V. "Prolific and Devourer: From Non-mythic to Mythic Statement in *The Marriage of Heaven and Hell* and *A Song of Liberty.*" *Journal of English and Germanic Philology* 70 (1971):207-19.

Jaffé, Aniela. *The Myth of Meaning in the Work of C. G. Jung.* London: Hodder and Stoughton, 1970.

Jones, James Land. *Adam's Dream: Mythic Consciousness in Keats and Yeats.* Athens: University of Georgia Press, 1975.

Jung, C. G. and Kerényi, C. *Essays on a Science of Mythology.* New York: Harper and Row, Inc., 1963.

———, et al. *Man and His Symbols.* Garden City, N.Y.: Doubleday, 1964.

Keefer, T. Frederick. "William Faulkner's *Sanctuary:* A Myth Examined." *Twentieth Century Literature* 15(1969):97-104.

Keppler, C. F. *The Literature of the Second Self.* Tucson: University of Arizona Press, 1972.

Kirk, G. S. *Myth: Its Meaning and Functions in Ancient and Other Cultures.* Cambridge: Cambridge University Press, and Berkeley: University of California Press, 1970.

Kitagawa, Joseph M. *Myths and Symbols: Studies in Honor of Mircea Eliade.* Chicago: University of Chicago Press, 1969.

Krieger, Murray, ed. *Northrop Frye in Modern Criticism.* New York: Columbia University Press, 1966.

Langbaum, Robert. "Browning and the Question of Myth." *PMLA* 81 (1966):575-84.

Larsen, Stephen. *The Shaman's Doorway: Mythic Imagination and Contemporary Consciousness.* New York: Harper and Row, Inc., 1976.

Leach, Edmund, ed. *The Structural Study of Myth and Totemism.* New York: Barnes and Noble, 1967.

Lévi-Strauss, Claude. *The Raw and the Cooked.* Translated by John and Doreen Weightman. New York: Harper and Row, Inc., 1969.

———. *The Savage Mind.* Chicago: University of Chicago Press, 1966.

———. "The Structural Study of Myth." *Journal of American Folklore* 78:428-44. Reprinted in De Garge, Michael, and De Garge, Fernande, ed. *The Structuralist from Marx to Lévi-Strauss.* Garden City, N.Y.: Doubleday and Co., 1972.

————. *Totemism.* Translated by Rodney Needham. Boston: Beacon Press, 1963.

Lewis, R. W. B. *The American Adam.* Chicago: University of Chicago Press, 1955.

Lidz, Theodore. *Hamlet's Enemy: Madness and Myth in "Hamlet."* New York: Basic Books, 1975.

Lyons, Charles R. "The Movement of the Creative Process from Playwright to Actor in the Avant-Garde Drama of the Sixties and Early Seventies." *Mosaic* 8 (1974):139-50.

Maier, Rosemarie. "The Bitch and the Bloodhound: Generic Similarity in 'Christobel' and 'The Eve of St. Agnes.' "*Journal of English and German Philology* 70 (1971):62-75.

McLay, Catherine. "The Dialogues of Spring and Winter: A Key to the Unity of *Love's Labour's Lost.*" *Southern Quarterly* 18 (1967):119-27.

McPeek, James A. S. "The Psyche Myth and *A Midsummer Night's Dream.*" *Southern Quarterly* 23 (1972):69-79.

Maranda, Pierre, ed. *Mythology.* Baltimore, Md.: Penguin Books, 1972.

Matthews, Honor. *The Primal Curse: The Myth of Cain and Abel in the Theater.* New York: Schocken, 1967.

Mellard, James. "Myth and Archetype in *Heart of Darkness.*" *Tennessee Studies in Literature* 13 (1968):1-15.

Merivale, Patricia. *Pan the Goat-God: His Myth in Modern Times.* Cambridge, Mass.: Harvard University Press, 1969.

Miller, J. Hillis. *Poets of Reality: Six Twentieth-Century Writers.* Cambridge, Mass.: Harvard University Press, 1966.

Montgomery, Marion. "Shadows in the New Cave: The Poet and the Reduction of Myth." *Southwest Review* 55 (1970):217-23.

Munz, Peter. *When the Golden Bough Breaks: Structuralism or Typology?* London: Routledge and Kegan Paul, 1973.

Murray, Henry A., ed. *Myth and Mythmaking.* Boston: Beacon Press, 1969.

Neuse, Richard. "Atheism and Some Functions of Myth in Marlowe's *Hero and Leander.*" *Modern Language Quarterly* 31 (1970):424-39.

Newman, Robert. "Myth and the Creative Process." *Centennial Review* 9 (1965):483-93.

Norris, Margot C. "The Function of Mythic Repetition in *Finnegans Wake.*" *James Joyce Quarterly* 11 (1974):343-54.

Orbison, Tucker. " 'This Distracted Globe': Self in *Hamlet.*" In *Perspec-*

tives on Hamlet, edited by William G. Holzberger and Peter B. Waldeck. Lewisburg, Pa.: Bucknell University Press, 1975.

Osterle, Heinz D. "Hermann Broch, *Die Schlafwandler:* Revolution and Apocalypse." *PMLA* 86 (1971):946-58.

Patai, Raphael. *Myth and Modern Man.* Englewood Cliffs, N.J.: Prentice-Hall, 1972.

Payne, Michael. "Origins and Prospects of Myth Criticism." *Journal of General Education* 26 (1974-75):37-44.

————. "Political Myth and Rhetoric in *Julius Caesar.*" *Bucknell Review* 19 (1971):85-106.

Peck, Russell A. "Public Dreams and Private Myths: Perspectives in Middle English Literature." *PMLA* 90 (1975):461-67.

Perry, John Weir. *Lord of the Four Quarters: Myths of the Royal Father.* New York: George Braziller, 1966.

Piaget, Jean. *Structuralism.* Translated and edited by Chaninah Maschler. New York: Basic Books, 1970.

Porter, Thomas E. *Myth and Modern American Drama.* Detroit, Mich.: Wayne State University Press, 1969.

Pratt, Annis. *Dylan Thomas' Early Prose: A Study in Creative Mythology.* Pittsburgh, Pa.: University of Pittsburgh Press, 1970.

Pratt, Samuel M. "Shakespeare and Humphrey Duke of Gloucester: A Study in Myth." *Southern Quarterly* 16 (1965): 201-16.

Rahv, Philip. *The Myth and the Powerhouse.* New York: Farrar, Straus, 1965.

Reck, Tom S. "Archetypes in LeRoi Jones' *Dutchman.*" *Studies in Black Literature* 1 (1970):66-68.

Righter, William. *Myth and Literature.* London: Routledge and Kegan Paul, 1975.

Ricoeur, Paul. *The Symbolism of Evil.* Translated by Emerson Buchanan. New York: Harper and Row, 1967.

Rosenfeld, Claire. *Paradise of Snakes: An Archetypal Analysis of Conrad's Political Novels.* Chicago and London: University of Chicago Press, 1967.

Roy, Emil. "The Archetypal Unity of Eugene O'Neill's Drama." *Comparative Drama* 3 (1969-70):263-74.

Rubinovitz, Rubin. "Myth and Animism in *Why Are We in Vietnam?*" *Twentieth Century Literature* 20 (1974):298-305.

Ryan, J. S. "Myth Criticism as Discipline." *Westerly* 2 (1973):49-58.

Santiago, Luciano P. "The Ulysses Complex." *American Imago* 28 (1971):158-80.

Santillana, Giorgio de, and von Dechend, Hertha. *Hamlet's Mill: An Essay on Myth and the Frame of Time.* Boston: Gambit, 1969.

Sanzo, Eileen B. "William Blake and the Technological Age." *Thought* 46 (1971):577-91.

Schechner, Richard, and Chwat, Jacques, eds. "An Interview with Grotowski." *The Dramatic Review* 9 (1968):29-45.

Sebeok, Thomas A., ed. *Myth: A Symposium.* Bloomington: Indiana University Press, 1967.

Segal, Charles. "The Raw and the Cooked in Greek Literature: Structure, Values, Metaphor." *Classical Journal* 69 (1974):289-308.

Slochower, Harry. *Mythopoesis: Mythic Patterns in the Literary Classics.* Detroit, Mich.: Wayne State University Press, 1970.

Slote, Bernice, ed. *Myth and Symbol.* Lincoln: University of Nebraska Press, 1963.

Spencer, Benjamin T. "Sherwood Anderson: American Mythopoeist." *American Literature* 41 (1969):1-18.

Spivack, Charlotte K. "The Journey to Hell: Satan, the Shadow, and the Self." *Centennial Review* 9 (1965):420-37.

Strelka, Joseph, ed. *Perspectives in Literary Symbolism.* vol. 1. University Park, Pa.: Pennsylvania State University Press, 1968.

Thorne, William Barry. "*Cymbeline:* 'Lopp'd Branches' and the Concept of Regeneration." *Southern Quarterly* 20 (1969):143-59.

Troy, William. *William Troy: Selected Essays.* Edited by Stanley Edgar Hyman. New Brunswick, N.J.: Rutgers University Press, 1967.

Uitti, *Karl. Story, Myth and Celebration in Old French Narrative Poetry, 1050-1200.* Princeton, N.J.: Princeton University Press, 1973.

Vargo, Edward P. "The Necessity of Myth in Updike's *The Centaur.*" *PMLA* 88 (1973):452-60.

Vickery, John B. "*The Centaur:* Myth, History, and Narrative." *Modern Fiction Studies* 20 (1974):29-43.

————. *The Literary Impact of "The Golden Bough."* Princeton, N.J.: Princeton University Press, 1973.

————. *Robert Graves and the White Goddess.* Lincoln: University of Nebraska Press, 1972.

————, and Sellery, J. M., eds. *The Scapegoat: Ritual and Literature.* Boston: Houghton Mifflin and Co., 1971.

————, ed. *Myth and Literature: Contemporary Theory and Practice.* Lincoln: University of Nebraska Press, 1966.

Vinaver, Eugène. *The Rise of Romance.* New York: Oxford University Press, 1971.

Vivas, Eliseo. "Myth: Some Philosophic Questions." *Southern Review* 6 (1970):89-103.

Voegelin, Eric. "The Turn of the Screw." *Southern Review* 7 (1971):3-48.

Waddington, R. B. *The Mind's Empire: Myth and Form in George Chapman's Narrative Poem.* Baltimore, Md.: Johns Hopkins University Press, 1974.

Waldmeir, Joseph. "It's the Going That's Important, Not the Getting There: Rabbit's Questing Non-Quest." *Modern Fiction Studies* 20 (1974):13-27.

Wasserman, Earl R. *"The Natural:* Malamud's World Ceres." *Centennial Review* 9 (1965):438-60.

Watson, George. "The Myth of Catastrophe." *Yale Review* 65 (1972):357-69.

Weisinger, Herbert. *The Agony and the Triumph.* Ann Arbor: Michigan State University Press, 1964.

Werner, N. W. "The Importance of Ritual in W. C. Williams' *Paterson."* *South Dakota Review* 8 (1970):48-65.

Wheelwright, Philip. "The Archetypal Symbol." In *Perspectives in Literary Symbolism,* edited by Joseph Strelka, vol. 1. University Park, Pa. and London: Pennsylvania State University Press, 1968.

———. *The Burning Fountain.* Bloomington: Indiana University Press, 1954.

White, John J. *Mythology in the Modern Novel: A Study of Prefigurative Techniques.* Princeton, N.J.: Princeton University Press, 1971.

Whitmont, Edward C. *The Symbolic Quest: Basic Concepts of Analytical Psychology.* New York: G. P. Putnam's Sons, 1969.

Williamson, Marilyn L. "The Myth of Orpheus in 'L'Allegro' and 'Il Penseroso.' " *Modern Language Quarterly* 32 (1971):377-86.

Yates, Frances A. *Shakespeare's Last Plays.* Boston: Routledge and Kegan Paul, 1975.

Zender, Karl F. "A Hand of Poker: Game and Ritual in Faulkner's 'Was.' " *Studies in Short Fiction* 11 (1974):53-60.

Index

347